The Development of the Pacific Salmon-Canning Industry

The Development of the Pacific Salmon-Canning Industry

A Grown Man's Game

Edited and with an Introduction by
Dianne Newell

McGill-Queen's University Press
Montreal and Kingston, London, Buffalo

Legal deposit third quarter 1989
Bibliothèque nationale du Québec

⬲

Printed in Canada on acid-free paper

This book has been published with the help
of a grant from the Social Science Federation
of Canada, using funds provided by
the Social Sciences and Humanities Research
Council of Canada.

Canadian Cataloguing in Publication Data

Main entry under title:
The Development of the Pacific salmon-canning industry
Includes index.
Bibliography: p.
ISBN 0-7735-0717-5
1. Salmon canning industry — British Columbia —
History. I. Newell, Dianne, 1943-
HD9469.S23B7 1989   338.3'72755   C89-090184-8

To H. Keith Ralston

Contents

Tables

Figures

Preface

As our past has been, so also we can expect [our] future. Ups and downs we have had, and doubtless will have again, but the industry in 56 years has expanded from one to 303 canneries and from 2,000 to 10,000,000 cases of an annual pack; with such a firm foundation established we have nothing to fear for the years to come. Today, the Pacific Coast salmon canning industry is far and away the greatest fishery enterprise the world possesses, and if we conserve and build up the salmon runs as they are capable of being built up, the day will come when the wise men from the far east will stop wasting their time on the toy fisheries of the Great Lakes and the Atlantic seaboard, and will come West, where they can splash in a real puddle and take their part in a real grown man's game. Henry Doyle, "History of the Pacific Coast Salmon Industry" (1920)[1]

This book looks at early modern business and its managers. It suggests the complexities of natural-resource management, explores the problems of West Coast seasonal labour and industry, and reveals the genesis of a private manuscript collection. The documents reproduced here are from the Henry Doyle Papers, University of British Columbia Library. As a young American entrepreneur with a thorough grounding in the pioneer fishing industry of the North Pacific, Doyle was the organizer and first managing director of a major amalgamation of salmon-canning operations, British Columbia Packers Association, founded in 1902. British Columbia Packers Association evolved into a highly successful enterprise, British Columbia Packers Ltd., one of the few of the pioneer fish-packing companies that remains in the same business today.

At first the press hailed Doyle as "one of the most energetic and shrewdest operators" engaged in the business of salmon canning in the West.[2] But he turned out not to be, to use modern jargon, "a team player." In the mid-1920s, when the salmon-canning industry of the Pacific was entering its peak, Doyle found himself out of the industry for good. Much had happened in the intervening years; when Doyle left, he took with him a rich body of notes, minutes, letters, reports, and statistics. He continued to collect and generate additional materials on the salmon-canning industry until his death, in 1961. Most of his business partners and many of his acquaintances in the industry achieved fame and fortune; Henry Doyle achieved neither. But in the end he had achieved something very important: he had kept the only comprehensive historical record of the industry during its great expansion phase. It is because of his keen sense of history and need to be remembered that this fascinating record has survived.

The Doyle collection of papers is significant in several ways. First, historically, this industry and period are immensely important for North Americans interested in economic and business development. The Pacific salmon fishery was one of the most valuable fisheries in the world, largely because of salmon canning. The rise of the salmon-canning industry occurred during the formative years of modern capitalism, the last quarter of the nineteenth century and the first quarter of the twentieth. Historian Alfred Chandler suggests that in this period the "visible hand" of management replaced what the political economist Adam Smith had two centuries earlier called the "invisible hand" of market forces – competition – in co-ordinating the activities of the economy.[3] Modern business enterprise and organized labour became powerful institutions in the economy, and their managers and officers highly influential groups of economic decision makers.

As this transformation in business and labour occurred, production and distribution in many areas of the economy became increasingly concentrated in the hands of a few large-scale enterprises. A major historical example of this phenomenon is the mass production of perishable products where domestication – and therefore, high-volume, year-round production – was possible, such as meat packing and milk, fruit, and vegetable canning. As will be seen, the canned-salmon industry did not fit the mould of these or other food-processing operations.

Second, the Doyle collection is interesting because it provides us with a comprehensive inside look at the entire salmon industry. The bulk of the collection focuses on the industry in BC and, tangentially, Washington State's Puget Sound district, the Columbia River, Alaska, and Japan. Whereas most studies of the Pacific salmon-canning industry focus on the two highest-producing districts, Alaska and the Fraser River – Puget Sound, Doyle's record provides a wealth of rarely surviving details on the fishery and cannery operations in the northern district of BC, a district quite different in character and history from the other two. His correspondence files and personal notebooks contain unique details on the physical location and day-to-day operation of the northern canneries.

They also show the inter-regional and inter-industry nature of the business of salmon canning and the range of problems the industry faced.

Third, Doyle was deeply committed to understanding the nature of the various species of Pacific salmon when very little was known about their life cycle and migratory habits. As a cannery manager and businessman, he was concerned that there always be an abundance of the raw resource, but he felt that simply regulating and restricting the fishing were inadequate measures and largely a waste of time. In fact, he was deeply suspicious of those government officials, fisheries experts, and cannery men who blamed the declining salmon runs on overfishing. Doyle advocated instead international regulation of the fishery, development of local hatchery programs (private and public), and application of new techniques for converting salmon waste into marketable products (thereby making more efficient use of the existing supplies of salmon). Doyle gave talks and prepared dozens of reports on his experiments with techniques for canning, smoking, pickling, dry-salting, and freezing salmon; for salting and reducing herring and pilchards; and for freezing halibut. These interests are themes which run through the record he generated during his active period in the industry.

Because Doyle recognized the heavy role that governments had and would continue to have in shaping the salmon-canning industry in BC, he wrote dozens of letters to fisheries officials and commissioners of fisheries over the years. Many of these letters amounted to substantial briefs dealing not only with the regulatory and business aspects of the salmon fishery, but with locational and biological aspects as well. He was elected a BC director of the board of the Canadian Fisheries Association in 1920 and sat as a member of two federal fisheries committees in 1922. A quarter of a century later, in the 1950s, he continued to write letters to newspapers and fisheries officials regarding the threat to fishing posed by the Japanese factory ships operating off the coastal waters and by the provincial government's support for building hydro-electric plants on all the important tributaries of the sockeye areas of BC.

Last, Doyle commented extensively on labour and technique in both the fishing and processing ends of the business. The Doyle collection is interesting for anyone who wants to study the use of ethnic labour in Western industries. Several researchers have investigated specific cases of the harsh labour conditions that were so common in the western regions of North America during the contact and early-industrial phases of development. Howard Lamar's recent survey of this literature led him to ask, "Was the American West and the Western frontier more properly a symbol of bondage than freedom when it comes to labor systems?"[4] In the salmon-canning industry of BC and Alaska, Indians, Chinese, Japanese, Filipino, and other ethnic minorities fished or worked for canneries in great numbers, and often entire families participated. The particular proportion of each group and the methods of payment for their labour and services varied considerably from district to district and over time. Doyle took a great interest in devising new forms of contractual arrangements with fishermen and labour contractors, in speculating on the short- and long-term impact of specific fishing methods, and in preventing and subverting strikes. He investigated labour requirements and costs, especially regarding the introduction of labour-replacing techniques.

Doyle was critical of the financial arrangements – including the controls exercised by commission agents and Eastern banks – which he believed led to the ruin of many cannery operators, including himself. Although he had a personal stake in half a dozen cannery operations, his papers are not confined to discussing those operations alone. He kept careful track of all his competitors' operations as well, although how he gained access to so much confidential information would be interesting to discover.

During the Depression he sold part of his collection to the Fisheries Research Institute in Seattle.[5] He added other items later. Eventually, the American collection comprised seventeen volumes of his scrapbooks containing newspaper clippings for the years 1877 to 1935, a volume of documents and letters covering the period 1905 to 1930, and a 1905 version of his manuscript on the history of the salmon-fishing industry.[6] The Institute transferred these materials, along with a scrapbook belonging to the BC Fisheries Commissioner, John Pease Babcock (1855–1936), to the University of Washington Libraries in 1968. Babcock was a Californian who served as BC Commissioner of Fisheries from 1901 to 1906, Deputy Commissioner from 1907 to 1910, once fisheries rose to become a department, and Assistant to the Deputy Commissioner from 1912 to 1933. He also sat on the important BC Boat Rating Commission of 1910, and chaired the International Fisheries Commission (to regulate the North Pacific halibut fishery) from 1924 until the year of his death, 1936.

The major collection of Doyle's papers is located at the University of British Columbia Library. Doyle and his sons originally donated the bulk of it to the university's Institute of Fisheries in the 1940s.[7] Virtually no one has written on the salmon-canning industry since the 1960s without citing the Doyle collection at the University of BC. Over the years, however, he had rearranged and reorganized his papers to the point where the original order and unity has been lost. Furthermore, substantial information on and personal insight into the day-to-day operation of canneries exist in the thirty diary-like notebooks that he kept over the period 1900 to 1922, but these are difficult to use: they are uncatalogued, their contents are disorganized, and the cannery operations being written of are often unidentified. As well, there are no solid recent background studies on the industry with which to understand or evaluate the significance of the Doyle documents, or even just to interpret the terminology used. The Doyle collection has therefore been greatly underused for research purposes.

Until I encountered Doyle's papers, while I was working on a separate project on the salmon canneries, I had no interest in publishing a collection of historical documents. In my view, however, this particular collection is special, and a heavily annotated selection of Doyle's documents ought to be of great interest to both general readers and scholars. Doyle himself was a practical, self-taught individual. He was constantly at odds with the "experts" and had no qualms about or apologies to make for the opinions he formed; he did his homework well and was correct much of the time. He wanted to educate the public about the salmon fishery, and, toward the end of his life, even wanted to publish his history of the salmon fishery with a major press.

My first thought was to edit and publish Doyle's 1950s history manuscript "Rise and Decline of the Pacific Salmon Fisheries,"[8] as I thought Doyle himself had wanted to do. But I soon came to the conclusion, reluctantly, that Doyle's manuscript was unpublishable. It was only a pale shadow of the robust, coherent, and provocative story which could be extracted from the original collection of papers. Thus, it is Doyle's original collection (but including excerpts from the history manuscript) that forms the basis of this book.

The Doyle collection of papers at the University of BC comprises six running feet of material, which makes it a physically large private collection by archival standards. Eighty percent of the material in the Doyle papers is letters and reports sent to or acquired by Doyle (1902–57);[9] Doyle's outgoing letters (1902–58);[10] his thirty thin, handwritten notebooks on cannery and fishing operations (1900–20);[11] two Mill Bay cannery account books (1905–10);[12] notes, reports, speeches, and writings by Doyle and others, and approximately one hundred photographs of canneries and cannery men (1902–20);[13] statistical tables for various cannery operations and canning companies (mostly BC, 1876–1942);[14] and miscellaneous records of the British Columbia Salmon Canners' Association (name varies, 1899–1922) and British Columbia Packers Association (1902–21).[15] The documents reproduced in this book represent roughly three percent of the total bulk of this material and relate to the period 1902 to 1928.

Although I have included the full range of categories of subject matter and types of documents, I have concentrated on particular subjects which I think make for an interesting and unusual story. Thus, I have included most of the material dealing with the history of individual cannery operations and cannery operators, with relations with the Japanese, Chinese, and Indians who fished or worked for the canning companies, and with occupational structure and technological changes. Discussions of the biology of salmon, of prices, costs, and markets for both raw and canned salmon, and of the politics of development have been sampled. In addition, materials which compare the industry in BC districts with foreign salmon-canning districts have been included where possible and practical.

The rest of the Doyle collection consists of a scrapbook of newspaper and magazine clippings (1935–45)[16] and miscellaneous printed material (1938–58);[17] carbon-copy transcripts of the proceedings and evidence of two federal committees on which Doyle sat in 1922 (the Select Standing Committee on Marine and Fisheries and the Parliamentary Fisheries Committee);[18] charts, maps, and plans;[19] and pack statistics and catch records for Columbia River, Puget Sound, and Alaska (1866–1921).[20] I have not included this material in the book.

In making the final decisions about the specific documents to include, I tended to select Doyle's own letters and reports over other people's, and I chose the longer, more comprehensive documents over the shorter ones. I have included a few lists of personal names, brand names, cannery operations, and inventories of cannery equipment because the material constitutes a unique body of information. Two series of telegrams have been included, in both cases to highlight the use of the medium in conducting business. For the most part, I selected only those items which were worth reproducing in their entirety, though on occasion I deleted small portions of the original text in order to eliminate repetitious material or useless information. An introductory overview of the industry, introductory essays for each chapter, tables, figures, plates, a statistical appendix, and an extensive glossary of terms are included to make the archival materials more comprehensible to readers. The documents are numbered consecutively in the book; each document number and title is accompanied by a "slash number" that refers to the archival arrangement of the document at the University of British Columbia.

I have shown missing and illegible matter by square brackets enclosing the conjectural readings. If only a portion of a word or a simple article is missing, it is silently supplied when there is no doubt about the reading. I have made minor changes in punctuation and format for the sake of clarity and style, but have attempted to retain the quality of the narrative and the manner of expression appropriate to the context. Thus, notebook entries read as notebook entries, telegrams as telegrams, and business letters as business letters. Likewise, I have kept the original spellings of geographical place names; the modern spellings are used in the subject index and my introductory essays. Copy-editing Doyle's own writing was a pleasant task. Doyle was an eloquent man, though a bit formal by today's standards; he had a very strong personality, obviously loved to write, and paid attention to details. However, this book is not intended as a biography of the man who kept the record, but rather as the story of the rise of the industry as told through the record of an observant insider.

Acknowledgments

I am grateful to Henry Doyle's family, especially two of his sons, Richard Doyle and A.D.M. Doyle, who consulted with the rest of the Doyle family about my project and granted me permission to cite freely from their father's papers at the University of BC. They and their sister, Frances Doyle Perram, also gave me additional information on their father. I wish to thank Anne Yandle, head of Special Collections, University of BC Library, for helping me to track down the Doyle family, and Karyl Winn, Manuscripts Librarian, University of Washington, and her staff. Joyce Tiplady and Vicky McAulay exercised patience and skill in typing the manuscript from edited xeroxes of old documents, many of which were hand-written. Brian Foreman and Arif Lalani provided invaluable research assistance, David Dmitrasinovic, Aparna Kurl, and Anda Phelps provided editorial assistance, Keith Ralston helped me with the glossary, and Lance Davis and Peter Baskerville read an earlier version of the book and offered important suggestions.

Funding for the research underlying the book came from the BC Heritage Trust and the Faculty of Arts, University of BC.

The Development of the Pacific Salmon-Canning Industry

Introduction

The Pacific Coast salmon fishery is ancient. Traditionally, the Indian population fished heavily in the coastal waters and tributaries for both food and trade purposes. With the arrival of European fur traders, in the eighteenth century, a small local salmon market developed in response to their provision needs. Then, in the wake of the famous gold rushes from California to Alaska-Yukon, the salmon fishery became an industrial enterprise, and the canning of salmon was continuous from 1864. By 1900, the entire northwest coast of North America, from Oregon to the Bering Sea, had become the base of the largest salmon industry in the world. Dozens of companies, hundreds of salmon canneries, and many thousands of fishers and shoreworkers were involved. Until after World War II, most of the commercially caught salmon was canned and, in the case of BC, exported to world markets. The creation of such a competitive, highly seasonal, scattered industry with mostly isolated locations along the coast, removed from the centres of industry, and faced with scarcities of labour, capital, and materials, was considered a great triumph of nineteenth-century entrepreneurship. The growth of the salmon-canning industry in the twentieth century had a ripple effect in every district, affecting politics and social life as well as labour, commerce, business, and scientific research.

Compared with Canada's four-hundred-year-old East Coast commercial fishery, BC's is a recent development. Nevertheless, it provides a good example of the history of Canadian economic development. The Canadian economy has always been small (in the industrial era about one-tenth the size of that of the United States) and open, so that the forces of the international economy directly influenced the pattern of economic change.[1] As an export economy, Canada's natural-resource regions have been especially vulnerable to shifts in markets and to the discovery of new external sources of supply. For Canadians, the prices of most traded goods have been established internationally rather than domestically. The United States has often influenced the world price of the goods and raw materials Canadians export; this was the case with canned salmon.

Canada experienced an export-led boom in the period 1896 to 1929. Historians generally attribute this boom to the rapid expansion of the wheat economy into the western prairies of Canada, but it was more broadly based on a new generation of staples and new forms of old staples, such as Pacific canned salmon.[2] Until 1900, canned salmon was the principal export staple of the BC economy. (After the rise of forestry, mining, and agriculture in the twentieth century, however, the BC fishery came to rank below these other major primary and resource-processing industries in terms of the market value of output and average net earnings of workers per diem or per annum.[3])

After 1900, the BC fishing industry accounted for more of the volume and value of Canada's total fishery production than any other province,[4] and by 1905, because of the growth of salmon canning, the BC salmon fishery ranked first in the Dominion, outstripping the combined output of lobsters, cod, and herring.[5] While the older Atlantic fishery was based on the production of salted and dried cod, fresh and smoked Atlantic salmon, and fresh (and some canned) lobster – relatively untransformed natural resources – canning required more domestic value added than salting, drying, or smoking. It was an intrinsically industrial solution to the problem of food preservation because it depended on tinplate production and full-scale factory organization. Everywhere along the coast, salmon-cannery operators dominated the fishery, both salmon fishing and the business of catching and processing all the other varieties of fish, including shellfish.

Canning, in contrast to other forms of processing, made possible the distribution of salmon on a world-wide basis and contributed to its popularity as a food.[6] Canning is a French process, dating from the 1790s, which consists of putting food in a container, sealing it, and subjecting the sealed container to the heat of boiling water.[7] Canning as a means of transporting fish to market probably began in the 1830s, in Scotland. From there it spread to the Atlantic-coast regions of Maine and New Brunswick, where lobster and salmon were canned beginning in the 1840s.[8]

New Englanders brought canning to California's Sacramento River in the 1860s.[9] The industry spread rapidly northward to the Columbia and Fraser rivers, into Washington's Puget Sound and up the BC coast into Alaska, and across into Siberian waters. Alaska became the world base for the industry, and BC the second most important region (see figure 1

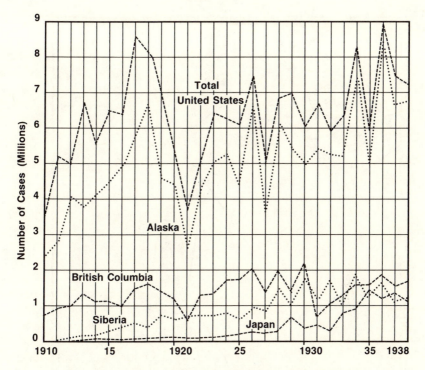

Figure 1: World Production of Canned Pacific Salmon, 1910–1938

and table A1). BC's salmon-canning industry always operated quite differently from that in the United States, however; the former was always export oriented, more diversified, more labour intensive, and more heavily regulated by the state.

BC's economic landscape greatly affected the early growth and spread of this and other provincial resource industries. The province's ocean ports helped to compensate for its geographic disadvantage with respect to the rest of Canada and much of the United States,[10] especially once the Panama Canal opened to traffic, in 1914. The BC coast occupies the whole of the sea front between the 49th and 55th parallels of north latitude. As seen in figure 2, like the coast of Alaska it is made up of a great number of sounds, bays, and inlets, many of which stretch inland for considerable distances, and is studded with islands. Except for a few areas, such as the Fraser River delta, the coast is rugged and montainous, with much of it inaccessible except by water. Because it is exceptionally well sheltered and contains large quantities of high-quality stocks of fish such as salmon and halibut, it has been one of the richest commercial fishing grounds of its size in the world.[11]

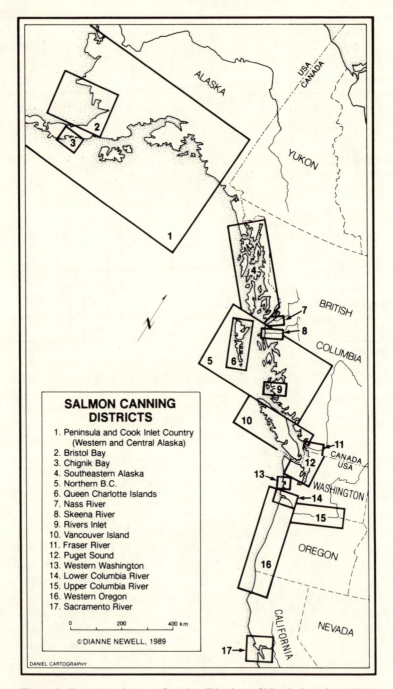

Figure 2: Key Map, Salmon Canning Districts of North America, 1904

On the Pacific coast, salmon migrate from their deep-sea habitat to their native freshwater streams to spawn in definite seasons and in cycles of from two to six years, depending on the species. Unlike the Atlantic variety (genus *Salmo*), which spawn many times, Pacific salmon (genus *Oncorhynchus*) die soon after spawning once and is highly suited to processing by canning. All five species of Pacific salmon are available in BC, though not in every district, and there are important differences in the life cycles, spawning habits, physical size, and quality of flesh – all of which influenced developments in the salmon-canning industry.

Heading the list is sockeye, or red, salmon. Its high oil content and the bright red colour and rich flavour of its flesh assured that the canned product would be highly marketable. Sockeyes, which run in four- and five-year cycles, are available normally in mid-summer, and only in the vicinities of the long river systems and major inlets along the mainland coast and a few places along Vancouver Island.

The runs of the other species occur at different times of the year and in a greated variety of regions. Pink, or humpback, salmon run before and more frequently than sockeye, every second year, but the individual fish are very small. Chum (keta), or dog, salmon mature every three to five years and run in the fall months. Both pinks and chums are highly suitable for drying and dry-salting, and together they comprised the traditional food fish of the West Coast Indians.[12] Coho, or silver, salmon run from July to November in three-year cycles, and are the most comparable to sockeye in flavour and colour. Lastly, spring (known outside BC as chinook, quinnat, king, or tyee) salmon are the largest, mature in their sixth year, and run almost continuously from spring to fall. Spring and coho were marketed principally as fresh or frozen fish.

As a general rule, the natural season for any given species lasts six to eight weeks and begins later, by several weeks, in the south than in the north. As can be seen in figure 2, sockeye runs on the Fraser River were enormous every four years, then declined in each of the succeeding three years of the cycle. And there were cycles within cycles: the "big run" years of 1897, 1901, and 1905 produced twice as many sockeye as the previous three big-run years. The other districts had smaller, but more regular and predictable annual runs of some or all the various species.

The spontaneous one-way drive of salmon to the spawning grounds, in great numbers over a short season, made an ideal situation for canning.[13] The fish could be caught cheaply and easily in the inshore waters and river estuaries, where they congregated before beginning their ascent to the spawning beds, or in the mouths of the rivers and inlets themselves.

Until the 1950s, gillnetting, which was the main method for catching sockeye, accounted for the largest part of the commercial salmon catch in BC and provided employment to the largest single group of fishers in BC,

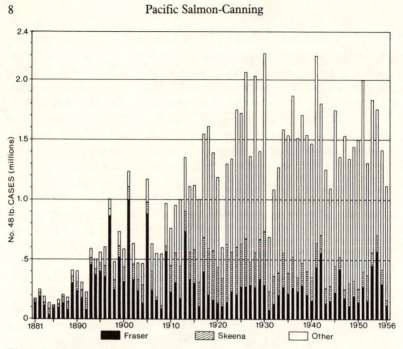

Figure 3: BC Canned-Salmon Pack by District, 1881–1956

Western Alaska, and the coastal states.[14] Gillnetting gradually changed after 1900 from a localized hand-and-sail operation, requiring a boat puller and a captain, to a motor-powered, one-person operation. As a fish-conservation measure, however, the BC and Alaska governments prohibited the use of gas motors on the gillnet fleet from time to time and in special regions. Even where gillnetting remained a hand operation, a major innovation was the introduction of steam-powered, later diesel-powered, packing and collecting boats in the early 1900s. This, and the use of artificially produced ice, enabled the gillnet fleet to range over greater distances and to stay for longer periods in the fishing grounds.

The other salmon-fishing methods included purse seining, for catching schooling fish – pink and chum salmon (and pilchards and herring) – trolling with hooks and lines, for spring and coho salmon, and long-lining, for cod and halibut. Purse seining came into its own in the early 1900s, with the introduction of power-driven rollers for hauling and shooting the net. Commercial trolling began as handlining from skiffs and rowboats in the late nineteenth century (and the practice continued right up to the 1940s); larger boats and powered trolling lines were introduced in BC salmon fishing during World War I.

The salmon fishery on the American side of the international border involved the highly efficient, low-cost trap method of fishing. In Puget

Sound, the impounding of sockeyes with properly set traps was so "efficient" and non-selective that not enough salmon continued their course to the Fraser River fishery and spawning grounds. As a conservation measure, the Dominion government banned the use of traps in commercial salmon fishing for most of British Columbia. Traps were not banned in Alaska until it achieved statehood, in 1958.

Fish conservation was and is a major issue in ocean fisheries. Fish in the ocean are a common property resource and are therefore difficult to manage – there is no incentive for individuals to conserve the stocks for, as the historian Arthur McElvoy suggests, "Every harvester knows that if he or she leaves a fish in the water someone else will get it, and the profit, instead."[15] Today we understand that a stock of fish is a renewable but exhaustible resource. Intensive harvesting leads to depletion; depletion erodes productivity, a situation further aggravated by the deterioration of the ecological environment. Improvements in the technical ability to find and catch fish may kindle profits in the short run, but lead to intensive overfishing, and eventually the collapse of the resource, in the long run. Before the 1890s, conventional wisdom in North America held that oceanic fisheries were so vast that they were practically inexhaustible; regulating anything other than the intensity of the fishing effort simply made no sense.[16] All this changed around the turn of the century with the development of the maximum-sustained-yield theory. The sustained-or steady-yield theory held that "the amount of fish that at any given level of harvesting effort will yield over the long run is a function not only of the intensity of fishing but the capacity of the stock to reproduce."[17] It guided most scientific thinking about fisheries, game and fur-bearing animals, and timber resources until the 1960s.

The post-World War II environmental movement forced governments to alter their strategies for dealing with resource issues.[18] Policies were now designed to maximize the economic return from fishing rather than maximize the raw yield of fish. As a result, officials worked to eliminate the common-property nature of the fishery, replacing it with a "limited entry" regime. Canadian government officials introduced license limitation in the commercial salmon fishery in the 1960s,[19] the same decade in which the provincial government began promoting the interests of fish farming and sport fishing over those of the commercial inshore salmon fishery. More recently, the Canadian government has severely restricted fishing access on the basis of gear type and area.[20]

It is best to manage the fishery on a large scale, because each fishery covers a huge area and fish migrate over the coast. In Canada, unlike the United States, the central government has always been responsible for the ocean fishery. Normally, it would not have regulated the shore-based commercial processing of ocean-fishery products. Yet the case of the

Pacific salmon fishery was an unusual one. Due to the peculiar migratory habits of the fish, its freshwater habitat came under Dominion jurisdiction, as did the operation of the canning plants themselves, since the cannery operators controlled the fishing through the method of cannery-owned ("attached") licenses.

The first major Dominion inquiry into the BC fishery, in 1891, dealt with conservation issues and salmon regulation on the Fraser. At that time, fisheries officials and cannery operators knew so little about the nature of Pacific salmon that they were unconvinced that the salmon die after spawning; most thought that this was simply an unfounded Indian legend.[21] They believed also that artificial propagation could both increase the amount of salmon available and even out the cyclical and seasonal variation in the runs. Between 1884, when the first government hatchery was built, and 1933, the government opened fifteen hatcheries (eight for the Fraser River system, two for the Skeena, one for Rivers Inlet, and four for the Vancouver Island district). A handful of others were built by the canning companies themselves, sometimes as a condition of receiving exclusive licenses from the government to fish. Most were built before World War I, and the majority cultivated sockeye.[22] The last of the early Dominion salmon hatcheries closed down in 1937; they simply were not cost effective without extensive environmental controls.

Conservation of Pacific salmon took many other forms. To conserve specific runs of salmon, the Dominion government, which had been licensing gillnet fishing since the 1870s, decided in 1908 to control the geographical spread and concentration of fish plants by insisting that provincial canneries obtain an annual license to operate from the federal fisheries department. The provincial government had licensed fish plants since it had become involved, in 1902. The practice of dual licensing lasted until 1928, when the Dominion government was successfully challenged in the Supreme Court of Canada by a prominent cannery owner, Francis Millerd. The Dominion government also introduced formal controls in the northern district, as a result of a 1910 commission, to curtail overfishing there. It is worth noting that during the 1910s the government actively examined conservation issues for several other categories of important natural resources in Canada.[23]

Beginning in the early 1900s, the industry's solution to the problem of overfishing was to impose a system of boat rating. This was a technique whereby each canning district, and each plant within the district, was limited to a specific number of fishing boats each season. The basis for allotment was the canning capacity of the plant as measured by the number of canning lines, the square footage of the plant, or the average size of previous packs. Once the industry spread into new districts the voluntary arrangement weakened, and the government became involved in enforcing a formal system beginning in 1910.

During 1913, the world-famous Fraser River spawning runs of sockeye, already under pressure from the Puget Sound fishery, were further endangered by an event unconnected with the salmon-canning industry, a major rockslide in the Fraser Canyon at Hell's Gate. As it happened, 1913 was a peak year in the four-year cycle for sockeye and in the two-year cycle for pinks. The slide prevented substantial numbers of both of these important species from reaching the spawning grounds that year. It would take many decades and the enforcement of a considerable body of fisheries regulations for the big sockeye runs to be restored.

After a brief lull during the post-World War I depression in Canada, the Duff Commission recommendations of 1922 led the government to open the fishery to independent fishers (white and Indian) and to remove all special restrictions on the northern salmon-fishing and -canning industry.[24] In Alaska, overfishing and overexpansion during the war had led governments in the United States to give ever more serious consideration to the regulation of their Pacific fisheries,[25] and eventually led to the signing of the international salmon fisheries convention of 1937, which aimed to regulate and protect the Fraser River salmon fishery.[26]

Because the Alaska salmon fishery, where the United States' industry had become concentrated, was enormous, and because the American salmon fishery was only loosely regulated before the 1920s, the United States was the major world producer of canned salmon. It produced at a low cost for its own domestic market and exported its surpluses, mainly to the largest international market for canned salmon, Great Britain.[27]

BC's canned-salmon production was considerably smaller than that of Alaska (roughly one-third, see table A1), and was high cost (mainly because of the conservation measures in place)[28] and export oriented, though stiff import duties effectively denied the province entry to the large American market. Until the end of World War I, BC packed mainly for Great Britain and was its main source of canned salmon; after the war, during the 1920s, the Japanese became unbeatable competitors in that market (table A6). In Japan, salmon canning had started up in a small way during the Russo-Japanese war (1904–05). These producers packed at a low cost, almost exclusively for export to Great Britain.

As the industry spread, even before the emergence of Japan (and Siberia) as a major producer, Canada and the United States had to find additional markets for their canned-salmon exports. By World War II, both nations were exporting canned salmon to over forty countries, though the principal destination in both cases remained Great Britain. Canada found major markets in the 1920s in Australia, France, and, to a lesser extent, New Zealand (see table A7) because of the special trade deals struck with these countries.[29] In addition, the Dominion fisheries department attempted to increase the domestic market for all Canadian fish products, including canned salmon, through its new publicity, transportation, and marketing division. As a result, the Canadian domestic market for canned salmon rose from virtually nothing, in 1920, to thirty-five percent of the pack, on the eve of World War II. Brokers and wholesalers sold the product in export markets using their own, or sometimes packing-company, brands.

In the formative years, the salmon fishery, along with other West Coast resource industries, had, understandably, to import huge amounts of capital from Eastern financial centres, California, and abroad.[30] Nevertheless, it was the BC port city of Victoria that made the major contribution to the early salmon-canning industry in terms of outfitting, including hiring white crews, provisioning, transshipping, and marketing. Victoria was also home to the head offices of most of the provincial canning companies in these early years. The city's commission merchants usually handled both imports and exports and dealt in a variety of commodities. Their direct trade with Great Britain could be traced back to the Cariboo gold rush of the 1860s. (Victoria played an even greater role for the pelagic seal hunt, which was concentrated in the ten-year period 1885–1905: during the 1890s Victoria was the world's premier sealing post.[31]) The foremost agent for the provincial salmon-cannery operators and sealers in the 1880s was the leading commission-merchant firm in the province, Welch, Rithet of Victoria, later renamed R.P. Rithet and Co.[32] In San Francisco the company operated as Welch and Co., and had a branch in Liverpool, England.

Capital and marketing agencies from San Francisco began moving into the Alaska and British Columbia salmon-canning industry in a major way in the 1880s; W.T. Coleman and Company of that city financed many of these new cannery operations.[33] In BC the American-backed ventures were soon outnumbered, however, by the dozens of Canadian- and British-backed companies and the mergers which came to characterize the industry after 1900.[34] By that time, Vancouver and Seattle were becoming the entrepôts of the industry in Canada and the United States, respectively.

In this industry, productive capacity was increased primarily by moving into new geographical areas and species of salmon, and by processing other fish, including shellfish, rather than by increasing the size of individual plants.[35] This was because of the extreme perishability of fish, seasonal and cyclical variation in yield, regional and total limits in volume of supply (both natural and man-made), and the existence of a cheap, flexible labour system. The entire year's supply of a given species had to be caught during the approximately six to eight weeks it was in season, and then, because of the extreme perishability, it had to be preserved within hours of being caught. The warmer the weather, the greater the distance from the fishing grounds to the processing plant, and the bigger the glut, the greater the problem of spoilage. High-speed ocean transport and efficient brine-refrigeration techniques were not available until after World War II, and before the 1950s it was technically not feasible to freeze and subsequently can salmon with no loss in quality.[36]

Salmon-canning plants everywhere had therefore to be built at tidewater sites close to the fishing grounds, which were widely scattered and vulnerable to resource depletion over time. Everything – fish, people, supplies, and canned salmon, even the canneries themselves – travelled by water. The canning plants functioned on a strictly seasonal basis, with a transient labour force. Some operated on one species, others on all five. Some simply canned salmon, others included fish-oil and -meal reduction operations, cold-storage and can-making plants, boat works, saw mills, and so on.[37]

From 1871, when the first cannery operated, to 1966, when the last cannery was built, over 220 individual cannery sites were established in BC – over half of them by 1905 (see table 1). Probably three times that number were established in the American section.[38] While dozens of plants operated continuously for thirty, fifty, or more years, others were

Table 1
Chronology of BC Salmon Cannery Districts by Year of Initial Site Development, 1871–1966

Location		Year of Cannery Construction		
District	Sub-District	First	Final	Total Sites
Fraser	Fraser R	1871	1965	74
	Vancouver	1901	1956	14
Skeena	Skeena R	1876	1929	20
	Prince Rupert	1882	1960	9
Naas River		1881	1918	12
Central	Rivers Inlet	1882	1932	14
Coast	Northern Outlying	1890	1927	11
	Southern Outlying	1890	1928	8
	Smiths Inlet	1883	1929	5
Vancouver I	East Coast	1881	1966	21
	West Coast	1895	1934	19
Queen Charlotte Islands		1911	1938	16
			Total	223

Source: Dianne Newell, "Dispersal and Concentration: The Slowly Changing Spatial Pattern of the British Columbia Salmon Canning Industry," *Journal of Historical Geography* 14, no. 1 (1988): 29.

short-lived or operated sporadically. Because of the frequency with which canning plants were idle for a season or more, were converted to other uses or moved to more suitable locations, or were burnt down or otherwise destroyed, in no season were more than a third of the total number ever built actually in operation.

Salmon canning on the BC coast during most of the nineteenth-century phase had been confined almost exclusively to sockeye because of that species' superior quality, hence value for exporting. Because the Fraser was one of the greatest sockeye rivers in the world, the mouth of that river was where the pioneer operations and cannery operators got their start beginning in 1871, the year BC became a province of Canada. During the 1880s and 1890s, the industry rapidly expanded on the Fraser and spread into all the main sockeye fishing districts of the province – the Skeena and Nass rivers (over 800 nautical kilometers away), Rivers and Smiths inlets, and Alert Bay off the northeast coast of Vancouver Island, and into the upper Puget Sound district of Washington State.[39] In Alaska the first cannery was built in the southeast, in 1880. A major sockeye fishery was created in the western region, which expanded tremendously in the period 1900–1910. Accompanying this was the opening of the pink-salmon fishing grounds, in the southeastern section, and the chum-salmon fishery, in the central region.[40]

After 1905, the industry in BC and Alaska spread into processing the cheaper species of salmon, and other varieties of fish and, as a consequence, into additional fishing grounds, the halibut fishery was on the rise in the deep, unsheltered waters of Alaska and northern BC. Halibut, like salmon, had a high market value. The commercial halibut fishery, in turn, stimulated the herring fishery, as herring was an important source of halibut bait. Because halibut was sold to fresh- and frozen-fish markets, cold-storage facilities were necessary for freezing both halibut and halibut bait. In about 1909, the Eastern Canadian market for fresh fish – especially spring and coho salmon and halibut – from BC opened considerably; it started to be shipped from Vancouver by rail. Prince Rupert became the principal halibut port on the north Pacific coast after the Grand Trunk Pacific Railway reached there, in 1914.

By 1911, when the first salmon cannery opened on the Queen Charlotte Islands, plants could be found in each of the major fishing grounds of the province, and all five species were important in the mix. The cheaper grades of canned salmon and the newly opened outlying districts were such major factors by this time that the combined pack of pink and chum salmon outstripped that of sockeye (see table A3). The canneries responsible for putting up the bulk of the non-sockeye pack were located outside the Fraser River district (see figure 3). Because the other species of salmon ran either before or after sockeye, herring ran in winter, and halibut ran in the spring, the active season for many individual canneries grew from a matter of weeks, when sockeye was the only species being processed, to a period of many months.

To meet the increasing demand for food during World War I, fishers and cannery operators everywhere along the coast rushed to exploit the stocks of pinks, coho, and the lowest-grade salmon, chum.[41] Also canned, for the first time, were herring and pilchards, a type of large sardine which disappeared from the BC coast during World War II. Herring and pilchards were, for a long time, considered too prized as a food and a bait for fish to be converted to oil and fertilizer; the Dominion government therefore banned their use for reduction until 1925, when the provincial salmon-canning industry entered its peak period of production.

As with most of the other resource-based industries in Canada, an economic recovery occurred in the BC salmon-canning industry in the mid-1920s. A series of large runs of salmon, high prices, good markets, and the government's new open policy for the fishery sparked a trend toward merging or consolidating firms and establishing larger-scale, regionally centralized, more diversified plants. Events in the salmon-canning industry mirrored the general business trends of the time. According to economic historians, almost two-fifths of all consolidations in the big movement between 1900 and 1948 in Canada occurred in the four years after 1924.[42] Nineteen twenty-eight was the single most remarkable year. Unlike the great wave of mergers which swept through the North American manufacturing sector at the turn of the century, which involved the simultaneous merger of many or all competitors in an industry into a single giant enterprise, these later amalgamations typically involved acquisition of one or more small firms by a large competitor.[43] In Canada, the formation of British Columbia Packers Association (1902) and its ultimate successor, British Columbia Packers Ltd. (1928), provides an example of both the early and later types of amalgamation.

Technological change did not play as large a role in this food-processing industry as it did in most of the others. Salmon-cannery operators adopted key mechanical innovations from the 1880s onward. These mainly involved straight transfers of techniques developed in other branches of the food-processing industry, and were first introduced in the American cannery operations. Mechanical filling machines and steam retorts, used for cooking canned salmon, had been developed for the fruit- and vegetable-canning industry in the United States by the 1880s; a salmon-butchering machine (the "Iron Chink", the only significant invention to originate with the salmon-canning industry) and, later, sanitary or solderless can-making machinery were introduced in the early 1900s; and the vacuum closing machine (developed for the coffee industry) was introduced in the 1920s. When perfected and adopted, these substantially increased the ability of each plant to handle all the fish available to it during periodic gluts without necessarily increasing the size of the plant or the workforce.[44] However, the perfection of the high-speed, continuous-processing machinery was a long process, and in BC adoption of the new techniques was both slow and geographically uneven.[45]

Indeed, when and if the operators adopted technological innovations in filling, cooking, fish butchering, and can-making, they tended to limit their choices to essential ones which eliminated waste or maintained or improved the quality of the pack. In theory, the workers who would be the most affected by the new technology would be the crews of Chinese males. When butchering machines were first experimented with, in 1901 in the Puget Sound region, the Chinese cannery workers walked off the job in protest.[46] They had genuine cause for alarm: the development and introduction of "labour-saving" machinery was intended not only to eliminate the problem caused by labour shortages in times of gluts, but to do away with the need for Oriental (and native) labour. Usually, in BC, however, the need for a quality pack for export, as well as the remoteness and isolation of many of the canneries, meant that hand-butchering and hand-filling lines persisted, especially for the choicest grade, sockeye, and for the small and irregular sizes of tins. This was equally true for some of the American districts.[47]

In BC, the seasonal demand for labour, especially in the early days and in isolated spots where little or no local labour pool existed, led the industry to rely on Indians and on labour contractors who supplied the far West with much of the labour for all types of seasonal and short-term work in general.[48] Cannery operators and regional associations of operators negotiated with the fishers through their bosses or unions, on pricing raw fish and before each season contracted with Chinese labour agents to put up the pack at each plant.

The opening prices for raw salmon were set, regionally using formulas which took into account the price differentials imposed by the market for canned salmon (see tables A4 and A5), the anticipated availability of each species in each fishing ground that season, and the relative bargaining power of the various organizations of fishers, tenderboat operators, and shoreworkers.

The labour contract, termed a "Chinese Contract," ensured the short-term skilled labour required by a cannery operator at the canneries. These contracts detailed the exact tasks, including undertaking miscellaneous work around the cannery, such as can-making, processing a minimum number of tins of specified weight and quality, and packing the cases for shipment. They also detailed the price per case and the payment schedule for such work, including the amount of the cash advance paid to the contractor and the penalties for poor workmanship. The labour contractor supplied supervision, food, clothing, bedding, and other necessities. The last Chinese contract was signed in BC on the Skeena in the 1950s.[49]

In the Alaskan canneries, Chinese crews completely dominated cannery work for the first few decades.[50] By the peak year of Chinese employment, 1902, over 5,300 out of the total Alaskan workforce of 13,800 were Chinese. By 1909, however, Japanese workers comprised one-third of the workforce. After that, Chinese labour contractors increasingly replaced the Chinese and Japanese workers with Mexicans and Filipinos, who formed part of the large group of migratory workers found throughout the food-harvesting and -processing industries on the American west coast.[51] Labour contracts ended in Alaska in the mid-1930s, under intense pressure from organized labour; while in Puget Sound, where an adequate local workforce was available, some cannery operators phased out the contract system as early as 1911, and hired white women and children for day wages.[52]

In BC, the Chinese bosses supervised the work of Chinese, Indians and, on the Fraser River after 1900, Japanese, who generally worked on a piece-rate basis. These workers were usually relatives of the fishers. The older men and women washed and cleaned the raw salmon. The women and young teenage girls filled the empty cans with pieces of fish. Children did light work.

Until World War II, the provincial government exempted all salmon-cannery workers from legislation, introduced in the 1920s, to regulate daily and weekly hours of work, minimum wage, and overtime pay for most categories of factory workers in the province.[53] The cannery operators, working on a company-wide or even a province-wide basis, privately negotiated benefits with the fishers and non-contract cannery crews. These benefits typically included free temporary housing for them and their families and, in good times, free return transportation between the home base and the canneries each season. The companies also furnished winter storage for the boats and gear of the independent fishers and company-owned boats, gear, and fishing licenses for their own fishers. Most fishers were paid fixed amounts on a per-fish basis. Companies provided advances to individuals in the form of either cash or trade with the company store, which supplied all the essential items, such as nets, ice, fuel oil, and groceries, and ran the post office and, often, a telegraph service. In supplying such benefits to their fishers and shoreworkers, cannery operators stood not only to secure an adequate supply of fish and a reasonable force of cheap short-term labour in advance each season, but also to make additional profits from the purchases at the company store.

The degree of organization and the prevalence of conflict in the history of the fishing industry in BC have been unusually high among fisheries, and have generally been attributed to the nature of the all-important salmon-fishing and -canning industry, with its concentrated, mass-production methods, many uncertainties and risks, and racially mixed workforce. "Competition and conflict," notes one study, "occurred frequently among fishers themselves, as well as with fishing or canning companies; among different racial or ethnic groups ... among different specialized occupational groups or branches of the industry ... and among boat owners or skippers and crewmen working on shares ... At the same time, there [was] intense competition among canning companies and other fish buyers for the output."[54]

Collective action on an industry-wide basis was impossible before the industry became geographically concentrated, which occurred after World War II. Yet, because of the shortness of the fishing season and the unpredictability of the runs, even the threat of strike action could be effective. From the 1890s to 1930, fishers formed over a dozen different unions (fish-cannery and reduction-plant workers did not form unions in BC or the United States until the 1930s), and there were dozens of strikes involving thousands of fishers and plant workers. The most violent strike of all, that of sockeye fishers on the Fraser in 1900, resulted in riots and the imposition of martial law. After 1903, as the industry expanded into the northern fishing grounds and became heavily regulated there, the North became the centre of strike activities; the strikes there were usually small and involved a single racial group.[55]

As a group, the Japanese were especially hard hit. From the 1890s to 1920, the proportion of fishers in British Columbia who were Japanese increased steadily. As early as 1902, when there were approximately four thousand Japanese fishers, "more fishermen were Japanese than were either white or Indian, though at no time were the Japanese actually in the majority."[56] The government began placing barriers to the advancement of this highly visible and successful group of fishers before World War I. When the government opened the fishery to independent fishers, in the early 1920s, its official intention was to eliminate Japanese from the industry over the next decade. The government eventually forcibly removed people of Japanese origin from the coast in 1942 as a war measure.

Racisim was equally apparent in the canning plants themselves. After the completion of the first transcontinental railways in the United States and Canada, which had used Chinese labour, anti-Asiatic sentiment ran high on the Pacific coast. Measures were taken in both countries to do away with the presence of Chinese workers and to prevent more from entering the country. The United States government barred Chinese from entering that country beginning in 1882. Under similar pressure from British Columbia, where over half of the total Chinese population in the country lived, after 1885 the Canadian government restricted the immigration of Chinese to Canada through the imposition of an exorbitant "head tax" and a virtual ban on immigration of Chinese females. In 1907, the Asiatic Exclusion League was formed in BC to combat what the public perceived as an invasion of the provincial workforce by Chinese, Japanese, and East Indians. Citizens in Vancouver rioted against these groups. The total Oriental population in BC was actually never large – only 9.1 percent of the total population in 1891; after that, though the numbers grew from nearly 9,000, in 1901, to over 23,000, in 1921, the proportion of Chinese to the non-Indian population in BC "constantly shrank in size and significance."[57] Nevertheless, labour, merchant groups, and, after World War I, returned soldiers in BC agitated against the presence of Asiatics in the province.

Canada's immigration regulations were, in principle, unrestrictive until the early 1920s. But the large numbers of immigrants to western Canada between 1896 and 1913, World War I, and the political and economic upheavals which accompanied the post-war depression led Canadian politicians to implement a much more restrictive "white Canada" immigration policy, which remained largely unchanged until the 1960s. One signal of the new "white Canada" policy was the passing of the Chinese Immigration Act, in 1923. That act effectively prevented the entry of Chinese into Canada for the next several decades. With the sanction of the various levels of government, attempts were undertaken in this same decade not only to eliminate Japanese from the fishery but to limit all Chinese, Japanese, and East Indian employment in mining, railway, and public-works projects.[58]

Only a handful of new cannery sites were developed in BC after 1930, and the absolute numbers licensed to operate steadily diminished. In the years after 1945, the investment per person in the primary fishing operation was doubled as fishers adopted innovations in fish-locating apparatus and in high-speed, all-weather, all-purpose transport. The fish-packing industry diversified and became geographically concentrated in a dozen large, integrated plants located in a few centres; these plants operated year round. A variety of new, lower-priced fish products, including canned tuna, came onto the market as substitutes for canned salmon. As a result, canning was no longer the main method of processing the salmon catch. In Alaska, unlike BC, the intensity of salmon fishing increased after World War II to the point of the decline and near-extinction of the salmon there. In both BC and the United States, the remote, isolated seasonal operations came to a permanent close. Today, a mere handful of salmon canneries survive as fish-packing plants. What follows is the story of the salmon canning in the decades before 1930, when the industry was very much on the rise.

CHAPTER ONE

Henry Doyle and the Formation of British Columbia Packers Association, 1901–1902

INTRODUCTION

The 1890s had been boom years on the Fraser: a succession of very large spawning runs of sockeye caused the number of cannery operations to triple, to forty-nine, by 1901. The stark, only partly mechanized, seasonal plants, adjacent outbuildings, wharves, and racially segregated housing quarters for the fishers, cannery gangs, foremen, managers, and others sat on pilings driven into the tide banks. These cannery camp-villages stretched from the city of New Westminster, where many of the first plants were built, to where the south and north arms of the Fraser empty into the Gulf of Georgia.[1] The early business boom ended in 1900, in what one historian calls "a crisis of over-expansion, marked by strikes and company mergers."[2]

The four-year sockeye cycle on the Fraser produced an unprecedently large canned-salmon pack for the 1901 season, which was sufficient to revive the industry temporarily; thirteen million salmon went into cans in BC that season. But the industry could not expect such an enormous spawning run again until 1905. It had to find a more permanent solution, especially since the provincial government had become involved in regulating the industry by organizing a fisheries department. As mentioned, the federal fisheries department had been administering and regulating the Pacific salmon fishery from the beginning. Within this dynamic situation of conflict and crisis, Henry Doyle approached the BC cannery owners and their financial advisors in December, 1901, with an ambitious proposal to amalgamate a majority of the individual operations of the province into a single new company.

The son of Irish immigrants, Henry Doyle was born in Paterson, New Jersey, on 8 September 1874. In the internal migration typical of the times in the United States, the Doyle family travelled westward to California in 1875. In those days, California was one of America's leading fishing states. The Doyles settled in San Francisco, the financial centre of the industry, where Henry Doyle, Sr., started up the firm of Henry Doyle & Co., dealers in fishing supplies. The firm's field of operation grew with the fishing and fish-packing industry itself. By the time of the senior Doyle's death, in 1898, the firm had branch offices in Vancouver, BC, Seattle, and Astoria, Oregon.

Henry Doyle, Jr., had joined his father's firm in the 1890s as a travelling salesman. This position provided him with a thorough grounding in the business and personalities of the pioneer phase of the industry as it spread northward along the coast. When the Vancouver branch opened, in 1895, young Henry was its manager. And when his father died, Henry assumed the position of general manager of the entire enterprise; he was 24 years old. In 1900, Doyle married Frances English, the daughter of one of BC's pioneer salmon-cannery operators, Marshall M. English. A partnership headed by English had established a cannery at Brownsville, across the river from New Westminster, in 1877. What happened to the Doyle family fishing-supply business after that point is unclear. Doyle himself settled in BC and entered the province's salmon-canning industry in a dramatic way.[3]

In Doyle's view, the time was ripe to attempt a major amalgamation of canning operations.[4] As far as he was concerned, the Fraser River operators – especially the newcomers – were conducting their business in a "suicidal fashion." They also had developed a bond of mutual dependency with the local bankers, which neither party could escape from easily. It was in the interest not only of the cannery owners and their bankers, but also of the local businessmen who were directly or indirectly involved in the industry – mercantile firms and agents who supplied twine, nets, tinplate, and other goods and credit for a commission and disposed of the canned product (also for a commission), insurance agents, labour contractors, sawmill owners, machinery suppliers, and shippers – to take immediate steps to place the industry on a firmer footing.

Earlier attempts at business consolidations on the Fraser had failed, and Doyle studied them carefully to determine why. He advocated replacing the traditional owner-managed cannery businesses with a modern company which would have many units operating at different locations. A hierarchy of salaried executives would direct each set of operations. Over them would be a top-level executive – Doyle himself – who would co-ordinate the entire enterprise, a board of directors, and the stockholders. The new scheme, which he promoted over the winter of 1901-02, was modelled on the highly successful Alaska Packers Association, founded in 1893. Doyle had become acquainted with the Alaska Packers Association while travelling the coast in the 1890s as a sales representative for his father's fishing-supply business. He was also familiar with another successful consolidation, the Columbia River Packers Association, founded in 1887.

At the heart of Doyle's scheme for the packers of BC was the need to reduce the size of the pack and to lower the cost of the operations. The scheme addressed the need to control the quantity and price of raw fish available to each individual operation and to strengthen control of the market for canned salmon. Although Doyle publicly discussed the economies of large-scale production which might come about by amalgamation and plant closures, he knew that little in the way of economies of scale were possible. The true purpose of the amalgamation was to eliminate internal competition for fish and seasonal labour. Competition not only raised the costs of production but lowered the quality and selling price of the final product. Doyle and many of the other canners saw competition as a major problem for the future growth of the industry.[5]

Doyle's proposal provided a full rationale for acquiring as many of the cannery operations in BC as possible. He was particularly keen to take over the northern plants, which he believed would eventually become more profitable than the ones on the Fraser. This was perceptive of Doyle, considering that the Fraser was one of the premier sockeye rivers of the world, and most people therefore regarded it as the permanent centre of the industry in BC. He also outlined a scheme for financing the purchases (see document 63). Two-fifths of the purchase value would be paid in cash. This arrangement would allow the cannery managers to clear the operations of debt and to finance improvements. The cash for purchasing the plants would be secured by a bond issue which Doyle himself would arrange with an Eastern financial syndicate. The remaining three-fifths of the purchase value would be paid in common stock, issued to the former owners at twenty percent below the par value of one hundred dollars. This was a strategy which Doyle believed would ensure the co-operation of the former owners and shareholders in the amalgamation.

Once Doyle acquired the majority of plants in the province, the next step would be to shut down a certain portion of them, remove the machinery and equipment to other plants, and convert the abandoned plants to fish camps and winter storage.[6] This was a sensible plan, which would become standard practice in the industry. Doyle openly criticized the industry for having no "first-class" plants; the largest plant in BC packed only half the daily output of a "modern" cannery in the United States (see document 7).[7] This lag, he believed, was the result of the lack of equipment and poor internal arrangement of the BC plants. In fact, however, the size of the pack in each district was limited primarily by the amount of fish available locally each season. The average amount of salmon in the major American districts – the Puget Sound and Alaska – simply was greater than that in BC. Although Doyle advocated modern organizational strategies, he apparently felt strongly that the operating plants should be managed by practical, experienced cannery men who would also serve as members of the board of the new company. Departments would be created within the company to handle the buying of supplies, to arrange for insurance and transportation, and to market the product according to geographical region.

Doyle obtained the approval of bank representatives in Vancouver, then travelled to Montreal and Toronto in February, 1902, where he submitted the plan to the Eastern head offices of the Bank of Montreal and the Canadian Bank of Commerce. These banks ranked among the top three in the country and carried between them ninety percent of the salmon canners' accounts. The Bank of Commerce had acquired its forty percent of the financing business when it absorbed the old British-owned Bank of British Columbia, in 1901. Molson's Bank held the remaining ten percent of the canners' accounts.[8] The banks saw the possibility of avoiding bankruptcies and agreed to encourage their clients in the business to join the association. The banks also pledged to finance the operating requirements of the new company.

It then fell to Æmilius Jarvis, an investment broker and banker acquaintance of Doyle's in Toronto, to form an underwriting syndicate with Toronto, Montreal, and Boston brokers to raise the capital ($2.5 million) with which to finance a merger of this magnitude. For tax and other practical reasons, Jarvis, with E.W. Rollins of Boston, organized the new company in New Jersey. Upon Doyle's return to the west coast, he secured options on the purchase of nearly sixty percent of the canneries in the province. On May 20th, 1902, the British Columbia Packers Association of New Jersey was officially formed.[9]

As was common practice, the promoters received payment for their services in stock and management positions in the new company. Doyle was paid $250,000 in common stock; the Eastern syndicate received an equal amount. The syndicate, in addition, could buy seven percent of the total preferred shares at twenty percent below the par value of $100. These were transferrable into common stock at $115.

Doyle became general manager of the association. Seventy-year-old Alexander Ewen, the pioneer cannery man in BC, became president, an office which he held until his death in 1907. Ewen had been active in the BC fishing industry since 1864. He owned or had interests in several major canning companies that operated plants on the Fraser River and also had investments in agricultural and mining ventures. There were four district supervisors, all of them former cannery men. Three supervised the Fraser River plants: George Alexander (the Ladner area) was a former partner of Ewen's in the Canadian Pacific Packing Co.; Ninian H. Bain (Steveston) was a former employee of Ewen's; and Duncan Rowan (North Arm) had, with his brother, John, built the Terra Nova cannery in 1892. W.A. Wadhams supervised the northern district. Within a short time, Marshall M. English, Jr., Doyle's brother-in-law, was brought in to manage the Skeena River district, and Robert A. Welsh the Puget Sound properties. George I. Wilson, the secretary, had been one of the principals in Brunswick Canning Co., Pacific Coast Packing Co., Alliance Canning Co., and Albion Canning Co. – each of which was bought up by British Columbia Packers Association. The local managers of the Bank of Montreal and the Canadian Bank of Commerce sat on the ten-member directorate.

At the time of incorporation, in the spring of 1902, thirty-nine canneries were under option (twenty-seven on the Fraser, twelve in the North) and options on four others were under negotiation. The combined packs of these canneries brought the percentage under option to roughly fifty-four percent of the total provincial pack in 1903: on the surface of things, Doyle's advice had been followed. In the final tally, the association acquired thirty-five cannery properties: twenty-four on the Fraser and ten in the North (document 9). The consolidation involved three of the largest interests in the industry in BC at the time: those of Victoria Canning Co. Ltd., of Alexander Ewen, and of George I. Wilson. The individual purchases included everything from land, buildings, machinery, and equipment to vessels, cannery-store inventories, and even product trade marks. Detailed inventories, appraisals, and statements of debts and credits for each operation under option were supplied as a part of the transfer arrangement.[10] The result was a new company that produced forty-one percent of the provincial pack in 1903.

In securing options on the canneries considered for amalgamation, Doyle's task had not always been straightforward. Some of the cannery men made token attempts to hold out, as is clear from the exchange of cagey telegrams between Doyle and the owner of the Cleeve cannery in 1902 (documents 3, 3a–3f). Other cannery owners were genuinely not interested in selling out to British Columbia Packers Association, and it would have taken a great deal to win them over. During these negotiations, Jarvis and Doyle were pestered by a host of sales agents and machinery manufacturers from all over the continent who had learned of the proposed big amalgamation through the businessmen's "grapevine" and saw a potential opportunity to corner new business for themselves. J. Alex Gordon's letter to Jarvis (document 4) mentions that Gordon's Eastern Canadian buying agency already controlled the major share of the Eastern Canadian market for canned salmon. Yet the amount cited, 25,000 cases, represents less than two percent of the BC canned-salmon pack for 1901; besides, a portion of the 25,000 cases may well have been purchased for export, since there was almost no domestic market for Canadian canned salmon until the 1920s.

The first act of the British Columbia Packers Association directors was to launch a full-scale independent financial and logistical survey of the Fraser River and northern canneries (document 6). They instructed the evaluators to pay particular attention to the size, condition, and character of each cannery operation, to any special features, such as a cold-storage plant, and to its location and value. The difference between the option figures and the evaluators' valuations was considered the price to be paid for the company's goodwill and brand names.

Like Henry Doyle, the evaluators noted several important potential advantages to exploiting the northern district. Their detailed observations likely proved very instructive to Doyle, both as general manager of British Columbia Packers Association and, later, as a cannery manager and part-owner in his own right. First, the runs of sockeye, the main species being canned at the time, did not fluctuate as much in the four-year cycles in the North as they did on the Fraser. Second, the supplies of sockeye were not as vulnerable to competition from American fishing interests as they were in the Fraser River district, where the highly productive Puget Sound industry depended upon intercepting the runs of salmon headed for the Fraser River spawning grounds. Finally, a "poor year" in the Fraser district could often be offset by a "good year" in the North.

There also were locational advantages for the northern cannery operations. Because of the greater isolation from populous centres and the abundance of Indian fishers and shoreworkers, there appeared to be fewer problems in controlling fishers and cannery labour in the North than on the Fraser River. Moreover, a large, profitable cannery-store trade was to be had with Indian employees and fishers. Unlike those in the Fraser River district, most of the northern cannery sites had abundant supplies of fresh water for processing, domestic use, and power requirements. Lastly, the projected construction of the new transcontinental railway through Skeena country to the coast would connect the northern fish-packing operations to the Eastern markets.[11]

In the fall of 1902, Doyle visited the northern district and provided British Columbia Packers Association with his typically detailed observations and recommendations on each salmon-fishing ground, salmon cannery, and potential new cannery site in the major arms, inlets, and river estuaries (document 7). His speculations on the various fishing grounds accurately anticipated future trends in the industry, which were to include processing new species of salmon and other available varieties of fish and shellfish, and using other processing methods than canning. His recommendations included suggestions about which canneries to shut down and which to expand and/or upgrade, and why. He paid particular attention to the site location in relation to the prime fishing grounds, to plant arrangement, and to the quantity and quality of processing machinery and equipment for each of the existing operations. As this was a major turning point in the history of technology for the salmon-canning industry, his detailed descriptions of the physical plant make these key documents for historians. Doyle also staked every available, suitable, unclaimed cannery site for foreshore and land-application rights in the areas he was able to visit. In staking claims he used the names of British Columbia Packers Association personnel, including some of the previous owners of association canneries, and of members of his own family. Doyle provides some background history for most of these people. in documents 8 and 10. These staking activities paralleled developments in the young forest and mining industries; in the first decade of the century there were major staking booms for both timber and mineral claims along the coast.[12]

Several of the best cannery locations spotted by Doyle were on Indian reserve land. This should come as no surprise: given the traditional coastal orientation of and the importance of salmon to the Indian population of the Pacific Northwest, it would have been difficult to have chosen a good site for a salmon cannery that was not also located at or near an Indian village or fish camp. What is astonishing to us today, however, is the apparent casualness with which Doyle staked claims for cannery locations even when he suspected that they were located on Indian reserves. In at least one case, he negotiated with the Indians concerned for a lease on their land and a guarantee of employment for local Indian fishers and shoreworkers should a cannery ever be built there.

Doyle took a genuine interest in knowing the cast of characters involved with the early days of the canning industry (document 8). In BC a more varied group could not be imagined. Many of the pioneers were ordinary, industrious men who had worked their way up through the ranks of the canning business – though more than one of them, including Doyle himself, certainly had not harmed their prospects when they chose a pioneer cannery owner's daughter or sister as a bride. A colourful partnership of brothers-in-law was that of George Dawson and Fred Buttimer, who built three canneries in the province – each named "Brunswick."[13] There were exotic characters, too: foreign noblemen of the likes of Sir Thomas Cleeve and Sir Thomas Lipton, for example. Both Cleeve and Lipton became involved in the Pacific canned-salmon industry because they operated major food-import and wholesale businesses in Great Britain and wished to pack canned-salmon to their own requirements. One of the New Westminster cannery owners was a wealthy Chinese merchant named Lam (or Sam) Tung, who supplied many of the canners with the Chinese labour they required. Robert Ward was a prominent Victoria commission merchant and broker whose company, Robert Ward & Co. Ltd., owned the Imperial cannery and whose brother was general manager of the Bank of British Columbia.

Some cannery proprietors were former traders with the Hudson's Bay Company who had operated posts on the coast. Others were ex-Cariboo gold-seekers. Included among the latter were some of the most prominent names in the canning industry – J.H. Todd[14] and E.A. Wadhams – and a black cannery owner of the 1870s, John Sullivan Deas, after whom the island is named.[15] A few representatives of the so-called "cannery clan," notably Robert Draney and his wife and the Rev. Alfred E. Green, were highly popular personalities on the coast. Not all of the cannery people were respected figures; Doyle regarded a few of them as manipulative or unscrupulous. He knew them all.

THE TRANSFER ARRANGEMENT

1. 1/14 "Memo for Mr. Doyle"   *1902*

The arrangement in regard to the transfer [of plants to the British Columbia Packers Association] is as follows:

The plant passes at a fixed value and includes all buildings, machinery, steamers, boats, scows, and nets which have been in use and as detailed in your inventories at the close of last year.

The packing and fishing material consisting of cans, tinplate, new nets, twine and rope, and all other canning material, as per your inventory, to be taken at cost landed.

The new material supplied since inventory was taken is also to be taken over at invoice cost.

The goods in the store are to be taken over as per inventory and all new goods supplied this year assumed at invoice cost.

The credit sales since inventory are to be assumed by the new company, and cash accounted for [should go] to it for all cash taken in exchange for goods.

The outlay in cash in connection with the business for this year incurred up to date is to be assumed by the new company.

The outstanding debts as per your last inventory are to be collected by the new company and accounted for to us; and the inventory liabilities are to be paid by us.

It will be necessary for you to go over the inventories with the company's [BC Packers Association] representative, and to satisfy him that everything is on hand as detailed in the last inventory.

The statements required [of the cannery under option] are:

1st-   Valuation of goods in store as per inventory at cost landed; new goods since taken into stock at invoice cost.

2nd-   List of material such as cans, new nets, twine, rope, etc. carried over from last year as per inventory, with inventory values. List of new packing and fishing material received either from ourselves or others since inventory was taken, at invoice cost.

3rd-   Statement of all moneys expended and advances given to fishermen, Chinese contractors, and others. Cash paid out for freight and passages and all other cash outlay.

4th-   List of outstanding debts to be collected for our account.

The contracts made with the fishermen, Chinese contractors, foremen, etc. are to be assumed and carried out by the new company in exactly the same way as if the cannery had remained in our hands. We enclose a statement of account to date, showing all cash paid out by us and supplies furnished, so far as we have them charged up.

WORKING OUT THE DETAILS

2. 1/13 Letter: R.P. Rithet & Co. Ltd. to Doyle   *Victoria,*
                                                                      April 16th, 1902

Dear Sir:–

We hand you herewith the inventories of Messrs. R. Cunningham & Son's buildings, plant, etc., four sheets; inventory of boats, scows, etc., one sheet; nets, twine, etc., one sheet; and packing material, etc., one sheet – seven sheets in all. As we understand it the option given by Mr. Cunningham is for the buildings and plant, including boats and nets in use, but not new nets, nor any packing material such as solder, lead, cans, labels, etc. etc.

We also enclose a diagram and description of the land in connection with the cannery, but this was made in our office according to information given by Mr. Cunningham, and is not to be taken as a correct and legal description, but only as indicating roughly the land which is included in the option given you. When a deed is to be prepared it will probably be necessary to employ a surveyor to furnish a proper description.

A photograph of the cannery is also mailed you herewith.

We remain yours faithfully,

      R.P. RITHET & CO. LDT.
      "?.H. Landen"
      for (vice-pres.)
      Encls.

3. 1/6 Letter: Cleeve Bros. to Doyle   *Limerick,*
                                                                      May 10, 1902

Dear Sir:–
   We herewith enclose confirmation of cables passed between us.
   We are writing Mr. Mulhall this Mail instructing him to convene the
necessary meeting to confirm the sale.

3a. Cable: Doyle to Talbot c/o Cleeve, Limerick   *May 2, 1902*
Cleeve asking price entirely out of proportion other canners or what
could duplicate plant for our valuators consider the value to be seventy
five thousand including Cold Storage and Tug our Company incorporated will start in a day or two taking plants over must know immediately
whether Cleeve accepts price named third cash balance stock advise by
telegraph.

3b. Cable: Cleeve to Doyle   *May 5th, 1902*
Offer subject immediate reply cannery cold storage tug 100,000 dollars
third cash 5,000 dollars less half in cash.

3c. Cable: Doyle to Cleeve   *May 6th, 1902*
In determining value your figure tug cold storage were accepted by our
valuators entire difference lies in nets boats cannery plant which can
duplicate entirely new much under your value the best offer I can make
85,000 dollars third cash offer subject to immediate reply otherwise
cannot arrange this season.

3d. Cable: Cleeve to Doyle   *May 6th, 1902*
We will accept subject to immediate reply by wire 31,633 dollars cash
792 shares.

3e. Cable: Doyle to Cleeve   *May 7th, 1902*
Offer subject immediate reply 30,000 dollars cash 700 shares this post-
ively best will do advise by telegraph.

3f. Cable: Cleeve to Doyle   *May 7th, 1902*
We will accept 30,000 dollars cash 700 shares.

4. 1/8 Letter: J. Alex Gordon to Æmilius Jarvis   *Montreal,*
                                                          April 1st, 1902

Dear Mr. Jarvis: –
   I see by the papers that you have formed a company to be called The British Columbia Salmon Canning Association. We have acted as Agents for the sale of Salmon (British Columbia) for the last twenty years, and we are therefore thoroughly conversant with the business, and are in touch with all the principal buyers of canned salmon. We may say that in former years we have sold as much as 25,000 cases a season in Montreal alone, but latterly competition from other Packers and Commission men in British Columbia has somewhat reduced our sales, but from what we hear and see, your Syndicate intends consolidating into one big combination, some 62 independant fishing companies with exclusive privilege on the Fraser, Rivers Inlet, Skeena, and other Rivers, this will of course naturally put your Company in a very strong position, and we see no reason why it should not get 75% of all the business done in Canada. My object in writing is to ask if you will kindly use your influence with your friends to allow my firm to represent you, or I should say your Company, in Montreal, for the taking of orders for salmon. I am not quite sure if you will remember my name; I have often met you at the Yacht Club at Dorval, and on the Yacht "Chaperon" – I saw Charlie Porteous a day or two ago, and he gave me your address. I may say that I know Montague Allan and also Herbert Holt very well, and feel sure that they would all use their influence on my behalf.
   Mr. Borget advised my writing to you at once. I would very much like to represent the Company, as I feel sure I could do a large business here, knowing all the Wholesale Grocers intimately, and they are, as you are doubtless aware, the largest buyers of canned salmon. I am selling agent for St. Lawrence Sugar Refining Co. which brings me every day in touch with the Trade. I may say that the Wholesale Grocers all say, that should I get the agency, they will support me.
   Thanking you in advance for anything which you are able to do for me in this matter.

5. 1/8 Letter: Gordon to Doyle   *Montreal,*
                                          April 29th, 1902

Dear Sir: –
   We received your letter of the 17th April, acknowledging ours of the 4th inst., with copy of letter to Mr. Jarvis.
   We note that you are not appointing one selling agent in each city, and that brokers will handle the pack of individuals canners, same as hereto-

fore. We thank you for saying that our interests will be properly protected, but if you should change your mind, and appoint a selling agent
in each city, we trust you will kindly consider our application for the
agency. If necessary, as well as the names we have given you as refer-
ences, we can give you all the merchants in the wholesale grocery trade
here.

FINANCIAL AND LOGISTICAL SURVEY
OF BC CANNERIES, 1902

6. *11/12 Report: D.J. Murray and C.P. Larsen,*   *May 8, 1902*
   Evaluators to Æmilus Jarvis, Chairman
   of Subscribers Paid Stock, British
   Columbia Packers Association

Dear Sir:

In accordance with the general lines laid down at a meeting in Vancouver on the 11th ultimo at which Messers. Nichols, Murray, Rintoul,
Doyle, and yourself were present, we at once proceeded to visit the
various canneries on the Fraser River in order to obtain a general idea of
the condition, their character, their locations, and the value thereof. For
all practical purposes it was deemed unnecessary to examine and then
appraise the many items of the plants, and it would have been impossible
to do so within the time allotted, as we were to be supplied with inventories later. Our observations were therefore confined to the size and condition of the cannery buildings proper, and the quality and capacity of the
equipment of each concern.

For convenience the canneries on the Fraser River are discussed
herein under that District name as distinguished from the Northern
District.

Fraser River Canneries

Land. Outside of the City of New Westminster, in which there are four
canneries located chiefly on leasehold frontage from the city, the land
occupied by canneries has no special value other than for the canning
business. The best situations have been selected, of course, and so keen
has the competition become for available water frontage at Steveston,
that actual transfers of property have been made there at a rate equivalent to $10,000 per acre. For that frontage we allowed $250 per lot or
$2,500 per acre. Lots at the rear of the canneries obtain value from the
fact that from six to eight thousand people are congregated there during
the fishing season. These are graded down in our estimates according to

location. A cannery site of sufficient area should contain about three acres, the value of which we usually placed at from $300 to $500 per acre. Cannery sites convenient for securing fresh fish and having the channel of the river deep and unchangeable are not numerous beyond what are already occupied. It was not without difficulty that we were able to arrive at what we considered would be a relatively fair valuation upon land held by each cannery concern.

Buildings. Cannery buildings proper vary in size from 16,000 to 70,000 square feet of floor space including lofts and wharves, the average being about 25,000 square feet. The foundations put in are invariably of a most substantial character. In all cases these are of cedar piles or mud sills, the life of which is practically unlimited. The superstructures may be said to be simply large, plain, wooden buildings having many sky-lights and windows and generally containing loft space for empty tins, nets, etc., and in some cases for can-making. The walls are usually of battened rough boards, though a number of them are of drop siding. The roofs are covered with cedar shingles, excepting a few which have split-cedar shingles. The Deas Island cannery is an exception. It is covered throughout with corrugated galvanized iron. Generally speaking, the buildings appear to be kept in reasonably good repair. A few gave plans from which we were able to calculate the cost closely, and in a number of instances we were aided by plans and descriptions of the floor space and capacity of each cannery. These have been furnished by the managers to the Fraser River Canners' Association and upon which a committee of that organization allotted to each cannery for several years past the proportion of fishing-boats out of the total number deemed sufficient for their requirements, and at the same time avoided unnecessary competition for fishermen. The plan worked satisfactorily. Net racks and wharves are included under these headings. Local prices at the present time for labour and material were adopted, and we believe that buildings of equal capacity can be constructed at the figures given by us.

Plants, machinery, etc. This heading embraces the complete equipment of the canneries excepting their fishing outfits. With two or three exceptions the machinery appears to have been well cared for. Manufacturers' prices at present are used as a basis of valuation and, as an offset for depreciation, no allowance is made for freight on machinery or the cost of putting it in place. The value of boilers was estimated from their condition as stated in the particulars given in the last report of the Provincial Boiler Inspector.

Many of the inventories were incomplete or defective in their descriptions. In some cases it was necessary for us, in order to obtain an idea of value, to add equipment which we knew to be indispensable to the operation of a cannery and which we believed to be there. Owing to these circumstances, it is fair to assume that our valuations are under cost. Care should be exercised by your company in taking over the plants to see that everything which usually pertains to them is accounted for whether specified in the inventories or not, and also that all items of plant are in reasonably good condition.

Boats, nets, etc. Valuations upon these were of necessity largely conjectural. To minutely examine and value each item would require a great deal of time. Large fishing-boats, when new, cost from $60 to $110 and skiffs from $30 to $40 each. The outfit of each would cost from $20 to $30 additional. An allowance for depreciation was made in our valuations by the arbitrary average price fixed upon of $35 for skiffs and $90 for boats with complete outfits. Nets, when new, cost from $75 to $110 each. After being used we placed them at $40, which is an especially conservative estimate. In some cases boats and nets were not accounted for and are, of course, not included herein. Fish scows we averaged at $150 each.

Steamers and tugs. There are 18 of these included in the options taken from 39 canneries. From the time given to us it was impossible to minutely examine them. We arrived at a value upon a few of them by their size, general appearance, and condition. From the familiar knowledge of Mr. Munn with cannery steamers and tugs on the Fraser River and many also in connection with the Northern canneries, the opinion is expressed that the price allowed for them as a whole is reasonable.

Cold storage. The two ice-making and cold-storage plants, one of the Federation cannery, and the other of the Cleeve cannery, were considered by us. Undoubtedly these would be useful adjuncts to the company's canning operations as well as for the export of fresh fish which may be contemplated. To have an abundant supply of cheap ice available during a heavy run of salmon would greatly assist in avoiding deterioration of those on hand before being canned, apart from the important consideration of how much the pack may be increased by carrying a supply forward to be canned at greater leisure from a fluctuating run.

Neither one of your subscribers felt that he was competent to value these plants without having an opportunity to obtain prices of the machinery installed and to minutely inquire into the details of construction. Inasmuch as their owners could not be induced to give options upon their canneries without including these plants, it is desirable, in our opinion, to have them taken in at the price quoted.

Northern Canneries

These canneries were not visited by us. In comparing their inventories of machinery, etc., at hand, we found them having an average value of about 23% less than the Fraser River canneries. This is due chiefly to a shortage of modern machinery. Indefinite and incomplete inventories, with few exceptions, rendered the task of appraisement unsatisfactory. This applies similarly to the boats, nets, etc. The value of their land and buildings according to their own estimates varied greatly, and neither of your valuators could give the benefit of personal observation. It was necessary, therefore, to find a method which would justify us in giving our opinion of their value as a whole, rather than in individual cases. In doing this we have based our decision chiefly on the continued earning power of these canneries in the past. This earning power we ascertained by taking the average price paid for salmon and cost of supplies, making due allowance for additional charges for freight [which do not apply to] the Fraser River. Inquiry elicited the fact that canneries operating both in the North and on the Fraser River packed [one-pound] "talls" for sundry reasons only in the North. Obviously it would be wrong to take the class of cans producing the smallest profit as a basis of calculation. Profits per case usually increase on the other styles of cans, over the profits on "talls," as follows:

Pound "Flats"   – One Shilling to One Shilling and Sixpence.

Half Pound "Flats" – Two Shillings and Sixpence to Three and Six.

Ovals   – Three Shillings and Sixpence, and upwards.

Taking the average pack of twelve canneries of 102,542 cases for the past four years, there is, is our opinion, ample justification for assuming that $1.00 per case per annum is a reasonable estimate of profits for the Northern canneries. Upon the option price of these twelve canneries, viz. $470,000, the percentage of profit per annum at $1.00 per case is 21.8%. Upon the amount of cash payment it is 37%, and upon our valuation of $377,000 a percentage of 27% per annum.

It will be observed that between the option prices and our valuations there is a difference of $93,000 on the twelve canneries, or 20%, which may be regarded as the price asked for goodwill and brands, a price which is not considered exorbitant by us under all the circumstances. Having in view the above percentages and the opinions expressed to us by one canner concerning another's property, as well as opinions obtained from disinterested sources, together with our own estimates of several canneries from inventories, plans of buildings, etc., which were quite complete, we feel that we are amply supported in the basis of value arrived at from these canneries, viz., about $30,000 on an average for each canning plant.

On the Naas [sic] River, we are credibly informed, all the available cannery sites are included in the property of the three canneries under consideration. Possession of these would therefore give your company a virtual monopoly on the river. The salmon of this stream are regarded as superior to those of any other in northern British Columbia and quite the equal of Fraser River salmon in quality. A large trade is also said to be carried on there with the Indians.

Speaking of the North generally, there would appear to have been less difficulty in dealing with fishermen and labour generally than on the Fraser River by reason of its greater isolation from populous centres. A further advantage is that the sockeye salmon runs do not fluctuate as much in the quadrennial cycles as they do on the Fraser River, and not in frequently does it happen that there is a good season in one district when it is a poor one in the other.

It has been already noted that the supply of sockeye salmon each season varies more on the Fraser River than it does in Northern waters. The supply, however, has not apparently diminished from the corresponding seasons for many years past. The total pack of the Fraser River is not smaller, although, in individual cases it is less, owing to the supply of salmon being distributed amongst a greater number of canneries. Meanwhile, a canning industry of even greater magnitude than on the Fraser River (in respect to size of pack) has been created on Puget Sound, and it depends almost entirely upon the catch of salmon that ascend the Fraser River. In respect to the Northern District, their supply has undoubtedly not diminished and should be more easily maintained as a result of consolidating the canning interests. There is no doubt that the land acquired in connection with the canneries generally will always be a valuable asset, owing to the purpose for which it was selected, and having in many cases in the North the advantage of freshwater privileges for power and otherwise.

Another item which may be mentioned here is that the construction of the projected Canadian Northern Railway to Port Simpson on the Pacific Coast would greatly facilitate your company's operations in the North.

In respect to the advantages of consolidating the various canning plants under one management, these are very numerous and various. By reducing the number of canneries operated, the tension upon the labour market during the height of the season's run should be considerably relieved by the adoption of more machinery and equipment in enlarged plants and with much less labour for the same production. The number of fishing boats could be reduced materially, and so enable the fishermen to at least earn as much in a season at a smaller figure per fish than by the fishing grounds being overcrowded. The capacity of a sufficient number of existing canneries is great enough with the expenditure of a few hundred dollars upon each to enable you to reduce the number of canneries by at least one half and leave the total capacity as great at least as at present.

The item of insurance also offers an opportunity for a large saving, especially in the case at Steveston, where the canneries are crowded together and the rates are very high. The risk of fire originating would be greatly lessened by closing down a number of them.

The canneries on which options have been obtained have each packed an average of 10,000 cases per year for four years past. The saving upon each cannery that could as well be closed down is fairly represented as follows:

Conclusion

Summary

	No. of Canneries under option	1901 Pack (cases)	Option Price ($)
Fraser River District	27	525,499	952,500
Northern District	12	94,391	470,000
Total	39	619,890	1,422,500

The amount, 619,890 cases, represents 50.4% of the total pack (exclusive of the Clayoquot cannery, on the west coast of Vancouver Island), which amounts to 1,230,172 cases.

Negotiations have been practically closed on four more canneries, the packs of which will increase the percentage under option to about 54%. It is desirable that all canneries should be included if possible, so that no combination of those remaining out could materially interfere with the general policy and conduct of your company's management.

It should be understood that the option prices and inventory values of the canneries (with two exceptions) were withheld from us until after our estimates were completed, as presented in the statements already referred to. The difference between our valuations and option figures is regarded as the price to be paid for goodwill and brands, and as such, have been carried forward. We found it desirable in some cases to make reasonable allowances for this item, and, in our opinion, these are fully justified, with the exception of the Victoria Canning Co.'s option, which is about $20,000 in excess of what has been allowed to others. A reduction of this amount should be secured if possible. Still, it is more important that the firm which controls these canneries, R.P. Rithet & Co., should not be left out of the consolidated interest.

We regret that the illness of Mr. H.N. Rich prevented us from having valuable assistance from him.

Finally, we beg to report that we believe our valuations to be conservative throughout, and that for all practical purposes they can be relied upon as accurate. There is a good prospect of securing from time to time all of the canneries not included at present, excepting possibly the canneries of the Anglo-British Columbia Canning Co. This Company has six canneries on the Fraser River and three in Northern waters, representing 15% of the total pack of the province. We understand that you have entered into a satisfactory working arrangement with them for the ensuing season. This enables us to express unhesitatingly our opinion that the percentage secured is sufficient to warrant embarking in the business with safety.

With good management there is every reason to expect that the profits in future will be entirely satisfactory.

We confidently approve of the undertaking, and believe that you are amply justified in proceeding with the organization of your company and in taking over the various canning plants secured by option, without delay.

THE RUSH NORTH

7. 11/12 "BC Packers Canneries Reports, November 1902," by Henry Doyle

Alert Bay Notes

Alert Bay is situated on the west side of Cormorant Island, in the Johnstone Straits [sic]. From a fishing station standpoint, it is one of the best on the coast, being directly opposite the mouths of Kingcumbe [sic] Inlet, Knight's [sic] Inlet, and numerous smaller sounds and inlets, as well as being within three miles of the Nimpkish River, which is very fairly supplied with sockeye salmon. Strictly speaking, Alert Bay cannot be considered as a sockeye location. By having sufficient crews and tugs to exploit the grounds successfully, it is very probable that an average of 10,000 cases of sockeye could be obtained at Alert Bay, but the bulk of the fish put up would be of the coho and humpback variety, and, if proper care was taken to catch these fish, Alert Bay should be good for from 40,000 to 50,000 cases annually. The fish are practically all caught in seines, the crews of which are paid so much per month, which brings the cost of raw fish down to a very low figure, so much so that there is an exceedingly handsome profit on the cheaper varieties packed at this plant. The store trade, also, is very good. Alert Bay is in a district containing a large number of Indian villages, the inhabitants of which draw almost all their supplies during the winter months from the Alert Bay store, so that the business to be done at this point (unlike other canneries), is an all-the-year-round trade.

The cannery at Alert Bay, in its present condition, is totally inadequate for a proper development of the fisheries. Its present capacity is about 400 cases per day, whereas if it were increased to 2,500 cases per day, and proper fishing equipment given to it, no difficulty should be experienced in running the plant to full capacity. The present buildings, in addition, have been put up piecemeal, and consequently, although there are some portions older than others, the buildings themselves are very badly arranged. The warehouse and part of the main cannery building are in a very good state of preservation, and could be utilized without much alteration. I would recommend, therefore, that the present fish wharf be torn down, and a much larger and better-equipped one built on this place, and that the present bathroom be removed and a modern one established in its stead. For machinery I would recommend the putting in of all the labour-saving machines that we would place in other canneries, and that the plant be equipped with two full lines.

During the sockeye season, at least one tug should be used in connection with the Alert Bay plant, and later on, when cohos are running there, and operations on the Fraser River have slackened up, it would be advisable to send still another tug to Alert Bay, so that the fall fishing at that point could be developed to its full capabilities.

Aside from its salmon, Alert Bay is a splendid point for canning clams, and, I believe, crabs as well. It is also situated very close to the halibut banks, and during the months of October to January, inclusive, a great deal of halibut fishing is done nearer to Alert Bay than any other prominent northern point, so that from a halibut standpoint it has its advantages as well.

A proper investigation should be made of the herring fisheries in the adjacent waters, with the idea of putting them up as sardines, for which there is a large demand.

Taken as a whole, I believe Alert Bay to be the most capable of development of any of our plants, not only from a canning standpoint, but from a cold-storage point of view as well, and I would recommend that the changes suggested should be made with as little delay as possible.

Burke Channel Notes

Burke Channel, from Fitzhugh Sound to North Bentwick [sic] Arm, is about 50 miles long by an average width of 1½ miles. There seems to be nothing in the way of fishing locations until about 2 miles above Kelp

Point on the opposite shore. Here there is quite a fair-sized stream, and a good grass beach. The fish ascending the stream are said to be principally humpbacks and dog salmon. We did not do any staking here.

Kwatna Sound is said to be a very good coho inlet, having at least one good stream running into it. We did not go into the Sound, so consequently no staking was done. The place, however, should be investigated at as early a date as is possible. The same applies to Kwaspala Cove, which we also neglected to visit.

Opposite Labouchere Channel, and on the southerly shore of Burke Channel, are two small bays, divided by a small neck of land. The streams emptying into them are small, but the beaches are good, and right in the path of fish going up the Bentwick Arms. These beaches we staked in the name of Allan Cameron for the bay to the eastward and the bay to the west in George Cassidy's name, and staked posts for application for the land itself in their respective names. [Cameron and Cassidy were owners of the Acme cannery when it was sold to the association.]

China Hat Notes

The China Hat [or Princess Royal] cannery is small, but until it proves itself more as a fishing centre of salmon suitable for canning purposes I would not recommend any additional expense being incurred outside that necessitated by the installation of labour-saving machinery. The present plant is very well laid out, and credit is due the management. If the Association had more men to whom its interests were important as [the owners] Toms, Morris, and Fraser consider them, we would have reason to congratulate ourselves.

While we cannot yet judge China Hat as a canning location, it is unquestionably well located for salting dog salmon. The fish are very large and uniform in size, and seemingly unlimited in number. The quality also surpasses any I have seen elsewhere. The market for salted dog salmon is only in its infancy, but already it can easily take 10,000 to 20,000 tons. On the Fraser River the Japanese can afford to pay 7¢ for the raw fish and still make handsome profits. At China Hat bigger and finer fish are obtained for 2¢ each, so that if the Fraser River Japanese can make money at 7¢ we should be able to undersell them, if necessary, and still make an exceedingly handsome profit if we only realized a sum equivalent to the cost price of the Fraser River product.

I would strongly recommend that full enquiries be made into the market conditions for this fish, with the view of putting up a good many thousand tons at China Hat next year, and I would further recommend putting any increase to the plant that might be necessary in view of salting being done on a large scale.

Gardner Canal Notes

This inlet is about ¾ mile wide, on the average, from its mouth at Devastation Channel to the head, or the total length of the arm from the head to McKay Reach and Grenville Channel, the main passages to northern British Columbia waters, would be about 80 miles. The water is very muddy as compared to other northern streams, which would make gill-net fishing very easy, owing to the cloudy condition of the water concealing the net in the daytime, and preventing it from being lit up by phosphorous at night. The Canal is fed by 4 large rivers, the Crab, Brim, Kermano, and Kitlobe [sic]. The last two, owning to the shallow water at the mouths, are unsuitable as cannery sites, although fish go up them in large quantities. Both the Brim and Crab rivers are excellent cannery locations, having plenty of water and good beaches, with ample room for boats, netracks, and all outbuildings, as well as the cannery itself. Of the two, I should recommend Crab River as being the best, owing to its central location, although the Brim River is also to be recommended, owing to its excellent waterfall, from which sufficient power could be obtained to produce 200 horse power. It is, however, about 20 miles up the inlet from its mouth, which is a drawback, as compared to Crab River, which is situated right at the mouth.

The only available site outside of these is that occupied by the old Price cannery, which was within five miles of the head, and which could only be recommended owing to its splendid water power. In all other respects it was too far away to take full advantage of the fish, as they were not in as good condition by the time they reached there as they would be if caught nearer the mouth. In addition, the runs of fish that enter the Kermano, Brim, and Crab Rivers leave the Canal before the Price's site is reached. Price operated his plant for some three years, but absolute ignorance and gross carelessness were displayed in the management, which resulted in the plant being closed down in 1894, and the company disbanded. The largest pack secured was 6,500 cases in 1893, but it was the opinion of those familiar with the place that Gardner Canal should be good for 15,000 to 20,000 cases, if properly managed. The fish are largely sockeye, although quite a large number of cohos are also to be had, as well as a few humpbacks.

After going over the ground carefully we staked out Brim River as a cannery location in the name of E.E. Evans, and that of Crab River in the name of G.I. Wilson, and with these secured, we do not think there is danger of anybody else being able to successfully operate on Gardner Canal. And, while I would not recommend the erection of a cannery this year, I think the Association should take steps towards securing these locations with the idea of eventually utilizing same.

Outside of salmon, Gardner Canal is noted for the enormous quantities of oolichans which frequent the Kitlobe, and if in the future anything is done toward the packing of this fish, Gardner Canal would be the proper place to establish a fishery for same.

Kimsquit and Dean's [sic] Channel Notes

Kimsquit Inlet from Labouchere Channel to the head is about 40 miles long, by an average width of 1–1½ miles. For the most part it is lined by precipitous cliffs, but on the westerly shore, about 5 miles from the mouth, is a good beach and stream. Twenty miles further, on the same shore, is another good beach, while at the head itself is the Kimsquit River, a good large stream in which the sockeye salmon are found. It has also a fine beach, fully one mile in width. Five miles down from the head, and on the easterly shore is another river, near which Draney's cannery [Kimsquit] is situated. This plant is small but well arranged. With sufficient effort made to fish this inlet it should be good for at least 10,000 c/s yearly, of which two-thirds should be sockeye grade. As Draney was already on the ground and as prospects did not warrant two plants, we did no staking on the inlet.

Dean's Channel itself does not seem to possess any fishing points of merit, but to the north are quite a number of inlets, which undoubtedly contain good salmon streams, but these we did not visit, so no staking was attempted. In Lama Passage, on the way to Bella Bella, cohos were numerous, but no beaches of consequence were noted. These waters deserve a thorough investigation, which would probably warrant the erection of a plant somewhere near the junction of Johnstone Channel and Cousins Inlet.

Lowe Inlet Notes

The [Lowe Inlet] cannery is well situated and fairly well laid out. It requires the fish wharf better arranged, in order to permit the use of any labour-saving devices, and the capper wants to be shifted so as to give it a better draft for the carrying off of steam. This would prevent this waste steam heating the can loft as it does at present, thereby causing a large number of rusty cans.

The bathroom also wants a complete rearrangement. At present, the first cooking is done in kettles, which should be replaced by retorts. For last cooking, they have one retort. Another should be added. The changes to be made in this plant the coming season should be comparatively inexpensive, as with the possible exception of increased width to the fish wharf and some alteration to the bathroom lean-to, to accommodate the changes there, I can see no necessity for any work to be done in the way of building.

The Lowe Inlet pack can, I think, be largely increased by the adoption of an energetic policy, and by their keeping in close communication with the Skeena River, so as to take advantage of any surplus of fish there. Until such time, however, as purse seines are permitted, Lowe Inlet's advantageous position cannot well be proven, and therefore any extra expense of enlargement cannot be recommended for the coming season.

The tanks for water should be replaced by better constructed and larger tanks, as those now in use are small, poorly built, and have out-lived their usefulness.

Naas River Notes

The Naas River fishing grounds extend for about 15 miles above the mouth, but owing to the large sand spits and shallow water there are no cannery locations worth having above the Mill Bay plant. Sites on the Naas River are very scarce, and are practically all taken already.

Mill Bay is on the north shore, about 4 miles from Lowe Point at the river's mouth, and has a small harbour and a fair beach. There is a stream flowing down that gives ample water for ordinary cannery pur-poses, and as regards the present fishing grounds, it is well located. The fishermen can fish both tides as [the tides] turn right at the cannery.

Naas Harbor is one of the finest sites in the Province. The harbour is well sheltered and has a splendid place for an unlimited quantity of fishing boats, while its water supply is right at hand and very plentiful. It also possesses a very good beach.

Echo Cove is also well sheltered from all severe winds, has a splendid anchorage for small boats, but is lacking in a good water supply, as the three neighbouring streams are small, and in summer are very likely to run dry.

There is a good stream at Kinkolith [sic], also a large area of flat land, most of which is held by the Indian villagers. But the mud flats in front make it practically impossible to have a large boat land there, which renders it useless as a cannery site, even were the land obtainable.

Below Kinkolith and just at the southern side of North Point there is a good level plot of land and a fair stream, but as is evidenced by the immense quantity of driftwood piled upon the beach, it is so exposed to the winds that sweep up Portland Channel that it is practically out of the question as a cannery site. Furthermore, the freshwater stream almost immediately enters property belonging to the BC Canning Co., so that the latter company would be in a position at any time to seriously cripple any competitor locating there.

Apart from those mentioned above there are practically no locations on the Naas River proper, so that competition there is bound to be limited to two, or at most, three parties. The river is full of ice in winter, although Naas Harbor and Echo Cove are free from it. Much damage is always anticipated from it, but up to the present very little actual harm has been experienced.

As a fishing stream the Naas River has never been properly exploited. It can easily accommodate three times its present number of boats and a good pack of 50,000 c/s per annum obtained, if the business was in the hands of people alive to their opportunities.

Naas River Cannery Recommendations

Mill Bay. If this plant belonged to the Association I would advise closing it at once, and using the location as a camp for Naas Harbour. For this purpose it is well adapted. The main cannery building seems very good, and well laid out, although small, but the outbuildings are poor. In equipment the cannery is sadly lacking: no capper, washer, nor power knife, and kettles instead of steam boxes for the first cooking. The boiler is allowed 85 lb., is in fair condition, and about 15 years old. This year 49 boats were fished, most of which were round bottomed.

Naas Harbour. The situation is very poor, the cannery having been built entirely on mud sills. The water line at low water is over 200 feet in front of the cannery, thus necessitating a long wharf and warehouse. Both of these could have been rendered unnecessary had the cannery been farther out, or on the opposite shore of the Harbour, where deep water is easily obtainable. The cannery is a badly arranged, much patched-up affair, with equipment similar in all respects to Mill Bay, but by no means as well laid out. The boiler is about 18 years old, in fair condition, and is allowed 90 lb. steam. The number of boats fished this year was 32, but in addition, all the sockeye caught in the 10 nets fished by [Port] Nelson [saltery] were also turned in to this plant. Most of the boats were round bottomed.

The Cascade plant is the worst in arrangement that the Province possesses. The store, sleeping houses for the white labour in the cannery, and the net house are fully 200 yards away from the cannery, and being around the bluff are at present only accessible at low tide. Outside of their situation they are in bad condition, and at their best were unfit for the purposes intended.

The cannery building itself, while rather light in construction, seems in very fair condition. All the original buildings are set on sills, which are dry at low water. The addition put on the front rests on six rows of driven piles, which should be renewed before the building is used. The outbuildings near the cannery are absolutely useless. If this plan is operated in another year, I would recommend extending the building another 75 feet. Proper mess houses for whites and Chinese should be built adjoining the cannery, and suitable fishermen's houses also erected on the same ground, which is ample for all such requirements. Thus the old places farther up the Cove could be torn down or abandoned, and by putting a boom across the end of the cove a splendid harbour for small boats would be readily secured.

The only real drawback to the Cascade as a cannery site is the lack of water, but this could be very much improved by employing suitable storage tanks, and a pipe of respectable dimensions (the old pipe is ¾″ iron). For the fish wharf, salt water could be used if necessary.

At present there is practically no machinery in the cannery. The one retort and the boiler are in good condition, and the frame of a square shears also seems good. There are a few cannery trucks (high) around, but with these exceptions practically everything would have to be put in new.

North Bentwick Arm Notes

This arm is about 10 miles long by an average width of 1¼ miles. At the south end there is a grassy beach about 1½ miles wide, through which the Bella Coola River enters the inlet through several mouths. The approach is very shallow, and large vessels cannot get within a mile of the delta lands. The river is very swift, being only navigable by spoon canoes. Sockeyes and cohos go up the Bella Coola River, following the northerly shore. The tide lands at the head belong to John Clayton, and we staked, with his knowledge and consent, three foreshore claims in front of his property, said claims running westerly from the mouth of the main river, and being located in the names of W.A. Wadhams, R.C. McDonald, and Jos. McDonald, in the order named. [The McDonald brothers owned the Westham Island cannery before selling it to the association.] These locations have good bottoms, and should be suitable for trap fishing.

About a mile further toward the mouth of the river and on the northerly shore, a fair-sized river enters the inlet. There is a very fair beach, and the foreshore may be valuable as either a trap or seine location. There is plenty of fresh water, and a cannery could easily be erected here. There is a report that someone has already located this place, but we staked a foreshore claim in the name of Geo. Alexander. We did not stake for an application for land, although it might be well to do so, as cannery sites are scarce on the inlet, and securing this would lessen the chances of competition. The stream is said to be good for cohos and humpbacks, but no sockeyes.

At the entrance to the inlet, and just inside Shoot [sic] Point is a splendid beach, which we staked for foreshore rights in the name of Alex Ewen, although told that someone is reported to have previously applied for it. We did not stake for land claim, although it would be advisable to do so, as the land is very suitable for a cannery site, being exceptionally well located, and with plenty of fresh water. The principal run is cohos.

This and the two preceding beaches, together with the site the cannery occupied, represent about the only places on the North Bentwick Arm for a cannery to locate, so that control of them would probably guarantee control of the Arm. Properly run and enlarged, both in packing capacity and number of boats, and with live, energetic, and progressive management, which is sadly lacking at present, the cannery here should be good for an average pack of 15,000 to 20,000 c/s divided as follows:– spring 2,500 to 3,000 c/s; sockeye 5,000 to 7,500 c/s; cohos 5,000 to 7,500 c/s; and humpbacks 2,000 to 2,500 c/s. The quality of all grades seems very fair, the spring being especially good. With seine fishing or traps the output should be materially increased.

Observatory Inlet Notes

This inlet, from its mouth to the head of Hastings Arm, is about 40 miles long by an average width of about one mile. Twenty-five miles from the mouth, Alice Arm branches off and extends northeasterly about 12 miles, with the same width as main arm. About 18 miles above the mouth of the inlet, on the western shore, is Salmon Cove. This has a splendid gravel beach, fine flat land, and a good stream. This is an excellent coho stream, but the whole place is an Indian reservation, so could not be staked. A little above, and on the opposite shore, are three little coves, two of which are without streams, while the third and far-thest one up possesses a good stream. This is probably an Indian reserve, but as no posts could be found we staked it for both land and foreshore in the name of F.M. English.

Just below Parry Bay there is a splendid beach, well adapted in every way for a cannery site, but this, also Parry Bay itself, is included in an Indian reserve. Just above Hans point on Alice Arm is a small beach and a little stream, which we staked in the name of O.E. Darling, and made application for the land in his name also. From this [point] on there are no streams up which fish would probably go until the head of the arm itself is reached, but we did no staking there, as the three streams emptying into it pass over mud flats for a distance of probably 2 miles, so that it would be impractical to locate a cannery there.

Returning, there is a good beach but no stream at the end of Way Point – the junction of the two arms – nor nothing beyond that again on the right hand or easterly shore until within 6½ miles of the head of Hastings Arm, where there is a splendid beach, with a very good stream. There was an Indian hut on the property, which, while vacant, probably denotes that the place is an Indian reserve, but, being unable to find any posts, we applied for the foreshore and land in the name of A.V. Darling.

Hastings Arm head is like the head of Alice Arm in respect to the large mud flats in front of the good land. There is a very good river emptying into the salt water, but we made no stakings. The salt water is discoloured for many miles down both these arms, and while sockeye are not known to frequent Observatory Inlet, the cohos are reported to be very plentiful, and this inlet should be a splendid auxiliary to a Naas cannery.

Just above Frank Point there is a large bay or inlet, known locally as Goose Bay. There is a splendid waterfall there, but no very large streams. Cohos and humpbacks predominate in this bay. From Goose Bay there is practically nothing of consequence until about 2½ miles up from North Point on the easterly shore. Here a good bight exists, with a fine beach, low lands, a good stream, and quite close at hand a waterfall that might be utilized for power. This bay is known as the Scow Ban [sic] Indian reservation, but upon enquiring at the Kinkolith Village I learned that only the mouth of the creek and a strip of land on both sides of it were included in the reserve. On the northeast side there is quite a large piece of beach land, not included in the reserve, while on the opposite side a small piece of beach was also left out. These we staked for the Company in the name of F.E. Doyle, and as regards the reservation itself, I obtained from the Indian Council at Kinkolith a lease of it for $200 per year for 25 years, with the option of renewal at the expiration of that time.

As the cannery location, this is one of the best situations for Naas River fishing, being nearer to the fishing grounds than either Mill Bay or Naas Harbour, besides being well protected from winds, and free from ice, which latter is the great fault with plants situated on the Naas River proper.

Observatory Inlet Recommendations

As regards the different managements, the Federation canneries [Mill Bay and Naas Harbour] are in very poor hands. If the foremen – Chambers and Stapleton, respectively – were given a free hand they could probably make a better showing, but even then their lack of knowledge of an up-to-date plant and its operation would seriously handicap them in competition with even a second-grade Fraser River man. The Cascade [or Echo Cove] plant, of course, is not running, consequently has no management to criticise.

If the Observatory Inlet site can be obtained I would recommend that a cannery be erected there. It is more accessible than any on the Naas River itself, and as regards everything necessary for a cannery site, seems all that is desired, and is a far better location than either Mill Bay or Cascade. Of course, a plant, if erected here, would be entirely new as far as buildings are concerned, and also for quite a lot of the machinery, although a boiler, solder machine, retorts, etc., might be obtained from some of the plants closed down on the Fraser River. I would recommend that a good big cannery be erected here, equipped with two lines of machinery, and that at least 100 round-bottomed boats be fished. I told the Indians that in event of our building on the reserve we would expect them to fish for us, and as they profit by the rental from the land we lease they are more than willing to fall in with our views on this respect. As the bulk of this tribe now fish for the Federation Co., securing them would answer the double purpose of giving us the fishermen we require while crippling the operations of the competing company.

Portland Canal Notes

We did not go up this Canal any distance, as, owing to it being the boundary between Alaska and British Columbia, the fishing would have to be restricted to one side. From all accounts the best fish streams are on the American side, and as seines are freely used in their waters, they have a decided advantage. The Canal is free from customs inspection, and as therefore Americans can use their seines in British waters without danger of any interference, it is not a good fishing ground from our standpoint.

Our trip was only as far as Dogfish Bay, about 4 miles up the Canal. This place has a good stream, a nice beach, and lots of flat land. Judging from appearances, it is a splendid humpback location, and probably cohos also run here in considerable quantities. As the bay is about one mile long, we staked the foreshore in the names of J.M. and E.R. English, and applied in their names for the shore as well.

For fall fish, Dogfish Bay is a well situated and valuable accessory to Scow Ban, if a cannery is erected at the latter point.

Rivers Inlet Notes

Rivers Inlet is about 35 miles long, and averages 2 miles in width. The water is very deep and clear, except in sunny weather, when the muddy water from the river discolours it. The Wadhams cannery is the one nearest the mouth, is well situated, has plenty of water, a good beach, and excellent accommodations for fishermen and boats. About 1½ miles up the bay is the "Hole in the Wall," a natural basin, well adapted to store scows during the winter, and a good fishing round for humpbacks.

The Brunswick cannery is well situated on the opposite shore to the Wadhams cannery, and distanced about 9 miles. Both these plants can be altered with but slight expense so as to have packing capacity sufficient for the entire inlet.

The Wannuck [sic] cannery is badly situated and wretchedly arranged. The best thing to do is to close it as a cannery and simply use it as a fishing station, in conjunction with either the Wadhams or Brunswick canneries. The Green cannery should also be used for the same purpose.

While at the Brunswick and Wadhams canneries, investigations were made with the idea of utilizing the water power, but it was found that both the head and the volume obtainable were insufficient for practical use in this way, although ample for ordinary cannery purposes.

The situation of the Good Hope cannery is poor, but the cannery itself is well appointed. Those belonging to the BC Canning Co. are worse than the Wannuck, and had they belonged to us, the best thing we could do would be to close them as canneries, but operate one of them as a fishing camp.

Locations on Rivers Inlet are scarce. Outside of those already utilized there is a splendid place – Shotbolt Bay – owned by the BC Canning Co., also a very good place on Schooner Passage, owned by Jorgensen or Wadhams. One or two other locations have been taken up, but are not likely ever to be built upon.

There are no seining beaches on the Inlet, and but one fair trap location noticed. This latter lies from and between the mainland and Black Rock, near the mouth of the main channel. Purse seining, however, should be worked to great advantage all over the Inlet. Regarding the run of fish, sockeyes seem to go only up the O-Wee-Kay-No. The Kilbella River is good for cohos, while Moses Inlet is frequented principally by humpbacks.

Fishing with gill nets is, to a certain extent unsatisfactory, owing to the clearness of the water and the continuous rains. Purse seines should be obtained, if possible, as the output can probably be doubled if their use is permitted.

Rivers Inlet Recommendations

Wannuck Cannery. This plant is a patched-up affair that, in addition, is badly laid out and erected at a place very much exposed to the strong winds that sweep up the Inlet. It is the poorest plant, and worst situated of the three we had in operation on the Inlet this year. As the two others are better adapter to the changes we desire, I recommend the closing down and dismantling of this plant as a cannery, and its use in the future only as a fishing camp.

Wadhams Cannery. This is the best cannery plant in British Columbia, both as regards the cannery itself, and the accommodation for its cannery and fishing labourers. In floor space it is amply large for at least three lines, and I would recommend moving the Wannuck machinery down and increasing the Wadhams cannery correspondingly.

As the closing down of the one plant and increase of the other would also mean an increase in the number of boats operated by the Wadhams plant, it will be necessary to provide more accommodation for nets. To this purpose I would suggest the erection of a separate building 60 × 100 feet, to be used exclusively for nets. This would be ample, and would have the very desirable result of keeping the fishermen outside of the cannery itself. The space now occupied as a net-loft could be utilized for additional can-loft space and a can-making room, which, from a labour-saving point of view, should be situated on the same floor as the can loft.

Brunswick Cannery. This plant is also one of the best owned by the Association, and can easily be equipped for two lines without any additions being made to the building. There will practically be no expense for machinery, as that now in the Green [Vancouver] cannery can be moved to the Brunswick for use there. It will be necessary to build a proper mess house, which is badly needed at present, and at the same time it may be found advisable to build a separate net house.

This year the Wadhams cannery fished 180 boats, Brunswick 109, and Wannuck 98. My idea would be to increase Wadhams to 250, and Brunswick to 175.

Regarding the management of the Brunswick and Wadhams canneries, I am pleased to say that good, capable men seem to be in every department of both plants, and the workmanship of their packs was not excelled by anything I saw. I was not equally impressed with the staff at the Wannuck plant.

Skeena River Notes

Fishing on the Skeena River extends for about 15 miles above Port Essington, and from there out as far as Edye Passage to the west, and Tugwell Island toward the north. The salmon enter the river through the Slough, Blind Passage (between Smith and De Horsey Islands) and through Middle Passage, between De Horsey and Kennedy Islands. Practically no fish come up Telegraph Passage, on which the Standard cannery is situated. Fishing in the river itself can only be done on the tides. Outside, the tides are worked both ways.

Cannery sites on the Skeena River are scarce, and the best ones are already in use. Kirby has a site, but it is too small for a cannery of any size. It is situated between Carlisle and Claxton [canneries], and is the only one heard of not owned by a cannery now operating.

Whether trap fishing is practical around the Skeena River is problematical, owing to the great current caused by the large tides. Outside of this the conditions are very favourable, and after careful investigation we staked for land purchase and foreshore rights the southern end of De Horsey Island (two claims), the northern end of Kennedy Island (five claims), also at the southern end (three claims) on either side of the BC Canning Co.'s crown-granted property in Cardena Bay. We then staked all of Bay Island (four claims), Kitson Island (two claims), and the west side of Smith Island from tree point to Hellgate (ten claims).

Crossing over Malacca Passage we then staked two claims south from Grace Island, three claims on the south and southeast sides of Arthur Island, two claims on the south side of Prescott Island, opposite Snuff Island, two claims north of Henry Island, and one claim at the western end of Useless Bay. Some of these places had already been staked by others, but only for lease of foreshore. We found no notices for purchase of land nor posts for same.

The coast around the Skeena River is very sheer and rocky, and but few beaches are to be found. Fresh water also is rather scarce. Most of the fishing is done out of the river, the canneries having camps as far west as Edye Passage, twenty miles west of Smith Island.

Even if our applications for land and foreshore were the ones granted, and permission given us to operate traps, I would not recommend their introduction in the neighbourhood of Smith, De Horsey, or Kennedy Islands. To my mind there is no question but that, properly construed, these islands are within three miles of the mouth of the river, and were traps put in there so as to withstand the currents and tides, they could completely shut off from the Skeena River every salmon working toward that river. That such a result would be harmful to our interests, as well as others', goes without saying, and the attention attracted to the dangers that could be expected from injudicious trap fishing might result in an order from the government prohibiting their use in any part of the Province.

Skeena River Cannery Recommendations

Standard. The Standard Cannery is very badly arranged, so much so that good work when fish are running plentifully is practically impossible. It is also fully twenty-five miles away from the fishing grounds, is in a badly exposed place, and has no beach or other accommodations for boats. In my opinion the place should be dismantled and closed, as it would pay better to do so than to make a good plant out of it.

Cunningham. The location is a good one, but the building is old and small. It would be well to build an entirely new cannery here. One is much needed on the Skeena River, and there is room for such a plant as should be erected, although there will be no room to spare. The general plan of the present cannery is pretty good, but it was built in sections, is weak in construction, and is too narrow for practical work. The old hands left by Cunningham are too much in a groove for the Association's good, and I would recommend replacing them in another season with more active and up-to-date men.

Balmoral. The cannery is small and poorly laid out, as well as being too narrow. It will require practically a new plant to be able to call the cannery modern. Everything is run on a cheap order, which is a good illustration of the proverb "penny wise and pound foolish." There is plenty of good land, cleared, plenty of water, and good boat room for a modern plant here, and except from the standpoint of labour, I consider the location superior to Essington. This drawback [of labour supply], however, may be fully counterbalanced by the greater sobriety that would be there as compared to Essington, and also by the store business that could be obtained. On the whole, I think Balmoral the best place of the two. The management, however, would want to be put in more progressive hands, with whom future results would be of more moment than the petty savings of the present.

Claxton. This is unquestionably the finest location on the Skeena River. It has sufficient water power to run the whole plant, has splendid accommodations for boats, plenty of net rack room, and all the cleared ground necessary. None of the other places compare with it, except the two canneries belonging to the ABC Packing Co., which exceed it in floor space of cannery. This, however, can be easily overcome with but small expenditure. In my opinion the Association should secure this plant, if possible. Its control would give us command of the Skeena River situation and would remove what might be a dangerous competitor.

Carlisle. This plant is small, but well arranged and well situated. Next to Claxton, I consider it the best location on the River. Everything is in good order and reflects credit on the management.

Inverness. The cannery is very badly laid out, being shaped like the letter "L" with the packing room exceptionally long, and laid out entirely on the land, thus necessitating extra work in handling the pack. In other respects it is very fair, and could be made into a good plant. Its situation on the mouth of the "Slough" (the northern mouth of the Skeena River) makes the location an excellent one.

Northern [sic] Pacific & BC Canneries. Both these plants – the property of the ABC Packing Co. – are well equipped and fish a large number of first-class boats. (This year they had between them 144 boats, of which about 70 were fished by Japanese crews.) They are well situated, have ample room for their buildings, and do a very good store trade. They are excellently managed by Mr. W.R. Lord, and the packs put up were the best, as far as workmanship goes, that I saw north of Rivers Inlet.

Aberdeen. This cannery is fairly well laid out, and is the best-equipped property owned by the BC Canning Co., with the possible exception of their Fraser River plant. It is, however, to my mind, badly situated, being too far away from the early fishing, and out of the way also as regards general cannery purposes. It owned by the Association I would advise dismantling and closing down of the plant.

Herman. This is only an apology for a cannery, and if owned by the Association would never be operated. The work performed, however, reflects great credit on the management, and it is a fortunate thing for the slower-going concerns that the operation of this plant is hampered by its lack of space and the precarious financial condition of its proprietors.

Ladysmith and the *Alejanora* canneries I did not visit. They are, however, very small concerns, and are without proper financial backing. As packers they can hardly be considered as serious competitors.

The Association should have a cannery on the Skeena River that would have as great or greater capacity than the combined capacity of their present plants. It should fish at least 250 boats, and be modern in every respect. Its initial capacity should be at least two complete lines. After careful consideration, I think the site chosen should be that of the present Balmoral cannery.

In erecting a cannery, a cold-storage plant should also be added. This is practically essential, for [John] Wallace [Claxton cannery] enjoys the same position as regards Skeena River fishing as we do on the Fraser River as regards coho fishing, i.e., he is in a position to pay more than others can afford for his fish. He has the advantage, though of being able to do so on nearly all his catch, spring, steelhead, or coho, and his margin

on those grades is great enough to permit a substantial increase in the
cost of sockeyes, were he so inclined, which would mean for his competitors that they might have to pack [sockeyes] at a loss. We cannot afford
to remain in this position, and I would strongly urge that we fortify
ourselves by putting up a cold-storage plant that would leave us on even
terms with Wallace, and by working in harmony with him hold the
others in the place we desire to keep them.

Smiths Inlet Notes

Smiths Inlet proper starts about 30 miles from the entrance to Smiths
Sound, and is about 20 miles long by one mile in width. There is good
fishing all the way up, although the water is pretty clear. About 8 miles
up, and on the northerly shore, is a small arm, on which is situated
[William] Hickey's [Smith Inlet] cannery, a small affair resting on set
piles which is inaccessible to vessels except at high tide. There seems to
be an abundance of fresh water, and the surroundings easily admit of
plenty of enlargement being given the plant if so desired. At present the
capacity is not over 7,500 c/s. There is one retort for last cooking; first
cooling being done in kettles. The plant includes a washer (L&B), but no
capper.

Quashela [sic] Lagoon is off the southerly shore of Smiths Inlet, about
2–½ miles above the arm on which Hickey's cannery is located. The
easterly shore of the lagoon has a good grassy beach, and is well adapted
for [beach] seining, not only because the ground is suitable, but owing to
the fish taking that shore oftener than the opposite one. The westerly
shore has two small beaches cleared, but neither are of much value, and
are not likely to be used much in future.

With a seining license this place can be made to produce 5,000 c/s of
sockeyes each year, and by properly fishing the neighbouring waters a
cannery should pack 15,000 c/s yearly, of which one half at least would
be sockeye. If our property on Quashela was protected so as to prevent
trespass, and a close watch maintained to see that no fishing was done in
the lake, the present cannery would find its pack seriously curtailed.

We went up into the lake, and while there is undoubtable evidence
that the regular tides affect its waters, it is to such a small extent that
I think Mr. Sword's decision [to prohibit fishing in the lake] was a just
one. [C.B. Sword was Chief Inspector of Fisheries for BC from 1900 to
1911.]

South Bentwick Arm Notes

This arm is about 25 miles long by an average width of 2 miles. At the
south end there is a grass beach about one mile wide, and two small

streams, one on each side of the bottom land. There is a small Indian shack at present on the land which is suitable for seining and for a cannery site. Plenty of fresh water is obtainable from a waterfall about ¼ mile from the S.E. corner of the flats. The water runs off very quickly from the beach, over 100 feet being the depth about 100 yds. from shore. We staked this beach for foreshore rights in the names of Jas. Fowler and D. McWilliams, and posted notice of application for 20 × 80 chains of land in the name of Fowler. About two miles above the end of the arm and on the left-hand side going toward Labouchere Channel, there is a grassy plain extending along the inlet about two or three miles. Quite a large river comes in at this point, so that fresh water is plentiful. The beach seems well adapted for seining, and the land for a cannery site. We staked this beach for foreshore rights in the names of R.M. Currie, F. Bell, F. Boutilier, D. Rowan, and J. Rowan, in the order named, and posted notice of application for 20 × 80 chains of land each, in the name of Currie, Bell, and D. Rowan.

Almost opposite the last-mentioned piece begins the Indian reserve, which extends from the southern end of the flat land on the eastern shore to a point just beyond the Noek [sic] River. It thus embraces the delta land formed by the Tallyo [sic] and Noek Rivers, excepting about ½ mile from the latter river to the cliffs to the north. This ½ mile stretch we staked for foreshore in the name of E.B. Welsh, but owing to lack of an additional post it was not staked for the land. However, it is worth doing so later on. It would be well also to apply to the Dominion government for the foreshore of the reserve for fishing purposes.

THE CAST OF CHARACTERS

8. *Excerpt from Henry Doyle, "Rise and Decline of the Pacific Salmon Fisheries," vol. 2, 216-46.*

At the time the British Columbia Packers Association was formed it was no longer the general practice to operate as individuals, as was the custom of earlier years. Instead a limited-liability company was formed under a descriptive name than in many cases was geographical in origin, such as Victoria Canning Company, Lulu Island Packing Company, Pacific Coast Packing Company, Westham Island Packing Company, etc. From the standpoint of reminiscences, that was unfortunate since the individuals [who] comprised a limited-liability company lost their separate identities and so do not stand out prominently as did the earlier pioneers. There were, however, a few of the 1892-1902 decade that deserve notice and these I sketch hastily.

The Pacific Coast Packing Company was principally owned by Ninian H. Bain, a good competent canner who had started as bookkeeper of the Delta cannery, married the proprietor's (Thomas E. Ladner) daughter, and started in business for himself in 1893. He was highly thought of and under the amalgamation was made district manager for the Steveston district, but he resigned this position a few years later to re-enter the business on Rivers Inlet on his own account under the name of the Strathcona Packing Company.

Robert Ward & Company, from whom the Imperial cannery was purchased, was a very prominent Victoria commission and brokerage house established in 1864. William C. Ward, a brother of Robert, was General Manager of the Bank of British Columbia. The two worked in close cooperation, and it was generally recognized that if Ward & Company had the selling agency of a canning company, the Bank of British Columbia handled its financial affairs. At the close of the century both brothers returned to their native England to live. Shortly afterwards, Robert Ward & Company was sold to R.V. Winch of Vancouver, and has ever since continued in operation under the name of R.V. Winch & Company.

The original owners of the Imperial cannery were Short & Squair, relatives by marriage, the latter being the former's son-in-law. Neither man was experienced in the cannery business, and losing money, lost control of the cannery itself. Their agents took it from them in settlement of their debt. The location of the plant was excellent, and closely adjacent was the Brunswick No. 1 cannery. On the formation of the British Columbia Packers Association I had the Imperial's fish wharf enlarged and extended and a new section built, uniting the Imperial and Brunswick [No. 1 cannery] buildings, the latter being made the warehousing portion of the plant. Today [c. 1950] the Imperial cannery, greatly enlarged and improved, is the nucleus of the [British Columbia Packers Ltd.] operations in southern British Columbia.

John A. Hume & Company was owned and operated by the English brothers [William D. and Marshall Jr.], sons of the original pioneer, Marshall M. English. The name Hume was acquired on the suggestion of buyers in England, who had a clientele that favoured above all other the "Hume" brand of Columbia River packed salmon, and who thought they could hold that trade if they could offer a Hume brand of sockeye salmon packed on the Fraser River. When the Imperial and Brunswick No. 1 canneries were joined together to make the existing Imperial plant, the old Hume cannery was turned into the net house for the combined operations.

The Canadian Pacific Packing Company owners in 1902 were Alexander Ewen, George Alexander, and David Hennessey, all listed among the original pioneers. Mr. Ewen became president of the British Columbia Packers Association, Alexander became district manager for the Westham Island–Canoe Pass district, and Hennessey retired to spend his remaining days at farming.

Wursburg & Co. – an Israelite [Jewish] ownership – entered the business [Albion Island cannery] with no knowledge concerning it and insufficient capital; and in its struggle to survive it was a thorn in the side of all the other operators. Finally, in desperation, all its competitors, acting under an association known as the Fraser River Canners' Association, bought the Albion Island plant from its creditors and resold it to the British Columbia Packers Association when it was formed.

Of Currie, McWilliams & Fowler, the two first named had been bookkeeper and foreman, respectively, for Ewen and Munn at the Bon Accord cannery, while Fowler was an engineer on the Empress steamers, plying between British Columbia and the Orient. Later on Fowler retired to become the Lloyd's agent in Seattle. He never took an active part in the canning business. McWilliams returned to his native Nova Scotia when [the partnership] sold out to the British Columbia Packers Association, and Currie severed his connection with the business about the same time.

The Cleeve Canning & Cold Storage Company was owned by Sir Thomas Cleeve, an Irish baronet, who operated in Ireland on much the same lines as did Sir Thomas Lipton in Scotland and England, and who wished to pack his own salmon sales requirements. His British Columbia representative was a son-in-law, J.A. Talbot, who returned to Ireland to live once the cannery and cold-storage plant changed ownership [in 1902].

The Westminster Packing Company was owned by a wealthy firm of Chinamen, under the leadership of a most highly respected Chinese resident of New Westminster named Lam Tung. Besides owning and operating their own cannery [Westminster, or Lam Tung] in the Royal City [New Westminster], they were contractors supplying other canners with the Chinese labour they required. They made more money out of these contracts than from their own canning accomplishments.

The Terra Nova Canning Company was owned and operated by two brothers, Duncan and Jack Rowan, skilled canners, both of whom had long been employed at J.H. Todd & Son's Richmond and Beaver canneries. On the formation of the British Columbia Packers Association, Duncan Rowan was made district manager for the North Arm and, under W.H. Barker, was given entire charge of all the Association's Fraser River canneries. Jack Rowan was in charge of the Imperial cannery operations under his brother and for many years subsequent to the latter's death.

The Dinsmore Island Packing Company was owned and operated by William Hickey and William McPherson. In the year of its sale to the British Columbia Packers Association, Hickey, in partnership with Robert Kelly of Kelly, Douglas & Company, Vancouver, acquired the exclusive salmon-seining rights for Smith Inlet (despite the emphatic protests of Victoria Canning Company, from whom the Ottawa government had withdrawn [seining rights]), and built a cannery [Smith Inlet cannery] there. This was afterwards acquired [1911] by the Wallace Fisheries Ltd.

Of the Welsh brothers, who operated the Celtic cannery on the North Arm, Robert A. was made district manager of the British Columbia Packers Association's Puget Sound properties. His brother did not retain any connection with the business.

But of all the "newer pioneers" of Fraser River operations the most colourful was the partnership of two brothers-in-law George W. Dawson and Fred J. Buttimer. They were New Brunswickers and as different from each other as day is from night. They had enough money to build and operate a plant at Steveston, called the Brunswick No. 1, where Dawson kept the books and attended to the selling, and Buttimer managed productions. They were very successful. [In the late 1890s] with the profits they made [at the Brunswick], they built another cannery on Canoe Pass, known as Brunswick No. 2, and a third plant on Rivers Inlet, Brunswick No. 3.

Buttimer was a short, quiet-mannered man, shrewd in judgement but retiring by nature. Dawson was large and very distinguished looking, generally inclined to silence but a very fury when aroused, which happened quite often. When I first knew him he lived in a little cottage on the corner of Hastings and Westminster Avenue (the present Main Street) in Vancouver, where later on, when he became affluent, he erected the Dawson Building ...

During the crucial, anxious years which had marked the opening of the 20th century, the price of fish, the selling prices of the canned products, and the legislative problems affecting the fishing industry had brought into being amongst the canning companies a protective organization known as the Fraser River Canners' Association. It was maintained by assessments of so much per case against the respective companies comprising the Association. Along with other operators was the new firm of Buttimer & Dawson, which had re-entered the business a couple of years after George Dawson and Fred Buttimer had disposed of their original holdings to the British Columbia Packers Association. Buttimer & Dawson acquired a small cannery on Harlock Island, opposite Steveston, and in 1905 they bought sockeye from a fisherman who had contracted to sell all of his salmon catch to one of the British Columbia

Packers Association's canneries. A warrant for receiving stolen goods was taken out by the Fraser River Canners' Association against Buttimer & Dawson; although the latter were promptly acquitted, George Dawson afterwards had no use for the Fraser River Canners' Association and was very bitter towards all its members.

A few years later, when Fraser River packs had dwindled so that the assessments were inadequate to meet expenses, and when the preponderance of northern British Columbia packs made contributions from operations there essential, the members of the Fraser River Canners' Association changed the name of the organization to the British Columbia Canners' Association. Most northern operators, myself amongst the number, were not members of the Canners' Association, and I felt that if and when the members wrote or interviewed Ottawa or Victoria government officials concerning pending or desired legislation, it would be presumed that they spoke in the interests of the industry as a whole. I therefore prepared a memorial [sic] pointing out this probability and asking the authorities not to act on this assumption unless the independent operators concurred in writing with each and every position the Association presented. When finally completed and filed, our memorial represented operators which packed over 60% of the canned salmon pack put up in the province.

The firm of Buttimer & Dawson eventually acquired three canneries in northern British Columbia; the Carlisle on Skeena River, the Manitou on the Kimsquit Arm of Dean Channel, and at Kildala in Rivers Inlet. They also owned the Uchucklesit cannery [later Kildonan, originally Alberni] on the Alberni Canal [sic], Vancouver Island. The firm's head office was in Vancouver ...

One of the northern British Columbia canneries acquired by the British Columbia Packers Association was purchased from the Balmoral Canning Company, owned by Turner Beeton and George Burns, both of Victoria. When the Skeena River operations were consolidated, a new and greatly enlarged cannery [Balmoral] was erected on the Balmoral site, and the other plants in the vicinity were dismantled. M.M. English, Jr., son of the old Fraser River pioneer [and my brother-in-law], was for many years manager of the Association's Skeena River district.

The two other Skeena River canneries acquired were controlled by the Victoria Canning Co., or rather, the latter's agents, R.P. Rithet & Co., of Victoria, although the Cunningham plant was entirely owned by Robert Cunningham and his son George. The elder Cunningham was a real pioneer of the northwest coast. He was an English ex-prizefighter who "got" religion in his native land and was sent to British Columbia as an assistant to the Rev. Mr. Duncan at Metlakatla. Shortly after arriving, he lost what he had "got" and became an employee of the Hudson's Bay

Company at Port Simpson. Subsequently, he engaged in the general-store business, first at Woodcock's Landing (now Inverness) at the Skeena River's northmost mouth, and later at Port Essington, or "Spokeshute," as it is locally known. His Indian wife and eldest son drowned opposite Spokeshute while they were returning from a visit to their former home at Melakatla.

The China Hat cannery (owned by Toms, Morris & Fraser) was only two years old when I bought it for the British Columbia Packers Association. My associates, never regarding the purchase favourably, almost immediately dismantled and abandoned the plant. Subsequently, Morris became a cannery manager for J.H. Todd & Son and persuaded them to build a cannery [Klemtu] near China Hat. It has been a heavy and consistent money-maker for this company. Frank Fraser, the partner of that name, had charge of the net department at Imperial cannery for many years, and his son Kenneth is, at present time, the genial and efficient manager of the Imperial's vast operations, embracing canning, freezing, fresh, and smoked fish departments, and the intricate processes that convert into valuable commercial products that ⅓ of the gross receipts of raw material which in olden times was considered, and disposed of, as waste.

John Clayton, who sold his cannery [Bella Coola] to the British Columbia Packers Association, was an old Hudson's Bay Company factor who acquired title to that Company's assets in the Bella Coola area when the Company decided to close the Bella Bella and Bella Coola trading stations. He had represented the great fur company there for many years; during most of the period he was the only white man living in that vicinity. He was the most fluent linguist in the Chinook dialect I have ever known, and he had an enormous influence with the local natives.

Originally Clayton had no intention of engaging in the cannery business, but when Robert Draney, who had some years previous built and operated a salmon canning plant at Namu, expressed his intention of expanding by building at Bella Coola also, Clayton built to forestall him for fear of losing some of the local trade. However, his heart was never in the new enterprise. When I agreed to a proviso in the purchase contract that stipulated that the British Columbia Packers Association would not engage in general merchandising in connection with its Bella Coola operation, he was delighted to sell us the cannery.

While the British Columbia Packers Association did not at this time acquire the Draney properties, the subsequent development of Robert Draney's holdings makes it fitting to speak here of that gentleman and his connection with the salmon-canning industry. Robert Draney was a native of Ontario, and his first connection with a salmon cannery was as blacksmith at the Inverness cannery when that plant, the first to operate on the Skeena River, was built at Woodcock's Landing in 187[8]. In 1881 he, in partnership with Thomas Shotbolt, a merchant of Victoria, built the first cannery [RIC] on Rivers Inlet, at the head. This they sold in a few years to the British Columbia Canning Company, an English company that operated by long-distance through the firm of Findlay, Durham & Brodie, of Victoria, of which Matthew Trotter Johnson, a genial and cultured English gentleman, was resident manager.

After selling out on Rivers Inlet, Robert Draney in 1893 built a salmon cannery and saw-mill at Namu, on Fitzhugh Sound. The site was most judiciously chosen as it lay about halfway between Queen Charlotte and Milbank sounds, and all the territorial area between these waterways, with its immense fishery wealth, was tributary to the seat of his operations. Here, Draney settled and raised a family of six sons and a daughter. Once the sons attained manhood Draney decided to build a second cannery for their benefit. When Clayton forestalled him at Bella Coola, he built, in 1902, his Kimsquit cannery near the head of Dean Channel.

Robert and Mrs. Draney were noted all along the northern British Columbia coast for their genial and open hearted hospitality, and Namu in their time was always the mecca toward which all transient travellers turned. I tried very hard to secure the Draney properties when I formed the British Columbia Packers Association, but the directors felt that the $60,000 I proposed paying was more than those assets were worth ...

Of the other northern cannery plants secured by the British Columbia Packers Association when it commenced operating, the Vancouver Packing Company on Rivers Inlet was acquired from the Rev. Alfred E. Green, a pioneer Methodist missionary, who was well known all along the northern coast. His interests embraced far more than his profession indicated: he owned many mining claims and potential cannery sites. His later years were spent in retirement in Vancouver.

Stephen A. Spencer built the cannery and general store at Alert Bay in 1881. He was a typical backwoodsman storekeeper, although he had been a photographer in Victoria in his younger days. He had lived contentedly amongst the Indians on picturesque Cormorant Island that lays opposite the mouth of Nimpkish River, which was the source of all of his salmon supplies. When I was negotiating with Spencer for the purchase of his plant, I asked to see his books so as to estimate the value of his holdings. The old man's reply was: "I do not bother to keep any books. All I know is that every year there is about $10,000 more in my bank account than there was a year before. You can ask the bank manager if that is not so, and if it does not satisfy you I will keep the property. I do not know what more I can say." It did satisfy me for I knew the old man spoke the truth. The percentage return on the $30,000 I paid for his property made the deal quite worthwhile ...

The most interesting experience I had was in connection with old J.H. Todd's son, Charlie. The old man had only recently joined his forefathers, after having survived long enough to see his son live fully up to the reputation which Tom Ladner heard he had earned for parsimoniousness. When I explained my project he was deeply interested, studied it carefully, and promised to give me the option I desired. I still have, in his own handwriting, the memorandum of the prices he agreed to accept for each of the assets to be taken over. With his assurances of cooperating, I then returned to Vancouver ... The option promised was never given, although Chas. F. Todd repeated to the Underwriter's representative the assurances he had previously given me. The company is still operating under its original ownership, the oldest of all the existing companies in the salmon-canning industry either in Canada or in the United States ...

THE FINAL TALLY

9. *"The Properties Acquired by the British Columbia Packers Association at its Formation," Doyle, "Rise and Decline," Vol. 2, app. 1c.*

Fraser River

Ewen & Co. (Lion Island cannery), and Victoria Canning Co. (Delta, Wellington, and Harlock canneries), all on the main river; Colonial Canning Co., Canadian Packing Co., Pacific Coast Canning, Robert Ward & Co. (Imperial cannery), Dawson & Buttimer (Brunswick cannery #1), and John A. Hume & Co., all above Steveston; Lulu Island Canning Co. and Atlas Canning Co., at Steveston; Fishermen's Packing Co. (Port Guichon), below Ladner; Dawson & Buttimer (Brunswick #2), Anglo-American Canning Co., and Westham Island Canning Co., all at Canoe Pass; Currie, McWilliams & Fowler (Westham Island), and Wursburg & Co. (Albion Island), main river; Boutilier & Co., Cleeve Canning & Cold Storage Co., Premier Canning Co., and Westminster Packing Co., all at New Westminster; Terra Nova Canning Co. (Lulu Island), Dinsmore Island Packing Co., Ewen & Munn (Sea Island cannery), Alliance Canning Co., Provincial Canning Co., Welsh Bros. (Celtic cannery), Acme Canning Co., and Greenwood Canning Co., all on the North Arm, Fraser River. In addition, the Columbia Cold Storage Co.'s cold-storage plant in New Westminster was acquired, and, as the name indicates, another, but smaller, refrigeration plant was acquired with the Cleeve cannery.

Northern BC

Balmoral Canning Co. (opposite Port Essington), Robert Cunningham & Son (at Port Essington), and Victoria Canning Co. (Standard cannery), all on the Skeena River; Victoria Canning Co. (Wannock cannery), Dawson & Buttimer (Brunswick cannery #3), Vancouver Packing Co. (Vancouver cannery), E.A. Wadhams (Wadhams cannery), all on Rivers Inlet; Victoria Canning Co. (Queshela Lagoon, closed), Smith Inlet; (Cascade cannery, closed), Nass River; (Lowe Inlet cannery), Lowe Inlet; Toms, Morris & Fraser (China Hat cannery), China Hat; John Clayton (Bella Coola cannery), Bella Coola; and Stephen A. Spencer (Alert Bay cannery), Alert Bay.

Total: 43 operations.

CHAPTER TWO

Scramble for Control

INTRODUCTION

International control of the Fraser River system sockeye fishery – specifically, the rise of the Puget Sound sockeye fishery at the expense of the Fraser – was a major issue for the BC salmon fishery by the turn of the century. The salmon-canning industry of the Puget Sound district had started in the 1870s (document 10).[1] Most of the early canners there had received their start on the Columbia River, then had moved northward into the Sound and Alaska in the 1870s and 1880s. A boom occurred in the fisheries in the Sound and in the Fraser River district of BC in the 1890s.

The year that the British Columbia Packers Association started, 1903, witnessed the unexpected collapse of the Pacific Packing & Navigation Company on the American side of the international border. Pacific Packing represented a short-lived, ambitious attempt by the Puget Sound canners to amalgamate plants there and in Alaska into the largest salmon-fishing and -packing company to date. A major cause of the failure was that Pacific Packing was financially so over-extended that, with the poor sockeye runs of 1902, it became vulnerable to the campaign waged against it by its competitor, Alaska Packers Association, which had recently begun to acquire canning operations in the Sound area. But, as Doyle's account makes clear, one result Alaska Packers did not anticipate was that several financially strong competitors would replace the one that was weak: over time, Alaska Packers would lose ground to new packing companies such as Pacific American Fisheries, Inc. This was a typical pattern in the aftermath of the big merger movement that swept North American manufacturing in the 1890s and early 1900s. The results of operations for the big three early consolidations – Alaska Packers Association, British Columbia Packers Association, and Columbia River Packers Association – as shown in tables A8, A9, and A10, illustrate the trend.

The rapid expansion of the industry on the Sound was due not only to the usually large runs of sockeye, but also to the widespread use of trap nets, which, as Doyle points out, were used first on the Columbia River and then on the Sound by a handful of Fraser River canners as they began to expand into the Point Roberts and Upper Sound area. Trap nets were well suited to the fishery in the Sound. Except where the Fraser River outflow sweeps into the top, the salt water in the Sound is too clear to be fished efficiently using the traditional gillnet method.

Doyle addressed the threat posed by the Puget Sound fishery in a major brief he presented in 1903 to the newly appointed federal minister of fisheries, J.R.F. Préfontaine (document 11), and in the various papers he prepared on the biology of Pacific salmon. The Government of Canada repeatedly tried to negotiate a treaty for Fraser River sockeye, but the United States failed to ratify any such agreement until the 1930s. Doyle also developed and circulated his ideas about the spawning "instincts" of Pacific salmon (Doyle believed that salmon are guided to their native spawning grounds by a sense of smell) and about the threat posed by the sea-lion population.[2] Given what we know today, his theories were generally sound: it was later proven through tagging programs that salmon do return to their native habitat to spawn, and most scientists today believe that returning salmon are guided by a sense of smell. But in Doyle's day, the fisheries experts dismissed his ideas as unscientific (document 12).[3] Doyle also worked on the problem of recycling fish waste. Even before fisheries authorities insisted that cannery operators properly dispose of their fish waste rather than simply toss it into the chuck, Doyle was experimenting with ways to turn the waste into profitable by-products (document 13).

As well as attempting to influence fisheries policies, Doyle set to work outlining a strategy for the British Columbia Packers Association's first operating season (document 14). Acquiring the cannery operations was one thing; transforming them into a modern company was quite another. Doyle's papers provide rare details on the strategies employed and costs involved. He proposed a series of changes to the canneries owned by the Association in the various districts, estimated their cost, and suggested which of the changes could be delayed. Most of the changes he proposed involved improving the condition of the plants and equipment. He also worked out agreements between the British Columbia Packers Association–owned plants and the other cannery operators on the Skeena River, the Nass River, and Rivers Inlet (document 15). These voluntary agreements limited the number of boats fishing for each cannery and did away with the competition for the armies of fishers and shoreworkers that flocked to the various cannery camps and villages each season. No longer, for example, were individual cannery operators to "steal" Indians

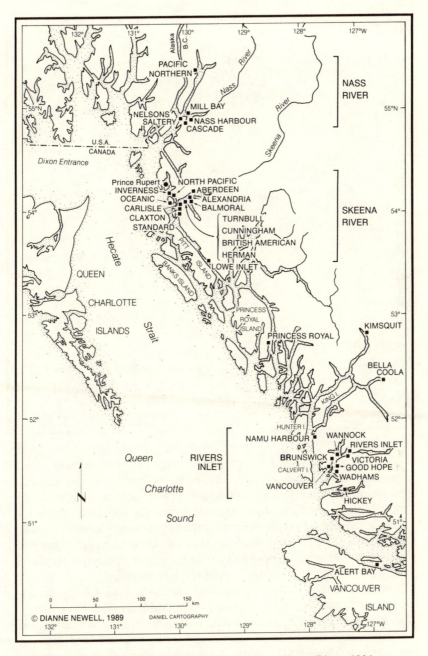

Figure 4: Location of BC Salmon Canneries other than Fraser River, 1904

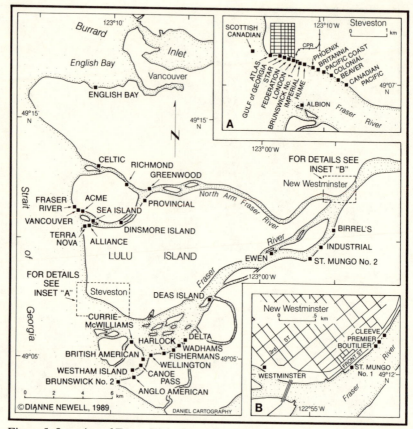

Figure 5: Location of Fraser River Canneries, 1904

away from other canneries by offering higher wages or better piece rates, a practice which had become common in the peak years for salmon. Although the Indians likely resisted this new policy (just as they did in the sealing industry), many of them were already obligated to fish for specific cannery operations because of the cash advances given to them at the end of the previous fishing season. Doyle recommended that the agreements for each district be signed on the same day and that bonds be put up by the various parties to bind the agreements.

The 1903 and 1904 canning seasons progressed along the lines anticipated by Doyle. His notebooks and correspondence files show him to have been an energetic and resourceful company manager, who reacted swiftly to the vagaries of the salmon-fishing season in each of the districts (documents 16–18). He hunted down details about the various operations up and down the coast. In a set of unique accounts, he noted the packing capacity of each plant (as measured by the number of canning

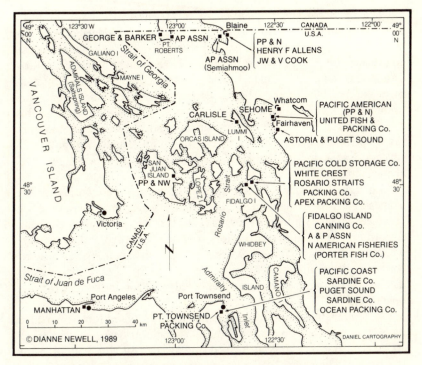

Figure 6: Location of Puget Sound Salmon Canneries, 1904

lines) in the Alaska, Puget Sound, Columbia River, and BC districts (document 19) and determined the exact variety and quantity of equipment and crew needed to put up a given size of pack for each line of packing capacity in 1904 (documents 20–20a). Apparently, packing the smaller sizes of cans cost more than packing the large size, because it took more tinplate and time to process the same quantity of fish. He noted, too, that the average capacity of BC plants was smaller than that of the American ones. This finding is hardly surprising, however, given the enormous size of the runs and the unregulated nature of the American salmon fishery – and thus greater ability to capture salmon – in this era. Because the key innovations in salmon canning were American, it is generally thought that the BC industry had to import cannery equipment from the United States, but, as Doyle's notebooks (document 17) show, when he outfitted the British Columbia Packers Association plants with the latest in canning machinery he was able to obtain most of it from local manufacturers in New Westminster (Schaake Machine Works) and Vancouver (Letson & Burpee [L&B] Ltd.).[4] The year in which Doyle outlined a state-of-the-art cannery operation, 1904, marked the tail end of the manual era of production in this industry.[5]

Doyle paid particular attention to the terms and conditions of all Chinese labour contracts (documents 22–23). In particular, he scrutinized the work of British Columbia Packers Association's main Chinese contractor, Lee Coy. Doyle seems not to have thought much of Lee Coy as a labour manager, though he did acknowledge his work as a union-buster in the 1904 season, when he earned a $2,400 bonus for "breaking unions." How common it was to use Chinese (or Japanese) bosses in this role is not known. In these years some of the Indian agents also were involved in labour issues; they tended to advise (usually without much success) Indians not to participate in union activities, especially strikes, at the canneries.[6]

Although the canneries paid the Indian women who worked in the canneries (called "Klootchmen") fixed hourly wages for cleaning the fish and piece rate for filling the cans, the Chinese "bosses" supervised them. Accordingly, the cannery operators routinely recorded Indian cannery workers' labour as "Chinese Work," or "China Labour." A precise record of their earnings and expenditures can be found only occasionally, usually in the surviving "fishermen's ledgers" for individual cannery operations.

The fishing and cannery agreements Doyle proposed for the northern district were based on those of the new trade association, the Fraser River Canners' Association, formed in 1900 to deal with conditions on the Fraser. The names of the various fish-processing associations in BC are a bit confusing. In 1902, the Fraser River Canners' Association merged with the British Columbia Salmon Packers Association, which had been formed in 1899 to replace "The Combination of Cannery Packers" of 1897, but it continued to be called the Fraser River Canners' Association until 1909. In that year it was renamed the British Columbia Salmon Canners' Association.[7]

Unlike in the North, where Indians remained important as commercial salmon fishers until after World War II, by 1904 Japanese fishers were rapidly replacing Indians in the Fraser River district and were moving into the northern district too. Their "bosses" were organized by this point and wanted the cannery operators to pay them a commission for their services. Their petition to the Fraser Rivers Canners Association in 1904 (document 25a), which was by then a province-wide organization, outlines their role in the industry and provides a rarely surviving list of names of Japanese fishers' bosses for 15 cannery operations on the Fraser.

The power of the canner operators' agreements for the northern district was tested in the 1904 season. In that year, a major strike of fishers occurred over fish prices. Several unofficial fishers' strikes had been held in the northern region before 1904, but these had involved Indians alone.

Eventually, as Japanese fishers began to move into the northern district, they also participated in strikes.

The 1904 fishing strikes on the Skeena and Nass rivers were the most determined of the northern strikes to that point.[8] Eight hundred Indian fishers and two hundred Indian women cannery workers, unaffiliated with any union, led the strike on the Skeena just as the runs of sockeye began. The cannery operators wanted a fixed-price agreement to cover this season and the next four-year cycle of good and bad years. They offered the fishers an opening price of seven cents per fish; the Indians wanted ten cents (documents 26a, 26c). The local operators were willing to compromise at eight cents over a three-year period, but the canners' association vetoed the move (document 26b). Initially, the Japanese fishers supported the strike, but their support was short-lived. Once the runs of fish picked up, some of the Japanese began to fish. However, because there were so few Japanese fishers in the North at the time, it was not possible for them to keep pace with the big runs on the Skeena that year.

As is clear from the flurry of telegrams passing between W.D. Burdis, secretary of the Fraser River Canners Association, E.H. Bridgeman, secretary of the managers' committee on the Skeena River, and the various cannery operators on the Skeena, some cannery operators eventually settled with the Indians on price – offering them eight cents or higher (documents 26a–26f, 28a–28n). The northern Indian agents got involved by organizing a meeting between the Indian chiefs and the cannery operators. By this time, however, many of the striking Indians had either returned to their homes or travelled to the Fraser River fishing grounds. On the Fraser, the Skeena River strikers were quickly employed in a few canneries, including even plants owned by the British Columbia Packers Association.

Doyle was angered by the cannery association's unwillingness to deal with the unco-operative fishers and cannery operators (document 29). As for the Indians who shifted to the Fraser, that season turned out to have poor runs. Doyle does not go into the details, but, according to the local Indian agent, most of the Indian fishers did not catch enough fish on the Fraser to repay their cash advances or to pay for their provisions for the season, "and in fact, some went away in debt to the canneries."[9]

By this time, Henry Doyle himself was at such odds with British Columbia Packers Association that at the close of the 1904 season he resigned from his position as general manager. According to Cicely Lyons, a long-time secretary with British Columbia Packers Ltd., who eventually became the unofficial company historian, Doyle's resignation came as no surprise to most of the canning interests in the province.[10] He had made enemies on the company's board. The Eastern directors had complained of the poor results obtained in the first few years after the amalgamation, and they believed that Doyle was to blame. The directors also were apparently angered that, at the time of purchase of the various cannery operations, Doyle had not extracted from each seller a formal agreement to refrain from engaging in the salmon-processing industry, except for the British Columbia Packers Association, for seven to ten years. Without such an agreement, many of the sellers started up independent operations almost immediately. Lyons writes that this lack of a formal agreement "caused a rift between Jarvis and Doyle which widened with the passing years – and earned for the British Columbia Packers' Association an unsparing critic."[11] Doyle was a critic of British Columbia Packers Association, to be sure, but he and Jarvis remained on friendly terms for the next two decades.

Another chronicler of the canning industry, Hugh McKervill, agrees that Doyle had a pernicious side to his personality. According to McKervill, Doyle could be "quite vitriolic and an unscathing critic of those who were not blessed with the same opinion as himself."[12] But unlike Lyons, who regarded Doyle as an incompetent businessman, a failing she claims was due to his inexperience, McKervill was immensely impressed with Doyle as an assiduous businessman who kept a detailed record of the industry throughout most of his career.

There is little doubt that Henry Doyle bore a grudge against the company for years. But his disappointment was not without justification, as becomes painfully clear the deeper one delves into the written record he left behind. Doyle's own version of his resignation from British Columbia Packers Association differs considerably from Lyons'. In a long letter to Jarvis, Doyle set out his complaints (document 30). According to Doyle, the shareholders considered his ideas about changes in plants, management, expansion, and diversification to be impractical, and therefore they never gave him the backing he deserved. All former owner/operators, for example, were supposed to be given first consideration for any cannery positions at the disposal of British Columbia Packers Association. Doyle carefully documented how the directors ignored this obligation. For this reason, the former owners were not to be blamed for starting up canneries on their own shortly after the amalgamation. As far as Doyle was concerned, there had been only an implied agreement with each of the sellers, which he considered to be unenforceable. This is difficult to believe, however, since the draft letter of agreement used to form the amalgamation included a sample of an indenture for securing options on canneries. The indenture contains the promise that the vendor will "not alone or in partnership, or as a shareholder, stockholder, director or trustee, engage in the business of packing or canning fish" for ten years within twenty miles of tidewater in the province.[13] Similarly, the local cannery agents who had helped persuade their clients to join the amalgamation were, "all things being equal," supposed to handle the supply and insurance requirements for British Columbia Packers Association. Doyle had given his word, and the offended parties blamed him when things did not work out according to the agreement.[14] Finally, in Doyle's view the "absentee" Eastern bondholders constantly interfered with the management of the company – they seemed to know nothing about the nature of the industry. It was for these reasons alone, claimed Doyle, that he resigned as general manager and director in 1904. The company president, Alexander Ewen, resigned too, and for the same reasons as Doyle, a matter which Lyons neglected to mention in her account of the Doyle resignation.[15]

Replacing Doyle as general manager was George I. Wilson, who had been the company secretary. Another director, Robert Ker, a Victoria businessman, replaced Wilson as secretary. These two appointments led to bitter complaints from Doyle, who considered the new appointees to be unknowledgeable about the technical aspects of the industry and incompetent as managers. He somehow convinced the directors to approach the Alaska Packers Association for advice. This led them, in 1904-05, to engage a prominent canner, William H. Barker, to investigate the problem. Barker was a principal in the American fish-packing firm of George & Barker Co. and former general superintendent of the Columbia River Packers Association. Following Barker's investigation, Ewen and Doyle were asked to withdraw their resignations from the board. Ewen rejoined; Doyle, however, did not; he strongly objected to the company's keeping Wilson and Ker on as directors. In 1905, Wilson was in fact replaced by Barker. Barker became president in 1907, when Ewen died, and held that position for the next twenty-one years, until his own resignation, in 1926.

Henry Doyle was out of the company for good. Having failed to have it operate along the lines of his original proposal and no longer able to manage it from within, he secretly attempted to interest a few investors outside the province, notably Edward Eyre in California, to create a new syndicate to take over control of both British Columbia Packers Association and Columbia River Packers Association in 1906 (document 31).[16] Doyle intended, of course, to manage the new bigger and better amalgamation thus created. But an economic recession was underway on the west coast. Since he had no substantial financial resources of his own and was encountering considerable trouble finding suitable backers in the United States, he quickly abandoned the idea for the time being and launched a new career for himself as manager and part-owner of half a dozen important cannery operations in the northern district of BC.

INTERNATIONAL COMPETITION FOR THE RESOURCE

10. Excerpt from Henry Doyle, "Rise and Decline of the Pacific Salmon Fisheries," vol. 2, ch. 15.

The Puget Sound Fishery

The first salmon cannery on Puget Sound was built in 1877 by Jackson & Myers at Mukilteo, a few miles south of where the city of Everett now stands. Its owners had started on the Columbia but thought that river was getting overprovided with canneries and that they could do better in the virgin territory lying to the north. They chose Mukilteo as a suitable location because of its close proximity to the Snohomish River, but its exposed position to storms sweeping down the Sound proved too great a handicap, and after a couple of years, they abandoned Mukilteo and rebuilt in the little town of Seattle. There, they had a sheltered site and were more centrally located for all the fishing areas of the Upper Sound. With the change of location, the ownership also changed, Myers buying out his associate, and thereafter Geo. T. Myers & Co. became the operational name. The firm grew, progressed, and eventually became large and successful, extending its operations to Alaska as well, with son succeeding father in name, business ability, and popularity.

My first recollection of Seattle was in 1882, when my father took me to M. Myers' cannery to see the little steamer he had nearing completion and which was to be employed in gathering up fish from the neighbouring salmon streams. Compared to present-day fish collectors, it was extremely primitive, but at that time people thought Toby Myers extravagantly daring to build so large a vessel and spend so much on its construction. However, its success fully vindicated his judgement ...

The second cannery built on Puget Sound was at Tacoma, the then aggressive rival of Seattle in a contest for supremacy. It was another Columbia River canneryman, James Williams, who inaugurated the new adventure; but his financial position was weak, the location unfortunate, and he was compelled to abandon the field after a season or two.

In those years there was hardly any demand for the cheaper varieties of salmon and, with the exception of a few spring, or chinook, no others were procurable in Upper Puget Sound. True, Indians at Lummi Island and the Point Roberts reefs caught sockeye in season with their crude reef nets, but the take of these primitive fishing appliances was small and the distance to Seattle and Tacoma too far for the transportation means then available. As a consequence, while it was known that sockeye salmon swam through the waters of the Lower Sound, they were not fished revise by the natives for sale or for their own use. Gill-nets were practically useless in the clear salt water; hand-operated purse seines too slow in setting to be closed before the fish sounded and escaped; and traps were, in these waters, an untried method of catching salmon.

Traps had, however, been introduced on the Columbia River, and while not overly successful there, gave promise of future benefits when better understood. A man named Goodfellow, residing at Point Roberts, and several others in that vicinity or around Lummi Island, experimented somewhat, and their success simultaneously decided E.A. Wadhams and Daniel Drysdale of the Fraser River to use the money received from the sale of their BC canneries to the Anglo-British Columbia Packing Company to build on the American side of the international boundary line, and to depend entirely on traps for their fish supplies. Wadhams built his cannery on the eastern shore of the tip of Point Roberts, Drysdale his on Semiahmoo Spit in Drayton Harbor, just off the town of Blaine.

For successful operation a trap must be set or driven so the line of its lead does not parallel but actually crosses, however slightly, the pathway of current, scent, taste, or other attraction the salmon are following on their journey back to their native river or stream. When off this mark, the fish will follow the lead but swim beyond its influence and the unlucky trap owner has the mortification of seeing his intended victims glide by in countless thousands while only a few stragglers along the inner edge of the shoal come within the orbit of the appliance set for their capture. In the first year of their operations in the waters of the Lower Sound this lack of knowledge of how a trap should be set often proved disastrous, and many a trap owner lost his all because the few sockeyes he captured nowhere near compensated him for the cost of installation and operation of his trap. Both Wadhams' and Drysdale's experiences were that their traps were improperly driven in the first two years, and it was not until the third try that they learned to set them to obtain the best results.

The Wadhams and Drysdale canneries were both built in 1891, and while each of them made money from the start, Drysdale's operations showed the greatest profits of the two. His Semiahmoo cannery made $15,000 in 1891, $22,000 in 1892, and then in 1893, with all the traps properly placed, the net return was $75,000, and could have been twice as great – so abundant was the take of fish – had his packing capacity been equal to the occasion. As it was, he sent to Seattle for scowloads of ice and iced down 80,000 sockeyes to be processed later, when the cans purchased from the Columbia River area arrived and were made available.

So great was the 1893 success of Drysdale and Wadhams that their field of operation engaged the attention of the Alaska Packers Association, and to enter, and, as they then thought, to control this new fishing area, they bought out the two individuals named and enlarged the packing capacity of both plants. Subsequent operations proved that economies could be effected by closing down the poorly located Wadhams cannery and adding its equipment to the plant at Semiahmoo.

The price paid Drysdale for the Semiahmoo cannery was approximately $300,000; Wadhams received about a third of that sum for his Point Roberts investment. All of this capital outlay was returned to the Association out of the profits made in 1894, 1895, and 1896. Taken as a whole, the Association's Puget Sound profits for its first two decades exceeded those made in the same period in all their Alaska canneries combined, thus vindicating Henry Fortman's foresight in acquiring these properties.

During the first 10 or 11 years for operations in the Puget Sound district the total cost of the pack at Semiahmoo cannery never exceeded $2.50 per case for 1-lb. talls. This was inclusive of the cost of fish – including the installation and maintenance costs of all their traps – all cannery supply costs, labour, management, and all the expenses of transport and shipping. After this time the cost of fish rose steadily. In 1906, contracts with independent trap owners were for 25¢ to 26¢ each for sockeyes, Bob Welsh paying the last named figure to Phil Cook for all the latter's Strawberry Bay trap-caught fish.

So successful was the Alaska Packers Association on Puget Sound, and so great was the confidence in its judgement, that it was not long before others followed them into this new fishing territory. Two enterprising youths, Young & Williams, built at Blaine, but their operations were not very successful. They were somewhat short of capital and, in addition, lost money through improperly setting their traps. Subsequently, they sold their cannery to J.W. Cook, the well-known Columbia River cannery pioneer, and under his ownership the traps were properly placed and the company made money. Cook's manager and part owner [of the cannery] at Blaine was Jarvis L. Smiley. Smiley had started on the Columbia River as foreman for the Eureka & Epicure Packing Company. When Cook finally decided, when in his 80s, that he was old enough to retire, he turned the entire Blaine property over to Smiley; the latter was even more successful in his sole ownership than he had been with the previous partnership. Some years later, he acquired an interest in the old Henry F. Allen Red cannery at Blaine, and also built and operated another plant in Alaska. Smiley was one of the most highly regarded and popular men in the business ...

At the time J.W. Cook bought the Young & Williams cannery at Blaine, he also acquired that of the Manhattan Packing Co. at Port Townsend, built and originally operated by "young" Joe Hume. Joe was the nephew of old William Hume, who was the cause of [Joe's] violent antipathy to Astoria and all Astorians. Port Townsend, however, was not suitably located for participation in the sockeye fishery. Shortly after acquiring it, Cook abandoned the plant and moved its equipment to Blaine.

Another pioneering canning firm in the Blaine area was Ainsworth & Dunn. [Ainsworth and Dunn] were amongst the most successful and highly respected men ever to engage in the business. The fathers of both men were associated with the Great Lakes fisheries, with headquarters in Buffalo, and the sons were inseparable friends and companions from childhood unto death. They came to the Pacific coast together, engaged together in the fresh-fish business in Seattle. They then expanded their operations by building a cannery at Blaine, which made them independently rich from its operation under their ownership. After some years, they sold out for $325,000 to the Pacific Packing & Navigation Company, when that ill-fated enterprise came into being. Three years later, at the receiver's sale [for the PP&N Co.], Ainsworth and Dunn re-acquired their former property for $75,000. Under their second period of ownership, they continued making handsome profits as of yore, but after the Fraser Canyon catastrophe [in 1913], they retired permanently from the business ...

Another pioneer canning firm in the Blaine-Point Roberts area was the George & Barker Packing Co., whose plant was on the west side of Point Roberts, one-half mile south of the International Boundary line. Like so many others, George and Barker were old Columbia River operators; had been partners in that area as well; and shortly after George became general manager of the Columbia River Packers Association, Wm. H. Barker assumed a similar position with the British Columbia Packers Association [1904].

Coming later to the district than most of the others, George and Barker were not as successful in acquiring choice trap sites as others in their locality, although some of the [sites] they did secure were fair. But what they lacked in this respect was compensated for by their close proximity to the Fraser River and its gill-net fishermen. As a receiver of stolen goods successfully smuggled across the international border, the company put up large packs and made handsome profits. In my first year as general manager of the British Columbia Packers Association, I was on a tour of inspection on one of our fish collecting vessels, and in passing Point Roberts paid a courtesy call on the manager, Henry Teller, an old Astoria acquaintance. As I approached the wharf, I saw nearly one hundred Fraser River gill-net fishing boats – among them 43 of our own – delivering to the George & Barker cannery fish caught in our nets on the British side and contracted to be delivered to us ...

It was always a matter of speculation how George & Barker evaded customs and regulations duties in this manner without the American authorities taking cognizance of their activities. The company remained unmolested for many years, but when finally some more efficient or honest customs official had charge of the district, action was instituted and a thorough investigation of all past irregularities was threatened. To avoid this, George and Barker agreed to pay a lump sum fine of $15,000 in cash in full settlement. The charge was dropped when this fine was paid and assurances were given that the offences would not be repeated.

With this illicit source of supply thus denied, the George & Barker cannery, its pack decreased to less than half its former volume, and the business no longer was as profitable. Barker had then long been president and general manager of the British Columbia Packers Association and, as such, arranged a sale of the Point Roberts cannery to the Canadian company for $150,000. Shortly thereafter, the plant was quietly permitted to cease operating altogether.

Proceeding down the Sound, the next cannery encountered was that of the Friday Harbour Packing Co., on San Juan Island. It was built with funds provided by my old friend, John A. Devlin, of Astoria, and was operated, with his advice and assistance, by two Astoria protégés of his, Fred Keen and Phil Cook.

The two latter, on going to Astoria, had set up the partnership of Keen & Cook to engage in the insurance business. They had little or no capital, but were genial and enterprising and attracted the notice and friendship of Mr. Devlin. The latter, then retired and possessing ample wealth, decided to set them up in the Puget Sound salmon-canning business. Their cannery at Friday Harbour was well situated, their traps spendidly located, and their operations very successful. Subsequent to Mr. Devlin's death, they sold their cannery and trap locations to the Pacific Packing & Navigation Company for a handsome figure. Keen then invested his share of the capital in choice Seattle real estate, which increased in value [greatly]. Cook bought back the Strawberry Bay salmon trap – one of the very best on Puget Sound – for a fraction of its worth, at the receiver's sale three years later, and he contracted its catch to R.A. Welsh's Bellingham Canning Co.'s plant. For many years this trap produced for Cook a net income of approximately $20,000 a year. Eventually, his widow sold it to the Bellingham Canning Co.

The shoals of sockeyes, Fraser River bound, all swim past Village Point, the westernmost projection of Lummi Island. [As a consequence, the Point area] was perhaps the most valuable trapsite on Puget Sound. A tremendous current swings past the Point, however, which makes it extremely difficult for a trap to hold fast. Time and time again, just when the waters were swarming with salmon, the current carried away a section of the lead and put the appliances completely out of action.

Here, at Village Point, a cannery was built, its owners being the same English shareholders who financed the Federation Brand Salmon Canning Co., with canneries on the Naas and Fraser rivers in British Columbia. Like most businesses managed at long distance, the English company could not operate as successfully as its locally owned competitors. In addition, it repeatedly had the principal trap washed out at the very height of the sockeye run. Thus, between ill fortune and poor management, the company lost money and sold the Carlisle Packing Co., the chief, and eventually sole owner, of which was Frank Wright. [Wright was] long prominent in the salmon-canning business of Puget Sound and Alaska, and was the man who built the first cannery ever to be operated on the Yukon River.

Crossing from Lummi Island to the mainland, one came to a cluster of little settlements adjacent to one another, bearing the names of Whatcom, Sehome, and Fairhaven, respectively. Their separate identities subsequently became lost when the three [settlements] merged into one ... Bellingham was the name chosen for the community's permanent cognomen.

In Fairhaven, the most southerly portion of the combined settlement, a man named Henry Newton started a company called the Fairhaven Canning Co. It never was successful while he was connected with it, but from it grew the Pacific American Fisheries cannery, once the largest in the world and for many years one of the most important. Newton was an Englishman, well educated and cultured, with an engaging personality and charming manners. He was well connected in his home country, but there was a streak of unreliability and trickiness in his compostion which led him to take advantage of those who trusted him ... [He originally settled in New Westminster, BC, then moved] to the town of Fairhaven on the other side of the international boundary, where he built the cannery ...

In Chicago, there was a firm of commission brokers whose principal business was the sale of canned salmon. The firm was Deming and Gould. In order to make connections with salmon packers, the senior partner, Ed Deming, paid a visit to the Pacific coast. He arrived in Fairhaven just as the curtain descended on Henry Newton's portrayal of a canning magnate, and [Deming] quickly saw that, properly managed, the enterprise had great possibilities. Taking advantage of the situation, he acquired for a new company, the Pacific American Packing Co., the cannery Newton had built and lost. When the Pacific Packing & Navigation Company was formed, Deming put his property into the amalgamation, getting as part of the *quid pro quo* the Chicago district selling agency of the new company. When the latter failed, and its assets were disposed of, Deming invested capital in a new company that acquired many of the Pacific Packing & Navigation Company's holdings, both on Puget Sound and in Alaska. This fresh venture was called Pacific American Fisheries, and Bellingham, succeeding Fairhaven in name, became, and still is, the company's headquarters. From there, all of their Sound and Alaska interests have been managed. It is today one of the largest and strongest financially of all ... [the] operators, and practically all of this is owed to Deming's guiding hand, shrewd judgement, and business ability.

Just west of the Fairhaven cannery another fishery plant was erected, no more successful for its original builder than Newton's had been for him, but which later proved a gold mine to its subsequent owner. This was the Ocean Packing Co.'s Washington cannery, built by B.A. Seabord, another Columbia River pioneer ... Unfortunately [he suffered a] deterioration of character ... and it did not take long before his readily available assets were exhausted, his credit destroyed, and no one would finance him. The property at Fairhaven lay idle for a season and then passed into the possession of Robert A. Welsh, who operated it for over a third of a century under the aegis of the Bellingham Canning Co.

Robert A. Welsh, an Englishman, had been one of the Fraser River cannery owners who sold their businesses to the British Columbia Packers Association. He was made, by that company, manager of its Puget Sound interests. In their deliberate ignorance of the worth of these holdings, the directors of that company preferred sacrificing to developing these American assets, and in their negligence, Welsh saw his opportunity. He took over the Association's Puget Sound holdings; leased the Seaborg cannery in 1905; made a profit that year of $25,000; then purchased the plant from the Seaborg creditors. And, through continued operations, he made a fortune which was expanded by reinvesting surplus profits in Alaska, where he was equally successful. He was an experienced canner, a good business man, and was extremely popular. For many years Deming, his neighbouring cannery competitor, was sales agent for the Bellingham Canning Co. as well as for the Pacific American Fisheries. It was the most unusual relationship, but its long continuation was evidence that both parties found the arrangement eminently satisfactory.

Around the shoreline from Bellingham, in the picturesque bight called Chuckanut Bay, another cannery is situated, built and operated by Columbia River pioneers. Its manager and guiding spirit was Daniel Campbell, the present beloved dean of the salmon-canning fraternity, and only recently retired after more than fifty years' participation in the business.

Dan Campbell, when I first knew him, was foreman at Marshall J. Kinney's Astoria cannery, and it was as the latter's junior partner that he built the Chuckanut plant. Some years later, Campbell took over the Kinney interest and from then on was the sole proprietor.

In most lines of business competitors may be on a friendly basis, but even so there is an element of restraint in their relationships. Such, however, was not the case with the Bellingham triumvirate. Deming, Welsh, and Campbell were close friends socially as well as in business. They pooled their resources when circumstances indicated that would be desirable, and jointly owned and operated canneries in both southeastern and western Alaska. They furnished a rare example of unity in a field that abounds in jealousies, broken promises, suspicions, and deceit.

Below Chuckanut, at Anacortes, were situated the southernmost of the pioneer Puget Sound sockeye salmon canneries. One of these was owned by the Anglo-British Columbia Packing Company, but, being located in American instead of British territory, it was operated as a separate entity known as the Fidalgo Island Packing Co. Like the parent organization, its management was in the hands of Henry Bell-Irving & Co., in Vancouver, BC. Mr. Bell-Irving was one of the first in seeing the value and importances of intercepting the sockeye runs before they crossed the international border, and this Anacortes plant was built in furtherance of that object. Afterwards, the Alaska field was invaded, still in the name of Fidalgo Island Packing Co., and under its auspices, and today it is only in Alaska that its operations are carried on. The Anacortes plant was closed down when trap fishing on Puget Sound was legislated out of business.

The year after the Fidalgo Island cannery was built, two other British Columbia cannery operators united to build almost alongside of the other cannery. These collaborators were J.H. Todd & Son, of Victoria, and R.V. Winch, of Vancouver ... "R.V.," as his intimates call him, spent his youth in Peterborough and Cobourg, Ontario, but was still in his teens when he headed west in search of fame and fortune. He worked his way toward this goal on a section gang of day labourers on the construction of the Canadian Pacific Railway. He reached Vancouver almost simultaneously with another Cobourg boy, George E. Bower, who had married one of R.V.'s sisters, and the two formed the partnership of Winch & Bower to engage in the green-grocery business. They ran this successfully for many years, but as the town grew into a city and opportunities expanded; Winch, by far the more enterprising and venturesome of the two, reached out for other fields to conquer. He met a man named Jacobsen, a small fur-trader at Nootka, on the west coast of Vancouver Island. [Jacobsen] told him of the vast salmon runs he had observed there and persuaded Winch to build a cannery at that place. Jacobsen

told the truth about the plentifulness of the salmon but, being ignorant
of the differences of species, did not know that those he had seen were
the dog [chum] salmon, not sockeyes. As there was no market then for
the cheaper grades, Winch did not can them, and his entire season's
output totalled only 112 cases. In the fall of his first season he closed
down and dismantled the plant, taking a heavy loss.

Next, with one Ed Port, he formed the firm of Port & Winch and
engaged in the fresh fish business in New Westminster. Their principal
operations were in icing down and shipping salmon, sturgeon, and halibut in carload lots to eastern Canada and the United States. Fishing
regulations and the opposition of cannerymen, however, limited and
restricted expansion. Winch dissolved the partnership to join Hennessey, Alexander & Ewen in building the Canadian Pacific Packing Co.'s
cannery just above Steveston on the Fraser River.

When Puget Sound gave evidence of becoming a big sockeye salmon
packing area, Winch decided to enter that field and so sold to his local
associates his interest in the Fraser River cannery. However, the capital
at his command was insufficient for the step comtemplated, so he went to
Victoria and succeeded in inducing J.H. Todd, who had ample funds, to
join him in the venture. This was in the year 1898. Their earliest experiences, like those of Drysdale, Wadhams, and others, were poorer than
expected due to their traps not being properly set ... At this time, old
J.H. Todd was far along in years and his mental faculties were weaken-
ing, also his imagination magnified his losses, present and [those which
could be expected in the] future. He became obsessed with the idea that
the Anacortes plant would never succeed in making profits and that the
losses experienced there would eat up all of his lifelong accumulations.
Son Charlie did not share these apprehensions, but he saw the old man
breaking down through worry, so he acquiesced in his father's wish to
dispose of the property before it ruined them. The Todds therefore
offered Winch their share of the capital stock of the Anacortes Packing
Co. for $26,000. [This was] the amount they had invested in the enter-
prise, and at this figure Winch and his brother-in-law Bower acquired
possession of sole ownership. Not having this $26,000 in addition to
what Winch had already put into the business, they borrowed it from
their bankers, the Merchants Bank of Halifax (afterwards, the Royal
Bank of Canada), who were also providing the coming season's working
capital ...

So heavy was that first run of sockeye salmon in 1899 that by the 16th
of July, when the run ceased as suddenly as it had begun, every can of
the 40,000-case pack prepared for by the Anacortes Packing Co. had
been filled. Bower was content to stop there, as was Bell-Irving, whose
pack at the neighbouring Fidalgo Island cannery was also completed.

But Winch was more sanguine and bolder. He purchases tinplate and supplies for 26,000 cases additional, and when the second run of the season came in he filled them all as well ...

The Alaska Packers Association, whose Semiahmoo cannery had done equally well and whose management realized how valuable the Anacortes Packing Co.'s trap locations were ... bought out Winch & Bower at a price somewhat in excess of $450,000, all cash, as the sellers declined to accept stock in the Association. Even at this huge cost the Alaska Packers Association did well. Their 1900 operating profits there netted them over $350,000, and although they rebuilt the plant entirely for the "big" year of 1901, they were reimbursed the amount it cost by the profit [the cannery operation] made that season. In the long run, however, only the trap locations proved to be really valuable. The new cannery had been built on piles driven in toredo infested waters, which made its upkeep unduly expensive. It was found cheaper to transport the salmon catches to their Semiahmoo cannery and process them there. The Anacortes property was therefore dismantled and abandoned. Ever since, all the Association's Puget Sound operations have been concentrated at the Semiahmoo plant ...

So plentiful were the sockeye salmon, and so cheap their cost when a trap was properly set to intercept their passage, that enormous profits were made, and it was easy to conceive that if a company was formed to purchase as many as possible of the trap locations and canneries then in operation, economies in cost could be effected that would make set earnings considerably greater. And, if this reasoning was sound as regards the acquisition of properties on Puget Sound, how much greater would be the lowering of costs, stabilization of prices, control of the selling market, and augmentation of earnings if the operations were extended to Alaska as well? The Alaska Packers Association had already proved that such a company could exceed individual operators in the profits made; an even larger company should be able to better the Association's record. And it might be, eventually, that the new company and its exemplar would amalgamate and effect what would probably be a monopoly of the salmon fisheries of Puget Sound and Alaska.

Thus reasoned Roland B. Onnfroy, a Frenchman of good education, commanding presence, and the possessor of a voluble and convincing tongue and most charming, insinuating manners. He had been an associate of Ferdinand de Lesseps and one of the latter's engineers in the ill-fated French attempt to construct the Panama Canal ... Quietly at first, and afterwards with great vigour and all the fanfare of showmanship, Monsieur Onnfroy went ahead securing options on cannery properties, trap location rights, steamers and sailing vessels used in the transportation of fishing and cannery supplies and for transferring the

packs from processing plants to railroad terminals. Where his own persuasions failed or were likely to fail, he sought other means and influences. He ascertained who were friends of the parties whose holdings he
wished to acquire and paid them lavishly for their assistance. He interviewed bankers and engaged their influences through intimations of their
securing a share of the new company's banking business. He brought
pressure through supply houses which hoped to be favoured with orders
when the new owners were at the helm, and he interested canned fish
brokers on his behalf by insinuating they were the ones he wished to
[have] act for his company in the region where they were located.

He pictured future operations in such vivid and entrancing colours
that Eastern investors almost insisted on being permitted to purchase
shares; and he succeeded in forming a company – the Pacific Packing &
Navigation Company – with an issued capital of approximately
$7,000,000, a large investment total for those days.

In acquiring canneries and fishing stations, trap locations, steamers
and other vessels used in the fisheries, and in any other purchases made,
Onnfroy did not haggle over values. Until his negotiations gained
momentum and publicity, the prices he agreed to pay were not unreason-
able. But when later he had to deal with those diffident in selling, or
more grasping than others, he paid almost any price asked and even
contracted for the seller's personal services with the proposed new company, on a commission or salary basis, on terms, in some instances at
least, excessively high.

Most, if not all, of the options he secured called for the purchase
consideration being paid in cash. As far as my knowledge goes, none
were paid for otherwise and, consequently, none of the original owners
were hurt when subsequently the amalgamated company failed ... When
Onnfroy had finally secured all he could persuade to sell to him, or
possibly all the capital he had for investment could be stretched to cover,
he exercised his options and the Pacific Packing & Navigation Company
came into being, just in time to commence operations with the "big"
pack of 1901. A subsidiary, the Pacific Selling Company, also emerged
from its chrysalis stage at this time to take charge of the Company's sales
department.

Amongst those who had assisted Onnfroy with their persuasions and
influence when options were being acquired, one of the most active was
Thomas B. McGovern of the firm of Delafield, McGovern & Co., New
York. His firm was one of the largest brokerage houses engaged in selling
canned salmon; its junior partner had learned the business as a clerk in
the employment of W.T. Coleman & Co., and his ethical education had
followed the lines taught in that school of experience. Richard Delafield
came of a well-known and wealthy New York family, was a director of

one of the largest banks in that city, and had been a boyhood friend of McGovern. [Delafield], to help [McGovern] along, financed the operations of the firm that bore their joint names, although himself taking little or no interest in its active management. Spurred on by McGovern, he invested a considerable sum of his own money in the new enterprise and induced some of his friends and banking associates to do likewise, until, directly and indirectly, he was financially involved to the extent of $700,000. [This sum] was lost by him when the Pacific Packing & Navigation Company went through bankruptcy and its assets were disposed of. For his assistance in securing this New York capital McGovern was given the sole agency for the North Atlantic territory, and it was to handle this business that the Pacific Selling Co. was formed. He was also given a responsible position in the sales department of the parent company's Seattle office; and, when the bubble burst, he became one of the receivers for the insolvent company.

[To accomplish] the grandiose plans Onnfroy had in mind, the new company tore down the old Fairhaven cannery and erected on its site a new main cannery building 260' × 350' and equipped with 9 full lines of packing capacity. Adjoining it was a warehouse building 360' long and in width, 280', tapering to 184'. Its storage capacity was 300,000 cases. It was widely advertised as the largest canning plant in the world. This was true then, although the more modern equipment and packing capacity of the canneries of today enable smaller plants to pack daily a greater quantity of salmon than this monster of its time ever achieved, or was capable of achieving.

It was in the "big" year of 1901 that the Pacific Packing & Navigation Company commenced operating and its combined Puget Sound and Alaska packs totalled 1,130,127 cases, of which 445,468 cases were red, or sockeye, salmon, and 684,659 cases were of the cheaper qualities. During the same season Alaska Packers Association put up 1,074,395 cases of sockeye quality, 199,171 of other grades, to total 1,273,566 cases.

While the Puget Sound sockeye pack of 1902 was only a third of that secured in the previous year, in Alaska that season's pack of 1,700,044 cases of red fish [sockeye] was larger than any previous year on record ... The world's markets could not suddenly absorb such large increases, and a big portion of the 1901 fish was carried over, unsold, to the following year to compete then with the latter season's pack in the field of sales. The Alaska Packers Association possessed long-established and favourably known brands; the Pacific Packing & Navigation Company's labels were only then placed before the public ...

All these combined circumstances made the Pacific Packing & Navigation Company very vulnerable to attack, and besides, its disbursements for fishing and canning assets had absorbed practically all of the funds originally secured from the sales of shares, leaving the company with little or no working capital. At the opening of the 1903 season, loans and accounts payable totalled approximately $5,000,000, with only about $1,500,000 worth of canned fish and other liquid resources available.

The Alaska Packers Association recognized its opportunity and took advantage of it. Most of its competitor's unsold pack consisted of the two cheapest grades, pinks and chums. The Alaska Packers Association cut the selling price of 1–lb. tall pinks to $2.00 and that of chums to $1.50 per case, both being far below their cost to any packer. [The Association] judged this action would make bankers over-cautious of financing a company whose pack must consist largely of low-grade salmon, and that, as a result, the younger company would be put out of business. In both these expectations its acumen proved correct, and shortly thereafter the Pacific Packing & Navigation Company passed into receivership.

Some very wild and fantastic projects were advanced seeking the fallen empire's rehabilitation, none of which were successful, partly because, in most cases, the promoters sought more after their own aggrandisement than for the welfare of the Pacific Packing & Navigation Company's shareholders or creditors. [One] example will suffice to illustrate the techniques employed.

In 1902 I had formed the British Columbia Packers Association with the Canadian Bank of Commerce providing one-half of the underwriting capital. In February 1903, T.B. McGovern, one of the receivers of the defunct company ... submitted to Sir Byron Walker, president of the Canadian Bank of Commerce, a proposition to form a company to acquire a controlling interest in three salmon-canning corporations, viz., his company [PP&N Co.], our company, and the Columbia River Packers Association of Astoria, Oregon, with which latter company McGovern did considerable business. Only a controlling interest in each company was contemplated ... [A] holding company [was] to receive a commission of 5% on ALL sales and IN ADDITION such brokerages as they may have to pay in effecting such sales. Under this arrangement no merger of the constituent companies was contemplated. Existing methods of independent administrations were to remain practically unaltered ... The holding company would absolutely control the marketing of packs; would do all the financing; make all sales; buy all supplies; and act in an advisory capacity with respect to the economical management of the constituent companies.

Sir Byron Walker and some leading Eastern shareholders of the British Columbia Packers Association received this proposition with some favour; but the former, knowing I was familiar with the affairs of all three of the companies, insisted on first submitting the proposal to me for approval, and I damned it on every count. I pointed out that McGovern's plan meant the shareholders of all three companies would be mulcted of 5% more on sales than they were then paying with no compensating gain to anyone except the proposed new holding-company shareholders. It was customary to pay 1% to agents for arranging and securing such working-capital advances as the season's work required, and while this was not mentioned by the promoter, it would undoubtedly be demanded. In the case of British Columbia Packers Association, at least, it could arrange such financing without the intermediation of any such company as McGovern was sponsoring. And finally, I mentioned that in all the years the Columbia River Packers Association had been in business up to that time, it had never paid any dividends, while the Pacific Packing & Navigation Company would, I predicted, be under a receiver's management before the year was out. On receiving my report the Eastern Canadians broke off all negotiations with McGovern, and in March of 1903, one month later, the Pacific Packing & Navigation Company filed a petition of insolvency and passed into receivership ...

Nothing having come of this, or any other refinancing programme, in September the Courts ordered that the assets of the Company be disposed of at public auction on 10th November that year ... The Alaska Packers Association had accomplished its objective and annihilated its largest competitor, but only at great cost to itself, its own losses exceeding $1,800,000. One result it had not anticipated was the creation of several financially strong competitors replacing the one which was weak. Prices realized at the auction were far below the cost of replacement, to say nothing of what the insolvent company had paid for them, and these newcomers could not be crushed as the Pacific Packing & Navigation Company had been. The largest and strongest of these new operators, the Pacific American Fisheries, Inc., today [1950s] ranks as the second largest salmon canning company on the entire Pacific coast.

With the passing of the Pacific Packing & Navigation Company, the pioneer era of the salmon-canning industry may be said to have come to a close. From then on, many new interests appear, also a trade magazine to record their activities, and those interested in further developments will find detailed accounts fully set out in the pages of the *Pacific Fisherman.*

11. 2/2 Letter: Doyle to Hon. R. Préfontaine,   *Vancouver,*
    Minister of Marine and Fisheries   *March 24th, 1903*

Dear Sir:–

In accordance with my promise to you, made during our interview last November, I herewith beg to submit the following report concerning the salmon-fishing industry, more particularly that portion relating to the

Fraser River fishing. This report has been delayed owing to my desire to embody in it the results of last season's operations, so as to show the comparative results on Puget Sound and the Fraser River in what is considered an off year. The canning industry in these waters may be said to have reached its maximum in 1901, which was a "big year", and last season having been the reverse, the two taken together will enable you to see the situation as it exists today.

As the tables covering pack [not included] will show, up to the year 1891 practically all the fishing was done on our side of the line, the percentage for Puget Sound having been only four and nine-tenths per-cent in 1889 and three and seven-tenths percent in 1890. In 1891 a cannery was built near the boundary line, and traps were operated on Point Roberts. This was the first introduction of trap fishing in Puget Sound waters, and from that time on the percentage of pack grew steadi-ly in their favour, until in 1898 for the first time the preponderance of pack was secured by the American canners, and ever since they have succeeded in maintaining their advantage.

I understand that in 1895 the Dominion of Canada and the United States, in appointing the joint commission to investigate the fisheries in international waters, laid down the rule that where the principal matters were equal, small questions should be decided in favour of the country having a preponderance of interest. At that time such questions arising in connection with the Fraser River fish would have been decided in our favour, we then represented sixty-seven and two-tenths percent of the total for that year, and having maintained the leading position up to that time. Today, however, should a similar recommendation be made, the Americans would have the advantage both on last season's showing as well as for the four previous years.

In considering how the preponderance of interest has been allowed to pass away from us it will not do to simply take the figures stated, as all of the pack obtained on the Fraser River does not represent fish caught in Canadian waters. Quite a percentage of our pack was obtained from fish caught in American traps, purse seines, and even gill nets, so that were steps taken today by the United States authorities to prohibit the exportation of fresh salmon, the percentage of Puget Sound would be increased, and ours correspondingly reduced. To illustrate this I would mention that while last season was a poor one, we imported from Puget Sound sufficient salmon to fill 30,212 cases, representing point zero-nine and two-tenths percent of our total pack.

The percentage that can be obtained by Puget Sound packers in poor years will be correspondingly greater than in years of a heavy run of fish. Whereas in the latter case, their traps become so full of fish that it is necessary to let down the web and let the fish escape, so as to prevent the loss of the webbing, in a poor season, where such a glut of fish does not occur, they can retain practically every fish that enters the trap, and thus our supply is curtailed. Again, on a question of quality the Americans have the advantage, as the bulk of their fish is in good condition on arrival at their canneries, as they are then in a state of physical perfection. By the time the salmon have run the gauntlet of all the traps, however, they have been so delayed that they are further advanced toward spawning, and are consequently softer than would be the case had their travels been free of interruption. Also in a big run, when they are released from traps in which they have been confined for several days, they are more or less bruised through having rubbed against the walls of the trap in their efforts to espape.

The quantities of fish that can be obtained at one time by trap fishing, and the fact that they can hold the fish in the traps until they are ready to handle them, enables the Puget Sound packers to prepare plants of larger daily capacity than can generally be done on the Fraser River. Traps are personal property, and can be depended on for a supply if the fish run. Gill-net fishermen cannot be controlled in the same way, consequently the Fraser River canners have had more risk in their operations, and therefore have contented themselves with smaller plants. Thus, while there were 42 plants operated on the Fraser River against 21 on Puget Sound – a difference of 100% – the value of the Puget Sound plants are only $185,567 less than those on the Fraser River.

The differences, however, extend still further, for while they have fewer plants, their packing capacity is equal to ours – as is shown by results – and to do the same amount of work they only require about 65% of the labour. This of course means cheaper packs on the average, as there are fewer demands for a share of the money expended. The Fraser River, in its efforts to maintain supremacy, has been increasing the number of gill nets operating, which not only means that the number of fishermen have increased, but that, in addition, the competition resulting amongst this vast army of fishermen has caused heavy advances in the price of fish.

The cost of trap fishing, has, if anything, been reduced, owing to the broader knowledge that has been acquired by experience, so that they have not suffered from the same cause. Our increased efforts moreover have not correspondingly increased our returns, for the percentage in favor of Puget Sound has continued to mount up.

The tables covering our gear operated show that on the Fraser River the increased value has been brought about by the increase in labour employed, and all this increase is chargeable to gill-net fishing alone. Puget Sound on the other hand has divided its increased investment in fishing appliances over various items. Gill nets in 1901, while in number only one-eighth of those fished on the Fraser River, are all the way from 400 to 600 fathoms long, as compared with 150 fathom nets on the Fraser River. So that while only the same amount of labour is employed in operating a net, the men have three or four times the chances of making catches, and consequently can afford to sell at a less amount per fish. Set nets, drag seines, purse seines, and even traps have been increased in effectiveness, so that the returns are greater, although the number of mem employed has not been increased.

Trap fishing on the Sound has also resulted in retarding the progress of the fish, so that local conditions have been completely changed. In former years salmon used to enter the Fraser River in separate and distinct "runs." Sometimes two, sometimes four or five runs would occur in the one season, from July 1st to August 25th. These runs generally, if not always, represented the fish ascending different tributaries of the Fraser River, and presumably those ascending first were making for those spawning beds farthest removed from the river's mouth. With the advent of trap fishing, however, all this was changed. The numerous obstacles encountered checked the progress of the early runs until they were joined by the later ones, and thus today our catches are all made in practically ten days' time, so much have the Puget Sound operations reduced our period of working time.

As is shown by the joint report of Prof. Prince and Mr. [Richard] Rathbun, the fish pass through Canadian waters before entering American waters, and, after passing Discovery Island, divide, some coming up Haro and others up Rosario Straits. Their report is in error, however, in stating that those fish coming up Haro Straits enter the Fraser River without going near Boundary Bay and Point Roberts. On the contrary, they travel in almost a direct line from the head of San Juan Island to Cherry Point on the mainland, passing Stuart, Spieden and Waldron islands en route, and sometimes taking the Saturna Island, and against Orcas Island shore, so that good-sized runs pass both places. Some of the best traps in Puget Sound are on the Stuart and Waldron islands, and along Douglas Channel.

A little careful study of tidal conditions will explain this point beyond any question. The natural instinct of the salmon compels it to seek fresh water when the spawning time approaches. The fish, entering the Straits of Fuca from the ocean finds the brackish water along the Vancouver Island shore, where it is driven by the heavy incoming tides, the current of which, owing to the shape of the passage, being directed toward the American shore. This forms quieter waters on the Canadian side.

The tides from the northern end of the Gulf of Georgia, crossing the mouth of the Fraser River, sweep the fresh water of that river in an easterly direction, past Point Roberts into American territory. This fresh or brackish water, still forced along by the tidal current, is carried down Rosario Straits, where it is met by the pressure of the current from Admiralty Inlet, and turned toward the Straits. This accounts for the greater body of fish taking the Rosario Straits passage instead of Haro Straits, which receive comparatively little of the Fraser River water except in big years, when the volume of fresh water descending the river is so great that a portion of it crosses the gulf and enters Haro Straits through Active Pass. This argument is further proved by the fact that practically no fish are found in the passages between San Juan, Orcas, Lopez, and the smaller islands composing the group separating Rosario and Haro straits, and the reason of their not frequenting those waters is easily shown by the shape of the northern end of Orcas Island, which acts like the bow of a ship in turning off the waters.

The gill-net fishing on Puget Sound is mostly restricted to that portion made muddy by the Fraser River outflow. Traps are situated wherever suitable driving ground for the piles can be found inthe course taken by the fish. Purse seines are fished in all portions of the Sound, wherever fish are seen jumping. Their operations embrace all the waters on the American side, from the Straits of Fuca to Point Roberts.

If purse-seine fishing is permitted on our side of the line from (and including) the Straits of Fuca to the 49th parallel, it not only will help to put our industry on a more even basis with Puget Sound (by extending the length of our season's operations), but will enable us to secure fish before they enter American waters. This applies not only [to the waters] around the southern end of San Juan Island, but also to the waters from Discovery to Saturna Island. The fish caught by this method will also arrive at the canneries in primer condition than those caught in gill nets after being delayed by the American traps.

Traps should be allowed in the same territory to enable us to regain at least a portion of our lost ground, but while these appliances would prove of immense advantage to us, not only as regards the percentage we would obtain, but also as regards cost of pack, the matter is one that should be dealt with after the question of foreshore jurisdiction is definitely settled between the Dominion and Provincial governments, and some fair and equitable measure agreed upon that will give due consideration to those vested interests that are affected by the existing state of affairs, and who have stood the brunt of the American attack ...

In southeastern Alaska all the canneries use purse seines to a very large extent in their fishing operations, and it may be questioned whether they confine their use exclusively to their own waters. To my knowledge one cannery alone fishes the waters within a radius of 150 miles of their plant, and operates some 24 purse seines. Their pack of 75,000 to 100,000 c/s yearly, as compared to the 15,000 to 20,000 c/s pack of one of our northern plants, is much cheaper, owing to the greater amount over which to distribute their labour charge.

If purse seines are permitted in the northern waters they not apply would result in giving employment to a greater number, and that with more opportunities to the fishermen, but in addition would put the industry upon a more permanent basis by increasing the packs and making them more uniform one year with another. In nearly all the northern fishing grounds the waters are very deep, thus presenting opportunities for purse seines where drag seines and gill nets are quite useless. This applies most particularly to fishing in rainy or cloudy weather (which is most prevalent), when the fish swim deeper than when the sun is shining. In this dismal weather, although the fish may be extremely plentiful the present methods prove unprofitable, which would not be the case with the first-mentioned method.

A careful study of the chart showing the rivers and inlets opening into Hecate Straits [sic] and its landward approaches will show the same conditions as regards fresh water and tidal influences as prevail in the Fraser River approaches. The fresh water from the Skeena River and Naas River, as well as that from the various smaller rivers and streams ascended by salmon, and which empty into such arms of the sea as Portland Canal, Observatory Inlet, Work [sic] Canal, Kitimatt [sic] Arm, Gardiner [sic] Canal, and many smaller inlets too numerous to mention, all eventually work their way into Hecate Straits, and the fish, being led by their natural instincts to follow this water, can be secured by purse seines in the Straits, whereas neither drag seines nor gill nets could be profitably used. It is more than likely too that fish heading for the freshwater streams in American territory – which streams also empty into Hecate Straits – could be caught in Canadian territory, and thus enable us to handicap the American operations in Alaska in a similar manner to their interference with the Fraser River.

As regards the use of drag seines, I would also suggest a decided change from present methods. Today drag seining is only allowed under special license, which gives the holder of such license exclusive fishing privileges over an extensive area. This policy is more detrimental to proper development of the industry, as in the first place I do not know of a single instance in which actual bona fide fishermen have secured the privilege; and in the second place, in a great many instances these licenses are sought after and obtained by parties having no intention of utilizing the privilege for legitimate canning purposes, but with the sole object of selling the use of the license to someone else. Thus they receive an income from something that costs them nothing, and for which if any sum was paid the Government should obtain the benefit of. Of course, the only parties capable of purchasing such rights are the cannery owners, for we have no fishermen here who could afford to pays from $150 to $200 for an outfit, and a further $200 to $300 per year for a license, and then find a market for their fish at profitable prices. If this fishing is to be as fully developed as it is in other parts of the Dominion I would suggest drag- and purse-seine licenses be granted to fishermen directly, under exactly similar conditions as those governing the granting of gill-net licenses. This would enable bona fide fishermen to own and operate these nets, and would build up a permanent and steady class of resident fishermen working to their own advancement, and the establishing of the industry upon a more stable basis.

In presenting this I would mention that our idea is to enlarge the industry, and, in doing so, benefit ourselves by the greater opportunities such action would give birth to. If the department sees fit to adopt our suggestions as to the elimination of the present special drag-seine privileges, they will be taking away from us alone probably half of the total number of seine licenses issued up to the present time. Naturally, we would not advocate depriving ourselves of these were it not that we believe we could gain more benefits by the greater number that would be operated by the individual fisherman were they placed in the position to avail themselves of such an opportunity.

There is one exception to this rule, however, which I think will be justified. That is that where the holder, or obtainer, of special territorial privileges for seining purposes will immediately erect and maintain at his own expense a hatchery for the propogation of salmon, his special privileges should be guaranteed him as compensation for his enterprise.

In concluding this report, which I trust covers the point upon which you desired information, I will refer once more to the growth of the Puget Sound industry at the expense of the Fraser River by giving the following quotation from the report just submitted to the Washington State Legislature by Mr. T.R. Kershaw, the State Fish Commissioner. Speaking of the salmon fishing he says:

Within the last few years the fisheries industry on the lower Sound has grown with great rapidity, until today the Puget Sound district furnishes over 82% of all of the capital employed in the state in the fishing industry; over 77% of the number of persons employed; over 79% of the earnings of labor employed; over 86% of the value of the output for the state, and over 85% of the taxes received by this office. The Puget Sound district should therefore be credited with about 80% of the fisheries industry of the entire state.

CONSERVATION

12. *1/13 Letter: T.M. Smith, Acting*   March 20, 1905
      Commissioner, US Department
      of Commerce and Labor, Bureau
      of Fisheries, to Doyle

Sir:

The receipt is acknowledged of your letter of January 28, together with the manuscript of your paper on "The Deep Sea Life of the Pacific Salmon."

The letter has been read with interest and your views, while rather novel, are found to contain much that is interesting and suggestive.

It is apparent, however, that the views are largely theoretical and not based upon any considerable number of actual observations or careful investigation.

The theory that the sense of smell is highly developed in salmon is wholly without support. The same is true in scarcely less degree regarding the "marvelous geographic instinct which enables salmon to return to the parent stream." Practically all trustworthy evidence indicates that they possess no such instinct or sense.

There is sent you under separate cover a paper containing the results of certain investigations concerning the food of sea lions. From this report you will observe that the charges that sea lions are very destructive to salmon or any kind of fish are largely without foundation in fact.

Thanking you for the privilege of examining your paper (the MS. of which is returned herewith).

13. *1/7 Letter: E.R. Edson, Edson Reduction*   *Cleveland, Ohio,*
      Machinery Co., to Doyle   *February 27, 1903*

Dear Sir:

Mr. Jessop forwarded us 52 lbs. of salmon shipped by you to him for the purpose of making a test to ascertain the value of the same when treated by our system [of fish reduction], and to see whether the preservative you had used had in anyway injured the fish. We are inclined to think that either the preservative or the fact of the fish being so long out of water did destroy a small percentage of the nitrogen or ammonia. Figuring on the basis of one ton of fish, the value of the fish you shipped us would be as follows:

Oil Extracted

181.5 lbs., worth at the present time about

4¢ $5.26

Guano
> 506.9 lbs., analysing Ammonia 10.73%,
> Bone Phosphate of Lime 6.14%, and this
> on analysis worth in eastern markets today
> $26.36 a ton $6.68
Making a value for material of this kind after being
treated with the preservative and held $11.94

or, practically $12.00 per ton of raw material. The fish contained, as you see, a little over 9% of oil, and a little over 25% of dried guano. The total yield of solids being 34.42%.

As a general rule we find the offal from such fish much richer in oils than the bodies, likewise richer in nitrogen or ammonia, hence judge that these fish, and the offal from them, if treated as a whole, would yield about 12% oil and 25% guano, and if treated fresh, the latter in our opinion would analyse over 12% in ammonia, and such guano having a value today of about $30.00 per ton. In other words, we judge that a ton of such fish, when fresh, treated by our process would yield a value of about $17.00 per raw ton, which we think is about the value secured from similar material on a former test made by us, a copy of which test we think you have in your hands. Evidently if the cost of preserving is not great it would be profitable to preserve the surplus offal and waste in large tanks, and treat the same after the rush is over with, and the catch becomes lighter. We trust the above will be satisfactory.

We received an inquiry a day or two ago from Mr. Kenworthy. Is he not the manager of the plant that now handles your refuse?

PREPARING FOR BRITISH COLUMBIA PACKERS ASSOCIATION'S
FIRST SEASON, 1903

14. 2/14 Letter: Doyle, G.I. Wilson, and   *December 15, 1902*
*   E.E. Evans, Executive Committee,*
*   to British Columbia Packers*
*   Association Board*

Dear Sirs:
Regarding the proposed changes to the canneries owned by our Association, in order to work them most economically during the season of 1903, we submit the following report and recommendations. The matter has been referred in each case to the District Manager, and he has been asked to submit the changes he would like made, and the estimate of their cost. These we give, together with the recommendations made by us as to how much of these changes should be made this season. Of

course, it would be a matter of economy were we able to make all of the changes that we desire this year, but in view of the fact that this would involve the expenditure of a large amount of money, also the fact that the season of 1904 is expected to be small, and consequently the number of canneries that we have at present would not, in any event, all be operated, makes it advisable to leave some of these changes until we can make the alterations out of profits, and will only require them for 1905 [which will be the next "big year."]

The changes for those are as follows: –

Mr. Bain's District

Brunswick cannery	$25,000
Pacific Coast cannery	3,000
	$28,000

We advise making the change in the Brunswick cannery to the extent asked for, viz. $25,000, but leave the Pacific Coast until some future date. The change in the Brunswick is essential, especially as by making it we are enabled to run in one plant the same machinery that is now represented by the London, Brunswick, Imperial, and Hume canneries.

Mr. Alexander's District

The improvements proposed there are as follows: –

Brunswick cannery	$9,000
Albion cannery	11,500
Currie-McWilliams cannery	2,500
	$23,000

We recommend making the improvement in the Brunswick at the expense of $9,000, Currie–McWilliams $2,500, and changes in the Anglo-American to the extent of $1,000, making a total of $12,500. It could be arranged, if necessary, not to make the improvements in the Currie–McWilliams cannery, but considering that next year is expected to be a good one, and that the changes in that plant are comparatively of little cost, in order to make it more than double its present capacity we would prefer seeing the changes made now.

Mr. Ewen's District

Mr. Ewen asked for $5,000 change to the Ewen plant, which we recommend. It is just as well to make this a 2-line plant, and the expense is not much.

Mr. Rowan's District

Mr. Rowan proposed the following changes: –

Terra Nova cannery	$ 3,250
Celtic cannery	5,700
Acme cannery	5,150
	$14,100

This would make a 2-line plant out of each one of the above, but we do not consider it necessary for the coming season to make all of these changes, so that we would advise changing the Terra Nova at the cost of $3,000, Celtic at the cost of $5,000 – total $8,500.

Mr. Wadhams' District

Changes to the Wadhams cannery proposed would be $3,500, Brunswick $5,000, total $8,500. The bulk of these changes lies in the introduction of new machinery, there being practically no building expenses to be incurred by either plant. As some of this machinery is not absolutely essential, we have cut down the Wadhams cannery to $2,500, and the Brunswick to $3,500, making a total that we recommend for Rivers Inlet of $6,000.

Skeena River

It is necessary to erect a new cannery there in order to properly look after our interests. We have had Mr. English figure on a 3-line plant, at an estimated cost by him of $20,000, but we recommend making the Balmoral cannery into a 2-line plant, at an estimated cost of $15,000.

At Alert Bay and Bella Coola the changes proposed by the managers are absolutely necessary, and we recommend that same be passed. These changes will be $10,000 at Alert Bay and $5,000 at Bella Coola.

To sum up, the changes will be as follows: –

District	Asked	Recommended
Fraser River	$ 70,100	$60,000
North	43,500	36,000
	$113,600	$96,000

By making these changes, and by the consequential closing down of other plants, without diminishing our daily packing capacity, we effect the following economies: –

	Management	
	1902	*1903*
Skeena	$ 4,500	$ 1,800
Rivers Inlet	6,420	3,000
Other Northern Points	7,200	4,500
Fraser	24,800	13,680
	$52,920 [sic]	$22,980

making a saving for 1903 of $29,940.

By closing down 7 plants on the Fraser River and 3 in the North (in excess of those closed down last season), and allowing for the additional men required for the increased-capacity plants, we estimate there would be a saving, exclusive of management, of $2,500 on each plant, this on 10 plants closed down would be $25,000, so that we would have in 1903, on the whole, the following result:—

Saving in management	$29,940
Saving in other labour	25,000
Total saving in labour	$54,940

In getting these figures no account has been taken of savings made in fuel, steam-boat hire, and general operating expenses, which, of course, would be considerable. In addition, the increased pack at the larger plants will in all probabilities bring down the cost of white labour over what could be expected in smaller-capacity plants.

15. 2/1 Letter: Doyle to H. Bell-Irving & Co.   *Vancouver, BC,*
Dec. 16, 1902

Gentlemen:—

We understand that it is your desire that we give you some idea of what we will be willing to agree to for Rivers Inlet and the Skeena River before a general meeting [of the salmon canners] is called, so that we would have some definite policy outlined before such meeting should be held. You would like us to give you a memorandun of this so that you could study same at your leisure.

As far as Skeena River is concerned, the agreement as proposed by Mr. Lord [probably W.R. Lord, manager of the North Pacific and British American canneries] seems quite satisfactory. This agreement we understand to be practically a re-enforcement of the agreement made on April 2nd, 1902 at Port Essington, with the addition of clauses covering the following points:—

1. Transportation of Japanese and white fishermen to be paid one way, but transportation of the Indians not to be paid either way.

2. That no advances shall be made to fishermen, whites, Japanese, or Indians, until the agreement is signed by them, individually, to fish at 7¢ for sockeyes, steelhead, and cohos, 25¢ for red spring caught in spring nets, and 21¢ for red springs caught in sockeye nets. Humpback, 1¢ per fish; all of the prices to be for [those using] cannery gear.

3. No change is to be made in this agreement before, say, Nov. 1st, 1903, unless made at a regularly called meeting of the local managers.

4. Bonds to be put up by the various parties to bind this agreement, such bonds being the same as those put by the Fraser River canners to bind their agreement with the Fraser River Canners' Association.

[As for] Rivers Inlet, we have gone carefully over the memorandum submitted by the managers after their meeting of Nov. 7th last, but our idea is that the agreement should be made substantially as follows:–

1. That pooling of raw material is not considered practical, owing to the trouble caused by the Klootchmen and Chinese contractors, and the difficulty in making distributions of fish, and the excess labour that it necessitates.

2. As for the question of controlling the fishermen, that is now a far easier matter, with only three parties interested, than was the case with seven independent operators. The agreement made on June 23rd, 1902, should be made part of this proposed agreement, viz: that the canneries that in the past two years have had the services of certain tribes are to be left in undisputed possession of such tribes to the same extent that they have enjoyed in the past. That is to say, that in case they have had the exclusive control over any particular tribe, they are to continue to enjoy same. But, where one concern has three-fourths of one tribe, and another the other fourth, the relative proportions should be maintained. Thus, your having the Bella Bella Indians, and Messrs. Findlay, Durham & Brodie having the Kitimatts, you would continue to have those, without any attempt on our part to try and induce, or to accept, the services of members of those tribes to fish for us; you treating our fishermen in the same manner.

3. That the boat rating for Rivers Inlet for the season of 1903 is the same as that for 1899, viz:

Wadhams cannery	103
Brunswick cannery	86
Wannuck [sic] cannery	71
Vancouver Packing Co.	67
Total	327
BC Canning Co.	142
Good Hope cannery	95

This, we might point out, is a reduction on the number of boats that our Company fished last year of 44 boats, while it is an increase to the BC Canning Co. of 14, and leaves your cannery with a decrease of 2.

4. In view of the two preceding clauses, which do away with the competition for fishermen and put the boats on a limit, we can see no reason for pooling the canned product, as all starting out on a fair basis, it would be unjust to the party which has the most industrious, or lucky, fishermen. With the two preceding points agreed to, the resulted pack should be dealt without the necessity of pooling same.

5. The price of fish to be 7¢ with cannery [owned] gear, 9-½¢ for men fishing their own nets.

6. That no sale of nets be made to any fishermen whatsoever, whites, Japanese, or Indians.

7. A runner to be allowed for each tribe, to be paid at the rate of $2.50 per day, time not to exceed two months.

8. Wages of Klootchmen to be 12-½¢ per hour for washing, etc., and 30 trays for $1.00 for fillers.

9. Transportation to be supplied Japanese and whites one way, and Indians, both ways.

10. If discontinuing of holdings may be too drastic, it might be advisable to allow a bonus of $10.00 per crew of two men. No bonus allowed to single fishermen.

11. No advances to be made to fishermen, whites, Japanese, or Indians until agreement is signed to fish at prices named for the season.

12. No change to be made to the agreement before Nov. 1st, 1903, unless made at a regularly called meeting of the local managers.

13. Bonds to be put up by the various parties to bind this agreement to be on the same lines as those put up to bind the agreement on the Fraser River with the Fraser River Canners' Association.

If these suggestions meet with your concurrence, we shall be very pleased to have a regular meeting called at any time that suits your convenience, or the convenience of the other canners. In making agreements for the North, as a matter of protection (not only to ourselves, but to the other companies interested in both places), we would want two agreements, one covering Rivers Inlet, the other the Skeena River, entered into at the same time.

THE 1903-04 OPERATING SEASONS OBSERVED

16. 4/notebook 21 Excerpts: Executive Committee notes

April 2 [1903]. [The] *Terra Nova* – If crew work in cannery when boat not engaged let her start work.

[The] *Mamie* – Have her report here directly finished at Lowe Inlet – China Hat work – See letters English & Curtis. Have Wadhams rush pressing work Rivers Inlet in time for *Muriel* take pile driver to Lowe Inlet on her way north – See letters Wadhams & Curtis.

Cancel all arrangements for both Spring & Sockeye fishing Knight Inlet & let Sockeye net & unsold Spring nets be forwarded to Skeena River canneries – See letter Groves.

Change *Eagle* from Alert Bay to Rivers Inlet & write Wadhams their boat is to be half for Alert after he finishes with her – See letter Wadhams. Make Collier for Pac. Northern Pkg. Co. an offer to sell him Cascade [cannery] skiffs at $10 each – See letter PN Pkg Co. Write Mathews re loan asked for. Arrange if get personal guarantee & reduction in limit to 1,500 per trap – See letter Mathews. Arranged insurance we carry as per notes made by Mr. Wilson.

Re [Puget] Sound boxes (Welsh's letter 6th telegrams 22nd & our telegram 22nd) await arrival Welsh's letter. Write Garden to call re immediate work connected with obtained lease foreshore – See letter Gardner...

April 23 – Notify Rowan will not take out *Terra Nova* at present time. Arrange shipment supplies by outside boats – See letter Rowan. Order 100m bxs from Anacortes mill with option on 100m additional. Deliveries bet. June 1st & July 15th or Aug. 25th & Sept. 10th – See letter to [Robert] Welsh. Questionable distribution trap fish discussed and while no positive decision arrived at, I deem inadvisable pack [Puget] Sound fish except at Brunswick, Currie, Albion, and Imperial canneries. Try and arrange accordingly ...

April 28 – Wilson absent. Evans & Doyle. Re Alert Bay pack change Chinese contract to day-labour contract on same lines as Spencer had in 1901. Notify Groves reduce pack to 8,000 c/s and hold surplus of 450 bxs in tin plate. See letter to Groves also Chinese contract ...

May 5th – Learned from Evans insurance question had already been settled – the business going to Rithet, Ward & EC&E share and share alike, also smaller portions to Malins McGregor, the Continental & Ceperley.

June 2nd – Foreshore question. Write WS&B to proceed with completion of applications for leases in Straits & to have survey instituted and application work completed re sites on Chatham and Discovery Islands. See letter to WS&B. Write Canneries that where managers or others have their wives and families living at the canneries they are to pay for board at actual cost to the Co. No charge is to be made for use of houses ...

Sept. 5th – E[vans], W[ilson], & D[oyle]. Decided that where Japanese houses had no security to offer to cover loans, no advances should be made on account [for the] coming season. As consequence notified Ewen cannery from whom inquiry came that no advances were to be made ...

SUPPLIES ORDERED FOR 1903 SEASON – MACHINERY

17. 4/notebook 20

Weighing Machines: Ordered from Schaake 24 machines @ $240 each to him & $36 additional to be paid on his a/c to Letson & Burpee. Shipping instructions as follows:

2 machines to	Balmoral	shipped	
1	"	Standard	"
1	"	Skeena	"
1	"	Lowe Inlet	"
1	"	Bella Coola	"
1	"	Brunswick R.I.	"
1	"	Wadhams	"
1	"	Cleeve	"
1	"	Westminster	"
1	"	Albion	"
1	"	Currie	"
2	"	Brunswick C.P.	"
1	"	Can. Pacific	"
1	"	Pac. Coast	"
3	"	Imperial	"
1	"	Terra Nova	"
1	"	Acme	"
1	"	Dinsmore	"
1	"	Celtic	"

Lye Washing: Ordered from Schaake 3 machines @ $410 each. S/I as follows:

    1 to Balmoral shipped
    2 " Imperial   "

Conveyors: Ordered from Schaake 3 sets machines @ $166 for each complete conveyor:

    1 set to Balmoral shipped
    2 "   Imperial   "

Coolers: Ordered from Van. Eng. Work March 19th @ 2.40 cents each. S/I given April 22nd:

    150 for Balmoral Cannery
    100 for Cunningham Cannery

Alert Bay: Ordered from Letson & Burpee:
    1 fish elevator shipped
    2 retorts   "
    From Schaake:
    7'6" attachment shipped March 25th

Wadhams: Ordered from Letson & Burpee
    1 Power Gang Knife shipped

Brunswick: Ordered from Letson & Burpee:
    1 Capper shipped

Bella Coola: Ordered from Letson & Burpee:
    2 Retorts   shipped
    6   "   trucks   "
    1 set Tall Dies   "
    1 7'6" Attachment   "
    3 Thermometers   "
    1 Filling Machine   "
    1 Power Knife   "
    1 Square Shears ?   "
    From Schaake:
    1 Capper   shipped

Lowe Inlet: Ordered from Letson & Burpee:
    2 Retorts   shipped
    1 7'6" Attachment   "
    From Schaake:
    1 Capper   "

Standard: Ordered from Letson & Burpee:
    2 Retorts shipped
    1 Capper   "   April 11th
    1 Washer ?   "

Cunningham: Ordered from Letson & Burpee:
    1 Fish Elevator   shipped
    1 Tray   "   "
    20 Tall Cylinders   "
    1 Tall Dies   "

Balmoral: Ordered from Letson & Burpee:
    8 Retorts   shipped
    2 Cappers   "   March 16th
    2 Power Knives   "
    1 Wiper   "   March 16th
    1 Engine   "   "
    1 7'6" S. Machine   "   April 16th

18. 4/notebook 21 Excerpts: Directors' Meeting notes

January 12th 1904: Balance sheet was submitted showing net profit of a
little over $8,000 after allowing for expenditure on capital account, de-
preciation in value United Canneries stock and depreciation on material.
Was simply a *pro forma* statement but was erroneous as considerable of
the amount charged to capital was properly chargeable to depreciation on
plant, representing as it did cost of tearing down old buildings and
repairs and renewals. It was stated that the cost of putting up the 1903
pack taking all sizes and all locations into consideration amounted to
$4.45 per case. Requirements for 1904 were considered and it was finally
agreed about $200,000 would be the total amount required from the
banks. It was also stated that the value of nets required was approximately $40,000 and of boxes and other supplies about $43,000 (consider both
amounts are very considerably underestimated) ...

April 12th 1904: ... Decided to get bonds from all clerks & local managers the Assn paying cost of same. Reported District Managers declined
to agree to stand reductions their salaries and decided would not press
matters further. Although questions of reduction in executive salaries
was also raised no mention of it occurred outside of agenda paper. Re
purchase Herman cannery, I explained [R.V.] Winch and I were shareholders, [W.A.] Wadhams and [Robert] Ward were not but that
Wadhams, as an employee, would manage property and Ward would be
agent. Murray then raised question of Wadhams' liberty to even act as
manager and Wilson explained he could even hold stock if he so desired
as the estate of EAW [adams] not WAW [adams] had sold out ... Resolution passed that Executive could make no expenditure on capital account
without authority of Directors. Question was raised re authority for
purchase pile driver and Steveston land from Brunswick C. Co. It was
explained [that the] former, which cost $1,636.62, was treated the same
as if material & had more than paid for itself since ...

Directors' Meeting May 10th 1904: Letters from [E.W.] Rollins were
read criticising methods and management, and offering suggestions for
future guidance ... Sweeny very properly remarked Rollins was exceeding his position in presuming to write as he had done. Letter from Jarvis
& Co. on same subject also read ... I reported having visited all canneries
except Bella Coola on my northern trip and suggested whitewashing be
done at once. I explained cost would be fully offset by saving of 15¢ per
$100 on [fire insurance] premium. No action was taken. I reported wharf
at Balmoral needed considerable repairs, also handrailings, as while it
would entail a little expenditure, an accident under Employers Liability

Act would cost far more. Secretary instructed to write managers for particulars but beyond this, no action was taken.

NUMBER OF CANNING LINES, COAST CANNERIES, 1904

19. 4/notebook 19

Columbia River [Washington & Oregon]

Col River Pkrs Assn Elmore Cannery	3 lines	
Kinney "	3	"
Rooster Rock "	1	"
Eureka "	2	"
George & Barker "	2	"
J.G. Meagle Co.	2	"
A Booth Pkg. Co.	2	"
Sanborn Cutling Co.	2	"
Gallant Grant Co.	2	"
[?] Fishermen's Co-Op Co.	2	"
C.J. McGowan Chinook Cannery	2	"
Ilwaco "	1	"
Warrendale "	1	"
Pillar Rock Pkg. Co.	2	"
Warren Pkg. Co. Warrendale Cannery	2	"
Cathlamet "	2	"
Senfert Bros.	2	"
B.A. Seaborg	1	"
Altoona Pkg. Co.	1	"
Smiley Sheldon Co.	1	"

Puget Sound Canneries [Washington]

Alaska Pkrs. Assn. Point Roberts Cannery	4 lines	
Semiahmoo "	4	"
Anacortes "	4	"
Pacific American F. Co. Fairhaven "	9	"
Friday Harbor "	2	"
North American Fisheries Co. Anacortes "	3	"
Fidalgo Island C. Co. [ABC]	3	"
Rosario Straits C. Co.	2	"
White Crest C. Co.	1	"
Apex C. Co.	1	"

Carlisle C. Co.			2	"
Manhattan C. Co.			1	"
Astoria & Puget Sound Co.			1	"
George & Barker Co. [Pt. Roberts]			1	"
International			1	"
Pacific Northwest Co.			1	"
J.W. & V. Cook Co.			1	"
Pt. Townsend P. Co.			1	"
[Ocean] Washington P. Co. (Seaborg)			3	"
Sehome C. Co.			1	"
W.A. Doherty & Co.			1	"
Ainsworth & Dunn Blaine			2	"

Alaska Canneries

Alaska Pkrs. Assn.	Nush[a]gak Cannery	(3)	6	lines
	Kogguing "	(2)	6	"
	Neknek "		6	"
	Kvishak "	see Kogguing		
	Egagak "		1	"
	Ugash[u]k "		2	"
	Chig[n]ik "		2	"
	Karluk "	(3)	6	"
	Alitak "		1	"
	Ugamuk "		1	"
	Kussilof "		1	"
	Odiak "		2	"
	Pyramid Harbor "		2	"
	Wrangel [Island] "		3	"
	Loring "		3	"
North Alaska Salmon Co.				
	Nush[a]gak "	(2)	1	"
	Kogguing "		2	"
	Egagik "		1	"
NP Fishing & Pkg. Co.	Klawak "		1	"
Bristol P. Co.	Ugashik "		1	"
Alaska Salmon Co.	Nush[a]gak "		1	"
Alaska Fishing & Pkg Co.	"		1	"
Alaska-Portland Pkrs. Assn	"		2	"
Col. River Pkrs. Assn.	"		1	"
PP&N Co. (?)	"		3	"
Red Alaska Salmon Co.	Eugashik		1	"
Neknek Pkg. Co.	Neknek		2	"
"	Eugashik		1	"

PP&N Co. (?) Orca	Orca	2	"
	Chig[n]ik (2)	2	"
	Uyak (2)	2	"
	Hunter Bay	2	"
Pac. Coast & Norway Co.			
Union Pkg. Co.	Kell Bay	1	"
F.C. Barnes	Lake Bay	1	"
Kasgan Bay Co.	Kasgan Bay	1	"
Thlinket Pkg. Co.	Hunter Bay	1	"
Columbia Can & Co.	Lynn Chanel	1	"
Alaska Fish & Lumber Co.	Shakan	1	"
Alaska Fisheries Union	Chilkat	2	"
Pacific Cold Storage Co.	Taku	1	"
Pillar Bay Pkg. Co.	Point Ellis	1	"
Fidalgo Island C. Co.	Ketchican	2	"
Takutat C. Co.	Alsek	1	"
Geo. Myers	Chatham	1	"
PP&N Co. (?)	Taku [Inlet]	1	"
	Chilkoot [Inlet]	1	"
	Santa Ana	1	"
	Dundas [Bay]	1	"
	Yes Bay	1	"
[Boca de]	Quadra	1	"
	Petersburg	1	"

Fraser River Canneries [BC]

BC Packers Assn.	Atlas	1	line
	Imperial	4	"
	Pacific Coast	1	"
	Colonial	1	"
	Canadian Pacific	1	"
	Albion	1	"
	Currie	1	"
	Anglo American	1	"
	Brunswick	2	"
	Ewen	1	"
	Cleeve	1	"
	Westminster	1	"
	Celtic	1	"
	Dinsmore	1	"
	Acme	1	"

	Terra Nova	1	"
	Alliance	1	"
ABC Pkg. Co.	Phoenix	2	"
	Britannia	1	"
	British American	1	"
	Canoe Pass	1	"
	Wadhams	1	"
	Birrells	1	"
Malcolm Cannon & C.	Gulf of Georgia	2	"
	Scottish Canadian	2	"
	English Bay	2	"
Canadian Can. & Co.	Star	1	"
	Fraser	1	"
	Vancouver	1	"
J.H. Todd & Son	Beaver	1	"
	Richmond	1	"
BC Can. & Co.	Deas (1905–2 lines)	1	"
St. Mungo C. Co.	(1905–2 ")	1	"
National P. Co.		1	"
Great Northern C. Co.		1	"
Industrial		1	"

Skeena River Canneries [BC]

BC Packers Assn.	Balmoral	2 lines	
	Cunningham (1905–2 lines)	1	"
	Standard (1905–2 lines)	1	"
ABC Pkg. Co.	British Am.	2	"
	North Pacific	1	"
J.H. Todd & Son	Inverness	1	"
B.C. Can. & Co.	Oceanic	1	"
Wallace Bros.	Claxton	1	"
Carlisle Pkg. Co.	Carlisle	1	"
Cassiar Pkg. Co.		1	"
Skeena River Com. Co.		1	"
Alexandria Cannery		1	"
Village I. Cannery		1	"

Rivers Inlet Canneries [BC]

BC Packers Assn.	Wadhams	2 lines	
	Brunswick	2	"
ABC Pkg. Co.	Good Hope	1	"
BC Can. & Co.	RIC	1	"

BC Coast Points Canneries

BC Packers Assn.	Alert Bay [Van I.]	1 line
	Bella Coola	1 "
	Lowe Inlet	1 "
R. Draney	Namu	1 "
	Kimsquit	1 "
Federation Brand C. Co.	Mill Bay [Naas R.]	1 "
	Naas Harbor	1 "
John Wallace	Naas River	1 "
Port Nelson Co. S. Co.	Naas River	1 "
Wm Hickey Can. & Co.	Smiths Inlet	1 "
Clayoquot Can. & Co.	Clayoquot [Van. I.]	1 "
Alberni Pkg. Co.	Alberni Canal [Van. I.]	1 "
Pidcock Bros.	Quathiaska Cove [Van. I.]	1 "

A TYPICAL ONE-LINE CANNERY OPERATION, BC, 1904–05

20. 4/notebook 1 "Cannery Machinery and Equipment Requirements"

1	Boiler – return tubular 16′ × 5′ with 54–4″ tubes and all fittings complete
1	Vertical Engine 10 to 12 HP
1	Pump
1	Power Gang Fish Cutter fitted for 3 sizes
1	Weighter
1	Washer " " "
1	Capper " " "
1	Finger Solder Machine 9′
1	Fish elevator
3	Retorts 10′6″ × 4′8″ ⎰no. required to take care of full
2	Steam boxes ⎱capacity of one line machinery
250	Coolers 37″ square by 2¾ deep
	Test Kettles 3′6″ × 3′6″ × 2′1″ of 3″ lumber
1	Iron Lye Kettle 3′4½″ × 3′4½″ × 1′6″
	Bathroom Trucks Wheels 17″ dia 1¾″ face
	1¼″ square shaft 1⅛″ dia for wheels length 2′6″
	Retort Cars 2½″ × 19½ × 6½″ high with 5″ flanged wheels
	Stove Trucks
	Square Shears

Presses
Can Formers
Combination Dies
Seamer Frames
Cylinders, talls
       ½ flats
       flats
Seamer Fire Pots
Bathroom " "
Air Tank
Gasoline Tank
Drip   "
Platform Scales
Jack Screws #11
Rithet brace with taps, drills, etc.
Drill Breast
  " Post
Grindstone 220# 3"
    "   Small
Set lightening taps & dies ¼" to 1"
  " # 4 Duplex Stocks & dies
  " Pipe Stocks & dies ¼" to 1" Arm
  " #2   "   "   Little Giant
Pipecutter
Pipe Vice #2 –2"
Pipe Tongs
Alligator Wrench
L Wrench
Blocks Patent Single & Double
Mandril
Bench Shears 7"
Bellows
Blacksmith Tongs
Anvil
Vices
Blacksmith Hammer
Monkey Wrench
Spanner
Iron Wheelbarrow
Tube Scrapers
100' tape line
Augurs
Extension bit

  Brand for marking tools, etc.
  Solder moulds
  Acid tank & jar with trough
6   Filling Tables for 6 fillers each
1   Butcher table
2   Chopping tables
1   Washing table
  Salting table
  Tall can trays (size 25″ × 16″ inside measurement)
  Flat   ″   ″   (3″ high. Sided 1″ bottoms ⅝″)
  ½″ flat   ″   (spruce.)
  Can Boards
    ″ Baskets
  Fish Scows
  C.R. [Columbia River] boats
  Pulleys, shafting, belting, etc.
  Oil aprons
  Rubber Boots
  Glass for Seamers (½ flats 2″ × 2″ plate ⅜″ thick)
  Acid Jars (8 gal. capacity crocks)
  ⅜ Round Iron (for coppers)
  Can filling shields

20a. "Cannery Crew Required."
To pack: 1,000 c/s talls or flats or 600 c/s ½ flats Daily

White foreman	1
Fish tally[man]	1
Machine line man	1
Bathroom man	1
Engineer–fireman	1
Book-keeper–storekeeper	1

1,000 c/s talls or flats, or 600 c/s ½ flats daily, 800 c/s ½ flats daily

Chinese	(say 50)	(say 62)
Fish cutters	4	8
″ picklers	2	4
Trucking fish	1	2
Fish Slitting Machine	1	2
Carrying Fish to fillers	2	2
Ticket punchers	2	2

Filling light cans	1	1
Carrying fish to wiper	1	2
Feeding wiper	1	1
Carrying cans to salting machine	1	4
Feeding tops	2	2
Crimper	1	1
Solder machine	1	1
Cooler fillers	5	4
Stopping off	[4]	4
Cold test	4	6
Mending leaks	2	2
Bathroom	8	10
Lye kettle	3	4
Klootchmen	(say 55)	(say 85)
Filling	30/35	45
In gut shed	20	40

NET MAINTENANCE

21. 4/notebook 1 "Oiling Nets"

Use only Winnipeg or other prairie oil, as coast oil is not pure linseed oil
but has fish oil mixed with it. Use double-boiled oil if obtainable. Each
net requires 5 gallons oil. Put [net] through ringer and spread out to dry
to avoid spontaneous combustion, which is the only danger.

After oiling net bluestone it in the ordinary way, and bluestone it
throughout the season to cut off the slime, etc. Oiled nets will take up
only about half the quantity of bluestone of dry nets, and this saving
about offsets the cost of oil.

21a. "Bluestoning Nets"

Dissolve 9 lbs of Bluestone & 9 lbs salt in hot water sufficient to cover
net. Apply for about 4 hours. When liquid is cold, net may remain in it
for 10 hours. When the preparation is dirty, it can be purified by boiling.

Keep nets in boat damp and free from wind and sun. 25 lbs Bluestone
to 1 net for season. 300 lbs Bluestone to bbl.

CHINESE LABOUR

22. 4/notebook 1 "Chinese Contract"

Making boxes cannery pays extra for labour. Prices are about 1¼ cents per case of 48 lbs for talls and flats, and 1½ cents for halves, 96 to case ... Labelling cans 2¢ per case extra [for the] 1 lb [size]. Labour per hour 14¢ to 20¢. Labour trucking salmon from cannery to wharf 25¢ per hour. Labour stowing salmon on steamer 35¢ per hour.

Contractor pays for filling cans:

	½ Flats	1# Flats	1# Talls	½ Ovals	1# Ovals
per tray of 28	(3)4¢			(2)4¢	
" " " 24		(3)4¢			2¢
" " " 24			(3)4¢		

Contractor pays for labour:
>20¢ (12½¢) per hour to Klootchmen
>20¢ (15¢)   Indians [men?] or Japs.

Punching Tops. A Chinaman will punch 8 bxs of tin plate in 11 hours (14 × 20) plate. At 24 tops to each sheet this is 56 c/s tops to each box of plate, or 448 c/s for an 11-hour day. At $2.50 per day, this is a shade under ³⁄₅¢ per case as cost after labour for making tops.

23. 4/notebook 19 "Chinese Contracts for 1904 and 1905 Seasons"

1904

Clayoquot
prepared for 8,000 c/s guaranteeing 6,000 c/s. Contract price 49¢ per case.
Albion
prepared for 7,000 c/s guaranteeing $2,800 to contractor. Contract price 53¢ per case.
Hickey
prepared for 8,000 c/s guaranteeing $3,400 to contractor. Contract price 50¢ per case and 2 cans [for] do-overs allowed to each case.
Mill Bay
prepared fo 10,000 c/s guaranteeing 7,000 c/s contract price 50¢ per case.
Naas Hbr
prepared for 12,000 c/s guaranteeing 8,000 c/s talls at contract

price of 50¢ per case and 1,000 c/s ovals to be put up by day
labour.

Observatory

prepared for 10,000 c/s guaranteeing if on day-labour basis 1st
man $150, 2nd man $75, and foreman $75. Indian labour 10¢
per case. Made $600 advance. In case contracts are made this
is to be changed into regular contract.

BC Packers

Contracts given Bing were Brunswick, CP, and Albion. No guarantee as
he not member [Fraser River Canners] Assn. [Bing] wanted Currie but
Packers would not give it.

Lee Coy received the following contracts with bonus mentioned for
breaking union:

Cannery	Daily Guarantee	Advance	Bonus Mentioned
Imperial	2,500 c/s		$500
Pacific coast	—		250
Can Pacific	—		250
Currie	1,200		250
Terra Nova	—		250
Acme	—		250
Celtic	—		250
Balmoral	—		400
Cunningham	—		—
Wadhams	—		—
Brunswick R.I.	—		—
Bella Coola	—		—

1905

Nov. 8th. Ewen. Contract for Britannia for 1905 is made already at
50¢ for flats, 85¢ for half flats, and 13¢ for ½ ovals.

Nov. 8th. Lee Coy. Contract for BC cannery (ABC Co.) for 1905 is
made already at 47¢ for talls, 49¢ for flats, 84¢ for ½ flats.

Nov. 8th. Ewen. Contract for Ewen cannery for 1905 is made already
at 46¢ for flats, 78¢ for ½ flats. Contract for Balmoral cannery for 1905 is
made already at 48¢ for 1 lb. talls or flats and 80¢ for ½ flats.

THE "BIG" YEAR, 1905

24. 4/notebook 19 "Northern Cannery Notes, H.D."

7th March 1905. Marsh says average advance [to fishers] as far as he can learn has been $5 per man, i.e., $10 per boat. He is trying to hold his men down to this but expects to have to pay more. Thinks advance may go to $20 per boat but hopes to hold it to $16. On the latter basis, and figuring on average for 5 months, the amount due on a basis of 25 boats (50 men) would be as follows by the end of the season:

25 boats @ $16 per boat advance money	$ 400
Oilskins, boats, etc. for 25 boats @ $25 per boat	625
General Store a/c for 25 boats @ $100 per boat (50 men @ $10 per month each for 5 months)	2,500
Japanese sauces [sic], etc. for 25 boats @ $22 per boat	550
Total outlay	$4,075

This is equal to $163 per boat and is conservatively figured. A fair average, allowing for incidentals, would be $170 per boat.

It will take 2,000 fish at 8½¢ each to clear the advances per boat. In 1904, the average catch was about 2,700 for Jap boats.

24a. 4/notebook 3 "General Notes, H.D."

Aug. 10th 1905. Steveston Trip: Went to Steveston to-day, visiting the Federation, Steveston, Imperial, Atlas, and Scottish Canadian canneries. Federation plant in great disorder and badly handled. Largest pack any one day yet was 1,100 c/s 1# flats. Total pack to date about 12,000 c/s. Steveston Can. Co. had almost all of their ½ flat cans packed and expected to furnish same by end of week. Their best day so far was 460 c/s.

Imperial cannery in great state of disorder. Filling was poor, workmanship coarse, and [they had] their same old trouble of wasting solder in stopping off. Pack in warehouse in very bad shape. Numerous swells visible all throughout pile, in some portions seemingly averaging full 33⅓%. From lower end of can pile arose a fearful stench which I am satisfied did not come from decomposed fish under the cannery, but from spoiled fish in the cans themselves. It will surprise me greatly if when going over the pile their swells to be thrown away do not reach startling proportions. Only three lines at one time have been worked this season. Pack to date about 37,000 lbs. Bain told me he was greatly exercised through fear of running short on solder. His estimates of requirements at beginning of season had been 13,000 c/s more than head office would allow. Now their economy has proven a false one and they are scouring the country for pig tin, paying as high as 39¢ per lb. for it.

The Imperial cannery is this season fishing 215 boats. When limit was enforced their full deliveries amounted to 42,000 fish per day.

Their net account is much heavier in proportion to others, and Fraser is employing a great deal of labour and the cost is far in excess of other plants under Bain's management. Buttimer & Dawson are purchasing fish openly from other cannery boats. On the 9th purchased from at least 8 Imperial contract boats and 5 Imperial lay boats.

Wilson, the foreman, said their great trouble has been with the bathroom conveyor. Claims it is too lightly constructed and has been breaking down on them. As it works splendidly in Ewen's and Balmoral [canneries] I am skeptical as to this, believing trouble is due to Chinese trickery, especially as it is known they tried to break part of the line of machinery, presumably so as to shift responsibility for lost fish from themselves to the cannery.

Atlas cannery in good shape, clean, and packing well done. Only cannery in Bain's district where contract quality was packed. Contract called for 800 c/s per day. Largest day's pack 880 c/s. Cans will be all filled this week (13,000 c/s) and Bain expects to send them another 1,000 c/s from Imperial. Saint deserves great credit for his work here.

Scottish Canadian in good shape, fish wharf especially clean. Malcolm says Chinese contract called for 2,000 c/s a day but they have never yet succeeded in getting up that quantity. It struck me their crimping was not sufficiently tight.

Met Col. Phillips of Canadian Cang. Co. going out on train. He says they are prepared for 60,000 c/s. If fill up do not expect to operate next year, but will run one cannery and use up material if any cans left over.

Adamson said Gardiner was asking Wilson and others for quotations. This [Adamson] resents as he considered Wilson his connection, and Gardiner's offer has inflated Wilson's ideas so that no business is possible at present. Adamson said Powell was the English selling agent for the ABC Pkg. Co., Malcolm Cannon & Co., and the Canadian Cang. Co. In addition, [Powell] was buying outside salmon for their own, or customers', account. Adamson said Lobb has purchased all told 37,000 c/s, of which 25,000 c/s are from BCPA and 5,000 from Windsor. Adamson wants us to make him an offer of $4.95 here, quality passed here, for Steveston Cang. Co.'s 1# flats. As goods are under offer to Gardiner until tomorrow, could do nothing with him now, but he is to come in tomorrow at 4 PM to see what can be done.

Adamson says Kelly Clark & Co.'s estimate of Puget Sound pack is 500,000 c/s, or possibly only 450,000 c/s if true returns of the ½ lb cans were known. (Deming's estimate according to Burdis is 600,000 c/s of 48-lb to a case.)

24b. 4/notebook 21 Excerpts: "Executive Notes, H.D."

August 4th 1904 – Re: Chinese contracts with Lee Coy. Talking to Barker to-day. He said he was disgusted with Lee Coy. He was the most useless contractor he had ever seen and he could not understand how any one could consider him good. I told him that was my own opinion too; that I had wanted to drop him in 1903 but was over-ruled. I did not consider him competent in any way and to make matters worse, the foreman [at Imperial cannery], Wilson, was not capable for the position he occupied. I did not think him good for one [canning] line to say nothing of four, but when I wished to drop him in 1903, Bain said it would not be fair to judge him by that season's work as the installation of new plant, adjustments of machinery, etc. had shown him to disadvantage. His work in 1904, however, made me absolutely sure of his unfitness, and it also showed me Bain himself was lacking in both proper knowledge and force of character for the position he occupied.

CLASH OF THE CANNERS AND THE JAPANESE FISHERMEN ON THE FRASER, 1904

25. 1/8 Announcement: Secretary, Fraser River   *Vancouver,*
Canners' Association, to the members   *June 3rd, 1904*

Please attend a meeting of the above Association
ON TUESDAY, JUNE 7TH, 1904, AT 11 AM
to consider a letter from the Japanese Fishermen's Bosses; also a letter from the Fraser River Canners' Association, London [Committee], of May 19th (copies of which are herewith enclosed); and such other matters as may then be submitted.
Awaiting the favour of your kind attention.

25a. 1/8 Attached. Petition: Japanese fishermen's   *Vancouver,*
bosses to the Fraser River Canners'   *May 14th, 1904*
Association

Gentlemen:
It is over ten years since we Japanese first came to the banks of the Fraser River. We bosses have been gathering men for the different Canning Companies. We did our best to help the Companies to be successful

but we have never received any pay for our services. We supplied men with their necessaries before and through the Fishing Season, and at the end of the season we tried to deduct the cost of living from their work, but you remember, like the last Season, fishermen could not pay us back as they made no profit from fishing and they had no property to depend upon. They promised, of course, to be here next year, but many of them scattered, some died, and others were called back to Japan to serve in the army, and a great many dishonest debtors went away and would not come back; the consequence was a great loss to us. We were not willing to bear these heavy expenses but we were obliged to do so. There is not one good reason why we bosses should be responsible for the expenses of these men.

While we have to bear these heavy expenses there is no remuneration for us from the Company; therefore, it is no more than just that the Company pay a certain commission for each man we get. Though we have been serving the Companies without any due regard, we are not able to continue it any longer, and if the Canneries tried to compel us to do the same as in the past years, we will be bankrupt in the near future, and the good feeling which has existed between us will be dissolved, and we may be obliged to choose some other livelihood. This will certainly be a disadvantage to both parties, so we would like to have the Company grant us a certain amount of reward to each boss for his work. This will make the people feel more friendly toward the Canners and will be an advantage for both parties. You, gentlemen, may ask us this question, "Why did you not ask for the commission before?" We will answer, in the first place when your pioneer Japanese fishermen came to the banks of the River, they did not know the business method, and have done as they were told without thought for the future, and the fishermen who came after them have kept up the same old customs even though they knew they were losing. Our second reason is that we had a certain profit out of fishing, and the necessaries [sic] then were much cheaper than they are now, so our income was able to meet our expenses without us receiving anything for our work. But [in] recent years the continuance of poor fishing increased our indebtedness, so that we cannot now meet our expenses without more income, and it will be extremely dangerous for us to take in these men who are entirely strangers to us. We trust that these two reasons may convince you, gentlemen, of the necessity of granting us a commission for our work of gathering men for the Fishing season.

We will be greatly obliged if you will give us an answer as soon as possible.

We are yours truly,

(signed)

Japanese Fishermen's Bosses for:
CPP Co. – T. Nishihara, H. Hagashi, E. Enana, Y. Takano, T. Tutemoto; Beaver Cannery – T. Morita, K. Nagata, K. Kawasaki, R. Nadakoro; Colonial Cannery – Y. Komatu, M. Tamuta; PC Cannery – M. Higo, K. Zawa, G. Shinono, T. Kimoto, T. Tanaka; Britannia Cannery – K. Takahashi, H. Hamasaki, Y. Mozoguchi, I. Susaki; Phoenix Cannery – Y. Nishi, S. Ogomu, K. Kama, N. Nagai, R. Kagiwara, E. Shimamura, Tanino; Imperial Cannery – Y. Maedo, S. Katai, M. Mukai, T. Machida, U. Murkamo, S. Miyanishi, T. Ekeda, T. Ikari, T. Asano, Y. Maedo, T. Uyede, K. Motsuzoka, Y. Ode, F. Hamanisho, K. Hayoshi, S. Katai; Lighthouse Cannery – U. Aoki, G. Nakomada; Currie McWilliams – C. Sasaki, K. Erino; Star Cannery – T. Hamaguchi, U. Kuroyama, T. Nakanisho, K. Shimoge; Gulf of Georgia – K. Yashida, H. Oura, S. Tanaka, S. Matshuha, S. Takinchi, F. Tanaka, R. Nasano, S. Nishi, T. Sakai, George Isomura; Atlas Cannery – T. Matsunaga, K. Ringin, K. Yoshida; Ewen Cannery – D. Kuromoto, J. Hashigowa; British American – I. Tasaka, Y. Mukai; Scottish Canadian – K. Ida, K. Kishino, T. Mio, S. Hamaka, T. Matsumato, E. Suzuki, T. Tanabe. Y. Taniguchi.

INDIAN FISHERMEN'S STRIKE ON THE SKEENA, 1904

26. 11/5 Fraser River Canners' Association wires

26a. C.F. Todd to W.D. Burdis
Victoria,
June 25, 1904

Wire received felt sure McDonald would not wire us as he did unless situation serious which is now confirmed. We wired Ker yesterday that should agreement be made should be 4 years so cover parallel bad year Fraser 4 years hence also to attempt 7 cents next year account big run Fraser this reasonable. Our opinion is accept proposal quick 4 years 8 cents or if possible 7 next year. Believe nothing gained delay situation will quickly grow worse you cannot hold some of the canners who will act independently. Wire us what reply you send Skeena & consult A.E. Todd now in Vancouver.

26b. Burdis to W.R. Lord
Vancouver,
June 25, 1904

Stand firm to old prices. Wish consult Doctor and Wilson expected tonight. Have fishermen agreed accept eight cents three years. Wire reason for hurry.

26c. Lord to Burdis   *Aberdeen,*
                                                       June 25, 1904

Your telegram of today to hand. Fishermen demand ten cents. Some concession must be made to them without delay. Position growing worse. Large majority Indians not here holding aloof not sure they will accept eight cents. Few sockeye running. Rush further instructions.

26d. Lord to Burdis   *Aberdeen,*
                                                       June 25, 1904

Canners meeting here now stand by will have to give fishermen decisive answer tonight.

26e. E.H. Bridgeman to Burdis   *Aberdeen,*
                                                       June 25, 1904

Agreement unanimous by cannery managers that situation very serious only way out is to offer eight cents with three years agreement if possible kindly rush reply.

26f. C.F. Todd to Burdis   *Victoria,*
                                                       June 25, 1904

Your wire received managers better able size up situation than we are consequently we wired you advising acceptance proposal don't believe would send it unless assured fishermen would accept. Managers will wonder at owners wiring asking what reason for hurry, must be indifferent, surely their wire plain enough that all unanimous believing only solution offer eight cents regret Wilson and Doctor not arrived you will find delay dangerous. Will be out of town tomorrow.

27. 11/5 Minutes, Fraser River Canners'   *June 26, 1904*
    Association

STRIKE ON SKEENA RIVER

A meeting of the Skeena River Canners was held in the office of the Fraser River Canners' Association, Vancouver on Sunday June 26th, 1904.

Present:– Messrs. G.I. Wilson, H. Bell-Irving, D. Bell-Irving, R.J. Ker, A.E. Todd, and H. Doyle.

The telegrams [documents 26–26f] which have passed between the Managers Committee on the Skeena River and the Vancouver office were submitted and considered, and the situation on the River explained by Messrs. Wilson and D. Bell-Irving.

The Secretary was instructed to telegraph E.H. Bridgeman as follows: "Canners meeting today. Your instructions are notify fishermen no ad-

vance will be made. Post-public notice on each cannery to this effect.
Keep us daily advised of run."

The meeting then adjourned.

27a. Attached Wire: C.F. Jackson & Co. Ltd.,   *Vancouver,*
    to Carlisle cannery   *June 26th, 1904*
Association decide after consulting Wilson stand firm by Association
price must not give way without further authority from us.

28. 11/5 Correspondence files: Fraser River Canners' Association

28a. Copy of letter from W.D. Burdis (?) to (?)   *Vancouver,*
                                             June 27, 1904

Mr. Oscar Brown forwarded me the following copy of a message he had
received from the Manager of the Cassiar Cannery: –

Message received from Mr. Moore Saturday night at Cassiar Cannery.

Oscar Brown, Water St.
"Offered fishermen eight cents. See Burdis for particulars. D.M. Moore."

I showed Mr. Brown a copy of the telegram sent yesterday to Bridgeman, and he forwarded the following message:

Manager Cassiar Cannery, Skeena River.
"Withdraw price eight cents, must stand by agreement with Association. Oscar
Brown."

28b. Wire: Henry Doyle, Vancouver, BC,   *Aberdeen, BC*
    from Peter Herman   *June 27 1904*
Canners decision mistake not understanding situation ultimatum 7 cents
now a proper mess. Indians determined, no distress. Wadhams understands. Jacobsen held out 2 weeks, bankruptcy to face. Canners no
sympathy. Twelve boats cuts no figure strike. Situation serious, reconsider today before too late.

28c. Wire: W.D. Burdis, Vancouver,   *Aberdeen, BC*
    from E.H. Bridgeman   *June 28th, 1904*
Public notice posted, few Japs fishing today, majority Japs demand written guarantee take all fish cloudy and wet fish slack.

28d. Wire: W.D. Burdis from Bridgeman   *Aberdeen, BC*
                                         June 29th, 1904
Conditions unaltered strikers set yesterday again wet fish slack.

28e. Wire: W.D. Burdis from Bridgeman   *Aberdeen, BC*
                                                          June 30th, 1904
Some whites fishing sockeye outside average one hundred turned fine.

28f. Wire: W.D. Burdis from Bridgeman   *Aberdeen,*
                                                          July 2nd, 1904
Weather holding fine general average yesterday hundred. Today fifty Indians not fishing.

28g. Wire: W.D. Burdis from Bridgeman   *Aberdeen,*
                                                          July 5th, 1904
Canners met Indian Chiefs at Indian Agents request. Situation unchanged. Some Indians leaving. Average Monday seventy Tuesday over hundred.

28h. Wire: W.D. Burdis from Bridgeman   *Aberdeen, BC*
                                                          July 6th, 1904
Delay, wires down, up last night. Fine outside. Average Lord one ought seven, English seventy four. Many Indians leaving Canneries.

28i. Wire: W.D. Burdis from Bridgeman   *Aberdeen, BC*
                                                          July 7th, 1904
Oceanic, Claxton paying eight half. Inverness, Carlisle, eight, bonus ten dollars. Cassiar eight, but will meet advance, General average over hundred. Holding fine.

28j. Wire: W.D. Burdis from Bridgeman   *Aberdeen,*
                                                          July 7th, 1904
Indians leaving fast. Fraser sending for men. Wallace, Brewster Moore report offering eight. Weather fine. Fish running well. Report strike Naas Cannery caved.

28k. Wire: W.D. Burdis from Bridgeman   *Aberdeen,*
                                                          July 9th, 1904
Majority Indians fishing general average about seventy. Weather fine.

28l. Wire: W.D. Burdis from Bridgeman   *Aberdeen,*
                                                          July 9th, 1904
Average four Canneries seventy five. Fine. Some Indians fishing.

28m. Wire: W.D. Burdis from Bridgeman   *Aberdeen,*
                                                          July 11th, 1904
General average outside about hundred. River fifty. Rainy, cloudy weather.

28n. Wire: W.D. Burdis from Bridgeman   *Aberdeen,*
                                                      July 13th, 1904

Raining. Average [fishing] outside about hundred, river fifty. Indians here fishing. Copy of telegram seen today:– "W.M. Musgrave send down by *Danube* one hundred women, forty men, bring nets, will pay fares here. Gulf of Georgia Cannery, answer. Joseph Bradley."

29. 4/notebook 21 Excerpts: "Notes"

Directors' Meeting July 7th 1904: ... Re strike on Skeena and taking Indians from there for the Albion, W[ilson] stated he was afraid that if he did not accept men Mulhall or the United Canneries [ABC Canning Co.] would have done so. He therefore had given orders to the [Canadian Pacific Navigation Co.] to bring down 55 men, we paying fares, which would be deducted from their earnings unless their catches were individually over 1,000 fish for season. (This statement differed somewhat from W's statement of July 2nd to Barker and myself, when no competitors' names were mentioned and his reason was simply the fear of what others might do. If they were bound to come, he would rather have them than let others do so, and he had therefore told the agent for the Indians he would employ them if they came. He told us the number engaged was 30 boats but said absolutely nothing about having agreed to advance the fares.) During the desultory discussion which followed W's statement I told Ker that were I in Bell-Irving's place, I would raise price to 10¢. The Tsimpsean Indians were engaged by Lord & English between them, and [Bell-Irving] was therefore the outsider who would suffer most, and would draw from the BCPA especially to make up the shortage his actions had occasioned. I also asked W why instead of acting as he had done he had not called a meeting of the F[raser] R[iver] C[anners] A[ssociation] and raised resolutions against any Fraser canner giving strikers employment. He claimed they had not the power. From this I differ as with ABC, Todd & F[indlay], D[urham], & B[rodie] that his support would be overwhelming and if majority cannot rule, the FRCA is a useless farce ...

July 9th 1904 – Saw Alexander after arrival of *Beatrice* with Northern Indians. Told me he had just paid fares for 76 men & 20 women for Albion cannery. Saw Bain at luncheon. Told me he was then arranging & expected to get all balance of the Indians and that there were some 120 men & about 75 to 80 women came down. Where accepting men now they are down. Bain expressed strong disapproval of the advisability of W's action. Saw Barker, who informed me he had overheard W on Friday telling CPN man he had agreed to pay fares for only 55 men and would not pay a single additional one. (This does not prove correct in view of Alexander & Bain's statements.)

July 11th 1904 – W told Bower Todd responsible for losing strike on the Skeena, he having broken away from the other canners despite his agreement and offering 8½¢. As no break occurred until men started for the Fraser inaccordance with W's arrangement to employ them, [this] statement not correct. Strike was lost owing to W's action.

DOYLE PARTS WITH BRITISH COLUMBIA PACKERS ASSOCIATION

30. 2/4 Letter: Doyle to Æmelius Jarvis   *Vancouver, BC,*
                                                              August 5th, 1905

Dear Jarvis:

After talking over the stock proposition with Mr. Ker, he informed me of the conversation you had with him prior to taking your departure for the East, and from what he said of your remarks I am sorry to learn you have so misunderstood and misjudged my motives in criticizing the actions of those at the head of the British Columbia Packers Association. Permit me to assure you that my attitude was not, and is not, dictated by any feelings of vindictive spleen, as you seem to imagine. Nothing is farther from my thoughts, and no one – not even yourself – takes greater pride, interest, and concern in the Association, more heartedly desires them to enjoy a measure of success greater in proportion than any of their competitors secure. To me the Association means more than it can to you. It is true you were directly responsible for securing the preference shareholders, but securing them on arguments based on my representations made me indirectly the object of any onus or praise that might be deserved. To me also was entirely due the securing of the various canning properties, and I would be ungrateful indeed if through private resentment I now attempted to injure those who made my own success possible.

Had I been animated by feelings of resentment toward the Association I could, by voicing my knowledge of their affairs, have caused them considerable trouble, annoyance, and unpleasant notoriety. To my mind I had ample cause for doing so, but I distinguished between the Association and its individual directors, and did not blame the former for things the latter were responsible for. My differences with the directors were largely questions of responsibility, veracity, and knowledge of the business. Of the first, I assumed my share, but refused to also bear the burden of some others equally responsible. Of the second, I was content to let actions and general reputation be the arguments by which people could judge who was to be believed. As to knowledge of the business,

Mr. Barker's report to the preferred shareholders, that neither Wilson nor Ker had technical knowledge of, or were competent to manage, the business, and his subsequent adoption – in every detail – of my plan of management, I consider ample evidence as to who was in the right in the previous unfortunate dissensions.

I admit that I felt both hurt and exasperated when, despite Mr. Barker's verdict, the directors, on the question of having a closed season [for salmon fishing] in 1906 and 1908, took the advice of the incompetents in preference to that of Barker and Ewen. I also felt rather bitter against Messrs. Rollins and Cronyn for having kept these men [Wilson and Ker] on the board after I had pointed out the very danger which was afterwards realized, and after they had promised both Mr. Ewen and myself that the removals would be put into effect.

Through all this, however, I distinguished between the company and its officers. For the former I have steadfastly worked, argued, and fought, and in doing so I have not spared the directors when their actions were at variance with the Association's welfare.

To you in Toronto, far removed from the scene of action, and unfamiliar with the surrounding details, I can understand how my actions may have appeared to you in an unfavourable light. But I, who am on the spot, have almost daily to listen to complaints of unjust treatment or unwise actions on the part of the Association; on me falls the unpleasantness of being brought into contact with responsibility for actions which I share in disapproving of; and had I any desire to be vindictively inclined toward the Association I would, at such times, have ample opportunity to hurt them.

Human forebearance has its limitations, however, and on the two occasions on which I wrote letters concerning the Association, I felt, and still feel, my action was both right and perfectly justifiable. I further believe you will agree in that opinion when you are acquainted with the details.

If you will recollect, when trying to get the option on the Dinsmore Island Canning Co. – which was one of the last secured – we found old [William] McPherson a very canny, cautious, and hard-headed Scotchman to deal with. He spoke of the profitable business his company had enjoyed, of their good financial condition, and of their belief in the future proving equally profitable to them if they remained independent. With the distinct understanding that selling out to us would not mean severing their relations with the industry, they gave us the option, and on the same understanding – in which you as well as I were personally represented – we accepted it. In the course of the numerous conversations we had with them, the binding nature of the ten-year prohibition clause was frequently discussed. They objected to this but agreed to leave it remain on our statements that, while we considered it binding in a moral sense, there were so many technical ways of evading its observation that we only looked upon it as an honourary obligation.

But after the amalgamation had been affected and the Association [was] an established fact, matters were not carried out on the lines we had led the holders of ordinary shares to believe would be the case. Instead of shareholders being given the preference in positions at our disposal, they were overlooked or set aside in order that former employees of Wilson and Ker might be provided for. Today over 25% of the Company's plants are in the hands of such employees to the exclusion of shareholders, who are in my opinion far more competent to do the work than are the favourites who were preferred. To the appointments as made I was opposed, and considered them as violations of the promises under which our success had been secured.

Amongst others thus treated were Messrs. McPherson and Wilkinson. They felt aggrieved, and told me so, nor under the circumstances could I blame them. Others recognized their worth, even though their own company did not, and McPherson was offered the management of the Canadian Canning Co.'s North Arm plants. In a manly fashion he came to us before accepting and tried to see what we would do. We did nothing, nor did we oppose his accepting the offer, as under the condition of purchase we had a perfect right to do. In overlooking this opportunity we may have been wrong, but our subsequent actions were no better.

In the sale to us of the R. Cunningham & Sons cannery, the owners deliberately deceived us as to what the sale included. As a consequence, I was desirous of closing down the Cunningham cannery, since they refused to do us justice. For this reason the Balmoral was made of its present size; the intention having been to install *3 lines* of machinery there. When Cunningham realized our intentions, however, he brought pressure to bear on us through Rithet & Co., who had formerly been his agents. Mr. Ker, as Rithet's representative on the directorate, threatened us that if we did not run the Cunningham plant, Cunningham would build a new one and *R.P. Rithet & Co. would finance him in his operations.* The directors weakened; the Cunningham cannery was run at needless expense to the Association; and the Balmoral cannery remains an unnecessarily expensive cannery for a *two-line* plant, but not so had the [original] object in building it been carried out.

When the Great Northern cannery was offered for sale, McPherson & Wilkinson purchased it. Shortly afterwards, the directors notified them they could not operate their purchase, and directly subsequent to this notification I wrote my letter dealing with this matter. You are, I know, aware of what my letter contained, but you are not aware of what caused its composition. McPherson & Wilkinson asked me for a letter stating that they had tried in the beginning to have that prohibition clause eliminated, and that I had given them my opinion on it. I gave them the letter asked for because in addition to their past treatment at the hands of the Association, I was aware that the Great Northern cannery had been *purchased for them by Mr. Evans* [a director] – who made $500 on the transaction – and that Mr. Wilson, while the directors were coming to a decision to contest their right of purchase, *had offered them an advance of $4,500 over cost to turn the cannery over to him.* These are facts you probably knew nothing of, but I, who did, saw the mockery of Evans, Wilson, and Ker – after their actions – passing judgement as directors on the affairs of McPherson & Wilkinson, and I felt justified in endeavouring to shame the board into doing something more conducive to the Association's honour than the action they then contemplated, and have since undertaken ...

I then listened to Mr. Ker's explanations as to the placing of insurance, and made him admit he had not even tried to have the resolution of June 9th, 1904 carried into effect. The resolution distinctly stated the insurance *companies* were to be asked to submit plans and terms, and he admitted he had not approached a single company on the matter. What he did was simply to approach *agents* of companies and insurance *brokers* and the result was just so much time wasted as I could have told him beforehand ...

I know positively that we can save at the very least $5,000 a year by adopting my suggestion. I know also that it is against the interests of Ker and Evans to do so, and consequently the resolution passed has been ignored. The insurance business of the BCPA alone is more than many first-class companies are now obtaining through their present agents, and I know there would not be a moment's hesitation on the part of such companies to transfer their agency to the BCPA. In this simple way our insurance rebates, or agents' commissions, would immediately be increased from 10% to 20%. On the basis of our last year's rebates (as set forth in the last annual profit-and-loss statement) this would give us $? [sic] to start with. In addition I know from personal experience that the outside insurance business which would come to us *unsolicited* by business houses anxious to curry the Association's favour, would show a handsome profit after paying every item of salary and other expenses made necessary by having an insurance-agency account. It is all nonsense to argue that this is not feasible; that one company having the entire account could not handle it all; and that in underwriting it with other companies, they would get but the minimum commission, and thus the average would be about the same as at present. I know positively that this is not the case. I know further that Bell-Irving has an insurance agency of his own, and his business is not near as profitable as ours. I know that before the Alaska Pkrs. Association decided to carry all their own insurance, they dealt entirely through one channel, and their business was larger by far than we have to offer. I know well that there will be no trouble to put into practical operation the resolution I had passed, but I am equally as positive it must be done over the head of those directors who desire the business for themselves.

In our advocating this plan no shareholder can object they are being dealt with contrary to promises made them when then company's formation was in progress. Our promise was simply that everything *being equal* they were to get the preference. None of them could do as well by us as the companies themselves can do, consequently they could raise no objection. I am not desirous of seeing Ward & Co. or anyone else given a preference over other shareholders, but I want to see the Association adopt and live up to an honourable and just course, and this they cannot say they are doing today while certain shareholders are cast out in the cold in order that others, and former employees of others, are enjoying more than they were contented to accept in the beginning.

I am sorry to have afflicted you with this long epistle, and it would have been avoided had I been fortunate enough to have seen you while you were here. However, I want you to feel that I am as anxious as you are to make the Association succeed. I am willing to bend all my energies toward attaining this end, and you can count on my cooperation in all legitimate ways and means. It is only when I feel that the company is losing its opportunities or is being lowered in the estimation of others by the ill-advised or self-interested action of those influential in the conduct of its affairs, that I voice my condemnation, and in such events I consider I would be derelict in the duty I owe those I brought into the company if I failed to oppose such actions. When I told Mr. Cronyn of my intention not to be a director last year, he tried to dissuade me from such a step, but I felt I could not conscientiously remain on a board with men I lacked confidence in, as my doing so would mislead those who were relying on me. I felt keenly sorry at having to sever my connection with the Association, but saw no other course open to me to adopt. From a financial standpoint the company has been nothing but a loss to me as it cost me far more than I ever received, or am ever likely to receive, from it; but if handled right, as Mr. Barker can handle it, if he is untrammelled by interference from self-interested parties, I know it will abundantly verify everything I ever claimed for it, and no one is half as anxious as I am to see this result obtained.

31. 1/8 Letter: Edward L. Eyre, Girvin & Eyre,   *Oakland, Cal.,*
        to Doyle   *May 16th, 1906*

Dear Sir:

I must apologize for not having answered several of your letters, but I was away from the office considerably part of the time prior to the late disaster [the San Francisco fire]. Your letter of the 17th ult. has not reached me, but I assume it was an inquiry as to whether or not I had any definite proposition to submit with respect to purchasing the control of the British Columbia Packers Association, to which I beg to advise you that under present financial conditions this will be impossible, and I would advise you to look elsewhere to carry out your scheme. I had been making considerable headway in interesting certain influential friends of mine, but the late appalling disaster puts every thought except the up-building of the city out of the question for the time being at least.

Thanking you for putting the matter before me.

CHAPTER THREE

Expansion and Diversification

INTRODUCTION

A major turning point in the industry was 1905, the "big" year for salmon all along the Pacific coast. Out of this boom season developed a thirteen-year period of expansion and growth, interrupted only briefly by economic downturns in 1907 and 1913.

Helping the spread and growth of the industry after 1905 was the rapid and unprecedented mechanization of the fish-handling and -canning processes and the use of powered boats and gear. In the 1905 season, as predicted, the existing canneries could not handle all the raw fish available; keeping up with the gluts in fish overtaxed many of the old plants. Not only were manpower and equipment insufficient to process properly all the fish available at the peak of the runs, but the cannery operators usually did not have sufficient materials and supplies on hand to process the total amount available over the season. In these years before automatic can-making techniques, it was common for cannery operators to try to economize by, for example, underestimating the tinplate and solder requirements for making cans, only, in the end, to find themselves unable to can all the fish available. Because such materials were expensive, required storage space, and quickly rusted if not used, overestimating the amount needed could prove just as costly as underestimating.

As in 1901, cannery operators in 1905 were forced voluntarily to limit the number of fish they could accept daily from the individual boats and to reduce the number of contract boats fishing for the cannery. Despite these precautions, a substantial amount of salmon was canned too hurriedly and therefore had to be re-done (document 24a). So many "do-overs" occurred that some Chinese workers made a separate business out of re-labelling the tins for canners (document 36). Besides the do-overs, a large portion of the pack was spoiled because of contamination. Whether the contamination occurred as a consequence of canning fish that was no longer fresh or of using improper canning methods, the result was the same: an unprecedented number of "swells" that had to be destroyed. Some cannery operators tried to pin the blame on poor workmanship and penalized the Chinese labour contractors accordingly. Ultimately, the huge supply of canned salmon and the amount of contaminated product that year caused cannery operators and their agents to scramble to dispose of the pack at the best possible rates (documents 24a, 36).

All salmon canners had to be sensitive to the issue of quality. Not only were contaminated products unmarketable and thus a loss to the operators, but bad canned salmon tended to affect the product's reputation and, therefore, its general marketability. A few years later, the meat-packing scandals in the United States led to tougher regulations and controls on the canning industry in general (document 32). Fish canners in particular were affected, as fish is one of the most perishable of foods; unlike meat, it does not improve with aging!

The need for quality controls, which were difficult to enforce in the remote and isolated cannery operations at the best of times, led to increasing government involvement in research into the biology and microbiology of salmon and salmon processing. The Biological Board of Canada was formed in 1912, and a Pacific Biological Station was established at Departure Bay (Nanaimo) on Vancouver Island.[1] The same year, the provincial fisheries department launched a long-term scientific project to study the nature of halibut and all five species of salmon, to attempt to unlock the mysteries of their migratory habits. Charles H. Gilbert, a former Stanford University zoologist, headed the project until 1924, when he resigned and moved to Alaska to continue his investigation there.[2] Drs. Wilbert A. Clemens and Lucy S. Clemens continued Gilbert's work in BC.

Another outcome of the 1905 boom was a major, lengthy federal inquiry into the industry, lasting from 1905 to 1907 (document 33).[3] It was called the Prince Commission, after its chairman, Edward E. Prince, who at the time was General Inspector of Fisheries for Canada and secretary of Canada's Marine Biological Board. Salmon conservation was examined, both the impact of the American fishery on BC's fishery and the dangers posed internally by overfishing in the northern waters of BC. An important lesson had been learned from the Sacramento River fishery in California, where salmon had already been fished out.[4] A similar lesson was being learned from the trends within the pelagic sealing industry, which had begun to wind down with the decimation of the herds and the consequent massive decline in catches that was evident by 1905.[5] In the final report of 1907–08, the commissioners recommended prohibiting construction of new canneries and the use of gas motors on gillnet boats in the North. The effect of the limitations (which began in

1908) on cannery operations gave the existing companies a virtual monopoly over the industry in District 2 (northern) and District 3 (Vancouver island). But the limitations did not have a conserving effect on the supply of salmon – the take of fish between 1908 and 1917 actually increased by roughly forty percent.[6] This was in part because, in spite of the ban on construction of new canneries, the government issued ten new cannery licenses during that period.

The economic recession in 1907, which coincided with a low year in the four-year sockeye cycle, caused cannery managers once again to impose a voluntary system of boat rating to cover the next two seasons. The history of boat rating is discussed in document 57. The scarcity of salmon in 1908 (a very poor season for sockeye) and 1909 (a big-run year that did not come up to industry expectations) led to fierce competition and, thus, to the breakdown of boat rating on a voluntary basis. The failure of the voluntary arrangement led the provincial government to impose mandatory boat ratings for the 1910 season. The province's action prompted yet another federal commission of inquiry into the Pacific fishery, so that regulations limiting a maximum number of fishing boats in certain northern areas were issued.[7] In 1912, the government retained a certain portion of fishing licenses for white fishers who were British subjects and owned their own boats and nets – a trend which would gather momentum over the next decade as anti-Japanese sentiment mounted in the province.

The men responsible for the spread of cannery operations into the new areas, for the expansion of older areas, and for the beginnings of diversification after 1905 were of many different types. There were some genuine newcomers to the field, but for the most part the original old canning families and firms simply expanded into the new areas. Then there were the experienced cannery men like Henry Doyle, who struck out on their own. They bought up old plants as they came on the market; when permitted, they sometimes built new ones. Some new consolidation activity occurred just before World War I, yet the salmon-canning business remained competitive, seasonal, scattered, and marked by a cyclical, fluctuating, and largely unpredictable supply of raw salmon.

Regardless of their individual background, all cannery operators, large and small, old and new, needed to amass a great deal of information about what Henry Doyle called "field conditions" (documents 34–35). They needed to know when the fish were headed for the spawning grounds and where they were going, what size and mix of pack their competitors were preparing for, what prices and terms were set with which fishers' bosses and Chinese contractors, and what the market conditions were. The more astute operators – Henry Doyle among them – also knew enough to investigate new fishing grounds, long-term trends in the availability of the salmon (see table 2), and new processing techniques. For this type of information, the cannery operators relied heavily on personal observation and on contact with other canners and their agents, with Indian fishers on the spawning rivers, and, as Doyle's notebooks reveal, with the itinerant Japanese fishing bosses, Chinese labour contractors, and Indian recruiters who themselves travelled up and down the coast to collect intelligence. Also investigated were the changing structure of the industry and of the markets. Although canned salmon for the English market predominated, other markets for canned salmon and also the fresh-, frozen-, and salted-fish trade were on the rise by this period (documents 37–38).

Henry Doyle spent his first year after leaving the British Columbia Packers Association, 1905, on the Nass River as managing director of the Port Nelson Canning and Salting Co.'s newly built plant. He became involved with two other canning operations in 1906. One was the Lighthouse (Federation) cannery (built in 1893 by the Federation Brand Salmon Canning Co.) at Steveston, which he and Daniel Drysdale, who was vice-president of Alaska Packers Association, leased for a few seasons and operated as the Royal Packing Company. The other was the old Herman cannery at Port Essington, on the Skeena, which Doyle and R.V. Winch purchased upon Peter Herman's sudden death. They operated it as the Skeena River Commercial Co. Ltd. Winch was a native of Ontario who, after arriving in Vancouver in 1886, founded a food-retail business (Winch & Bower) and managed the Canadian Pacific Cannery operation at Steveston from 1893 until it was sold to British Columbia Packers Association, in 1902. After a brief period in which he engaged in salmon canning in Washington State, he returned to BC. In 1909, Winch acquired and renamed after himself Robert Ward & Co., which had evolved into an insurance, real-estate, and mortgage firm, and financed several canneries in the province. Doyle purchased the Mill Bay cannery, on the Nass River, in 1908; he operated it as Kincolith Packing Co. In 1912 he, Daniel Drysdale, and Donald Moore (of the firm Peck, Moore & Co.) purchased two outstanding properties from Robert Draney, the Namu and Kimsquit canneries located in the central-coast area above Rivers Inlet. They operated these two under the company name of Draney Fisheries Ltd. At some point, Doyle seems also to have acquired a one-fifth interest in the Cassiar cannery, a Skeena River plant built in 1903.

Of all the canneries with which Doyle was associated, however, his true pride and joy seems to have been the small Mill Bay operation where he, as manager and president of Kincolith Packing, and various members of his family spent many of their summers from 1908 to 1922. The complex genealogy of the Mill Bay operation is fairly typical for this industry. The first cannery to operate on the site was H.E. Croasdaile's, beginning in 1879. Findlay, Durham & Brodie Ltd. acquired the property and built a new cannery in 1888. The next year the British Columbia Canning Co. Ltd. acquired it; then, in 1895, the Federation Brand Canning Co. Ltd. took it over and operated it until 1908, when Doyle purchased it. It was at Mill Bay that Doyle introduced a series of cost-saving measures which he termed the "Mill Bay system" (documents 39–41). At the heart of the system was the water-power installation, which powered everything on the site, including the cold-storage plant for freezing halibut. Doyle's records of the Mill Bay system constitute an interesting study of the diffusion of new technology and its impact on workers and on the work place.

Doyle claims that he was the first in BC to introduce an automatic solderless can-making system, in 1913. Yet, according to *Pacific Fisherman*, both Anglo-BC Canning Co. and M. DesBrisay & Co. Ltd. experimented with the new technology alongside the traditional soldering line in their Fraser River plants one year earlier, in 1912.[8] It is possible that Doyle may not have been aware of this, though he was an avid reader of *Pacific Fisherman*. Cicely Lyons writes that BC Packers Association installed the new can-making equipment at their Acme and Imperial canneries on the Fraser in 1913 (the same year as Doyle did), and that the Association's can-making lines were the first to be installed in the province.[9] Apparently, the president of British Columbia Packers Association, William Barker, and many other cannery operators had attended a demonstration of the process in Astoria, Oregon, in 1912.[10] It is not known if Doyle attended also. These quibbles aside, letters to Doyle such as the one written by Frank Burke, of Wallace Fisheries, on the sanitary can-making line at Mill Bay suggest that cannery operators in the North turned to Doyle for practical business advice (document 42).

Doyle's annual lists of fishers by name (for the Indians and whites only) and ethnicity (documents 43–45) provide rare insight into the social history of the northern salmon fishery, where the Indians and Japanese predominated. In the shore-based operations, foremen (except for the Chinese bosses), netmen, mechanics, watchmen, storekeepers, accountants, and the like were almost always "white" males; the cooks were Chinese (document 45). Although in this period the families of Japanese fishers increasingly replaced Indian and Chinese workers in the canneries on the Fraser, in the other districts of the province large numbers of Chinese men and Indian women, children, and elderly men predominated. Doyle's ledgers, including his cannery-store accounts, show that Indian women, as well as working on the salmon-canning lines at washing and filling, also pickled salmon, made and mended fish nets, and sometimes crewed ("pulled") for the Indian gillnet fishers (docu-

Table 2
Spawning Ground Reports of Sockeye Runs, 1904–1934

Year	Smith Inlet	Fraser River	Naas River	Skeena River	Rivers Inlet
1904				Very large runs	Magnificient runs
1905				Very large runs	Immense runs
1906				Very good runs	Runs very satisfactory
1907				Very good runs	Grounds heavily seeded
1908				Very large runs	Better than average
1909			Large run	Very large runs	Very well seeded
1910				Very large runs	Well up to average
1911			Heavy run	Very good runs	Abundance of fish
1912			Heavy run	Run very poor	Very heavily seeded
1913		Last "big" year, seeding poor	Very fair run	Very good runs	Extra well supplied
1914	Very heavy runs		Very numerous runs	Very heavy runs	Equal to last year
1915	Very heavy runs		Very heavy runs	Runs above average	Runs slightly under average
1916	Poor runs		Runs very fair	Runs below average	Up to last three years
1917	Runs only fair		Only fair		Runs very poor
1918	Poorly seeded	Better than 1917	Runs very poor	Runs below average	Runs very heavy
1919	Abundantly seeded	Best in several years	Seeding very poor	Largest in many years	Abundantly seeded
1920	Very well seeded	Good as 1919	Runs below average	Comparatively light	Seeding only fair
1921	Very poorly seeded	Only fair spawning	Average seeding	Very fair seeding	Seeding only fair
1922	Very fair seeding	Best seeding since 1909	Best in 5 years	Better than 1918 or 1921	
1923	Abundantly seeded	50% better than 1922	Run poor	Very heavily seeded	Similar to 1921 & 1922
1924	Only fair	Better than in 1923	Well seeded	Very large runs	Best in 10 years
1925	Very heavy runs	Up to average of recent years	Best in years	Splendid runs	Very heavy runs
1926	Excellent runs	Fairly satisfactory	Poor	Up to average	Better than average
1927	Exceptionally well seeded	Best in years	Poorly seeded	Very satisfactory	Abundantly seeded
1928	Splendid supply	Up to average of recent years	Poorly seeded	Very satisfactory	Satisfactory but under aver.

1929	Slightly below average	Best since 1917	Poorly seeded	Excellently seeded	Better than average
1930	Very well supplied	Early seeding poor but late seeding heavy	Heavily seeded	Splendid spawning year	Most satisfactory
1931	Best ever observed	Poorer than brood year	Disappointing	Good average seeding	Very heavily seeded
1932	Unusually good	Poorer than brood year	Satisfactory	About normal	Fair, average
1933	Splendidly supplied	Better than 1929	Fair	Fairly satisfactory	Well seeded
1934	Highly satisfactory	25% better than 1930	Heavily seeded	Fairly satisfactory	Average seeding

Source: UBC, Doyle Papers, box 6, file 23. This report, in Doyle's handwriting, was likely compiled from the annual reports of the Commissioner of Fisheries, Department of Marine and Fisheries (Canada).

ment 46). Their children filled trays with empty cans and often labelled the full cans; for this they earned tiny amounts of credit at the cannery store. As Doyle had predicted earlier, a cannery store could be quite profitable, especially in the remote areas where Indian families were the major customers (document 47).

Whether or not Doyle's improvements and management strategies at Mill Bay actually were unique or had the kind of impact that he implies they did, he filled a dozen notebooks with remarkably detailed accounts of the Mill Bay operation that suggest he was an innovative and shrewd, if somewhat hardened, manager. Just how typical a cannery manager he was we can only speculate, since none of the others left a comparable record.

1905

31. 4/notebook 19 "Northern Cannery Notes, H.D."

Adamson estimates 475,000 c/s to be Fraser sockeye pack and says Weston figures it 525,000. Each has cabled home these figures. Personally, I think Weston's figures correct. Adamson says the English buyers are going to stand present prices all right, as they are buying on the anticipation of this season's supply having to provide for 1906 as well. They also do not seem to have thought of the large quantity of Fraser talls, which will have to be used to cover shortage in Skeena sockeye talls ...

11 Aug. 1905. Have telegrams Gillespie offering on account of Grocers Wholesale Hamilton: – 400 c/s Lord Nelson Naas talls @ $4.40; 100 c/s cohos @ $3.75; 50 c/s humpbacks @ $2.75, which we [Port Nelson cannery] are wiring acceptance of.

Speaking to Evans, on the 9th inst., he said that Green of Gardiner [Gardiner of Green's cannery, Rivers Inlet?] was an old man very set in his ideas, working in a rut, and very much inclined to make concessions over whenever asked for by buyers, who more or less ran him. Gardiner does not pay much attention to business, only going to [his] office once or twice a week. Scott, Gardiner's man in Liverpool, he characterized as an unprincipled man of very unsavory reputation. He was supposedly used by Pelling Stanley & Co. as the tool by which they could put through all questionable transactions in which they desired to not appear. In exchange for this work, Scott practically controls PS & Co.'s salmon business, which means quite a lot to Gardiner. For general rustling up of trade, however, Gardiner does not stand as high as others.

Saw Barker and mentioned my suspicion of Imperial pack. He said he had noticed the same yesterday, had taken both Bain and Wilson there, and had given them h--1 for it. They claimed it was only a few cans and that they had had no time to turn over pack as yet, owing to rush of work. Barker says he is disgusted over the way things are going at the Imperial; there is nothing economical about its present management, their fuel bill is very high in proportion to other places, and their work is the poorest he ever saw; everything seems to go wrong. The Atlas he also had trouble to begin with, but it is doing first class now. The Pacific Coast [cannery] is also doing well. He also spoke highly of Currie-McWilliams's and Ewen's ...

Aug. 3rd 1905. Bella Coola Cannery Notes: Johnson told me the water supply ran so low that they could only get enough for drinking purposes. Was not even sufficient to wash [fish] with. Cannery obtained its sliming-tank supply by pumping from the inlet. Cannery pack is all sockeye. Could have packed more only ran out of cans. Johnson's said manager's house cost $2,000 and mess house $3,500 to build. Panzer left line of machinery where it stood instead of moving it forward as I had ordered. They had only 24 Chinamen and were at times very short of fillers. Their largest day's pack was a little over 600 cases.

STRICTLY PRIVATE & CONFIDENTIAL

32. 1/4 Announcement: W.D. Burdis to Doyle,   *July 9, 1906*
    Port Nelson, F&T Co. & Federation
    Cannery

BC Canners, Gentlemen:–
    Intimation has been sent me from Ottawa, furnished by a thoroughly reliable authority, that there is every probability of the meat packers in the United States (whose business has been so seriously injured in consequence of the recent revelations) sending spies to the canneries on the Pacific Coast during the present season, to watch the operations and lay charges of filthy and unsanitary conditions in connection with the packing and the physically unhealthy character of the Chinese and Indians who handle the fish.
    I have been requested particularly to draw your attention to the desirability of your managers taking extra precautions in respect to the cleanliness of the benches, tables & tools in use, and to see that these are kept scrupulously clean. Further, that no syphilitic Chinese or Indians are permitted to handle the fish, or work inside any of the canneries.
    On the Fraser River the offal is contracted to be taken away regularly, but no such facilities exist on Rivers Inlet or the Skeena or Naas rivers, where the offal is passed into the water.

I am credibly assured the Fisheries Department in Ottawa had received CONFIDENTIAL ADVICE ON THIS SUBJECT, AND HAVE PASSED IT ON TO ME IN LIKE CONFIDENCE. Whilst we have no doubt that the conditions are satisfactory, yet you will recognise the desirability of using extra precautions at the present time.

May I therefore respectfully ask you to give this subject your personal and careful attention.

I remain,
Yours faithfully.

THE PRINCE COMMISSION INTO
THE BC SALMON FISHERY, 1905–07

33. 1/1 Excerpt from Prologue to Doyle, "Rise and Decline"

In 1905 one of the usual farcical royal commissions was appointed to examine into and make recommendations for [among other things] regulating the Fraser River sockeye salmon fishery. Details of this will be found in my personal diaries covering the years 1905, 1906, 1907. In opposition to the Commission's recommendations [to close the Fraser fishery in the 1906 season] I was sent to Ottawa representing the opposing cannerymen and Mr. Ewen, president of the British Columbia Packers' Association, while Mr. Barker headed the delegation endorsing the Commission's position. Our side won the decision, and the half-century that has elapsed since then without the disasters our opponents predicted has amply endorsed and confirmed our viewpoint.

34. 4/notebook 5 Excerpt: "General Notes, H.D."

[c. 1904]. Lord says cost ABC Pkg. Co.'s improvements to Skeena River plants including cost new boats was $4,500 in 1903. Preparing in 1904 for 50,000 c/s. If fill all cans expected make $2.50 per case in his personal returns will be over $3,000. Lord says cost of nets per case in 1904 was about 34¢ for sockeyes against nearly 3 times as much for 1903. Japs are most destructive of all fishermen [with the nets] but do much better. In 1904, the general average for the BA & NP canneries were Japs 2,900 fish to boat, whites 1,750, Indians 1,350. [H.C.] Brewster said his Japs also averaged 2,900 but that his Indians were a close second. He fished Masset Indians.

35. 4/notebook 3 Excerpt: "General Notes, H.D."

Aug. 26th 1905. Naas River Notes: Went to Mill Bay to see Mr. McCullough. He gave me map of the Aiyansh section of the Naas, which in his opinion forms its present principal spawning region of the Naas River watershed. He has never been up the Si-aks River to the point where it issues from Si-dak Lake. Formerly the Naas River made a big bend just below Aiyansh and flowed over by the mountains to the left of the river as one descends. In time, however, the lava flowing from the neighbour-hood of the outlet of the Si-dak Lake pushed the Naas River farther and farther away from the mountain, until it forced it into its present channel ... Along the line of the lava bed the water has never been known to freeze, although both above and below it the river is covered with ice every winter. Mr. McCullough thinks that for this reason the fish may find their section most suitable for their spawning operations, for the Ksigingitl River and that lying next in a SE direction are noted spawning grounds ... There is a difference in the run of salmon each year, the Indians being able to note the different fish and to tell where they came from ...

Portland Canal Notes: Asked Conway about fish in the Portland Canal. He said that the only sockeye stream he knows of there is the Bear River ... Both the Bear and the Salmon rivers originate in glaciers ... [and] have good runs of the 3 poorer grades, the coho being sometimes very numerous and spawning in the lagoons and delta streams near the mouths of the rivers. The amount of cohos, humps, and dog salmon are large enough to warrant fishing, but the sockeye run is too small to consider. (I also think quality must be very poor – H.D.)

Aug. 28th 1905. Naas Notes: Stapleton told me that since he has been on the river the run has never been too large for them to handle in their canneries and they have never had to waste a fish. He thinks fish will never be found in big runs as on the Skeena.

Next year he does not expect to get over 60 boats and will advise preparations be made on that basis. He says 180 boats is all that can be expected to be obtained here, and, therefore, there is nothing to be gained by any one company preparing for a bigger pack than 60 boats will supply.

Sept. 2nd 1905 ... The regular mark adopted by the Port Nelson cannery for first-quality goods is $N^{P}C$. In the bottom space is put S for sockeye, R for red spring, C for coho, H for humpbacks, and P.S. for pink springs. For do-overs the mark is $C^{P\ N}$ and in the remaining space is put the grade marks as above. The 100 c/s ½# flats for Henry Berry are marked: H.B.
Brisbane

Sept. 25th 1905. Barker showed me on Saturday last a list of the Puget Sound packs totalling 782,000 c/s of 48 lb. ea. He said Cook, Sehome,

Welsh, Carlisle, and others would all lose heavily on their Chinese contracts as packs fell far short of guarantees.

36. 4/notebook 3 Excerpt: "General Notes, H.D."

Sept. 28th 1905. June says he met Henry Benlah on street, and was told by him George Buttimer had engaged him and all the old Brunswick [cannery] Indians to fish for him next year at the new cannery at Kildala. Long Jim was to have the Chinese contract both there and on the Skeena.

June says he learns from the Chinamen the Gulf of Georgia had trouble with swells again this year, and that at least 800 c/s of fish had to be thrown away. June says Lum Low c/o Sang Lung & Co. is the best man for labelling salmon at wharf and does all the BC Packers' work of that kind. His charge for opening cases, labelling, and re-boxing is 5¢ per case. If old labels have to be stripped off, the cost is 1¢ per c/s extra. Made contract with June for 1906 at 48¢ for 1# talls or flats & 80¢ for ½# flats, with a guarantee of 55 men besides himself and mess-house cook, and a daily-pack guarantee of 1,100 c/s 1# or 650 c/s ½# cans, June to remain at cannery throughout the season, acting as foreman. Advance prior to pack [is] $1,500 ...

Oct. 17th 1905. Ma Toi says Bell-Irving is preparing for the following Skeena River packs next season: BA cannery, 10,000 c/s ½# flats and 5,000 c/s each 1# talls & 1# flats, total 20,000 c/s; North Pacific cannery 8,000 c/s ½# flats and 7,000 c/s 1# flats, total 15,000 c/s. [Projected] total for the river [is] 35,000 c/s. Toi also said that out of 16,400 c/s packed this year at Good Hope, over 1,600 c/s were do-overs. This was due to bad Chinese work. June had the contract.

Oct. 30th 1905. Letter from McPherson just down (written on 19th) says cohos are still running in the Bay.

Nov. 1st 1905. June was in to-day and said the Carlisle cannery, Skeena, and Buttimer & Dawson's new Rivers Inlet cannery were both to prepare for 15,000 c/s. He understood the proportion was 3,000 c/s halves and 12,000 c/s 1#. In the Inlet probably 1# flats and on the Skeena 1# talls will be put up. Long Jim is the contractor for both places.

Good Hope pack is to be 15,000 c/s, of which 7,000 c/s will be ½# flats & 8,000 c/s probably 1# flats. This year the ABC deducted $600 from Chinese contractor for do-overs. The men are all down on Woods in consequence.

Malcolm Cannon & Co. have given their next-year contracts to Lee Coy, both for Scottish Canadian & Skeena plants. This year the Gulf [of

Georgia cannery] contractor could pay his men only 60¢ on the #1 as MC
& Co. charged them for swells, and also deducted $1,700 balance due
from last season. The 60¢ was paid over to the men direct by MC & Co.,
and the contractors are trusting to luck to be able to pay off remainder
from same outside source, or another season's profits. June says the
Scottish Canadian preparation for 1906 is to be 20,000 c/s and for the
Skeena 15,000 c/s.

Donald Moore told me yesterday that, up to this year at least, no live
fish were turned out of the hatchery at Lakelse despite the superintendent's reports to the contrary. Moore says he is positively right in the
matter. He estimates the number of boats next season at 1,500 and pack
preparations at 200,000 c/s. He mentioned the advisability of a boat
limitation being established on the Skeena by the Government, and
I believe he is working toward that end. His own pack preparation will
be between 10,000 & 12,000 c/s.

MARKETING NEW SPECIES AND PRODUCTS

37. 4/notebook 1 Excerpts   *(n.d.)*

List of Registered Brands & Owners
New Zealand

Alaska Packers Assn.	– Helmet	Nautilus
	Gold Coin	Export
	Hume's Flag	Cape Karluk
	Argo	
BC Packers Assn.	– Cutlet	Pine Tree
	Our Best	Rex
	◇©◇	Unicorn
	Arbutus	Swallow
	Darby	Polar Bear
	Red Feather	Peacock
	Sunset	Triangle
	Snow Shoe	Gold Ring
	Red Poppy	Cascade
	Clover Leaf	Arrow
	Eagle	Ewen & Co.
W.A. Anderson [sic]	– Silver Net	Chief
	Southern Cross	
BC Cang. Co.	– Chanticleer	Fisherman

J.H. Todd & Sons	– Sunflower	Tiger
J.J. Bostock	– Tecumseh	
ABC Pkg Co.	– Laurel Wreath	
J.R. Love (N.S.W.)	– Waratah	
A.S. Peterson & Co. (NZB)	– Golden Link	
North & Co. (NZB)	– Shib	

38. 4/notebook 19 Excerpts: Fresh Fish Dealers, Canada, c. 1906

Leonard Bros.	Montreal
D. Halton Co.	"
Maritime Fish Corporation	"
M. Doyle Fish Co.	Toronto
F.T. James Fish Co.	"
P. Burns & Co.	Calgary
W.J. Guest Fish Co.	Winnipeg
Winnipeg Fish Co.	"

"Foreign Buyers of Frozen Fish"

W. Waddell & Co.	London, Eng.	
Jno. Layton & Co.	"	
Freeman & Gishford	"	
Seddon & Dawling	"	
Baxter & Son #221 Billingate	"	
Chas. Petrie	"	
Geo Tabor, Ltd.	"	
Klevenhausen & Co.	Bremen, Germany	
C. Waldemann	Koeslin,	"
R. Kanzow	Hamburg,	"
Gottfried Friedrichs	Hamburg,	"
Earnest W. Kahn	Hamburg,	"

Jany. 11th 1906. Speaking to Kaneko to-day. He said the Japanese demand for humps is not likely to revive as the [Russo-Japanese] war [1904–05], and the consequent demand for canned goods, had built up the local industries wonderfully. Before the war there were only 5 or 6 salmon canneries [in Japan], whereas to-day there are over 90, and these do not restrict their operations to salmon, but can everything that is marketable. Owing to the cheapness of their labour and materials, their cost of production is much less than ours, and from present appearances the exports from here of canned humps is a thing of the past.

Speaking of [salted?] dog-salmon business, [Kaneto] said he sent 4 lots to Japan, two of which arrived in time, but balance too late for holiday trade. C.F. Jackson & Co. also sent 1,500 tons which arrived too late. The latter claim, however, that they are not the sufferers as their Yokohama connection took all the risk.

These large carry-over stocks taken in connection with the new supply to be expected from Japan's Sagahalien [sic] possessions (where dog salmon abound) will necessarily curtail the demand for BC goods. Kaneko thinks the orders will be both limited and at lower prices than prevailed this year. The cheapest purchase he made this year was $27.50 per ton, and prices ran from this to $30 and $35 per ton. Dry-salted herring, he says, is the staple food fish of the peasant classes, and as a consequence must sell very cheaply. He doubts if we can cure them at a cost sufficiently low to enable us to compete with the Japanese fish, which is both larger and of finer quality than what BC herring he has seen. He thinks China will prove a better and more remunerative market than Japan, as [the Chinese] are large consumers, have not as great a local supply, and are satisfied with the smaller-sized fish such as we can send from here.

DOYLE'S CANNERIES, 1906-14

39. 1/1 Excerpt: Prologue, Doyle, "Rise and Decline"

In buying Mill Bay [in 1908] I acquired a cannery that paid the highest insurance-premium rates of any cannery in British Columbia. In the first year's time I reversed this position from highest to lowest rate, and the saving effected more than offset the cost of the improvements. Up to that time, every cannery in northern British Columbia and Alaska was shingled roofed. [That type of roof] has to be snow-shovelled by hand several times every winter. With the exception of Wallace Bros' Claxton cannery, every cannery obtained its freshwater requirements from a V-shaped gravity-flow trough from the nearby creek.

I covered the old shingle roof with a sheeting of corrugated iron, which ended snow shovelling. I dammed up two small lakes 300 feet back of Mill Bay, and from this reservoir piped to the cannery enough power to operate both the cannery and, subsequently, the cold-storage plant, and replaced kerosene lighting in all outhouses with [electric lighting]. I tore down the fire-trap 10 by 12 cabins that lines the pathway that connected the cannery to all the living quarters and replaced them with a mess house large enough to feed and house the entire white population [at Mill Bay] ... These improvements paid for themselves within two years of their installation, and every new cannery built in northern BC and Alaska thereafter adopted the [so-called] Mill Bay model.

Mill Bay and Namu were the first [canneries] in British Columbia to install can-making machinery [?]. Mill Bay made all its own cans and in addition, those used in Arrandale cannery on the Naas and Cassiar on the Skeena. Namu made its own requirements as well as those of Kimsquit. (See correspondence with Burke [document 42] and Bell-Irving on my letter file.) Mill Bay also installed the first conveyance system from the soldering machines to the can loft and from the latter to the filling tables. Mr. Gould of the American Can Co.'s Alaska Service Station was so impressed he said it would make it his business to see every Alaska cannery under his jurisdiction would install the Mill Bay system before the next fishing season opened.

A 10-ton compressor cold-storage plant was built at Mill Bay in 1912, and halibut fishing added to the other fishery activities. Its construction cost was $30,000, and Mr. Robert Payne said it was a more efficient plant than the New England Fish Co.'s Ketchican [sic] plant [southeast Alaska], whose cost had been three times as great. Its operation was very successful from the start.

TECHNOLOGICAL EXPERIMENTATION AND INNOVATION

40. 4/notebook 3 Excerpts: "Cannery Notes, H.D., 1908"

Cosens is cooking in the retorts at 240°, fill time. He says Mr. Ewen always used to test whether the fish was sufficiently cooked by bending the small rib bones. If they did not break in two without the slightest sign of springiness, he had them cooked long enough to make them do so.

Mr. Ewen advocated cooking at 225°, full time, but found in practice it was not workable as with the numerous changes in contents of retorts it was liable to lead to errors.

Mr. Ewen always claimed there was more "fever" in the fish around the end of July and that they therefore required longer cooking then than previously. Cosens said that actual experience demonstrated the correctness of Mr. Ewen's views. Cosens says there is a noticeable difference in the cooking of fish in the centre of a retort car compared with that in the top or bottom rows of cans. Cosens advocates the use of iron instead of wooden test kettles. They are more satisfactory, and, when repairs on wooden test kettles are taken into consideration, are far cheaper.

After fish is cooked and cans go through the lye tank, Cosens tests them by sound with the mallet. Leaks are taken out and mended at once, but the mended cans, instead of [being] put back into pack, are kept separate until next morning, when they are put into the retort again and held there 15 minutes at 240°. This, he claims, kills any germ life which may have entered the can through the leak opening and prevents the can from becoming a swell head. The cans, after coming out of the retort, are put into pack without re-venting.

Cosens takes [the] leaks from the coolers every morning after packing and mends them. He then puts them in the retort for 15 minutes at 240° and puts them in pack as #1 fish. He claims these leaks are so small no oil is lost and as fish is fresh, possesses oil, and had all the air expelled it is fully equal to the balance of pack. Before putting them in the retort for the 15-minute cooking, he puts them in the steam box for 20 minutes, then opens the vent with a hot iron and stops them up again immediately the air has been expelled. Cosens leaves fish in the steam box for only 25 minutes at 218°.

41. 4/notebook 26 Excerpts: "General Notes, H.D."

13th July 1914. [Sanitary Can] ... Going through can loft Bell-Irving asked if we would be prepared to make tins for other canneries, and I assured him we would and in fact had last season suggested the idea to Mr. Walker.

Bell-Irving said they had hesitated about installing new sanitary lines as their old-style lines represented considerable value which they felt it would be too costly to discard. He seemed surprised when I told him I figured I had saved the entire cost of installing the new plant out of last season's savings alone. We then discussed figures on this season's Chinese contracts and figured out Mill Bay as follows: –

14 1st crew Chinamen @ $60 per m for 5 m	$4,200
10 2nd " " @ $55 " " " 2 "	$1,100
Total	$5,300

during which period we expected to pack $25,000 c/s. This is equal to 21¼¢ per case. Adding for sundries cost should not exceed 25¢ per c/s. Against this Arrandale working old style had 47 Chinamen under contract. They prepared for 8,000 c/s ½ flat, 5,000 lb flat & 10,000 1 lb talls. At Chinese-contract prices this means $14,500, equal to 63¢ per case average, or 38¢ per case higher than my cost. In addition, his men do nothing outside of the canning without being paid extra while my men have to do any kind of work I give them to do ...

5th Sept. 1914. Cost ½ Flat Cans, Sanitary vs Soldered: Estimated cost of making 9,000 c/s ½# flat sanitary tins as follows:

Tinplate for body making, $2,700 =	30¢ per case	
Factory-made tops & bottoms, $5,600 =	62⅕¢ " "	
15 Chinamen, 13 days @ 2.50 per day		
$487.50 =	5⅖¢ " "	
675 lbs solder @ 27½¢ per lb., $186 =	2¢ " "	
Oil, fuel, etc., estimated, $45 =	½¢ " "	
White labour, etc., estimated, $150 =	1¾¢ " "	
Total estimated cost completed cans	$1.01⅘ " "	

Above estimated cost includes freight Vancouver to Mill Bay on all supplies.

Estimated cost of soldered tins as follows:–

Tinplate	60¢	per case f.o.b. Mill Bay				
Solder	28¢	"	"	"	"	"
Other materials	7¢	"	"	"	"	"
Chinese Labour	15¢	"	"	"	"	"
White Labour	20¢	"	"	"	"	"
Total estimated cost	$1.30	"	"	"	"	"
Mill Bay sanitary ½ flats	1.01	"	"	"	"	"
Estimated saving in cost	.29	"	"	"	"	"

In arriving at above figures, in the case of soldered tins, the cost of solder for tops, stop off, etc., also tops themselves, are included. Tops also included in sanitary can costs. Only can-*making* labour was figured on in both cases.

  Wrote Burke of Wallace Fisheries, giving him comparative costs as [per above]. Also advised him I expected the Mill Bay pack for 1914 would be 30,000 c/s, of which 20,000 c/s would be labelled under contract system, cost of such a pack would be as follows:–

7,000 c/s ½ flats @ 83¢ per c/s	$ 5,810
23,000 " 1 talls @ 52¢ " "	11,960
Making 2,000 c/s ½ flats carried over	
@ 15¢ per c/s	300
Labelling 20,000 c/s @ 3¢ per case	600
Making 30,000 boxes @ 1¼¢ each	375
Total estimated cost soldered cans	$19,045

Instead of contract I engaged Mill Bay Chinese on day-labour system, paying $60 per month to 1st crew, $50 per m. to 2nd crew, and wages allowed foreman & cook in addition. I estimated pack when completed will cost as follows:–

amount earned by Chinamen, say	$10,700
" " " Indian women	3,500
Total	$14,200

This represents a saving of approximately $5,000, and in addition we use Chinamen preparing fish for cold storage, glazing frozen fish, making frozen-fish boxes, etc., and this outside work represents quite a respectable sum. Working from the above premises I figure my 1914 operating savings to be:–

On ½ flats (omitting 15¢ Chinese labour already figured in contract) 9,000 c/s at a saving of 24¼¢ per c/s	$2,182.50
On talls (omitting 10¢ Chinese labour already figured in contract) 23,000 c/s at a saving of 18³⁄₁₀¢ per c/s	4,209.00
On Chinese labour, say	4,608.50
Total estimated operating saving	$11,000.00

This saving I figured to exceed total cost of installing sanitary line, so that one season alone would cover the cost of making changes. I therefore suggested he should make all their plants "sanitary" at one time. I further suggested they should put can-making machinery in Strathcona [cannery] only and distribute made tins from there. By doing so their machinery installation would be greatly lessened and their labour disbursements reduced to a minimum, [with] only transportation of cans to other plants to provide for.

21st Nov. 1914. Mill Bay total pack was approximately 34,650 cases made up of 7,115½ flats and 27,535 cases 1 lb talls. On old contract system, cost of Chinese labour would have been as follows:–

7,115 c/s ½ @ 83¢ per c/s	$ 5,905.45
27,535 " 1 talls @ 52¢ " "	14,328.20
Making 34,650 bxs @ 1¼¢ " box	433.12
Labelling 8250 c/s @ 3¢ " c/s	247.50
Total cost old system	20,914.47

This is equal to 60⅖¢ per case.

On the day-labour system, and charging all time up to canned fish (although outside work was done by the Chinese crew), we are paying

to Chinamen	$10,509.72
" Indian women & other such labour	3,005.00
Total cost new system	$13,514.72

This is equal to 39¢ per case.

Thus, under the new system the saving in Chinese-labour account has been 21⅖¢ per case or $7,400.

42. 1/14 Letter: F.E. Burke, Wallace Fisheries   *Vancouver,*
             Ltd. to Doyle   *September 12, 1914*

My dear Doyle:—

I beg to acknowledge receipt of your kind favor of September 5th enclosing the data Re the sanitary and solder cans. I appreciate your kindness in this matter very much indeed and hope that I will be able to reciprocate at some time in some manner to you.

It is very pleasing indeed to me to be able to obtain figures which show the actual details as the ones you enclosed. While I have been told at different times by quite a number of people of the amount of saving obtained through the use of the sanitary can, this is the first time that I have been able to get anything that could show just exactly how the saving occurs.

43. 4/notebook 3

Naas Catch 1905 – Sockeyes
Port Nelson Cannery

Deliveries from June 1st Season ended Aug. 22nd
Indians

J. Clayton	J. Watts
Antone Green	John Moore
Timoth Danzala	Chas Alexander
Henry Arzicgh	Jacob Williams
Paul Sharp	Chas Yeomans
Alfred Johnson	Mathew Lisk
Silas Maxwell	A.M. Watts
Donald Bruce	Oscar Johnson

Adam D. Joule		Jas Robinson	
Henry Smith		Robt Stewart	
Wm Sutton		C. Smythe	
Herbert Barton		John Barton	
Stephen Barton		Richard Morgan	
Jos Benson		Wm Lincoln	
Arthur Benson		Solomon Bright	
Abel Ward		Albert Allen	
Sol Ward		Henry Wood	
Geo Ryan		Peter Stewart	
Cornelius Nelson		John Wesley	
Wm Smith		Stephen Allan	
Johnstone Russ		Timothy Adams	
Richard Morgan			
Sockeyes:	72,455	Springs:	2,162
aver. per boat	1,767		52

Japanese
(identified by twelve boat license numbers only)

| Sockeyes | 25,984 | Springs: | 2,390 |
| aver. per boat | 2,165 | | 199 |

| Nels Larsen (white) | 2,905 |
| Nels Pearson (white) | 2,004 |

44. 4/notebook 3

"Black List" 1908, Mill Bay

Harry Angus	Benj. Benson
Solomon Bright	Walter Haldane
John McNeill	Simon McKay
Moses McKay	Peter Nishiog
Isaac Robinson	Herbert Robinson
Jasper Ross	Enoch Sampson
David Ven (?)	Timothy Derrick
Henry Smart	David Doolan
Albert Welsh	Herbert Clayton
Herbert Barton	Sam Munro
Alfred Livingstone (Scotteen)	
Chas Elliott	Arthur Derrick
Wm Hymas	

45. 4/notebook 4

"Mill Bay, 1909" Employees

J.S. Cosens	foreman	$1,200 for season
J.A. Donnelly	net man	800 " "
M. Welsh	2nd " "	500 " "
W.D. Noble	storekeeper	55 per m. Nov to Feby
		75 " " Mch to Oct.
Chas Smith	Bathroom	70 " " Mch 15
E. Donehue	Watchman	60 " " May 7th
Alf Johnson	Launchman	65 " " from aft 31 Mch
Jno R. Angus	Saltery	100 " " June 1st
Thos Liston	Campman	65 " " Apr 1st
Woo Ton	Mess house cook	40 " " from 25 Mch

Boats Fishing 1909
Japanese (Machida)

H. Higashiyama	T. Tanahara
M. Fugishita	T. Matsuoka
S. Nishi	K. Nishi
N. Watanaba	M. Nakamesra
[no sockeye catch]	
R. Yamamoto	T. Hara
T. Naokuchi	R. Tsukomoto
T. Machida	Y. Tshhara [?]
S. Shirskama [?]	H. Okuno
M. Masmura	

total Sockeye – 40,129   Spring & Steelhead – 3,007
average per boat ([16] boats) sockeye – 2,508
[" " " (17 ")] spring & steelhead – 177

Boats Fishing 1909
Japanese (Isuruyama [?])

T. Kanata	K. Iwama
S. Shimoda	Nicemoto
T. Huayama	J. Nakamuta
	[no sockeye catch]
M. Kwada	K. Kikumaton
M. Koichito	M. Tomado

total sockeye – 23,286   spring – 1,954
average per boat ([9] boats) sockeye – 2,587
[" " " 10 boats] spring – 195

Boats Fishing 1909
Indians

John Willow	Alfred McKay
Frank Martin	Wm McNeill
Isaac Robinson [no fish]	Robt Lely
Wm Jeffreys	Peter Calder
Johnnie Moore	Jacob Moore
Leonard Douglas	Geo Whitfield
Jos Benson	Saml McKay
Henry Ardzah	Geo Tait
Josiah Wesley	Peter Williams
Chas Elliott	Mathew Naas
Thos Bryant	Peter Stafford
Wm Smith	Chas Davis
Peter Adam	Matthew Russ
Alf Robinson	Wm Leeson
Silas Robinson	Lazarus Moody
Geo Robinson	Sam Gray
Arthur Calder	Robt May
Rich Darrick	Paul Jelu
Wm Martin	Chas Alexander
Nath Robinson	Alf Mountain
Paul Klatah	Johnny Morvan
total sockeye – 72,415	spring – 1,168
average per boat (41 boats)	sockeye – 1,766
	spring – 28

46. *Oversize volume. "Account Book by Fishermen and Catch, Mill Bay, 1908, 1909 [and 1910]"*

[Names of Indian Women, Young Girls, and Female Children Listed in the Company Accounts for 1909, 1910]

Ellen Eli (1910)
Mary Ann Williams (1909, 1910)
Lydia Yeomans   (1910)
Nancy Wilson   (")
Catherine Robinson   (")
Hannah Kiah   (")
Martha Haines   (")
Louise Joule   (")
Jessie McKay   (")
Alice Klatah   (")

Mary Alexander   (″)
Annie Moore   (″) [also a boat puller]
Jennie Angus   (″) [″   ″   ″   ″   ]
Emma Leeson   (″) [″   ″   ″   ″   (with William)]
Alice Mitchell   (″)
Martha Ardzah   (″)
Catherine Simpson (Derrick) (1909)   [probably a child]
Mary Ann Williams   (″)   [″   ″ ″   ]
Agnes Russ   (1909)
Sarah Tait   (″) [also a boat puller (with George)]
Lavina Robinson   (″)
Elizabeth McKay   (″)   [probably a child]
Jennie McKay (1909, 1910)
Alice Moore   (″   ″)
Louise Adam (1909)
Cicelia Alexander (1909, 1910)
Matilda McKay (1909)
Mrs. Mark (Maggie) Tait (1909)
Katie Dennis   (1909, 1910)   [probably a child]
Lilly Douglas (″   ″)
Lucy May   (″   ″)
Lucy McKay   (″   ″)
Luella Stevens (1909)   [probably a child]
Eliza Leeson   (″)   [″   ″ young teenage girl]
Helen Stafford (″)
Agnes Williams (1909, 1910)
Martha Ven   (1909)
Lucy Axidan   (″)   [probably a child]
Ester McKay   (″)
Adele Whitfield   (″)   [″   ″ young teenage girl]
Johanna Russ   (″)
Annie Wilson   (″)
Martha McNeill   (″)
Louise Caulder   (″)
Elizabeth Oxidan (1909, 1910)
Amy Mountain   (″   ″)
Mary Alexander (1909)
Rebecca (and Annie) Calder (1909)
Lucy Martin   (1909)
Sarah Whitfield   (″)
Annie Lan (1909, 1910)
Helen Smith (1909)
Sophie Johnson (1909)   [probably a child]

Eliza Gray   (1909, 1910)
Johanna Moodie ("   ")
Mary Robinson   ("   ") [also a boat puller (with Alfred)]
Elizabeth Leeson ("   ")
Alice Ven (1909)
Lucy Duncan (1909, 1910)
Annie Bryant ("   ")   [also a boat puller (with Thomas)]
Laley Robinson (1909)   [probably a child]
Emily Jefferies & Alice (1909) [Alice a boat puller with Wm
                                                        and a part-time fisher]
Mary Lord (1909)
Emma Lily (1909, 1910)
Mrs Jonny Morvan (1909)
Mrs. John Willow (Esther, and Susan) (1909, 1910)
Alice Martin (1909, 1910)
Maud Robinson (1909)   [probably a young teenage girl]
Kitty Davis   (")   [a boat puller with Chas
                                                        and a part-time fisher]
Jeannie Turk (1909, 1910)
Anne Morvan (1909)   [probably a child]
Lydia Davies   (1909, 1910)
Annie McNeill ("   ")
Isabelle Simpson (1909)   [probably a child]
Sarah Seymour (1909, 1910)
Kate Robinson (1909)
Julie Stewart (1909)   [probably a child]
Matilda Martin (1909, 1910)
Emma Mack   (1909)
Emily Smith   (")
Amelia Williams Moore (1909, 1910)
Anna Caulder   ("   ")
Annie Smith   (1909)
Annie Moore   (")
Jennie Angus   (")
Marie Wesley (1909, 1910)

47. 6/14 *"Results of Store Operations at Mill Bay [1908–1913]"*

Gross sales for year 1908	$14,696.70
" " " " 1909	17,547.07
" " " " 1910	19,027.38
" " " " 1911	20,941.50
" " " " 1912	34,561.07
" " " " 1913	42,556.35

Net profit on store operations averaged about 18½% per annum. The decided increase in turnover during the past two years has been due to the purchases of fishermen and others which the cold-storage installation brought to Mill Bay, and also to the influx of settlers to the Naas district, most of which trade is contributing to our business.

CHAPTER FOUR

War and Post-War Depression

INTRODUCTION

The war and immediate post-war years were tumultuous times for Canadian resource industries. Supplies of raw materials became limited, and their prices soared. Labour became increasingly scarce and expensive as men either went off to the military front or shifted into high-paid work in war-related industries at home. But despite these problems, the canned-salmon industry thrived. Canned foods were ideal for wartime.[1] Once canned, foods were preserved virtually indefinitely, could withstand rough handling, and did not require special storage conditions. Canned salmon was a particularly important food ration because it was pre-cooked and ready to eat from the can. Moreover, it was a major substitute for meat, as meat became increasingly hard to provide under wartime conditions.

For the first two years of the Great War, British Columbia salmon canners had to compete with lower-priced producers in the United States and Japan. Then the Canadian Naval Service, which took over the Pacific fishery in 1914, and the Canadian Government War Purchasing Commission pressured Great Britain sufficiently to gain competitive prices and contracts for BC canned salmon. Contrary to conventional wisdom, however, because Britain tried to keep its own fishery alive during the war, the BC canned-salmon pack was not used for civilian consumption in Great Britain, but as rations for Canadian troops stationed in England and for the allied troops overseas.[2]

The year 1917 was a turning point for the industry in Canada in many respects. At the beginning of the war the Dominion government had begun a new policy whereby businesses had to be licensed annually in order to operate. As far as the ocean fishery was concerned, this wartime measure served both to control the growth of the fishery and to scrutinize the nationality of the owners of coastal enterprises. Then, in order to increase production to meet the new world demand for food, make up for the scarcity of the sockeye pack as a result of the ruinous 1913 Hell's Gate landslide, and relieve the pressure of excessive numbers of fishers at the mouth of the Fraser River (where over 2,600 fished in 1914), the northern sockeye areas had to be expanded. The same applied to the newly opened canning districts of the Queen Charlotte Islands and the Johnstone Strait, where pink and coho salmon abounded, and the west coast of the Vancouver Island district, where the runs of chum salmon were excellent. All of this required putting as many plants intro production as possible.

Between January and March of 1917, the Dominion government proposed a series of changes to open up the northern district. The pre-war restriction on new cannery construction was to be lifted (although, as mentioned, in spite of the ban, the government had licensed several new canneries after 1908). The limit on the number of fishing licenses (except for Japanese fishers) was to be lifted, as was the earlier ban on the use of gas motors for gillnet fishing in the North.

Opinions varied widely on these proposals. Japanese gillnet fishers from the Fraser River district, who wished to maximize their fishing opportunities, pressured to have the ban on gas boats lifted.[3] Joining them were the northern cannery operators, who stood to profit from the increased availability of raw salmon and sales of fuel oil. Northern Indian fishers, on the other hand, strenuously objected to the prospect of a sudden influx of gas boats into the district; they feared that it would practically eliminate Indian fishers from the industry. In spite of Doyle's rather cynical denouncement of it, the Indian petition against allowing gas boats accurately reflects their predicament (documents 48–48a). To make matters worse, to compensate for the commercial overfishing brought about by the introduction of gas boats into the North, the Indians' use of the traditional high-yield methods of food fishing for salmon in spawning rivers with weirs was to be severely curtailed.

The smaller operators such as Henry Doyle favoured the idea of issuing new cannery licenses. Opposed were the large consolidations, such as British Columbia Packers Association (documents 49–51). As canneries came on the market, the company had been purchasing those in strategic locations in the North, and it therefore wished to protect its comparative advantage there. On all these issues Doyle and his colleagues enlisted the support of an experienced former manager of Clayoquot Cannery who was now a provincial politician, H.C. Brewster, in 1916. Brewster, who later that year became provincial premier, personally brought the cannery men's case before the Dominion government in 1917.[4]

In response to the canning industry's concerns, yet another fishery commission was held. This, the ninth inquiry of its type in BC, was appointed as a royal commission on July 2, 1917, specifically to study fishing conditions in the North.[5] As a result, the move to increase the number of cannery licenses in the province and lift the ban on motor boats in gillnet fishing in the North was to be delayed for five years, and there was to be no increase in the current number of boats allowed.

Because their labour was in great demand in other industries on the coast, the Japanese fishers, through the Canadian Japanese Association, pressured the cannery operators to raise the price for sockeye salmon in District 2 (the North) from 17½ cents to 20 cents (document 52). Since the prices paid for fish varied over the season, it is difficult to tell if the Japanese petition was effective. The reported price paid for sockeye in the North that season was 22½ cents for fishers using their own gear, and 15 cents for those fishing under attached (cannery) licenses.[6]

Doyle, seeing the wartime emergency as an opportunity to eliminate the pressure for high opening prices for salmon and also the traditional pattern of upward bidding on salmon supplies during the canning season, turned to the office of the Dominion Food Controller. It was the Food Controller's job to co-ordinate and control food production and, where necessary, prices in Canada during the war. Doyle suggested to the chairman of the fish section of the Canned Food Board, Henry B. Thompson, that he set a fixed price for salmon. Thompson was well acquainted with the BC salmon fishery: he has a Victoria wholesale merchant who had served as BC's representative on the 1917 Dominion Fisheries Commission. Thompson quite sensibly suggested that a fixed price be set on the finished commodity – canned salmon – not fish (documents 53–54). When food rationing was imposed in Canada that year, canned salmon was rationed and its price fixed.

The wartime demand for all grades of salmon had had two important consequences for the industry in BC. First, the wartime expansion broke the dominance of the British Columbia Packers Association, which, when it started up in 1902, produced almost forty-five percent of the total BC pack; over the next two decades its share slipped to sixteen percent. A new consolidation would have to occur before the company regained its ground (see table A8). Second, the war, reinforced by the Hell's Gate landslide of 1913, shifted the industry permanently into packing and marketing other species of salmon than sockeye. In the immediate post-World War I period, BC was putting up two-and-a-half times the pack of pinks and chums as the average before the war; Alaska was putting up four times the pinks and three times the chums (see table A3).[7]

Among the cannery operators who took part in the tremendous, if reckless, expansion of the canning industry during the war were Henry Doyle and R.V. Winch.[8] The story of their dealings was fairly common for the industry during the expansion phase. After he acquired the Draney properties (Namu and Kimsquit canneries), in 1912, Doyle encountered financial difficulties because of the failure of his partners to furnish their share of the capital investment during the economic slump of 1913. Accordingly, he became rather uncomfortably dependent upon the goodwill of his selling agents in England: first Balfour Gutherie & Co., then Evans, Coleman & Evans. In 1915, when Doyle was once again in short-term financial difficulty, R.V. Winch & Co. Ltd. came to the rescue and acquired a 52 percent interest in Doyle's Draney Fisheries Ltd. In 1916, Doyle's Kincolith Fisheries Ltd. (formerly Kincolith Packing Co. Ltd.) passed to Winch & Co. as well. Winch added Tallheo cannery to his holdings in 1917. Winch and Doyle then formed a new company, Northern British Columbia Fisheries Ltd., in 1918 to amalgamate the assets of Kincolith Fisheries Ltd. and Draney Fisheries Ltd., and to absorb R.V. Winch & Co.'s Kimsquit, Skeena River Commercial, Kumeon, Tallheo, and Port Edward canneries. Doyle was vice-president of the new company. His notebooks and correspondence files for the war years contain very detailed discussions of all these cannery operations.

With the high prices and market demand for the entire pack, including the cheaper grades, many of the cannery operators did well during the war, although their business records do not always reflect that fact. According to Doyle, the imposition of the stiff Business Profits War Tax on the larger salmon-cannery operations in 1916 (retroactive to 1915)[9] drove a few of the packing companies to engage in some creative bookkeeping in order to pay only small amounts, if anything, to the government (document 49).

In 1918, the Canadian War Purchasing Commission announced that the British Ministry of Food had commandeered the choice grades and small tins of BC salmon; the cheaper grades could be sold on the Canadian domestic market (Britain would get its cheaper grades from the United States). Thus, in spite of the 1917 fisheries-commission recommendations, the pressure from cannery operators to take advantage of the increased wartime demand for canned fish led the Dominion government to license eight new salmon canneries to operate in 1918. Accordingly, the largest number of canneries in a single season in the history of the industry in BC – eighty-seven – packed that year. The same phenomenon occurred that year, and for the same reason, in the United

States districts; in Alaska alone the number of plants rose sixty-seven percent during the war.

Doyle's notebook account of British Columbia Packers Association's opposition to licensing a new cannery for Bella Coola in 1918 suggests the ways in which government policies developed in response to the expediencies of war could be seen as having longer-term consequences for the industry (document 49). In the wartime scramble to supply the growing demand for food, the established cannery operators tried to control competition by restricting the activities of the newcomers. British Columbia Packers Association claimed that because of the licensing of new cannery operations over the past few years, it had already lost its hold on the fishing territory around the village of Bella Coola. This probably was in reference to the Tallheo cannery, which was built on North Bentinck Arm in 1916, and was acquired by R.V. Winch & Co. in 1917. In 1918, British Columbia Packers Association faced additional competition when the government granted a license to Winch to build a new cannery at Bella Coola (documents 50, 50a). The Association felt it was being discriminated against because the majority of its shareholders lived outside the province; the government appeared to give preference to BC-owned firms. For some reason, however, no new cannery was built at Bella Coola.

Because it needed additional revenue, the Dominion government boosted its license fees for salmon-fishing and -cannery operations by between one hundred percent and one thousand percent, depending on the category, and imposed a small war tax on each case of salmon produced. Cannery operators scrambled to introduce new machinery to speed up the processing lines, though, as already discussed, the extent to which machines replaced hand labour, or even reduced the need for skilled and semi-skilled labour, in the salmon-canning industry must not be exaggerated. As Doyle himself observed in a paper he wrote on the industry at the end of the war, in the small-scale and remote operations it usually was not economical to invest heavily in new machinery (document 61). Besides, with every year of the war, cannery operators found it increasingly difficult to obtain new machinery and equipment.

The world-wide recession which followed the war resulted in many cannery operations being idle one or more seasons from 1919 to 1923.[10] Despite this cutback in production, most of the cannery operators were stuck with huge surplus stocks. In 1921 there were on hand, including the carry-over from 1920, 750,000 unsold cases of salmon.[11] The war had created such hardship in so many countries that people bought only the necessities. These countries also lacked foreign exchange with which to purchase North American goods. But these were temporary setbacks. A more serious long-term problem was that Japanese producers were becoming unbeatable competitors for the prime market for red salmon – the United Kingdom, where "the country of origin [was no longer] a factor in selling goods" (document 56). The BC canners had no choice but to actively market the premium grades abroad and to develop additional markets – France and Australia, for example – for the cheaper grades. They did so by strengthening the British Columbia Salmon Canners' Association, forming it into a type of combine[12] to streamline and limit production in the industry. Cut backs were to be at the expense of the Indians, Japanese, and Chinese who fished and/or worked for the canneries. To represent their interests in the United Kingdom market, the Canners' Association engaged F.H. Cunningham, the newly retired Dominion Chief Inspector of Fisheries. All of this is described in the records of two of the more significant Canners' Association meetings (documents 55–56).

As for the fishers of Japanese ancestry, in 1920 the Dominion government dropped the pre-war policy of limited-entry licensing in favour of an "open door" policy of granting unlimited licenses to white and Indian fishers only – Japanese fishers were to be eliminated completely. Petitions such as Doyle's, two extensive reviews of the history of BC fisheries regulations which ultimately argue against opening the salmon-canning industry (documents 57–58), and those of several "interested parties" and of members of the BC Salmon Canners' Association (documents 59–60) led to yet another Dominion inquiry into the fishery. This, the Duff Commission of 1922, recommended that the Japanese be phased out from the salmon fishery "in the shortest possible time without disrupting the industry,"[13] that fishing licenses be no longer "tied" to canneries (thus reducing the cannery operators' control over who fished), and that the practice of issuing licenses for exclusive fishing in certain districts be ended. These changes were intended both to discourage Japanese from settling up-coast by eliminating them from the fishing industry, and to attract potential white settlers to the North with opportunities for seasonal employment in the commercial fishery.

The opening of salmon fishing and canning in BC to all "qualified" individuals and companies was ostensibly to promote fishing by Indians (whom Department of Indian Affairs officials wanted to be economically self-sufficient) and whites, especially the thousands of returned soldiers who wished to settle in BC after the war. (Similar incentives were developed to settle returned soldiers in the clay belts of northern Ontario.) The new policy resulting from the Duff Commission report severely reduced the number of Japanese fishing (and dry-salting) over the next three years, after which the government was forced to abandon the policy, in 1928.[14]

While Indian Affairs did not want Indian fishers eliminated from the commercial salmon fishery, Indians were not treated on equal terms with whites. Indian fishing licenses were concentrated in the North. As the numbers of licenses issued to Japanese declined each year over the 1924–27 period, only the number of licenses issued to whites increased; the number issued to Indians remained roughly the same, simply reinforcing the trend of the earlier period. In order to keep up the supply of Indian cannery workers it became customary in the major districts for cannery operators to use only those Indian fishers who had female relatives who could work at the cannery; even then, the Indian fishers reported, they often received insufficient and substandard gear.[15]

Among the packing firms that did not survive the financial and competitive chaos of the war and the post-war recession was the Doyle-Winch concern, Northern BC Fisheries Ltd.[16] As well as being hard hit by the depression, the firm had, like many others, overextended itself financially and become heavily indebted to its banker. In 1921, representatives of the local branch of the Royal Bank took over management of the company's assets. A few years later, the bank began selling off, or leasing and eventually selling off, all the assets for a mere fraction of their worth (document 64g). Doyle felt betrayed by the toughness of the bank officials, and it is interesting that author Cicely Lyons, though no fan of Doyle's, agrees with him on this point.[17] Northern BC Fisheries Ltd. ceased business in 1923. Its holdings went to large, established packing companies, who were themselves the products of amalgamations: Gosse-Millerd, Anglo-BC, Wallace Fisheries (which bought the Mill Bay operation), and Canadian Fishing Company.[18] Mill Bay and several of the other canneries eventually ended up in the hands of British Columbia Packers Ltd. R.V. Winch himself remained active in the industry through a new company he formed in 1924, Queen Charlotte Fisheries Ltd., until his death, in 1952. As for Henry Doyle, and many small players like him, he was finished in the industry.

WARTIME CONTROLS ON THE INDUSTRY

48. 2/8 Letter: Doyle to W.A. Found, Deputy   *May 7, 1917*
       Minister of Fisheries

Dear Sir:
    I enclose herewith copy of letter from Rivers Inlet, which is being circulated there and which will doubtless reach you in due course, and

I am writing you in connection with this letter so that you will have a full understanding of the situation when same reaches you.

In the first place (as I think I have pointed out previously) the permitting of gasoline engines in District No. 2 will mean that a majority of the gasoline boats now operated on the Fraser River will seek northern waters, thereby relieving the congestion on the Fraser and enabling the men to make more money in the northern fishing, with which they can liquidate the indebtedness they are now under to the Fraser River canners.

The argument advances in the fourth paragraph of the enclosed letter as to the poor condition of the Fraser River fishermen, and the contrast of their situation to those in northern waters, fully illustrates my contention, and the very fact that these Fraser fishermen are in such an unenviable position is greater reason for their being permitted to improve their condition by getting a return from their investment, which would follow the permitting of gasoline engines in the waters of District No. 2.

Paragraph two of the letter refers to the boats now in use not being strong enough for engines, but in this connection I would point out that all of the boats fished on Rivers Inlet are owned by the canners, so that the fishermen would have no property loss should they be discarded.

In no other section of District No. 2 will there be found many fishermen willing to sign this letter. The reason that it is put forth in the Rivers Inlet District is explained when they state in their letter: "that the salmon fishing season is so short that we would have ... a very expensive boat and outfit that we could only use about two months in a year." Rivers Inlet is the one place in District No. 2 where the fishing is practically restricted to the sockeye species of salmon, and no other fish are taken in the Inlet in commercial quantities, consequently the industry there only occupies them for the period stated. Nearly all of the Rivers Inlet fishermen are farmers or settlers in the neighbourhood of Cape Scott, Sointula, and Hunter Island, and devote the balance of the year either to the taking of halibut and cod or to agricultural pursuits. If they have a motor boat available for work in their home waters their earnings would be considerably augmented.

The last of their letter is rather contradictory as they ask that you have the use of power boats in District No. 2 prohibited for five years with the expectation that by that time they may have saved enough to fit themselves out. If the use of these boats will be so detrimental to their interests, why should they wish to save for the purpose of acquiring power boats?

I think the whole letter can be traced back to some of the canning interests who are using – to further their own selfish ends – the ignorance of the fishermen as to what use the power boats would be to them in their ordinary industry.

48a. Petition (copy, attached)   *Rivers Inlet, 1917*

Sir:

We, the licensed fishermen of District No. 2, fishing for salmon at Rivers Inlet, respectively petition your honourable Department to retain the present regulation which prevents the use of power or gasoline engines in fishing boats.

If they are allowed to be used, all must have them, or those not using them would be at a decided disadvantage. Most of us are poor men, and have no means to purchase an engine and boat. The boats now in use would not stand the engines, as they are not built strong enough.

On account of the War prices of lumber, materials, and engines are greatly advanced so that cost is about prohibitive. The engines would be imported from the United States.

If we have to go to the cannery owners for the necessary money, we would be tied up with contracts and agreements. Another reason is that the salmon fishing season is so short that we would have for the balance of the year to store and care for, to us, a very expensive boat and outfit that we could only use about two months in a year. The fishing season is so short we are compelled to find other employment for the balance of the year. Few of us know much about machinery, and we fear it would be expensive learning to operate an engine, and for which we would have to go in debt. This we know from the experience of the salmon fishermen on the Fraser River, who are nearly all very heavily in debt for gasoline engines and boats. Very few of the Fraser fishermen are able to pay their bills even with a good season, whereas in the North we are well off and contented with present regulations.

It is generally believed that the use of many motor boats on the fishing grounds make the salmon swim deeper, and in other ways make them more difficult to capture, and for this reason as well as from economy we prefer to continue fishing at present with the cheapest possible effective fishing boat.

For the above reasons, we earnestly beg your Honourable Department to not allow power boats in District No. 2 for five years; perhaps by that time we may save enough to fit ourselves out. We fully believe that if power boats are allowed, we will be forced to get them, and also be forced to go into debt for them, which would be very bad for us in every way.

Trusting you will favour our petition we will ever pray and remain

Your humble
servants,
[no signatories listed]

49. 4/notebook 27 Excerpt: "General Notes, H.D."

19th Mar. 1917. BC Packers re Bella Coola: In conversation with Cunningham on the 16th inst., he told me the BC Packers, through Jarvis, protested against any new cannery being licensed for Bella Coola on the ground that they were especially being handicapped through permission being given others to operate in [fishing] territory which originally had been exclusively controlled by them. The value of their investment had been detrimentally affected by such action, and the preference shown local BC parties was ascribed by them partially to the fact that but little of their "shares" were owned in this province. While this was true it was also true that most of their shareholders were Eastern Canadians and they looked to the Dominion Govt to prevent these parties being discriminated against.

Jarvis also stated they were [falling] behind, and as proof of this assertion claimed their surplus at the close of 1916 was $90,000 less than at the end of 1915. While this was true he overlooked telling the Department their annual statement showed a profit for the year of over $257,000 (after writing off $352,000 to depreciation on plant) and that the reason their surplus showed $90,000 reduction was that they paid out dividends of over $171,000, wrote $79,000 off to a special "depreciation" (?) [sic] a/c; paid the Government $34,000 Business Profits War Tax for *1915* and charged up the entire loss of two halibut steamers ($58,000) to the 1916 operations.

50. 3/4 Letter: F.H. Cunningham, Chief   *New Westminster,*
     Inspector of Fisheries, to B.F. Jacobson,   *8 May, 1917*
     c/o R.V. Winch & Co.

Re Cannery License – Bella Coola

Sir:

I beg to inform you that your application for a cannery license at Bella Coola has been approved, subject to the requirements covered by the regulations governing the issuing of new cannery licenses as set forth in Section 8 – a of the amendments to the British Columbia Fishery Regulations (copy enclosed) as per clause marked. Will you please comply with the said requirements by forwarding me a statutory declaration of acceptance therewith.

I am further directed to inform you that no fishing privileges will be granted in connection with this license and you will kindly inform me that the license is acceptable to you on these conditions.

50a. Attached: Excerpt from Pamphlet: *14th April 1917*
British Columbia Fishing Regulations
Amendments, Department of Naval Service.

Section 8a

1. Before a cannery license shall be granted the applicant therefor shall make a statutory declaration setting forth, in the case of an existing cannery, if it is owned by a company or firm, the name of such company or firm and whether it is a Canadian company or firm licensed to do business in the province, or if not owned by a company or firm, the name or names and nationality or nationalities of the actual owner or owners of such cannery, and in the case of a new cannery, if it will be owned by a company or firm, the name of such company or firm and whether it is a Canadian company or firm licensed to do business in the province, or if it will not be owned by a company or firm, the name or names and nationality or nationalities of the person or persons who will own such cannery, and that in either case the applicant or applicants have the necessary capital to erect and operate such cannery.

2. A new salmon cannery shall be completed and ready for operation within 18 months after the date of the issue of the license therefor.

51. 1/6 Form letter, Office of the Food Controller   *Ottawa,*
    In your reply refer to L–2   *March 14th, 1918*

Re – Wholesale Fish License

Dear Sir:

You are on our mailing list as a fish canner and under a recent order of the Board a license must be taken out by you if it is your intention to continue in business during the coming season.

An application to apply for a license is enclosed herewith, the Regulations governing the issuance of same will be found on the reverse side of this form. You will please note that if your business is in excess of one thousand pounds for any one calendar month, it is imperative that you take out a license. The penalty for an infraction of this order is one thousand dollars ($1,000) or imprisonment for three months, or both.

Please reply to this letter promptly, advising us in your reply what your intention is. If it is not necessary for you take out a license, please state your reasons.

P.S. If you are already licensed as required, please disregard this notice.

52. 2/8 Copy: Can. Japanese Association Branch   *Port Essington,*
         to British Columbia Salmon Canners'   *Jany. 20/17*
         Association

Dear Sirs:

Since there was a rumour that the canners of District No. 2 are of opinion that the price of sockeye this year will be 17½¢, it gave alarm to Japanese fishermen and contractors, disappointing them greatly, the rumour being supposed to have leaked from one of the canners.

At the meeting of contractors who are in this city here, including those of Skeena, Rivers Inlet, Naas, and others, held on Friday and Saturday last, it was resolved to the effect that it must strongly be appealed to the canners of District No. 2 to establish the price of sockeye at 20¢, and humpback, dogs, and spring salmon as requested first, otherwise to refuse their contract this year on the ground that they are unable to secure men.

There is great demand of Japanese labourers for logging, railway, and factories outside of city, and particularly at the distant places at good wages, and hundreds have left Vancouver already and hundreds are being expected to leave in near future [going] to where they can earn from $2.50 to $3.50 a day through [the] year. Conditions being so, unless the price of fish be advanced as requested, the contractors can hardly fulfil their contract, which caused them to resolve as above.

It is my hearty desire that you will be pleased to accept their request that they may continue their services, and ensure their loyal and energetic efforts in carrying [out] their contract with the canners.

And be pleased to understand that these contractors are very much anxious to secure good men in order to give the canners satisfaction, and unless they think they can get men, they prefer not to contract.

Trusting you will kindly consider the matter at the meeting of the Canners' Association, and hoping this matter can be settled through your help as soon as possible in order to hold men from leaving this city, I remain ...

53. 1/5 Letter: H.B. Thompson, Chairman,   *Ottawa,*
         Canada Food Board, Fish Section   *February 16, 1918*

Dear Doyle:

Re Fish

I beg to acknowledge receipt of yours of February 6th.

I am taking up your suggestion relative to the fixing of the price of raw fish, which I presume could be endorsed on the back of the licenses issued to the fishermen, but in order to be perfectly fair, the fixed price should be placed on the finished commodity turned out by the canners. I think it could be arranged that were this done a market could be found for the entire pack by the Allies, which would insure speedy transportation overseas, and would relieve the canners of the difficulty they are now under in the question of finding tonnage. Of course, nothing could be done without a conference with the Minister of Marine and Fisheries, and acting in accordance with his wishes. I will endeavour to obtain an appointment with him before long and see what his views are upon this question.

I have to thank you for all your good wishes, but I can assure you this job is no matter of congratulations, and I often wish myself back in British Columbia.

54. 1/6 Letter: Thompson to Doyle   *Ottawa,*
                                                        November 4, 1918

My dear Doyle:

I beg to acknowledge receipt of your letter of October 28th with enclosures, relative to the British Ministry of Food and the Canadian War Purchasing Commission. I have no doubt as you have written both of these bodies, they will take the matters dealt with in your letter up, and reply thereto.

As regards the Government naming some price to protect the Canadian trade, I think this was only natural that this should be done because, with the bulk of the pack commandeered, the natural deduction was that some canners might take advantage of the situation and increase prices to the Canadian trade, which would cause considerable criticism, and in order to expedite matters, rather than wait for the final prices to be settled by the Canadian War Trade Board they adopted the offer that was made by the Canners to the British Ministry of Food as the maximum prices.

THE CRISIS OF 1921: REDUCING THE
COSTS OF PRODUCTION IN BC

55. 11/2 Minutes, British Columbia Salmon   *February 8, 1921*
    Canners' Association

A General Meeting of the BC Salmon Canners was held in the Association rooms on Tuesday, *February 8th, 1921*, at 2.30 p.m.

Present: Messrs. H.B. Bell-Irving (Chair.) R.G. Johnston, T.H. John-
son, Alex Sutherland (Prince Rupert F. & C.S. Co. Ltd.),
H.O. Bell-Irving, J.M. Whitehead, B.C. Mess, P. Wallace,
R.C. Gosse, F.A. Hamilton, A.E. Carter, C.A. Crosbie, Wm.
Hickey, J.S. Eckman, R.R. Payne, R. Chambers (Westen Sal.
Packing Co.), D.T. Sandison, (Maritime Fisheries), J. Lamb
and W.D. Burdis, Secretary.

On motion, Mr. Bell-Irving presided over the meeting.

The Notice convening the meeting was read ...

The "Recommendations" were then considered in the sequence made.

1. CURTAILMENT OF PACKS OF PINKS AND CHUMS DURING
   1921.

Messrs. Whitehead and Mess having suggested that a better plan
would be to prepare a schedule (based on the average respective packs of
Pinks and Chums during the past 2 or 3 years) which could be made a
basis for a general measure of curtailing the packs this year.
Moved by H.O. Bell-Irving, Seconded by J.M. Whitehead, and carried
unanimously.

> "That the matter of Pinks and Chums to be packed in 1921 be
> referred back to the Committee to prepare a schedule to be
> presented to a subsequent meeting."

2. DATES FOR FIXING PRICES FOR RAW SALMON.

Moved by J.M. Whitehead, Seconded by P. Wallace, and carried unanimously.

> "That about May 1st for Spring salmon and June 1st for Sock-
> eyes in North – and about May 1st for Spring salmon, and July
> 21st for Sockeyes on the Fraser River – shall be the dates when
> prices for raw salmon shall be fixed."

3. UNIFORM FISHERMEN'S CONTRACT.

Moved by H.O. Bell-Irving, Seconded by Wm. Hickey and carried
unanimously.

> "That this recommendation be approved, and the Committee be
> asked to prepare a form of Contract for 1921 and that when it is
> approved and adopted, all the fishermen shall be required to
> sign same."

4. INSTRUCTIONS TO MANAGERS TO REFRAIN FROM BUYING
   SALMON FROM BOATS EMPLOYED BY OTHER CANNERIES.
Moved by H.O. Bell-Irving, Seconded by R.C. Gosse, and carried
unanimously.
   "That this recommendation be approved, and that it be acted
   upon by the Canners."

5. BOAT RATINGS FOR SKEENA RIVER.
These submitted for 1921 were:–

Balmoral	82	Oceanic	60
Dominion	26	Carlisle	34
Cunningham	21	Sunnyside	45
Brit. Amer.	57	Prince R.	36
North Pac.	40	Haysport	40
Skeena Com.	35	Inverness	45
Port. Ed.	26	Claxton	60
Cassiar	35		

Total 642

An exception was taken by Mr. Whitehead to the ratings for his Com-
pany's plants, and Mr. Crosbie declined to accept the ratings suggested
for his two canneries, and as the Carlisle Cannery was not represented at
the meeting, it was:–
Moved by R.C. Gosse, Seconded by Peter Wallace, and carried.
   "That the ratings for the Skeena River as submitted by the
   Committee be accepted as a basis, and that further efforts be
   made by the Committee to adjust the slight differences with the
   BC Fishing & Packing Co. [previously the British Columbia
   Packers Association] and Northern BC Fisheries, and to induce
   the Kildala Packing Co. to come into the rating for Carlisle
   Cannery."

5b. BOAT RATING FOR RIVERS INLET.
These submitted for 1921 were:–

Wadhams	19	Kildala	12
Strathcona	12	R. Inlet	17
Good Hope	13	McTavish	10
Beaver	13	Provincial	10
Brunswick	15		

Total   121

As exception to the ratings for Wadhams cannery was taken by Mr. Whitehead, and Mr. Mess desired to have the Chinese help in his Company's sawmill provided for, it was:–

Moved by R.C. Gosse, Seconded by H.O. Bell-Irving, and carried.

> "That the ratings for Rivers Inlet be adopted, and that the canners there endeavour to arrange a satisfactory settlement with the two companies as to the respective ratings."

5c. BOAT RATING FOR NAAS RIVER.

These submitted for 1921 were:–

Port Nelson & Arrandale	55	Kumeon [sic]	19
Naas Harbor	39	Wales Isl.	39
Mill Bay	27	Somerville	28
		Total	207

Moved by H.O. Bell-Irving, Seconded by J.M. Whitehead, and carried.

> "That the ratings for Naas River be approved as a basis and if any objection is taken, it be left to the Committee to be arranged."

6. THAT ADVANCES TO JAPS BE CURTAILED IN 1921 AND CUT OUT IN 1922.

Moved by R.C. Gosse, Seconded by C.A. Crosbie, and carried. Mr. Mess dissenting.

> "That recommendation No. 6 be approved, subject to a date being fixed for determination of the agreement."

7. REDUCTION OF BONUS TO JAP CONTRACTORS.

Moved by J. Lamb, Seconded by J.M. Whitehead, and carried.

> "That this recommendation be changed to read – 'One cent for each Sockeye, Red Spring, Cohoe and Steelhead, with a guaranted minimum of $12.50 per man.'"

8. RE: STOPPING ADVANCES TO INDIANS FOR LABOUR OR REDUCING SAME TO A SET AMOUNT PER RUNNER FOR EACH ADULT.

Moved by J.M. Whitehead, Seconded by J. Lamb, and carried unanimously.

> "That advances to Indian labour shall not exceed $2.00 per adult, and runners shall not be bonused more than 50¢ per adult supplied."

9. & 10. ONE-MAN INDIAN AND JAP CREWS ON THE NAAS AND
RIVERS INLET.

Mr. Crosbie said his Company favours two men on the Naas. Mr. Chambers favoured fishing one man per boat if possible.

Moved by J.M. Whitehead, Seconded by R. Chambers, and carried.

"That one Indian and Jap to a boat be allowed on the Naas, but that two men be used if possible."

11. REDUCTION IN PRICES OF CHINESE CONTRACTS.

"That recommendation of 70¢ for Halves and 50¢ for Talls be approved, and that no extra costs of washing or filling be paid by the Canners."

12. & 13. REDUCTION IN PRICES FOR INSIDE AND OUTSIDE
LABOUR.

Moved by T.H. Johnson, Seconded by J. Lamb, and carried unanimously.

"6¢ per tray for filling.

35¢ per hour for washing.

30¢ per hour for inside labour.

30¢ per hour for ordinary Jap labour.

40¢ per hour for Jap carpenters on boats or buildings, and that no advances in these prices shall be made until after approval by a meeting of Skeena managers."

14. REDUCTION IN WAGES TO GAS BOAT CREWS.

Moved by B.C. Mess, Seconded by T.H. Johnson, and carried.

"That the recommendation be approved, viz. to reduce the rates of wages, and whenever possible, *not more than three men shall form a single crew.*"

15. RE: PAYING FISHERMEN'S FARES TO THE CANNERIES.

Moved by R.G. Johnston, Seconded by D.T. Sandison, and carried unanimously.

"That one deck fare to the cannery be paid, *when the man has to make the journey,* but no return fares to be paid, with the exception of Indians, who may be returned to their homes if necessary."

16. RE: TRANSPORT FOR WIVES OF FISHERMEN.

Moved by C.A. Crosbie, Seconded by T.H. Johnson, and carried.

"That one way single deck fares may be paid to Japanese women when actually working in the cannery."

17. RE: ONE WAY FIRST CLASS FARES TO JAP CONTRACTORS AND THEIR WIVES.

"That this recommendation shall be changed to read 'That first class single way fares may be paid to Japanese contractors *only*.'"

18. PROTEST AGAINST THE HIGH PRICES FOR CANS AND COAL.

Moved by J. Lamb, Seconded by Wm. Hickey, and carried.

"That the Committee prepare a list of the number of boxes likely to be required this season, and that concerted efforts be made to secure reductions in the prices of cans, boxes, and coal."

19. RE: EFFORTS TO SECURE REDUCTIONS IN PASSENGER AND FREIGHT RATES.

"Resolved that this matter be referred back to the Committee, or a deputation appointed by the Chairman to take such steps as it may deem necessary."

20. RE: BONDS FOR PERFORMANCE OF THE AGREEMENT.

Moved by B.C. Mess, Seconded by R.G. Johnston, and carried.

"That this meeting agrees to abide by the resolutions as herein passed today, until the calling of a meeting to receive the report from the Committee respecting its success in adjusting the boat rating differences, such meeting to be called within ten days."

The subjects 1 to 6 inclusive referred to in the agenda were then taken up in serial order.

1. RE: SUBSTITUTING "BLUE BACK" FOR "COHOE" ON LABELS ON CANS CONTAINING BLUE BACKS.

Referred for future consideration.

2. PRIZE FOR FISH DAY DISPLAYS.

The Secretary was instructed to issue cheques to the amount of $50.00 for prizes.

3. JAP CONTRACTORS APPLICATION FOR ADVANCE TO $50.00 BONUS.

The Secretary was instructed to notify them of the resolution passed for a bonus not to exceed $12.50 per man.

4. WIRELESS STATION ON RIVERS INLET.
This matter was referred to the Chairman and a small committee to be
selected by him for investigation and report.

5. RE: REQUEST OF CHIEF INSPECTOR MOTHERWELL FOR
   RATES OF BOARD AND LODGING FOR INSPECTORS AT CAN-
   NERIES.
The canners present stated they had communicated their ideas to the
Chief Inspector in reply to his direct request.

6. H.G. WHITE'S OFFER OF SERVICES AS EUROPEAN
   SALESMAN.
This matter was deferred to a future meeting.

After a hearty vote of thanks had been accorded the Chairman and the
Committee for the valuable services rendered in respect to the various
recommendations submitted, the meeting adjourned.

SCRAMBLING FOR EXPORT MARKETS, 1920–22

56. 11/3 Minutes, British Columbia Salmon   March 15, 1922
Canners' Association

A Special Meeting was called for Mar. 15, 1922 to receive a report from
Col. F.H. Cunningham of his mission to England in the interests of the
BC pink salmon, and receive suggestions how best to continue the advantages secured by his work – and subsequently to consider desired reductions of the cost of the Coast passenger fares, and also certain suggested
changes in license fees submitted by Major J.A. Motherwell for the
consideration of the canners.

Present:– Col. F.H. Cunningham, and Major J.A. Motherwell, by in-
          vitation, and Messrs. F.E. Burke (Chair), Wm. Hickey, R.G.
          Johnston, R.V. Winch, J. Rice, D.T. Sandison, J.M. White-
          head, R.C. Gosse, F. Millerd, R.R. Payne, W.E. Anderson,
          W.R. Lord, M. Desbrisay, H.B. Bell-Irving, and W.D.
          Burdis, Secretary.

On motion of Mr. J.M. Whitehead, Mr. Burke presided.

The notice convening the meeting was read.

Col. Cunningham reported how he found conditions in England and what he did. He found large stocks of salmon and no demand, and the brokers and dealers very pessimistic. He held a meeting with the canned-goods section of the Chamber of Commerce in Liverpool, explained his mission, and suggested its financial and moral support. The brokers made it apparent that the producers must pay all advertising expenses. He went to London, where he met importers and wholesalers and found a large Siberian advertising enterprise on foot. The brokers *et al.* advised joining a general campaign for salmon of all grades and countries. The Alaska Packers Assn. would not come in, but opened up an independent campaign for Alaska Reds which got good results, and the pack of 1921 and 1922 was all sold. They will do the same this year.

It was impressed on him that the object of his efforts must be the retailer; 120,000 dealers had to be reached. He invited the editors of the trade journals to meet him at a luncheon. The luncheon was attended by the editors or representatives and favourable notices were published in several trade journals, which brought many inquiries. This was followed up by personal visits to retailers in many towns. 1921 was a favorable year to the canned goods trade, as strikes and shortage of fuel combined in increased consumption of canned goods. He issued 10,000 pamphlets and used his knowledge to disabuse the public minds of prejudice against all light coloured salmon. He found the opinion prevalent that *spawned fish* were used or some other fish packed and designated "Pink Salmon." There was also a prejudice against "medium reds" either red or pink – people could not understand it was another species of fish.

He occupied space in the Grocers Exhibition in London, where large crowds inspected the exhibits of canned salmon and models of fish, and innumerable inquiries were answered daily. In preparing the exhibits and attending to visitors he was ably assisted by Mrs. Cunningham, who contributed greatly to the success of the enterprise.

The Government injured business by selling parcels of salmon at reduced prices at intevals during the year, but finally all government stocks were cleaned out.

Siberian salmon will continue to be the most powerful competitor as it is red in color and is sold under the best known labels, which agrees with English prejudices. The Siberian packs are financed in England and all goods are inspected in the canneries. There is no business sentiment in England – quality and price is everything. The country of origin is no factor in selling goods, though, subject to equal quality and price, the preference would probably be given Empire products. Other countries realize this and Australia and Africa are taking notice, while the United States, by persistent efforts, has secured a great hold on the markets. Another reason is the Americans "stock" salmon in England, where quick delivery is demanded. Spot goods are a great factor in England, France, and Belgium, and must be considered in any efforts to secure a sure hold on English trade. He received no help from brokers or wholesalers, who were solely "business machines" and have no sympathies in business.

There is no market for chums in England. France, Belgium, and possibly other European countries are markets for these goods and should be cultivated.

Asked whether Siberian red salmon will not supplant British Columbia sockeye salmon in the English market, he expressed the opinion that the high-class purveyor will always shelf the genuine sockeyes, as their best customers call for it, and are prepared to pay the price for what they want. And though there are no standard prices per can in the retail stores, he found that sockeyes sold for about sixpence a tin more than Siberian or Alaska red salmon, which lack the oil and flavour of the BC sockeye product. Unscrupulous dealers might label Siberian salmon as sockeyes, there being no law to prevent them.

He did not think a marking act, demanding that tins be stamped with the country of origin, is likely to be enacted, but a preferential tariff in favour of British Empire products may be possible.

He made good use of moving pictures supplied by the Hon. Wm Sloan, [BC Commissioner of Fisheries], and found the public very much interested in them. During the Grocers Exhibition, two exhibitions were screened each day, and drew limit crowds that listened attentively to the lectures given.

He desired to express his deep indebtedness to Mr. F.C. Wade, Agent-General for BC, who had found him splendid accommodation in BC House, as well as the use of an entire window on Regent Street for the display of a BC salmon exhibit. And in every other way he had afforded him the most hearty cooperation and assistance.

He was pleased to state that as the result of the efforts of Mr. Wade and himself, BC canned salmon was placed for the first time on the list of goods for which tenders are called by the Admiralty. In consequence, sixty percent of the orders for pinks this year was filled by BC pinks, and more would have been taken had spot goods been available ...

Moved by J.M. Whitehead, Seconded by H.B. Bell-Irving, and carried unanimously.

> "That a hearty vote of thanks be accorded to Col. Cunningham for the excellent services rendered by him in England during the past year, which they realize have had a highly beneficial influence on the business, and for the interesting report they have just heard ..."

FROM BOAT RATING TO UNLIMITED LICENSING

57. 5/6 "Dominion Government Fishery Regulation for Northern BC" by Henry Doyle, 1919

In the early days of the industry, fishing was almost entirely restricted to gill nets. This was due to most of the canneries being located on the larger rivers where the runs of sockeye and spring salmon enabled satisfactory packs to be procured at comparatively little expense. In District No. 2 – by which title the northern BC district is designated – only three canneries procured their fish supply from other than gill nets. These plants depended on creek sockeyes for their packs and made their catches with small drag seines. Their average annual packs were 5,000 to 10,000 cases. The seines were operated under licenses, and the area covered by each license was approximately 15 miles of coast line. As a protection to the operators and to prevent excessive fishing, only one license was issued for any given area.

About 15 years ago the cheaper grades of salmon became valuable for canning purposes, thus creating more of an incentive for both canners and fishermen to operate in the waters of District No. 2. The number of gill nets fished increased considerably, and both the government authorities and established canners feared that if they were not limited to reasonable portions, over-fishing was bound to ensue. In 1908 the canners, by mutual agreement, appointed a Commission of three disinterested parties to establish a boat rating for each cannery in district No. 2, and the operators agreed to abide by the decision of this Commission.

The boat rating that resulted was on the whole a very fair one, but any agreement based on the voluntary action of individual canning companies could not in the nature of things be lasting. The Government recognized this fact, and in order to protect the runs from over-fishing, and official boat rating was established in 1910, under which a definite number of gill nets were allotted to each river or sub-district. The total for each sub-district was approximately the same as the canners themselves had agreed on, and naturally the division of licenses amongst the operators followed (with but few exceptions), the unofficial division that had formerly prevailed.

In order to make the regulations applicable to all fishing in District No. 2, seining licenses also were limited, and those already issued were confirmed to the holders. No additional licenses were permitted in areas covered by existing licenses.

These government regulations, unquestionably, were in the interest of the preservation of the fish, but they also had the effect of creating a vested interest for those fortunate enough to be license-holders prior to the establishment of the limitation. It of course followed that no new canneries could be erected, since all fishing licenses were attached to the plants already operating, and this in itself limited the market open to fishermen for the disposal of their catches.

For a time the new regulations worked very satisfactorily. But by degrees the pressure from applicants for new cannery licenses, and the desire of fishermen for more competition amongst buyers, became more and more pronounced. It was charged that the government was working in the interests of the established companies, had created a monopoly in their favour, and were stifling the development of one of our most important natural resources. In the case of gill-net fishing, this argument was rather far-fetched because the canneries then operating in gill-net districts were of sufficient capacity to handle practically all the fish taken by the gill netters, and to increase the number of nets (save in one or two isolated instances) was not conducive to fish preservation.

In seining areas, however, the case was somewhat different. The three existing plants were built primarily for canning sockeyes and had not sufficient capacity for packing any large quantity of the cheaper species, which also were available in the waters covered by the licenses held in connection with these plants. It was contended, and proved, that the quantities of pinks and chums procurable in these waters would support several more plants than were then operating, and that in many cases no attempts whatever were made by the license-holders to make use of the available fish.

Under the pressure brought to bear, the government gradually let down the bars. First, they granted cannery and seining licenses in sections not previously allotted – principally pink and chum areas. Next, they took some of the attached licenses away from the canners and issued them unattached. Then, they granted a few new cannery licenses, leaving it a matter of competition between the old and new operators as to which secured the unattached fishermen.

As a result of these changes, the number of cannery licenses issued in BC increased 50% between 1910 and 1918, but with no increase during that period in the number of gill nets permitted. This meant increased competition for the fish caught. It also meant that companies that formerly had fished a large number of boats, and had found themselves so curtailed as to fishermen that half their equipment lay unemployed. They naturally complained long and loud to the government, thereby adding their tumult to the volume with which the government was assailed. At last the authorities, for the sake of peace and quietness, in 1918 took off all restrictions as to cannery licenses and made fishing licenses, both gill nets and seines, open to all white and Indian fishermen who are British subjects. The only existing limitation is as regards Japanese: the latter being restricted to the number of licenses held by them prior to 1918.

These changes have, on the whole, been satisfactory to all concerned, but this has been due more to existing market conditions than to any real merit they contain. Only one new cannery has since been erected, but doubtless this will be followed by others when financial conditions improve. In gill-net areas, such as Skeena and Naas rivers and Rivers Inlet, the number of fishermen have increased approximately 25%. To-day's packing costs are so excessive that canners are not encouraging any large increase of fishermen, but when profits are realizable a still greater number of fishermen will be employed. These remarks are equally applicable to seine fishing. There has already been some increase in the number of seine licenses issued, and more will be called for when pinks and chums again command a profitable market.

It is perfectly obvious that with such increases in fishing appliances there will be more fish caught. Doubtless for a time this larger volume will mean greater profit to both fishermen and canners, but the experience of Alaska demonstrates that over-fishing means depletion of the spawning beds and ultimate extermination of the fishery. The Canadian government realizes the danger that threatens and are attempting to offset it by increasing the weekly closed season in proportion to the increase of fishing gear employed. Thus, in Rivers Inlet, when 700 boats operated, they had a 36-hour weekly closed time. Such measures, however, are simply temporary make-shifts. Carried to a logical conclusion, it means that eventually half the week may be closed time, and if this happened no cannery could afford to operate. It would also mean that, with such idle time on their hands, fishermen would be tempted to violate the regulations, and as a body, they would work to defeat the object of the law. With public opinion, as represented by both fishermen and canners, opposed to such drastic regulations they would be as difficult to enforce, and as frequently violated, as are the prohibition laws of the US at the present time.

It appears that despite warnings given them fishermen and canners the world over work on complacently at exterminating the industry that supports them and give no thought to the future until the disasters that have befallen others are experienced by themselves. Then they will howl for relief and call upon the government to take action to save them from themselves. To-day, those interested in the salmon fisheries in northern BC are quietly working under the new regulations the government has

put into effect. Tomorrow, the inadequacy of these regulations to maintain the fisheries will be apparent, and then the unrest and dissatisfaction
will be as great or greater than it was prior to 1918. As they are administered to-day, the regulations governing fishing in District No. 2 are not
satisfactory; they do not protect the supply of raw material, nor can they
conserve the fish.

We in British Columbia feel most strongly that hand in hand with
unlimited fishing must go artificial propagation on a scale commensurate
with the commercial drain on the supply. We feel that it is not enough
that these propagation efforts be confined, as they are at present, to
practically the one species – sockeyes – and that only the most important
sections, such as the Fraser and Skeena rivers, should be so taken care
of. We have over 1,000 rivers and streams, each the breeding ground of
one or more species of salmon, and on only four of these has our government attempted hatchery propagation. We feel that each individual
stream that is being depleted of its salmon life should have that life
restored and maintained by artificial propagation. And we feel that unless or until such protective measures are inaugurated the regulations
that are in force to-day are incomplete, inadequate, and unsatisfactory.

No one interested in the fishing industry questions the earnestness,
sincerity, or real desire of our government authorities to preserve and
build up our fish supply. Those in charge, both locally and at Ottawa,
are painstaking and hardworking, and they have given an immense
amount of time to the problems that confront them. But control lies in
Ottawa, 3,000 to 4,000 miles away from the actual seat of operations;
local knowledge is lacking; distance precludes quick action; fisheries are
regarded as a minor consideration; and political interference is rampant.
Until a change of policy occurs, no real relief is possible. Our fisheries
must be placed in the hands of a disinterested local Commission, possessing full administrative and executive powers; a Commission that would
devote all its time and all its energies to the solution of the industry's
needs, and with such intimate local knowledge of conditions that any
situation which may arise can be dealt with intelligently and without loss
of time. Until such a Commission does function, no regulations of real
value can be laid down, nor be properly administered. The most essential
need of to-day is one which will bring about such a change of administra-
tion. When that is accomplished the rest will follow as a natural sequence, and the industry will be established on a basis that will assure
profitable returns for the operators of to-day, and permit them to hand
an unimpaired supply down to posterity.

58. 5/6 "Unlimited Licensing in Salmon Fishing," by Henry Doyle, c. 1919

If the Government persist in their announced intention of throwing open cannery and fishing licenses to all British subjects the following results – amongst others – will ensue:–

1. In 1918, the British Ministry of Food had commandeered practically all the British Columbia salmon pack, with the exception of the "Chum" grade. Prices asked by Canadian packers were so much higher than American goods of equal grade were obtainable for that the British Ministry of Food demanded arbitration on prices. The arbitrators appointed by the Dominion Government were the War Purchasing Commission, and this body was furnished with all possible data covering costs of packing of both American and Canadian salmon canners.

The War Purchasing Commission awarded Canadian canners:–

> $12.50 per case for 1 lb. tall springs, against the American commandeered price of $11.00 per case.
> $11.50 per case for 1 lb. tall cohos, against the American commandeered price of $6.60 per case.
> $8.00 per case for 1 lb. tall pinks against the American commandeered price of $9.00 per case.

The Canadian price of tall chum salmon was $6.75 per case, but as American goods were obtainable at $6.40, the British Ministry of Food made all their purchases of this grade from the American packers.

The War Purchasing Commission, in setting these prices, recognized that owing to their larger individual packs (45,000 cases to the cannery in southeastern Alaska against 15,000 cases to the cannery in northern British Columbia), American salmon canners could produce

> Red Spring 1 lb. talls for $1.50 per case less than Canadians.
> Coho   " "   "   " $2.50 "   "   "   "   "
> Pink   " "   "   " $1.40 "   "   "   "   "
> Chum   " "   "   " $ .35 "   "   "   "   "

The United States is the largest consuming country of canned salmon in the world, taking over 60% of the total production. The control of this market is safeguarded for American canners by a 15% duty on canned fish. On to-day's selling values this protection by tariff mounts to:–

> Spring talls, $16.00 per case @ 15% $2.40 per case protection.
> Coho   " $12.00 "   "   "   " $1.80 "   "   "
> Pink   " $ 8.00 "   "   "   " $1.20 "   "   "
> Chum   " $ 6.40 "   "   "   " $ .96 "   "   "

Adding to this tariff protection the fair difference in packing costs as figured by the War Purchasing Commission, we find that, as far as the United States market is concerned, American packers are protected from Canadian competition to the following extent:—

Spring talls, $3.90 per case, or 25% of sales value.
Coho   " $4.30   "   "   "   "   "   "   "
Pink   " $2.60   "   "   "   "   "   "   "
Chum   " $1.31   "   "   "   "   "   "   "

From the above it is plainly to be seen that if unlimited fishing licenses are granted in Districts Nos. 2 & 3 [Vancouver Island], American canners could outfit a sufficient number of British subjects (?) [sic] with fishing gear and equipment to make it worth their while to send collecting boats for the take of fish and transport same to southeastern Alaska or Puget Sound. And owing to the protected trade they enjoy in their home market, they could pay prices for raw fish which the British Columbia packers could not possibly meet. This is already actually the case in District No. 1, where unlimited licenses are granted, and where Americans are securing practically all the fish while Canadian operators stand idly by, unable to meet the competition.

2. Under the proposed International Treaty, the use of purse seines is prohibited in the main sockeye fishing areas of Puget Sound. Being shut out of these waters, the owners of this class of fishing appliance find themselves possessed of seine boats and seine nets worth $10,000 to $20,000 per outfit and no place to operate them in. They face immense loss, when along comes a benevolent Canadian government offering an unlimited field in British Columbia for these American outcasts. In the name, and under the guise, of British subjects they will fish our waters. American buyers will quite naturally be given a preference in the purchase of their catches, and both fish and the money paid for them will go across the International Boundary line for the enrichment of the United States at the expense of Canada, and through the direct instrumentality of the Canadian government.

3. Fishing on the Fraser River during the sockeye season is no longer profitable, but with a limit on licenses in District No. 2, Fraser River fishermen were shut out of the North. In 1919, 1,337 gill-net licenses were issued for the Fraser River district, nearly 900 of which were taken out by Japanese. These men are bona fide fishermen of long experience, and all of them would unquestionably go to District No. 2 for sockeye fishing (returning to the Fraser River for the profitable fall fishing season) if the limit on licenses were abolished.

These Japanese engage solely in fishing for their livelihood, while with white men and Indians fishing is but a seasonal occupation. As a consequence, through closer application and working for a longer period the Japanese fisherman obtains greater catches, and naturally fish buyers – whether cannery owners of otherwise – prefer dealing with the labourer who produces the most results.

The results of throwing fishing licenses open to all British subjects will best be illustrated by taking Skeena River for an example. In 1919, about 950 licenses were issued for this river, of which 650 were held by Japanese, leaving 300 to cover both whites and Indians. Now, assume that the Skeena River canners – in anticipation of a great increase of fishermen through unrestricted licenses – should build and equip 600 new boats. This would give a total of 900 boats available after the 1919 Japanese fishermen were provided for. The past season on Skeena River was very profitable for the fishermen and naturally most of the exodus from the Fraser River would be to the Skeena River. Assuming that these 900 Fraser River Japanese fishermen went to the Skeena River to fish, it would mean that for the 900 boats the canners might have available, there would be 900 Japanese applicants – each owning his own net brought from the Fraser River – and say, 300 to 500 whites and Indians, practically all of whom would want a net as well as a boat from the cannery owner. Given these circumstances, anyone placed in the canneryman's position would act just as the canneryman will act. They would give preference to the Japanese to whom the smallest advance would have to be made and from whom the largest return could be anticipated. The result would be that Skeena River gill-net fishing would become a complete monopoly of the Japanese, and whites and Indians would have to seek some other occupation to make a living.

What would happen to the Skeena River would prevail throughout the Province. To-day the Indians of District No. 2 earn large sums each season, which they spend in Prince Rupert and other such centres. White fishermen also are gradually settling in Prince Rupert so as to be near the seat of fishing operations, and their monetary disbursements contribute largely to the welfare of the community. But with Japanese driving them out of business, neither whites nor Indians would make their present earnings; no money would be available for local tradesmen; and even the sums paid the Japanese for fish would mostly be sent out of the country – to enrich Japan at the expense of Canada.

4. While the above deal more particularly with the question of fishing licenses, the removal of limitation of cannery licenses would be equally disastrous. Two successive Governments admitted they lacked sufficient knowledge upon which to decide what was best for the British Columbia salmon industry, and therefore appointed Commissions (1905 and 1917)

to investigate and advise them what should be done. Both of these Commissions came out flat-footed in pronouncing restrictive measures absolutely necessary for the preservation of the industry. Since the 1917 Commission sat, conditions have become worse instead of better. Rivers Inlet has failed to put up satisfactory packs for three years in succession. The installation of traps near Cape Fox, Alaska, has seriously decreased the Naas River runs. Freshet conditions in 1917 (October) scoured out the streams from Seymour Narrows to Skagway, destroying the recently deposited spawn. The result of this freshet was a 50% decrease in the 1919 pack of pink salmon (the shortage is from 1,500,000 to 2,000,000 cases); a similar percentage of decrease can be looked for with cohos and chums in 1920; and a partial decrease in sockeyes in 1921 and 1922.

The 1917 Commission advocated a five-year period without further increase in licenses for either fishermen or canneries, and Nature has since emphasized the need of same. But with the end of the war it was essential our returned soldiers should not only be given employment, but should be encouraged to engage in occupations that promised them the greatest remuneration. The Government very wisely and very justly made a place for the soldiers in our fisheries. Many men engaged in the industry in 1919, and on the whole made good money despite their inexperience. They gained sufficient skill and knowledge to insure themselves greater profits in the years to come. The men in the days of their ignorance as to fishing conditions had been strong in their advocacy of unlimited licenses, but one season taught them the fallacy of this idea, and before the Department sprang their latest surprise the returned soldiers' organizations already had petitioned the Government to make no change from the conditions that prevailed in the 1919 season.

There *must* be a proportionated ratio between the number of canneries and the number of fishing licenses. Too few canneries would prevent the fishermen disposing of all their catches and waste would ensue. Too many canneries would mean some would go to the wall, and by the survival of the fittest the proper ratio once more become established – but only after unnecessary hardships and losses. In 1908, a boat rating was established to divide the fishermen amongst existing canneries so each would have sufficient to ensure profitable operation. Thus for fishermen and canners was the industry placed on a just and stable basis. But *since 1908 the Government has increased the number of canneries 50%* without a corresponding increase in the number of fishermen, and to-day, in some areas, the canneries are operating at a loss. To further increase the burden on established canneries by granting still more cannery licenses, without also increasing the fishermen, would cause those to fall who are already tottering on the edge of disaster ... [It is necessary to increase the amount of salmon available to fishermen. Government officials] travel along the same old Departmental rut, apparently unable to see what is going on except in the well-worn path before them. For 35 years they have been operating sockeye hatcheries on lines directly opposed to the natural habits and instincts of the species; their hatchery operations have been more responsible than any other cause for the depletion of the Fraser River fishery; and yet when one of their own hatchery superintendents demonstrates the fallacy of their present system and points out other methods which contain abundant promise of success, they make no effort to substitute the new plan for the old one. With eggs and hatchery men both available for rearing sockeyes by the new method, they are criminally wasting the precious eggs in the obsolete style that for 3½ decades has shown no beneficial results. With the "upper" Fraser River waters barren of sockeye runs from which new schools might be established, they are taking no steps to establish such runs by planting eggs shipped in from other points. With American traps threatening the extermination of Nass River sockeyes, they exhibit no effort to stay the destruction. But when it comes to legislation that nobody wants, to policies that seemingly are only half considered, and to measures that, while benefiting none, work hardships on all, the Fisheries Department shines forth with such a strong light and creates such an intense heat (of indignation) that we in British Columbia think Hell is but another name for Ottawa.

59. 11/1 Petition from BC Merchants and   *Feb. 1920*
        Manufacturers to Minister of Marine
        and Fisheries (copy)

Sir:–

We, Merchants and Manufacturers, not in any way directly connected with the salmon packing or fishing business, but vitally interested indirectly as we supply the salmon packers with anything they need in our line, respectfully ask that your Department postpone for one year any change in the regulations regarding the catching and packing of salmon.

We understood that you have stated that the fisheries were to be thrown open, that is, anyone could build or operate Canneries in any part of British Columbia or could obtain fishing licenses.

We feel that the effect of over-fishing would soon deplete our fisheries and do away with this business, and in that manner affect us and the whole of British Columbia.

                                         Yours respectfully,
                                         (signed)

David Spencer Ltd.
C. Spencer, Director

Canadian Pacific Railway
  Co.
F.W. Peters, Genl. Supt.

Kelly Douglas & Co. Ltd.
Robert Kelly, Genl.
  Manager

W.H. Malkin Co. Ltd.
W.H. Malkin, Manager

Western Grocers Ltd.
A. Badenich, Manager

The McClary Manufacturing
  Co.
J. Galloway

J.A. Tepoorten Ltd.
J.A. Tepoorten, President

Gault Bros. Ltd.
Henry A. Stone, Mng. Dir.

James Thompson & Sons,
  Ltd.
H. Thompson, Director

Macay, Smith Blair & Co.
  Ltd.
Gilbert Blair, Sec. – Treas.

J. Leckie Co. Ltd.
R.J. Leckie

F.R. Stewart & Co. Ltd.
A. Brenchley, Director

Gibsons Ltd.
Robert Gibson

Simpson Balkwill & Co.
  Ltd.
A. Twing, Sec. – Treas.

McLennan McFeely & Co.
  Ltd.
E.J. McFeely, President

Wood Vallance & Leggat
  Ltd.
J. Dunsmuir, Accountant

Ames Holden McCready
  Ltd.
Fred A. Richardson, Mgr.

Damer Lumsden Co.
F.J. Lumsden, Secretary

Union Steamship Co. of BC
  Ltd.
E.H. Beazley, Managing
  Dir.

The A.R. Williams
  Machinery Co.
F.S. Renson, President

American Can Co. Ltd.
H.G. Bigger, Sec. Treas.

Ross & Howard Iron Works
  Co. Ltd.
John Ross

The Robertson-Godson Co.
  Ltd.
A.S. Godson, President

The Canadian Fairbanks
  Morse Co. Ltd.
G.K. Towers, Manager

Wallace Parson & Farmer
  Co. Ltd.
J.B. Farmer

Edward Lipsett Co.
E. Lipsett

Crane Ltd.
J.E. McIlresey, Local Mgr.

Vancouver Lumber Co.
  Ltd.
E.S. Saunders, Manager

Camel Laird & Co. Ltd.
N. Thompson, Manager

N. Thompson & Co. Ltd.
N. Thompson, President

Imperial Oil Co. Ltd.
C.M. Rolston, Manager

Smith, Davidson & Wright
  Ltd.
W.E. Davidson

J. Hanbury & Co. Ltd.
J. Hanbury, President

Credit Foncier
  Franco-Canadien
Robert Craine, Manager

Ceperley Rounsefell & Co.
  Ltd.
F.W. Rounsefell

Gulf Steamship & Trading
  Co. Ltd.
John Gault

Canadian Bank of
  Commerce
J.V. Holt, Manager

The Merchants Bank of
  Canada
A.C. Fraser, Manager

The Bank of Montreal
R.H. Hogg, Acting Supt.

The Imperial Bank of
  Canada
J.M. Lay, Mgr. Vanc.
  Branch

The Bank of Nova Scotia
J.A. Siott, Asst. Manager

The Molsons Bank, Vanc.
  BC
J.W. Swaisland, Manager

Standard Bank of Canada
F.N. Sutherland, Manager

Union Bank of Canada
G.S. Harrison, Manager

The Home Bank of Canada
D.B. Nickerson, Manager

The Royal Bank of Canada
Thos. Peacock, Manager

Bank of Hamilton, Vanc. BC
J.W. McCane, Manager

The Dominion Bank of
  Canada
A.H. Bizett, Asst. Manager

The Bank of Toronto
J.K. Ball, Manager

60. 11/1 Resolution: British Columbia Salmon   *February 17, 1920*
          Canners' Association

The following resolution was passed at a meeting of the British Columbia Salmon Canners' Association held in Vancouver, Tuesday, the 17th day of February, 1920:–

"That as the proposed regulations for 1920 are considered by the Canners of British Columbia to be likely to hasten the destruction of the Salmon Fisheries of this Coast, it is strongly urged that with a view to giving time for the Government to reconsider and readjust these regulations for 1921, the 1919 regulations be adhered to for 1920, and that the Government be requested to take immediate action as to these recommendations and, further, that the Ministry of Fisheries be requested to immediately get in touch with the Fishing Interests with a view to the formulation of regulations which will coincide with the wishes of all the interests concerned."

WE CONFIRM THE ABOVE RESOLUTION:–

Wallace Fisheries Ltd.
F.E. Burke, Genl. Mgr.

Preston Packing Co. Ltd.
W. Hickey, Managing
    Director

The British Columbia
    Packers Ass'n.
Wm. H. Barker, General
    Manager

Cassiar Packing Co. Ltd.
By F.W. Johnstone, Sec.

Ocean Packing Co. Ltd.
A.L. Russell, President

Defiance Packing Co. Ltd.
W.E. Hodges, Liquidator

The Anglo-British Columbia
    Packing Co. Ltd. Agents
D. Bell-Irving

Northern BC Fisheries Ltd.
C.A. Crosbie, General
    Manager

M. Desbrisay & Co.
H.V.O. Chatterton,
    Secretary

Western Salmon Packing
    Co. Ltd.
A.S. Arkley

Kildala Packing Co. Ltd.
Geo. W. Dawson

Canadian Manufacturers'
    Ass'n., British Columbia
    Division
Hugh Dalton, Secretary

Redonda Canning & Cold Storage Co. Ltd. P.J. Russell, Secy. – Treas.	Manufacturers Association of British Columbia Jas. Hart, Secretary
Lummi Bay Packing Co. Ltd. J.E. Rice, President	J.H. Todd & Sons
Sidney Canning Co. Ltd. Chas. F. Goodrich, Manager	British Columbia Canning Co. Ltd. B.C. Mess, Manager
Nootka Packing Co. Ltd. J.O. Morris, President	St. Mungo Canning Co. Ltd. Jas. Anderson, Manager
Glen Rose Canning Ltd. J.M. McDonald	British Columbia Salmon Canners' Ass'n. W.D. Burdis, Secretary

DOYLE ON CANNING

61. 5/6 *"The Process of Canning Salmon,"*   15 *September, 1921*
    by Henry Doyle

Salmon are usually delivered to the canning establishment in scows which are moored alongside the "fish wharf." From the scows they are lifted in fish elevators of various descriptions to the cannery floor, where the different species are separated so that each can be processed in turn.

In the smaller canneries men known as "butchers" or "slitters" take the fish, decapitate it, remove the fins, slit open the belly, and finally cut off the tail. They then pass the carcasses through an opening into a fresh water tank or bath, where other operators receive them, remove the entrails, clean and scrape the belly cavity, and with a scrub brush rub the skin side of the fish to remove the surplus slime. In large canning establishments a machine known as the "Iron Chink" performs all the above described operations, and only a few washers are required to examine the fish, as it comes from the machine, to remove any matter which may still adhere to it.

After the salmon is cleaned it is generally passed into a brine of about 100 degree salimeter strength, where it remains about 20 minutes. In this time it absorbs sufficient salt to give it flavour. In some establishments instead of brining the fish a small quantity of dry salt is put in the can along with the fish, but while this answers the purposes as far as flavouring is concerned, it is not as desirable as brine cuts off some of the fish slime, which under the dry-salting process remains in the fish and is retained in the can.

From the brine tank the salmon is transferred to a drain table where it is allowed to remain until the surplus brine or water, as the case may be, runs off. It is then conveyed to the "fish cutter," a machine with revolving circular knives set at distances apart that correspond to the size of can the fish is intended for.

After leaving the fish cutter the salmon is put in the container either by hand filling or by a "filling machine." Once the can has received its contents the remaining process is a mechanical one. The cans travel on a belt conveyor to a weighing machine which automatically throws out "light weights" to be re-filled. Thence to a clinching machine, which puts on the lid and clinches it so it cannot be removed, although still leaving it loose enough to enable the interior air to be expelled.

From the "clincher" the can travels to the "exhaust box," in which it is conveyed up and down lateral passages, all the while subjected to a steam heat of approximately 200° for about 14 minutes. During its passage throught the exhaust box the fish receive a preheating to about 150°, which is sufficient to expel the air from the can and establish a vacuum. In many canneries the speed with which the cans travel through the exhaust box is such that the journey is completed in 9 or 10 minutes, but this is not recommended, as the shorter exhaust does not give a good vacuum, nor does the fish receive a sufficient amount of pre-heating.

After leaving the exhaust box the cans enter the "closing machine," which tightly closes the clinched lid and hermetically seals the container. From the closing machine the can travels to a "washing machine," which rinses the tin and removes any particles of fish, dirt, or grease which it may have picked up in the processing to this point. From the washing machine the cans pass into big iron trays, technically knows as "coolers," where they are arranged in an orderly fashion. The coolers when filled are placed on low cars in stacks of sufficient height to fit into the retorts, and when a sufficient quantity is ready to fill a retort, the cars are rolled into same, the retort is closed, steam turned on, and the actual and final cooking takes place.

In the retorts a steam pressure of 15 to 16 pounds is maintained and the cooking temperature is 238° to 242°, the latter being preferable. For one lb. tall cans the cooking period should be 1 hour and 15 minutes; for ½ lb. flat cans one hour and a half. This is for retorts of 3-car capacity – the standard size. For retorts of 4- or 6-car capacity (which are also used to a limited extent), a corresponding longer cooking period is necessary, as such retorts contain from 50% to 100% more cold fish through which the heat must pass before it warms sufficiently for the regular cooking process to begin.

When the fish is thoroughly cooked the coolers are removed, rinsed in clean water – which in some canneries is supplemented by first being dipped in a weak solution of lye – and then stacked to cool. They are generally left until the following morning, by which time the tins are thoroughly cooled and can be removed from the coolers by hand. In some modern plants, however, the cans are cooled in running water immediately on leaving the retorts, and then the remaining process can be proceeded with at once.

After the tins are cooled, either by air cooling or water cooling, they are taken to the lacquering machine, where they receive a thin coating of lacquer to prevent danger of subsequently rusting. After being lacquered the tins are labelled, either by hand or machines, and finally are placed in cases, ready for shipment to any part of the world.

IN THE SWIM AT FISH CONVENTION

Vancouver Daily Province, 5 June 1920. This cartoon accompanied a report on the Canadian Pacific Fisheries Convention held in Vancouver. A representation of Doyle appears in the lower left.

Portrait of Henry Doyle c. 1920. (Courtesy of Richard Doyle)

Original Cannery, Mill Bay, Naas River BC, 1905. (UBC, Doyle Papers, vol. 5, file 16)

Mill Bay Cannery, Naas River, BC, 1913. This is the canning plant that Doyle built.
(UBC, Doyle Papers, vol. 5, file 16)

Water Supply System, Kumeon Cannery [Naas River], Installing, 1916. L to R: Henry Doyle, Jr., Henry Doyle, Dick Courtland, and Hal Peck. (UBC, Doyle Papers, vol. 5, file 5)

Naas Harbour Cannery, Naas River, c. 1912. (UBC, Doyle Papers, vol. 5, file 18)

Salmon Fishing on the Fraser River, BC. Oar- and sail-powered gillnet fishing with a two person crew, 1906. Several cannery operations appear in the background. (Charles Mathers, Provincial Archives of Alberta, B9852)

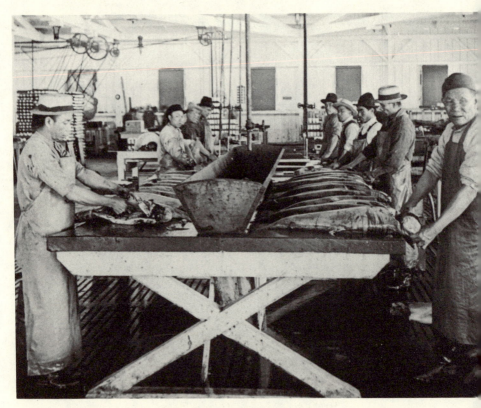

"Interior of a Canning Factory, Puget Sound," n.d. Each Chinese-contract fish butcher could process as many as 400 salmon by hand per day. (Keystone View Co. [Meadville, PA] Stereograph N13625, courtesy of Robert M. Vogel)

Indian women hand-filling tins of salmon on the Skeena River canning district, c. 1890. This is a rare, if not unique, nineteenth-century view of Indian women engaged in industrial work in British Columbia. It was taken by a talented amateur, Robert Reford. According to Ralph Greenhill and Andrew Birrell (*Canadian Photography 1839-1920* [Toronto: Coach House Press, 1979], 127), Reford purchased a Kodak camera as soon as they appeared on the market in 1888, making amateur photography possible, and used it extensively on his two-year trip to BC. (National Archives of Canada [NA]

Soldering tins by steam. Ewen & Co.'s Cannery, Fraser River, c. 1890s. (Wm. Notman & Sons, Montreal, NA PA120396)

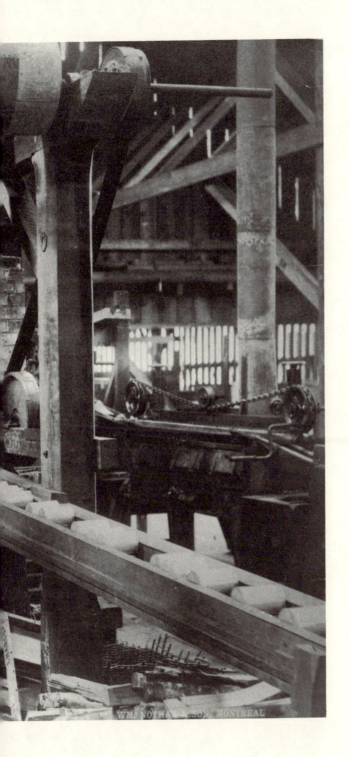

CHAPTER FIVE

Winners and Losers

INTRODUCTION

Henry Doyle attempted to re-enter the industry immediately after losing control of his canneries in the early 1920s. First, he tried to orchestrate a new amalgamation from outside the province. The person who would publicly arrange for financing and secure the options on the British Columbia canneries had to be an impartial party who could act, as Doyle had twenty years earlier, quickly, without tipping off the individual cannery operators. Doyle himself was now so intimately involved in the industry that he had to operate strictly "behind the scenes."

In 1922, Doyle asked a few Vancouver businessmen to approach potential backers in Toronto and England.[1] When nothing came of this, he approached George Armsby, of Blair & Co., New York, with the scheme (document 62). Armsby had been instrumental in forming the California Packing Corporation in 1916; the company had quickly acquired Alaska Packers as a subsidiary operation. California Packing represented the very different business trend in the United States salmon-canning industry in the twentieth century, when the large integrated packers that dominated the fruit-, vegetable-, and meat-packing trade, such firms as Libby, McNeil & Libby, Armour, and Swift, merged with American fish-packing operations.[2]

The main American company that Doyle approached in 1923, 1924, and again in 1925, was California Packing Corporation itself (documents 63–65a). When he wrote to California Packing in 1924 and 1925, Doyle exaggerated the importance of the extent to which the Alaska salmon fishery was in serious difficulty[3] and he insisted that good potential existed in Canada for a sizeable domestic market for canned salmon. He pointed out that by operating plants in Canada the American firm could take advantage of the new Australian-Canadian and Franco-Canadian preferential trade agreements to ship canned salmon to those two countries. He also assured California Packing – falsely – that the Canadian government would prevent any new canneries being built for at least ten years. But all these attempts failed.

Although his schemes were not successful, his extensive files of memos and correspondence on this issue provide an invaluable and unique opportunity to compare and contrast the state of the industry in 1924–25 with its state in 1902. Of particular interest, they show how most of the consolidations formed in the 1890s and 1900s quickly lost their positions of market dominance. While the scheme for a massive horizontal amalgamation which Doyle prepared in 1924–25 was similar to that which he had developed to form British Columbia Packers Association in 1902, there were several important differences. First, the industry had undergone extensive diversification and geographical spread, so, though Doyle's first plan was to amalgamate only the northern BC canneries, he eventually included every cannery operation in each of the major sockeye areas in the North (Skeena and Naas rivers and Rivers Inlet) and most of the canneries in the major non-sockeye fishing grounds (Vancouver Island and the outlying districts), for a total of eighty-five percent of the operations (documents 63–63a). The proposed amalgamation involved sixteen companies and sixty-one fish-packing operations. As always, some independent packers would be allowed to operate in the field without interference. These were the smaller firms that usually operated in the marginal, less productive areas. Second, whereas his much earlier report emphasized the importance of site locations and the quality of plants and equipment, his 1920s assessments emphasized quality of managers. Several new companies had entered the field, Canadian Fishing Co. Ltd. most prominent among them. Yet many of the original canners and/or their families continued to manage and own canneries in the province. As far as Doyle was concerned, the older the head of the family, the easier it would be to buy out the family business.

In Doyle's estimation, the assets of the Gosse-Millerd and Wallace fish-packing concerns would be prime targets in any amalgamation scheme – and he was correct. Combined, their assets rivalled those of the single most important company, British Columbia Packers Association, which had been re-organized as the British Columbia Fishing & Packing Company in 1920.[4] The Gosse-Millerd and Wallace interests together equalled approximately the same number of plants as British Columbia Fishing & Packing, but were financially "trimmer" operations and were located in more districts than British Columbia Fishing & Packing. Moreover, the Gosse-Millerd and Wallace interests had been hard hit by the post-war depression, and the former was plagued with internal dissension at the management level, so these two companies seemed to be ripe for a takeover. Doyle wanted to acquire other packing operations as well under the proposed amalgamation. Some were desirable because they involved modern and well-equipped canning plants and included special facilities, such as cold-storage plants, fresh- and frozen-fish-handling facilities, herring canneries or salteries, box- or can-making plants, or fish-reduction works for the manufacture of fish meal and oil. Others would be assets because of their location in special fishing areas of the coast that Doyle thought were essential to control. But in more than one case, Doyle wanted to bring certain plants into the amalgamation simply because he considered their owners too aggressive or dangerous to be left as competitors.

It was quite certain that the current long-time president of British Columbia Fishing & Packing, William Barker, would resist any form of consolidation (document 64a). Barker was both sceptical of the financial feasibility of a new consolidation and fearful of public outcries against the monopolistic behaviour it might lead to. Moreover, he was by now a man in his seventies and in poor health; perhaps he did not care for the intrigue. The company's vice-president was Doyle's old friend Æmilius Jarvis. Doyle knew that Jarvis would support such a consolidation, but Jarvis was at the time in a Toronto jail on charges of bribery, theft, and conspiracy concerning his stock-and-bond business in Ontario.[5] For Doyle, Jarvis would have been more of a liability than an asset to the proposed new company!

While Doyle himself was unsuccessful in forming a new amalgamation of salmon-cannery operations, the essential scheme he proposed in 1924 and 1925 was carried out by others over the period 1926–28. In 1925, Jarvis, now out of jail, spearheaded a successful campaign to have British Columbia Fishing & Packing purchase Wallace Fisheries Ltd. The purchase, in March 1926, included a subsidiary, Wallace–Diesel Ships Ltd., which British Columbia Fishing & Packing's subsidiary, The Packers Steamship Co., later absorbed.[6] Following this, rumours circulated in the industry that the directors of British Columbia Fishing & Packing had offered to sell the company to California Packing; nothing seems to have come of this.[7] Then, in 1928, British Columbia Fishing & Packing merged with the Gosse Packing Co. (incorporated in 1926 as successor to Gosse-Millerd Ltd., after Francis Millerd had disassociated himself from the management of the latter, in 1922), and quickly purchased the assets of Millerd Packing Co. Ltd. (incorporated in 1927). This major new consolidation incorporated as the British Columbia

Packers Ltd. in 1928, when it produced nearly one-half of the provincial pack. Missing in the deal was Anglo-British Columbia Packing Co. Ltd., a highly successful medium-size enterprise that had survived intact since its incorporation, in 1891, having refused to join the original consolidation to form British Columbia Packers Association in 1902. Meanwhile, as Doyle had predicted, William Barker resigned as president of British Columbia Fishing & Packing in 1926 in protest over the purchase of Wallace Fisheries. Æmilius Jarvis, his fortunes apparently repaired, stepped into Barker's shoes as president.

When it became known that British Columbia Packers Ltd.'s, general manager, J.M. Whitehead, was to resign on 20 April 1928, the ever-watchful Henry Doyle saw a chance to regain his stature in the packing industry. He began writing to Jarvis and the company directors suggesting – and then insisting – that he, Doyle, be appointed general manager of the new company. One of the more substantial and significant letters is reproduced here (document 66).[8] It shows Doyle's particular view of the requirements of a canning-company executive, the extent to which he was prepared to use the written record he had collected over the years to get what he wanted, and, sadly, the depth of his lingering bitterness and disappointment over his treatment by British Columbia Packers Association directors decades earlier and, more recently, by his bankers. Jarvis, the recipient of many of Doyle's letters, tried to sidestep the issue by claiming that, while he supported Doyle's reinstatement, other directors were against it, but Doyle learned otherwise from his friends in the business. Jarvis appointed R.C. Gosse, the former president of Gosse Packing Co. Ltd., general superintendent instead of Doyle.

Determined as ever, Doyle eventually forced a showdown with Jarvis by offering his services as a sort of vice-president in charge of operations, but lost. Doyle then had no choice but to give up hope of ever taking a direct role in the industry in the future. But he certainly never lost his interest or enthusiasm for the battle. A few sentences written during this difficult period to a friend who was sympathetic to his cause reveal Doyle's attitude toward what was by now a substantial private archive. "If you have any further use for the copies of correspondence [with British Columbia Packers Ltd.] I sent you," he wrote, "it would be well to retain them, but if not I would like to have them again as it will save me making other copies should the occasion arise to use them later on."[9] Clearly, for men like Henry Doyle knowledge was power. And the most useful knowledge was that which was recorded on paper and stored for future use.

INVITING A NEW CONSOLIDATION, 1924

62. 2/3 Letter: Doyle to George N. Armsby, c/o   *101 Winch Building*
Messrs. Blair & Co., New York   *Vancouver,*
                                                                       14th August 1924

Dear Sirs: –

I am sending you through the registered mail certain data respecting the salmon-canning industry in British Columbia, and what could be accomplished with same if capital can be secured for floating a new company to absorb at least 60% of the present operators.

The situation existing in this industry to-day is almost identical with what I understand you faced in forming the California Packing Corporation. As you know from experience, the industry is on a very sound basis, but, like everything else, periodically suffers reverses. Such occurrences led to the formation of the Alaska Pkrs. Association in 1893, the British Columbia Pkrs. Association in 1902, and the California Packing Corporation in 1916. These consolidations have all been financially successful.

Left to themselves packing companies, whether of fish or fruit, seem incapable of arriving at a fair basis for amalgamation. Each fears the competitors trying to bring all together will get the best of the deal, or the plums of management, if they are successful. In the past this has blocked all efforts at agreement amongst themselves.

For several years prior to 1902, the salmon canners of British Columbia tried to get together by mutual agreement, but could never reach an understanding. Then the writer (who was in the fishing-supply business), undertook the floatation ... I have heard that your experience and procedure in forming the California Packing Corporation was similar to mine in forming the British Columbia Packers Association, and that, like myself, you were only successful when you brought pressure through the banks to compel the operators to form the amalgamating company.

The situation to-day in the British Columbia salmon-canning industry is similar to those recited above. All operators agree amalgamation is desirable, in fact necessary, if they are to meet the competition of Alaska, Puget Sound, and Siberia on an even cost basis. But though talking amalgamation for the past three or four years, they are no nearer to accomplishing it than when they started, since each is suspicious of the other, and of the others' motives, in suggesting an amalgamation. As I am one of those interested in operating companies I cannot to-day do what I did 22 years ago, when I was a disinterested party. I can advise and direct an outsider what should be done, but if my participation (or that of any other interested person) was made public, the proposal would not succeed.

Under these circumstances, if an amalgamation is accomplished it must apparently be engineered by some disinterested person, and it is with this in mind I am writing you. If you undertake the task it will be necessary for you to secure the finances *and then* appoint some one or more representatives to come here to obtain the options. I am prepared to assist these representatives by furnishing them information as to the companies; the best way to approach them; what arguments or pressures can be used; and what would be fair purchasing prices to option their properties at. But in doing this I must remain "behind the scenes" until all the options are secured, or the proposition will end in failure.

The banks have already been sounded on the matter. They realize the necessity of amalgamation, are sympathetic, and where their present customers are in a position where bank pressure will influence a favourable decision they are prepared to exert that influence. They are also prepared to finance the new company for its operating requirements in the same manner they finance the British Columbia Fishing & Packing Co. to-day. No working capital will be required for the new company outside of what, if any, remains in the treasury as proceeds from the preference issue, after disbursing what cash is required to pay for the properties.

At the present time the Bank of Montreal finances nearly 40% of the operators, the Canadian Bank of Commerce about 20%, and Molson's Bank about 10%. The two former I have reason to believe would jointly undertake the entire financing of the proposed new company's operations, although possibly it may be desirable to give Molson's Bank some of the business. None of the other banking institutions would have to be considered, nor would their participation be desirable, as none of them are sufficiently interested to-day to familiarize them[selves] with the industry and its requirements.

The capital required for this amalgamation cannot be obtained in Canada. In the first place, the two banks which would finance packing operations are the bankers to-day of most of the wealthier companies. While anxious to see an amalgamation effected, they take the ground it would be *infra dig* for them to participate in putting their customers into such an amalgamation unless they first obtained the consent of the said customers. And it is essential to the success of the undertaking that these customers are not given that knowledge.

In the second place, Montreal and Toronto are the Canadian centres for obtaining capital. They are 3,000 miles distant from here and have no knowledge of the salmon-canning industry, save what they know of the British Columbia Fishing & Packing Co., the one listed company on their Stock Exchanges. With no dividends paid for three years past, no immediate prospects of resumption of dividend paying, and with the unnecessarily big slump in the value of this company's shares, the apparent evidence before them is not conductive to enthusiasm for another floatation in the salmon industry.

In the United States, however, the period of depression has already passed, your salmon-canning companies are again showing profits, and confidence in the industry has been restored. Since the federal government has now restricted the industry in Alaska, there is no room for further expansion in your country. Here, the opportunity still exists. Our fisheries have not been depleted – this season's pack, now nearing completion, promises to be one of the largest ever secured, and well above the average for the past 8 years – and our regulations are broad and well administered. If an amalgamation is effected, we have governmental assurances that the industry will be held in its present status and no new canneries will be permitted for a period of at least 10 years.

In 1901, when both of us were residing in San Mateo, California, I occasionally met you, but this is so long ago you doubtless have no recollection of me, and will naturally want some information concerning me and my knowledge of the Industry. While for the reasons already set forth it is necessary my connection with this matter be not disclosed for the present, I can refer you for information as to my reputation and knowledge of the industry to Mr. Henry Fortman or Mr. Wm. Timson, or our mutual friend Balfour Adamson. The latter especially can give you information, as he was here at the time I formed the British Columbia Packers Association, knows the situation that existed then, and can corroborate my statements as to what I then accomplished.

If you favourably consider this proposition and think it necessary for me to go to New York to submit the matter in greater detail, I am prepared to do so, but it is better to avoid this if possible as my absence from here might give rise to suspicion that I have a finger in the pie.

In the event of a favourable decision I cannot impress upon you too strongly the advisability of early action. The situation here is brightening, pack sales to date are greater than to the same period in any of the past six years, and with the return of prosperity, many who to-day are anxious for amalgamation would be reluctant to sell. Furthermore, under the best of circumstances it will take some time to get the new company organized and in operation, and all this should be accomplished before the end of this year so the economies proposed can be effected in time for the packing season of 1925.

If, on the other hand, the data I am submitting and the time spent in formulating this proposition have not succeeded in persuading you to personally undertake this amalgamation, would you be kind enough to recommend some firm whom I might approach in the matter with reasonable chances of success.

In conclusion, I would ask that before you reach a decision you show me the courtesy of personally examining the data I have herewith sub-mitted. It has taken many days and much labour to get these documents into presentable shape, and I would not like my efforts to go for naught because only a cursory examination was made of the proposition, or it was studied by someone, no matter how painstaking or conscientious, who lacked your knowledge of the canning business, its requirements, and its possibilities.

Communications sent to my office address might betray my connec-tion with the proposed new company, and should you give the matter favourable consideration, I would suggest your answer be sent me c/o Bank of Montreal, Kerrisdale, BC. So addressed it will reach me as promptly as if sent to the office.

A MERGER OF NORTHERN CANNERIES, 1924

63. 6/22 "Proposed Amalgamation of BC Salmon Canneries, 1924,"
     by Henry Doyle

The proposal is to effect an amalgamation of all the canneries in northern British Columbia, locally known as District No. 2, taking in with same the canneries in other sections of the province that are under the same ownerships. If successful in this undertaking, the new company [would have] 84% of the industry in the province. As there is a possibility, however, that some may prove unobtainable, it is proposed the new company should function if a sufficient number to represent 60% of the industry are secured ...

Savings on operating costs. Closing down half of the canneries included in the amalgamation, and putting up the same total pack in the remaining plants, would materially cut down packing costs. A conservative estimate of this saving is 25 cents per case. In addition, there would be a large savings in the cost of head-office maintenance. At the present time the 16 companies proposed for amalgamation maintain 16 offices, with head-office managers and clerical staffs, all of which require an expenditure of at least $250,000. More than half this amount could be saved under an amalgamation.

Anticipated profits. When forming the British Columbia Packers Association in 1902 I estimated the profits would average $1.00 per case. For the past 22 years in which they have been in existence, and against the existing competition (representing 78⅓th of the industry against their 21⅔ths [sic]), their actual profits averaged $1.03 per case. In only one year (1923) did they occur a loss.

The new company would represent between 60% and 84% of the industry; would put up packs per cannery over 100% larger than the British Columbia Fishing & Packing Co.; would save on packing costs and head-office maintenance; and would be in a position to secure higher prices for their products. They would practically control the total output for British Columbia and could eliminate the past needless and senseless price cutting, which was such a large factor in causing the heavy losses of the past 4 or 5 years.

Mr. Barker, of the British Columbia Fishing & Packing Co., in discussing amalgamation with some of his competitors, admitted that such an amalgamation would produce an increase of at least 35% over present profits. This estimate is generally considered conservative by other large operators. For the purpose of estimating profits for the new company, and to do so on a safe and conservative basis, I am not taking into account the additional savings referred to above. I am simply estimating for the new company the same profit of $1.03 per case that the British Columbia Fishing & Packing Co. have actually averaged for the past 22 years. For convenience, I have used the round figure of $1.00 per case in these calculations.

Payment for plants. It is estimated that the total purchase price of the plants desired will not exceed $6,500,000. Of this amount, some cash will be required by most operators to clear them of outstanding liabilities. In other cases, the purchase price will have to be paid entirely in cash. Based on past experience, probably one-third of the total purchase price will be in cash and two-thirds in stock of the new company.

In forming the British Columbia Packers Association, the cash necessary for its organization was obtained by selling 7% preferred shares to an underwriting syndicate formed by Montreal, Toronto, and Boston capitalists. This preferred stock was underwritten at $80 per share (par $100) and was transferable into common stock at $115. The canning companies entering that amalgamation were paid part cash and part common stock. The latter was $100 par value, but was issued to the canners at $80. It is proposed for the new company to follow the same procedure, although possibly both preferred and common stock could be floated at $85. Based on an issued price of $80 per share, the amount required to pay for the plants would be approximately: –

$2,750,000   7% preference shares of $100   par   value.
5,500,000   common   "   " $100   "   "   .

to which would be added whatever amount of common stock it is seemed advisable to pay for promotion.

In the case of the British Columbia Packers Association the capital stock of the company was $4,000,000, of which $1,250,000 was in preference shares and $2,750,000 in common. Of the common stock, $500,000 was paid to the promoters, half of which went to Jarvis, Rollins, and their associates in the Eastern underwriting syndicate, and the other half was paid to me. On the same basis for the new company, the common stock allotted for promotion would be approximately $1,000,000 par value. In the case of the British Columbia Packers Association formation, the only cash payment to the promoters was for travelling and other personal disbursements, and the costs of incorporating the company and legal expenses, including searching titles, etc.

If the same procedure is followed in the present case, as was adopted in the former amalgamation, the capitalization of the new company would be as follows: –

$ 2,750,000 in 7% preference shares – to furnish
                                                    $2,200,000 cash.
5,500,000 "   common   "   – to complete payment
                                                    for plants.
1,000,000 "   common   "   – for promotion.
  750,000 "   common   "   – to be held in treasury.
$10,000,000 total capitalization.

This capitalization for 61 canneries compares very favourably with the issued capital of the present operators. The British Columbia Fishing & Packing Co., representing less than a third of the percentage it is expected to secure for the amalgamation, has an issued capital of $4,291,800. At the same ratio for the proposed new company, this would mean about $12,500,000 capitalization. I therefore think the $10,000,000 capitalization proposed is conservative.

63a. "Canneries Operating Now Compared to What is Proposed to Operate Under an Amalgamation," c. 1924

Skeena River. Skeena River pack for the past 8 years averaged 334,785 cases, with 15 canneries operating. An average annual pack per cannery of 22,300 cases. Eight canneries should put this pack up at 44,600 cases average per cannery. Under amalgamation the canneries proposed for operation would be the following: –

Balmoral cannery of the BC Fishing & Packing Co.
Oceanic   "   " " "   "   "   "
Inverness   "   " " J.H. Todd & Sons Ltd.
Claxton   "   " " Wallace Fisheries Ltd.
Carlisle   "   " " Kildala Packing Co.
North Pacific "   " " Anglo-BC Packing Co.
Sunnyside   "   " " Gosse-Millerd Co. Ltd.
Cassiar   "   " " Cassiar Packing Co.

Rivers Inlet. Rivers Inlet pack for the past 8 years averaged 98,022 cases, with 9 canneries operating. An average annual pack per cannery of 10,891 cases. Three canneries should put this pack up at 33,000 cases average per cannery. Under amalgamation the canneries proposed for operation would be the following:–

Wadhams cannery of the BC Fishing & Packing Co.
Brunswick "   " " "   "   "   "
Kildala   "   " " Kildala Packing Co.

Naas River. Naas River pack for the past 8 years averaged 105,521 cases, with 6 canneries operating. An average annual pack per cannery of 17,585 cases. Three canneries should put this pack up at 35,170 cases average per cannery. Under amalgamation the canneries proposed for operation would be the following:–

Mill Bay cannery of the Northern BC Fisheries Ltd.
Arrandale   "   " " Anglo-BC Packing Co. Ltd.
Wales Island "   " " M. Desbrisay & Co.

Other Locations. Under amalgamation the other canneries proposed for operation would be the following:–

Imperial cannery of the BC Fishing & Pgk. Co. on the Fraser River.
Ewen   "   " " "   "   "   " "   "   "
Vancouver   " " " Gosse-Millerd Co. Ltd.   " "   "   "
Esquimalt   " " " J.H. Todd & Sons Ltd. on Vancouver Is.
Kildonan   " " " Wallace Fisheries Ltd.   "   "   "
Alert Bay   " " " BC Fishing & Pkg. Co. at Alert Bay
Knight Inlet " " " Anglo-BC Pkg. Co. Ltd. on Knight's Inlet
Seymour   " " " "   " " " "   "   " Seymour Inlet
Smith's Inlet " " " Wallace Fisheries Ltd.   " Smith's Inlet
Namu   " " " Gosse-Millerd Co. Ltd. at Namu
Bella Coola " " " Northern BC Fisheries   " Bella Coola
Manitou   " " " Kildala Packing Co.   on Dean's Channel
Bella Bella " " " Gosse-Millerd Co. Ltd. at Bella Bella
Butedale   " " " Canadian Fishing Co.   " Butedale

Lowe Inlet	" " " BC Fishing & Pkg. Co.	" Lowe Inlet
Masset	" " " Wallace Fisheries Ltd.	on Queen Charl. Is.
Skidegate	" " " Maritime Fisheries Ltd.	" " " "
Lagoon Bay	" " " Canadian Fishing Co.	" " " "
Lockeport	" " " Lockeport Canning Co.	" " " "

Gosse-Millerd Co. Ltd. and Wallace Fisheries Ltd. If these two companies were taken over the new owners would easily be the largest operators in the province, would have nearly as many operating plants as the BC Fishing & Packing Co., would put up approximately the same sockeye pack and larger packs of other species than the latter company, and would have less than half its capitalization. Its plants would cover a wider territorial range and would be more equitably distributed. This is shown by the following: –

	Gosse-Wallace plants	*BCF&P Co.* plants
Fraser River	1	4
Skeena River	2	4
Naas River	1	1
Rivers Inlet	2	3
Smith's Inlet	1	0
Vancouver Island	2	0
Queen Charlotte Islants	1	0
Outlying districts	3	3
	13	15

The reason for believing these two companies can be purchased is that the Wallace Fisheries Ltd. has never paid a dividend, Gosse-Millerd Co. Ltd. has not done so in recent years; and while both are making good profits now, they were heavily hit during the recent period of depression. It will take them some time to make up for past losses and get on a dividend-paying basis. Furthermore, there are divided factions in both companies. The Wallace Fisheries Ltd. recently dismissed the former manager, and while this has resulted in more successful operations, there is friction with the present management also. The active management of Gosse-Millerd Co. Ltd. is in the hands of the younger Gosses, but their convivial habits affect their activities, and it is reported that recently the directors have intimated that unless there is a speedy improvement in this respect, a change of management will be made.

Summary. The 61 canneries hoped to be secured for the amalgamation packed an average for the past 8 years of 1,076,135 cases. An average annual pack per cannery of 17,641 cases. Thirty-three canneries should put this pack up at 32,600 cases average per cannery. The saving in packing costs in putting up this larger pack per cannery should be at least 25 cents per case,

Comparison With Other Salmon Canning Countries.

The average annual pack per cannery	in Alaska is	37,200 cases
" " " " " "	on Puget Sound	42,100 "
" " " " " "	in Siberia	44,000 "

Since 1893, the year of its formation, the Alaska Packers Association (APA) has packed a total of 30,952,587 cases. Crediting *all* the profits prior to 1918 to canning operations, and taking the actual canning results since then, the net profits total $12,662,795. This is an average annual profit of 40 cents per case on an average annual pack for the past 8 years of 49,000 cases to the cannery. As against this, the leading British Columbia packing company made an average annual profit of $1.03 per case with an average annual pack for the past 8 years of but 15,600 cases per cannery.

64. *Report: "Explanatory Notes Covering each of the Existing Companies it is Hoped to Secure for the Amalgamation," by Henry Doyle, c. 1925*

64a. 6/1 Notes [The original report was split up and the various sections filed alphabetically by company or cannery name.]

Anglo-British Columbia Packing Co. Ltd. This company [of English capitalists] commenced business in 1891, having acquired by purchase 7 canneries on the Fraser River and 2 on the Skeena River. Their interest at this time represented 25% of the industry in the province. Subsequently, they built the Good Hope cannery on Rivers Inlet and a cannery on Seymour Inlet, and purchased the Arrandale (for $50,000), and the Port Nelson (for $37,000), both on the Naas River, and the Knight's Inlet cannery. Despite these additions to their original holdings they have steadily lost their commanding position. Today, their 7 Fraser River plants and one on the Naas are dismantled or idle, and they represent only 9% of the industry in the province.

The company shares are largely held by the Bell-Irving interests, and the local management is in the agency of H. Bell-Irving & Co., which controls the insurance, receives a 2½% commission on purchases, and gets 5% for selling the pack (out of which they pay any brokerages necessary). This agency agreement has been so profitable to Messrs. Bell-Irving & Co. that in the past they were opposed to having the Anglo-British Columbia Packing Co. Ltd. amalgamate with others, thereby cutting off their agency profits. But Henry Bell-Irving is now well up in years and independently wealthy. Since 1921 the losses are known to have greatly exceeded $500,000, and the company's shareholders are very dissatisfied with the situation. Under these circumstances, Bell-Irving & Co. now express themselves as agreeable to join an amalgamation and, it is thought, will come in on reasonable terms. Their shares have a par value of £10 and, as the stock is listed on the London Stock Exchange, its present selling value can be easily ascertained.

The Anglo BC Packing Co. Ltd. also own the Fidalgo Island Canning Co., with one cannery on Puget Sound and several in Alaska. It does not, however, propose to dispose of any of its American interests. Most of the shareholders are residents of Great Britain, and it is understood they are prepared to sell even if their Vancouver connections were opposed. Under the circumstances it is possible that the control of stock could be purchased directly from the British holders for less than would have to be paid through negotiating with the Vancouver office. If this were done, a considerable saving may be effected in securing this company for the amalgamation. (Since commencing business in 1891 the company has paid out in dividends to shareholders approximately $2,000,000 or about 4 times the amount of the subscribed capital.) In 1924 the company purchased the Port Essington cannery from the Northern BC Fisheries Ltd. for $45,000. The new cannery is meant to replace their "BA" cannery which had been destroyed by fire and has not been rebuilt.

British Columbia Fishing & Packing Co. Ltd. Since commencing operations in 1902 the company has packed a total of 5,305,194 cases, on which the net profit has been $5,510,764. This is an average annual profit of $1.03 per case. 1922 was the only year in its history that the company has shown a loss. Since 1902 the company has paid in dividends to shareholders the sum of $2,3[?]4,696.

Originally this company was known as the British Columbia Packers Association, and was an amalgamation of 24 canneries on the Fraser River and 10 in northern BC. The amalgamation was formed by Henry Doyle of Vancouver, with the financial assistance of Toronto, Montreal, and Boston capital, represented by Æmelius Jarvis & Co., of Toronto, and E.W. Rollins & Co., of Boston. At the time of its formation the company represented 60% of the industry in British Columbia. Subsequently they acquired, by purchase, the Dominion [in 1909] (for $50,000) and Alexandra [in 1910] canneries on the Skeena River, and the Naas Harbour cannery (for $85,000) on the Naas River. In 1924, they also purchased from the BC Canning Co. the Oceanic cannery on the Skeena River, and the "RIC" cannery on Rivers Inlet, paying $62,000 for both properties. Despite these additions to their original holdings, the company to-day represents only a little over 21% of the canning industry in the province. In addition to their Canadian interests, the company in 1914 purchased the George & Barker cannery on Puget Sound, paying $150,000 for this property.

For stock-market purposes the present company was floated in 1921, each share of the British Columbia Packers Association stock [having been] exchanged for two shares of stock [in the new company], the British Columbia Fishing & Packing Co. Ltd. As shares of both companies had a par value of $100, this exchange was equivalent to a 100% stock dividend. Practically all of the stock is owned in eastern Canada, and it is understood to be widely distributed in small holdings, principally with the French Canadian population around Montreal. Since 1921 no dividends have been paid to shareholders [owing to the unsatisfactory packing and marketing conditions], and with no demand for the stock, the market value is very low. Recently it was down to $9, and today is quoted about $16. As the liquid assets alone are worth over $2,000,000, equal to over $50 per share, there is no valid reason why the market quotation is so low except for there being dissatisfaction amongst the stockholders.

Of the original 24 plants on the Fraser River, only 4 are now in operation, the balance having been closed and dismantled. Their northern plants are mostly well situated and in fair condition, although generally they are below the average as far as up-keep is concerned.

Since 1905, the management has been in the hands of Mr. W.H. Barker, formerly of the George & Barker Packing Co. and the Columbia River Packers Association. Mr. Barker is a thoroughly experienced packer, with exceptionally good executive ability. He has been very successful in his management of the company, and deservedly stands high with his shareholders. He is inclined, however, to be too conservative, and the average annual pack per cannery of his company if the lowest of any of the large operators in the province. Without a radical change in policy the company cannot compete on an even-cost basis with competitors that pack two or three times as much per cannery, more than this company has put up in past years. Mr. Barker is well along in years, is in poor health, and, for some time past, has been anxious to retire. He opposes an amalgamation, although his principal shareholders favour it. Negotiations, to be successful, would have to be transacted with the eastern Canadian interests, or control would have to be secured through Stock Exchange purchases. The latter course would unquestionably effect an enormous saving in the purchase price of this company's assets.

The stock is listed on the Montreal and Toronto Stock Exchanges, and Mr. Æmelius Jarvis of Toronto has been the active representative of the shareholders. Mr. Jarvis has recently been interviewed and agreed to put the company into an amalgamation if one can be effected. His idea is that if the fixed assets are thus disposed of, the liquid assets can be converted into cash and a dividend of over $50.00 per share paid to the shareholders of the present company. If Mr. Jarvis was reasonably sure the amalgamation would be effected he would doubtless acquire considerable [amounts] of the stock on his own account, therby making a handsome profit through his inside knowledge of what is transpiring. If, on the other hand, the underwriting syndicate formed to finance the amalgamation bought controlling interest on the open market, they could either make this profit for themselves, or utilise the sum realized from liquid assets to furnish part of the capital required for the new floatation. It is understood that at the present time Mr. Jarvis is not personally so heavily interested in the British Columbia Fishing & Packing Co. Ltd., having disposed of his holdings before the company ceased paying dividends.

Under ordinary circumstances it would be advisable to invite Mr. Jarvis's co-operation in forming the new company, since the British Columbia Fishing & Packing Co. are such large factors in the situation and he is personally anxious to have an amalgamation take place. But recently Mr. Jarvis has obtained considerable unenviable notoriety in Ontario. Since the disclosures were made public in the bond-purchasing matter, he has disposed of the business of Æmelius Jarvis & Co. and retired from active participation in the stock-and-bond business. Under the circumstances, his co-operation in floating the new company might prove more of a liability than an asset.

The capitalization of the British Columbia Fishing & Packing Co. Ltd. is $5,000,000, in 50,000 shares of $100 par value each. Of this, 42,918 shares have been issued. Purchasing a controlling interest on the Stock Exchange, and allowing for advancing prices which stock activities would stimulate, the average cost for sufficient to control should not exceed $30 per share. Presuming 60% of the issued capital stock was acquired in this way, it would entail an investment of $771,000. When subsequently the present liquid assets were converted into cash and divided amongst the shareholders, this 60% interest would receive about $1,250,000, leaving a profit of around $500,000 after repaying the amount used in purchasing the shares, besides leaving the buyers with 25,800 shares to be exchanged for such shares as they would be entitled to receive in the proposed new company. The directors of the British Columbia Fishing & Packing Co. Ltd. are as follows: W.H. Barker (Vancouver, President); Æmelius Jarvis (Toronto, Vice-President); J.M. Whitehead (Vancouver, General Manager); Campbell Sweeny, E.E. Evans, H.H. Morris (all of Vancouver); A.C. Flumerfelt (Victoria); Mark Workman, Dr. Milton L. Hersey, Geo. H. Smithers (all of Montreal); and E.W. Rollins (Boston).

Since the above was written, the company has not yet resumed dividend paying, yet the shares have advanced in value and are now (Sept. 1925) quoted on Exchange at 48½. The directors remain the same except that Sir Henry M. Pellatt, of Toronto, a large shareholder, has been added to the board. Æmelius Jarvis was found guilty in the bond transaction and sentenced to six months' imprisonment, which he served. He was also fined $200,000 and had to pay same before his release from gaol.

Despite their purchase of the BC Canning Co. interests, which nominally increased their percentage of the industry to 21⅖%, the percentage they put up of the 1924 pack was but 15⅖%. This is the smallest percentage they have represented for any year since the company commenced operating.

64b. 6/3 Notes

Canadian Fish & Cold Storage Co. This company originally confined their activities to fresh and frozen fish, having built a very large cold-storage plant at Prince Rupert. In 1913, they built a salmon cannery [Tuck's Inlet cannery] on the opposite shore of Prince Rupert harbour, about 1½ miles distant from the cold-storage plant. It is only the cannery that it is proposed to secure for the amalgamation.

The cannery, while depending on the Skeena River for its fish supply, is not on the river itself but is some 10 miles away. Nevertheless, they have secured good packs, their average comparing very favourably with plants better located. The plant is modern in every respect and is equipped with both tall and half-flat [canning] machinery.

In the past the company has not made a very good showing, although the canning branch has done as well as competing canneries. The cold-storage branch has been a "white elephant," having been erected at a far too expensive cost, and being greatly over-capitalized. Three cold-storage plants, each of equal capacity, could be erected for what was spent on this one alone. It is doubtful if the company ever will show satisfactory profits on the capital invested.

The company, however, does a large business in fresh- and frozen-fish products and is a very important factor in this branch of the fishing industry. Although acquiring its cold-storage interest is not contemplated, it might be a good investment if the plant could be obtained at a reasonable price. This might be effected since the shareholders (largely residents of Great Britain), cannot be satisfied with their present investment, and should be willing to merge them at a reasonable price with the amalgamated company. As far as known, the company has never paid a dividend, nor discharged the [large] special loan [it has acquired].

Canadian Fishing Co. Ltd. In 1868, Boston wholesale-fish dealers organized the New England Fish Co., with a capital of $5,000, for the
purpose of conducting the halibut industry as a co-operative organization. In 1877, several New York firms were admitted to membership. In
1894, the New England Fish Co. commenced operations in Vancouver,
BC, for the purpose of controlling the halibut industry on the Pacific
coast. About 1908, the New England Fish Co. was re-organized. Its
capital stock was greatly increased, its co-operative features eliminated,
and its operations conducted on ordinary business principles for the
benefit of its shareholders. Today, the company includes amongst its
shareholders nearly every dealer of consequence in the cities of Boston
and New York, and it is the largest individual factor in the fresh- and
frozen-fish industry in the United States.

In 1908, the Canadian Fishing Co. Ltd. was incorporated to handle
the New England Fish Co.'s Canadian interests, which at that time were
limited to fresh- and frozen-fish products. In 1918, the Canadian Fishing
Co. built a cannery [Home cannery] in connection with their cold-storage
plant at Vancouver. In 1922, they operated, under lease, the Ocean
Packing Co.'s plant at Lagoon [Bay], Queen Charlotte Islands. In 1923,
they purchased that cannery and also the three canneries of the Western
Packers Ltd., situated respectively at Shushartie Bay (Vancouver Island), Marguerite Bay (on Smith's Inlet), and Butedale (near Wright's
Sound). The purchase price for the Western Packers plants is understood to have been $202,000.

The Vancouver canning plant is poorly situated from a salmon-
canning standpoint, all the [fish] supplies having to be brought from
some distance to be processed. But it is handy for the company, since
they use large quantities of salmon for their fresh- and frozen-fish trade,
and these have to be brought to Vancouver in any event. After selecting
such [fish] as are suitable of these departments, the remaining are utilized by the cannery. The Shushartie and Marguerite bay canneries are
situated in areas where no very large packs can be looked for, but the
plants are modern and well equipped. Under an amalgamation, both of
them would probably be closed, and their machinery and plants utilized
to enlarge some plants more advantageously situated for profitable operation. The Butedale cannery is the best cannery asset the company owns,
and is capable of considerably greater development than its past operations would indicate. The plant is well situated, modern, and is operated
by water power. A cold-storage plant is included in the property, and
this also is capable of considerably greater development.

The Canadian Fishing Co., and its parent organization, the New England Fish Co., have but recently become interested in the salmon-
canning industry. However, with the large capital at their command, the

knowledge of the fishing industry [they possess], and the splendid management they [exhibit], this company promises to become a leading and aggressive factor in the industry, at least as far as British Columbia is concerned. For this reason, it is very desirable that their canneries be secured for the amalgamation if at all possible.

It might be advisable to try and get the Eastern shareholders of the New England Fish Co. to become members of the underwriting syndicate and to have them merge their British Columbia canneries (they also operate two in Alaska) in the amalgamated company, retaining for their existing company the fresh and frozen fish branches of their activities. It is possible, but not probable, that they would dispose of their cannery interest on a sale basis, but they might be willing to let this department of their present business receive the benefits and increased profits which the amalgamation would effect. By becoming shareholders in the new company in the same ratio their present canneries bear to the canning industry in this province as a whole they would continue as operators, but they would make more on their investment than is possible under the conditions existing at present.

Mr. A.L. Hager is the manager of the New England Fish Co.'s and Canadian Fishing Co.'s investments on this coast. He is one of the best-informed fish dealers on this continent, a hard worker, of great executive capacity, and is highly regarded in the business community. Should his company's cannery interests enter the amalgamation, Mr. Hager would undoubtedly continue to manage the remaining interests of his present companies. This should not[, however,] preclude his taking an active part in the management of the new company's affairs. His co-operation would be an asset which should be secured if at all possible.

If the proposal is put before the Eastern shareholders of the New England Fish Co., and if it is made clear to them that what is desired is the segregation of their canning interests from their other investments, and their transfer to an amalgamation where its earnings will be greater, and if it is further proposed to have Mr. Hager take an active interest in the management of the amalgamated company, there should be no great difficulty in securing their co-operation. Since they would be an aggressive and dangerous competitor if they remained independent operators, it is very desirable that every effort be made to include their canneries in the amalgamation.

Early in 1925 the company purchased the three plants owned by the Kildala Packing Co. Purchase consideration was approximately $225,000 cash. As the Kildala Pkg. Co. averaged 45,572 cases for the 8 years 1916–1924, it gives the Canadian Fishing Co. a substantial increase in their yearly output.

Cassiar Packing Co. Ltd. The company was formed in 1903, and from then to 1923 inclusive there were packed 347,543 cases, on which the net profit was $356,661. This is an average annual profit of $1.03 per case. In only two years did the company show a loss. Since 1903 the amount paid out in dividends has been $278,600 on an original investment of $12,000.

The [Cassiar] cannery is situated on the Skeena River, on the line of the Grand Trunk Pacific Railway, with which it has spur connections. It has both tall and half-flat lines and is operated by water power. The plant is modern in every respect, well built, well situated, and it has the lowest insurance rate of any cannery on the Skeena River. The General Appraisal Co. of Seattle appraised the company's assets in 1921 at $130,000 replacement value. Cassiar Packing Company is owned by Col. J.M. MacMillan (⅖ths interest), Mrs. MacMillan (⅕th), A. Wallace (⅕th), and Henry Doyle (⅕th).

64c. 6/4 Note

M. Desbrisay & Co. This company, a private partnership, has for many years owned the Gulf of Georgia cannery at Steveston, on the Fraser River. The cannery is one of the largest and best situated of all the Fraser River canneries, but during recent years the owners have made no attempt to secure their share of the fish, and despite the advantages they possess, the packs obtained have been less than the average for the river.

In 1911, the company purchased, for $5,000, the cannery on Wales Island, Portland Inlet, which was built and operated by Americans prior to Wales Island becoming Canadian territory through the decision of the Alaska Boundary Arbitration Tribunal. The cannery is a large one, well situated, and capable of obtaining bigger packs than it has put up in past years. This season instead of operating it themselves, Messrs. Desbrisay & Co. have leased it to the Canadian Fishing Co. Messrs. Desbrisay & Co. are anxious to have an amalgamation effected and no difficulty is anticipated in securing their plants at a reasonable figure.

64d 6/6 Note

Gosse-Millerd Co. Ltd. The principal shareholder of this company is Capt. R.E. Gosse, originally a building contractor, who erected many of the canneries in this province. In 1909 he purchased the Burrard cannery on the Fraser River (subsequently burned down and not rebuilt). In 1914 he bought the Vancouver cannery and the Fraser River cannery of the defunct Canadian Canning Co., paying $45,000 for the assets, which included a complete line of Bliss can-making machinery, which had been installed at a cost of $40,000. In 1915, the company purchased the East Bella Bella cannery [Bella Bella #1], situated near Milbank Sound, paying $27,000 for same. In 1916, it built the Sunnyside cannery on the Skeena River. In 1919, it built the McTavish cannery on Rivers Inlet and the San Mateo cannery on the west coast of Vancouver Island. And in 1924, it purchased, for $180,000, the Namu cannery from Northern BC Fisheries Ltd.

The Vancouver and Fraser River canneries were adjoining plants, and under the present ownership have been operated as a single unit. Here all the cans used at their various canneries have been made. The location [Sea Island] is one of the best on the Fraser River, the plant is modern and up to date in every respect; and the can-making plant is one of the best assets the company possesses. The East Bella Bella cannery was purchased for much less than its real value, the former owners not realizing its possibilities. Under the present management the plant was greatly enlarged, and the packs secured have been uniformly big and much in excess of the general average for the province. In December of 1923, the cannery was totally destroyed by fire, and with the money received from the fire insurance, the company purchased the Namu cannery, 25 miles distant from East Bella Bella. The company has also partially rebuilt the East Bella Bella plant, and ultimately expects to have a new cannery here of still greater capacity than it formerly possessed.

In purchasing Namu at $180,000, Gosse-Millerd Co. Ltd. secured an asset which the General Appraisal Co. of Seattle had valued at $332,000. Namu is considered the best plant in British Columbia, both for its location and for the value of its assets. The cannery is one of the largest and best equipped in the province, and under proper management can pack 75,000 to 100,000 cases annually. In addition, there is a sawmill and box factory at which all the company's requirements in salmon boxes, etc., are manufactured.

The Sunnyside cannery on the Skeena River is situated on the Grand Trunk Pacific Railway, with which it has spur connections. The location is good, the plant modern and up to date in every respect, and the packs obtained in the past have been above average for this district.

The McTavish cannery on Rivers Inlet is modern and well equipped, though small. The location is also good. But under an amalgamation this plant would be dismantled and its equipement used to enlarge one of the larger and better-situated canneries on the Inlet. This season the McTavish cannery is not being operated, but its boats are fishing and the pack is being made at Namu.

The San Mateo cannery was built primarily for packing chum salmon. Owing to adverse market conditions, it has never been operated to capacity. The plant is modern and the location is good, but, under an amalgamation, the cannery would be dismantled and the plant used to enlarge one of the other canneries in that vicinity.

While Gosse-Millerd Co. Ltd. have recently become the second largest factors in the salmon-canning industry in this province, their activities have placed a great strain on their available capital. Like all their competitors, the company lost heavily during the late depression. It is heavily in debt to its bankers, and some of its shareholders are very dissatisfied. This dissatisfaction recently resulted in Mr. Millerd's retirement from participation in the company's management, although he still retains his interests as a shareholder.

Although the company is aggressive in its operations, is a good packer, and has built up some excellent marketing connections, there is every reason to believe it could be brought into an amalgamation. To leave it out would be dangerous, since its holdings are well distributed in all the important salmon-canning centres; it understands the business thoroughly; and it is a hard competitor to fight. On the other hand, if it was secured for the amalgamation, along with some of the other large operators, the packs which could be made would be so large, per cannery, that smaller competitors could not pack at an equal cost and would therefore be compelled by this fact to work in harmony with the amalgamated company.

Capt. Gosse is well advanced in years and is in poor health, and while it has been largely due to his ability and aggressiveness that the company has advanced so rapidly, he is now leaving the active management to his two sons. They are "chips off the old block," and, having been born and brought up in the fishing business, are experienced cannerymen. Their services would undoubtedly be required by the proposed new company. [As a final note,] early in 1925 the company purchased the Kimsquit cannery from the Northern BC Fisheries Ltd., the purchase consideration being $20,000 cash.

With the acquisition of Namu and Kimsquit the company now owns 7 canneries situated as follows:– Vancouver (Fraser River); Sunnyside (Skeena River); McTavish (Rivers Inlet); Namu (Fitzhugh Sound); [East] Bella Bella (between Fitzhugh and Milbank[e] sounds); Kimsquit (Dean's Channel); and San Mateo (west coast of Vancouver Island). These plants give the operators representation in every important sockeye-fishing district except Naas River, and most of [these districts] are particularly well situated as regards the cheaper grades. The combined annual packing capacity easily exceeds 350,000 cases, and fish are available for this output.

In addition to salmon canning, the plants at Namu and the Fraser River have ample can-making capacity for all the company's requirements, while Namu has a complete saw mill and box-making plant. At the San Mateo plant, they have installed a Hiller Reduction Unit for manufacturing oil and fertilizer from pilchards. This branch of the fishing industry promises to be extremely profitable. In addition, pilchards suitable for canning are plentiful, and the company, in former years, put up many thousands of cases of canned pilchards and herring. It can do so again at any future time when market conditions warrant. Dry-salting of herring for the Chinese trade has also been done on a large scale at the San Mateo plant and this branch of the business has produced excellent returns.

64e. 6/7 Note

Kildala Packing Co. Ltd. This company commenced operations in 1906 by purchasing the Carlisle cannery on Skeena River for $30,000. The operators subsequently built the Kildala cannery on Rivers Inlet and the Manitou on Dean's Channel. All three plants have been money makers, and the company has been one of the most successful in the province.

The Carlisle cannery has one of the best locations on the Skeena River and has a complete Troyer Fox can-making line, with which are manufactured the cans used in all three plants owned by this company. This can-making machinery represents an investment in itself of about $45,000. The Kildala cannery is almost equally as well situated on Rivers Inlet, but the Manitou, which is near the head of Dean's Channel, would be better situated if near the mouth. All three canneries are well equipped, modern, and in a first-class condition as to up-keep.

The company is owned by Geo. W. and S.E. Dawson (⅖ths), A.J. & G.A. Buttimer (⅖ths), and D. Groves and T.P. Lake (⅕th). Geo. Dawson is also a brother-in-law of the Buttimers, and they have been jointly interested in the salmon-canning industry for the past 31 years. In 1919, however, differences of opinion occurred between Geo. Dawson and his brother-in-law and resulted in such bitterness that they are no longer on speaking terms. In the quarrel, Groves and Lake sided with the Dawsons, giving the latter a majority of the stock, and the Buttimers have since had no say as to the company's operations.

George Dawson is a man well up in years, of an almost ungovernable temper, and extremely difficult to get along with. He is hardly on speaking terms with any of his competitors. Under the existing state of affairs he dictates the company's actions. He is anxious to sell the business – to which the Buttimers were originally opposed – but will only consider selling on a cash basis. The price asked for the three canneries is $175,000. Owing to the fact that Dawson will not declare a dividend to disburse any of the company's surplus – which includes over $300,000 in Canadian War Bonds – the Buttimers are now agreeable to having the company sold.

The company has made money consistently since commencing business. For the period 1916–1919 inclusive, the net profits made were $384,000, after providing $153,000 for Reserve, Depreciation, etc. The pack secured during this period was 200,326 cases, and net profits amounted to $1.91 per case. Even during the recent depression they have continued to show profits, owing to the revenues derived from their outside investments and their ability to finance without borrowing from their bankers to any great extent.

Considering the locations and good condition of their plants, [the fact that they own] their own can-making plant, and the good reputation [they have] as packers, the property, at the price for which it is offered, is one of the best bargains in the province.

64f. 6/8 Notes

Lockeport Canning Co. Ltd. The Lockeport cannery was built in 1918, but after operating for one season the company went into liquidation and was lost to the original investors. In 1923 the plant was operated under lease. It can be purchased at a very reasonable figure.

The cannery is located at Lockeport, near the southern end of the Queen Charlotte Islands. The waters in its vicinity contain good quantities of salmon of the chum and pink varieties, although pinks run only every second year. The location is much better than the packs obtained in past years would indicate. Under proper management, the property could be made a good and profitable investment.

Maritime Fisheries Ltd. [The company] owns and operates 2 canneries. One is located at Haysport, Skeena River. Haysport cannery was built as a cold-storage centre in 1913, and then made into a cannery in 1919. The price paid for the site and buildings when acquired from the former owners was approximately $10,000. The site is on the Grand Trunk Pacific Railway line, to which a spur connection has been laid. It is also well situated as regards fishing. The other cannery is located at Alliford Bay, Skidegate Inlet, Queen Charlotte Islands. The present owners bought all the assets located at Alliford Bay belonging to the defunct BC Fisheries Ltd. The price paid was $50,000, and the book value of the properties acquired was claimed to be $1,000,000. The receiver of the BC Fisheries Ltd. values same in 1914 as follows:– land, buildings, etc. ($60,000); cannery buildings and plant ($50,000); fertilizing buildings and plant ($120,000); saltery ($45,000); oilery ($50,000); tugs, boats, etc. ($175,000); stores ($50,000); machinery purchased in England ($60,000); other assets ($30,000), for a grand total of $640,000.

The properties were purchased from the receiver by Sir Thomas Lipton in his own name, but it is understood that the Maritime Fisheries Ltd., the real owners, comprise the following shareholders: – Sir Thomas Lipton (London); Andrew Weir (Glasgow); C. Williamson Milne (London); and D.T. Sandison (Vancouver). Sandison is not supposed to have much of an interest himself but represents the other shareholders mentioned. He is the manager of the company, but is rather weak and has no real knowledge of salmon canning. Under his operation they have not taken advantage of their opportunities, which, especially in the Skidegate plant, are exceptionally good. The Old Country shareholders cannot be satisfied with the results achieved so far, and there is but little doubt that they would join an amalgamation at a reasonable price. The Maritime Fisheries Ltd. has an authorized capital of $500,000 of which $350,000, it is claimed, had been subscribed and paid up in cash.

64g. 6/9 Note

Northern BC Fisheries Ltd. This company was formed in 1918, being an amalgamation of the seven canneries previously operated independently, but all owned by R.V. Winch & Co., Henry Doyle, and their associates. R.V. Winch & Co. owned the controlling interest, acted as managers and financial agents, and dictated the policy of the company.

Prior to the formation of the Northern BC Fisheries Ltd., Winch & Co. acted in a like capacity for the individual companies. Up to 1918, the properties had consistently made a good profit, most of which was used for the enlargement and improvement of the plants. But, in the depression period, the company was caught with heavy stocks of canned fish which they were unable to dispose of. To add to their difficulties, the company's bankers [Royal Bank] that year superannuated their former manager, who was familiar with the salmon-canning industry, replacing him with a man from eastern Canada who was totally unacquainted with the industry. The result was constant friction with, and interference from, the bank that prevented the company packing to capacity, as their competitors did. As a result, costs were higher than necessary, and the company made further losses. In 1921, the bank took the management into its own hands, with the usual result of ignorant mismanagement, and still further losses were made. In 1924, the bank decided against all further attempts to operate the properties, offering them for sale or lease. The Namu plant, the company's best asset, was sold for about half of its value; the Port Edward plant was abandoned to a mortgagee (holding a mortgage of $21,000 against the property appraised by the General Appraisal Co. of Seattle at $153,739, replacement value); and the Port

Essington and Bella Coola canneries were leased to competitive companies for nominal rents.

It may be mentioned in passing that the action taken by this bank was identical with all the other salmon-cannery accounts it financed. Every other banking institution has stood by its customers and is seeing them through the present period of depression. Practically all canning companies made heavy losses during this period. Had other banks followed the same course this bank pursued, two-thirds of the operating companies would have been put in a similar condition to this bank's customers. Under the circumstances, the Northern BC Fisheries Ltd. cannot be blamed for bad management. That their properties are of equal value to competitive plants is shown by the fact that it has been former competitors that have purchased one of the plants and leased the others.

Although the Port Edward cannery was abandoned by the bank to the mortgagee, the latter is friendly to the Northern BC fisheries Ltd. shareholders, and is carrying the mortgage for their individual account. This property therefore can be considered as one of the canneries which Northern BC Fisheries Ltd. would be prepared to put into the amalgamation along with their remaining properties.

The plants under lease have provisos whereby the leases are cancelled in the event of a sale being made. Therefore, these leases are not a bar to the properties being included in an amalgamation.

All the properties owned by the Northern BC Fisheries Ltd. are modern, well equipped, and operated by water power. In equipment and condition of up-keep, they compare favourably with any in the province. The Mill Bay and Kumeon plants are located on the Naas River, the former at the head of the fishing area, the latter at its commencement. Mill Bay, the largest cannery on Naas River, has put up the greatest packs. It is cheap to operate, and has a cold-storage plant of 2,000,000 lbs. capacity, also operated by water power. Kumeon is a smaller plant, and under an amalgamation would be dismantled and its equipment transferred to another locality. The Port Essington and Port Edward canneries are on the Skeena River. The former is better located than the latter, but both plants are comparatively small. Under an amalgamation they would be dismantled and their equipment placed in larger and better-located canneries. Kimsquit cannery is on Dean's Channel opposite the Manitou cannery of the Kildala Packing Co. Under an amalgamation it would probably be dismantled and its equipment added to the Manitou, as one cannery can handle the entire pack for this area. The Bella Coola cannery possesses the best site for a cannery in its vicinity. Under an amalgamation which included the British Columbia Fishing & Packing Co., the latter's Bella Coola cannery would be dismantled and its equipment added to this one. The Bella Coola fishing area has never been properly developed; it is capable of producing far larger packs than anything obtained in past years. [It should be noted than] subsequent to the sale of Namu cannery to Gosse-Millerd Co. Ltd., that company puchased the Kimsquit cannery for $20,000. Port Essington cannery was sold to ABC Packing Co. for $45,000, Port Edward to Pacific American Fisheries Co., of Bellingham, for $45,000, and the Mill Bay cannery to Wallace Fisheries Ltd., also for $45,000.

Even under the restraints on operations caused by the bank's interference, the company ranked second in production amongst all operating companies in the province. The pack figures do not, however, give a true indication of what the plants are capable of packing. Under proper and unimpeded management the company could have packed 200,000 cases annually, as the fish were available and the canneries possessed the necessary capacity. Properly run, the company could show larger profits proportionately than most of their competitors, since their average pack per cannery would be greater, and the cost correspondingly reduced.

64h. 6/10 Notes

Provincial Canning Co. Ltd. This company commenced business in 1917, the owners being Mr. Wm. Todd, of J.H. Todd & Sons, and Robt. Johnston, who is the manager of Messrs. Todd & Sons canneries in northern British Columbia. It has therefore to be treated as if part of the latter company's interests, since its inclusion in an amalgamation would be contingent on Messrs. J.H. Todd & Sons' properties also being acquired.

The cannery has a good location, is well equipped, though small, but under amalgamation would be dismantled and its machinery installed in one of the larger plants on Rivers Inlet.

Standard Packing Co. Ltd. This company, owned by Frank Inrig, Rivers Inlet manager for the BC Fishing & Packing Co., and his associates, secured a license in 1922 and commenced operations the season of 1923. From an operating standpoint it is of little value to include this company in an amalgamation, but its value to the latter lies, first, in the fact that it has a license to operate; second, all the Rivers Inlet canneries should be absorbed by the new company (in order to give them control of that district); and third, Inrig has been manager for the BC Fishing & Packing Co. for about 15 years and is so familiar with fishermen and fishing conditions on the Inlet that it would not be abvisable to leave him an independent.

What price would be paid depends on the amount of money they have already invested. This is understood to be small and it is felt that $40,000 is more than sufficient to cover. Perhaps their assets can be secured for a considerably lesser sum ...

64i. 6/17 Note

Summerville [#2] Cannery. This cannery is on the Naas River. It is owned by Evans, Coleman & Evans of Vancouver, who built it in 1918 at a cost of approximately $90,000. Evans, Coleman & Evans were largely interested in the canned salmon industry as distributors of the pack, but entered the packing business as operators. This adversely affected their standing with the older operating companies. Furthermore, they lacked practical experience and secured but mediocre packs. The depression in the industry was just commencing when they undertook the enterprise. As a consequence, the investment has been a losing one. In 1923, they leased the plant to Mr. Frank Millerd, who has since operated it. The cannery is modern and well equipped, though small. The location is fair, but the water supply is limited. Under amalgamation the plant would be dismantled.

There would be no difficulty in securing this property for the amalgamation as Evans, Coleman & Evans are anxious to get out of this branch of the business, and Mr. Millerd is favourable to an amalgamation of both this plant and his interests in the Gosse-Millerd Co. Ltd. properties.

64j. 6/10 Notes

J.H. Todd & Sons Ltd. In continuity of operation, Messrs. Todd & Sons is the oldest operating company in the province, having [acquired] its first cannery [the Richmond], on the Fraser River, in 1882. It is a private company, immensely wealthy, and its brands are well established and favourably known throughout the British Empire. Next to the BC Fishing & Packing Co., it enjoys the largest trade in Canada.

The company owns three canneries, one on the Skeena River, one on Rivers Inlet, and the third at Esquimalt, near Victoria. The latter obtains its principal supply from fish traps on the Juan de Fuca Straits – the only part of British Columbia in which trap fishing is permitted. In addition the company had a cannery [Richmond] on the Fraser River, near its mouth, but this was destroyed by fire in the spring of 1924[?].

The Inverness cannery has one of the best sites on the Skeena River, is on the line of the Grand Trunk Pacific Railway, and is large, modern, and up to date. Under amalgamation this would be one of the plants operated, with its capacity increased by the installation of machinery from some of the plants to be dismantled. The Beaver cannery on Rivers

Inlet is also well located and modern, but under amalgamation would be closed and dismantled. The Esquimalt cannery is well situated for handling trap-caught fish, but until the Fraser River sockeye run is restored, large packs cannot be looked for. There should, however, be a good profit made, as trap-caught fish should average less in cost than fish taken elsewhere with gill nets.

If these properties are acquired, and their acquisition is most desirable, it would have to be on a cash-purchase basis, and in addition to payment for their physical assets, payment would have to be made for their brands and goodwill. As independent competitors, Messrs. Todd & Sons Ltd. would be dangerous. Their wealth, and the trade they command, make them formidable, while their methods have always been selfish and competitors have never considered them reliable.

While very close and anxious for profit themselves, they apparently hate to see anyone else make money. When the British Columbia Packers Association was formed, they verbally agreed to enter that amalgamation; but once its formation was assured, they repudiated their word and remained free lances [sic]. Recently, like their competitors, they made heavy losses and expressed themselves as anxious to sell out. But when solicited to amalgamate with others, they declined to join, in the belief that with the others amalgamated, but as independent operators themselves, they could repeat their former successes.

If it became known to them that an amalgamation was contemplated they would not sell out even on a cash basis, and the only way in which their plants can be secured for the new company will be to deal with them first, buying their assets and business as if this was the only property the purchasers contemplated acquiring. Messrs. Todd & Sons will not give an option on their properties, and cannot be relied upon to live up to an agreement to sell unless they are tied hard and fast when negotiations are first entered into. For this reason, only a cash-purchase proposition can be successful. Once it was made known that the Todd interests had been secured, the way would be made much easier for securing other companies. Many would hesitate to join with Messrs. Todd & Sons as free lances, while anxious to amalgamate if this company's interests were secured.

Mr. J.H. Todd has been dead many years, but his son, Mr. Chas. F. Todd, and the latter's sons continue the business. The younger men are not adverse to joining an amalgamation, but the father dictates the company's actions and is the stumbling block to its participation. He is a man of about 70 years of age, but active and shrewd in business. He has few friends, and is simply a money-making machine – albeit a very successful one. Under ordinary circumstances it would be impossible to get him to sell out, but he hates to make losses, and if advantage is taken of this before an improvement sets in, and he is approached in the manner suggested, there is a good chance that the interests of this company may be acquired.

Wallace Fisheries Ltd. This company was formed in 1911, when the Claxton cannery on the Skeena river was purchased from the Wallace Bros. Packing Co., for approximately $200,000; the Alberni cannery from the Alberni Packing Co., for about $60,000; the Strathcona cannery on Rivers Inlet from the Strathcona Packing Co., for $150,000; and the Hickey cannery on Smith's Inlet, for $300,000. The money to pay for these purchases was provided by a bond issue of $750,000, and the issued share capital of $1,500,000 was given as a bonus to the syndicate taking up the bonds.

The company has been over-capitalized from the beginning, the management has not been good, and heavy losses have been made. No dividends have ever been paid, and at the present time $500,000 worth of bonded indebtedness still remains, and the company is heavily in debt to its bankers.

Originally the principal shareholders were as follows: A.D. McRae, Davidson & McRae, Jno. A. Hombird [sic], Geo. C. Howe, E.J. Palmer, J.M. MacMillan, Peter Wallace, and A.D. Davidson. A.D. McRae was the leading spirit in the organization, Howe was his father-in-law, Davidson his partner, and Hombird and Palmer business associates in other enterprises. Through these connections, McRae controlled the company, put in his own manager, and dictated the company policy. Since then, Howe, Davidson, Hombird, and Palmer have died, and their heirs and the executors of the two last mentioned are dissatisfied with the showing made under the McRae regime. Wallace and MacMillan are practical and experienced cannerymen and have always been dissatisfied with the management, and with the estates of Hombird and Palmer now supporting them, they control the situation. Owing to illness, Mr. F.E. Burke, the general manager, has been given a year's leave of absence on half pay, and Peter Wallace is now acting manager. It is doubtful if Mr. Burke will again occupy the position.

All the properties are good. Properly managed, the company should be one of the best revenue producers in the industry. Claxton cannery has the best situation on the Skeena River, and puts up the largest packs. It is large, up to date, and well equipped in every respect, and has a cold-storage plant in connection with it. Both cannery and cold-storage are operated by water power. Under an amalgamation this plant would be the most valuable of its assets on the Skeena River.

The Strathcona cannery on Rivers Inlet is also a first-class plant, modern and well equipped, but under amalgamation would be closed and dismantled. The Smith's Inlet cannery is equally good. Under amalgamation – and if the Canadian Fishing Co.'s Marguerite Bay cannery is secured – this plant would receive the Marguerite Bay machinery and equipment and do the company's packing for that area. The Alberni [Kildonan] cannery has been entirely rebuilt and a large cold storage erected in connection therewith. This property would do the new company's packing on the west coast of Vancouver Island, receiving the machinery and equipment from Gosse-Millerd Co. Ltd.'s San Mateo cannery. In addition to salmon canning and freezing herring for halibut bait, it would carry on with the dry-salting of chum salmon and herring for the Japanese and Chinese markets. This dry-salting business has assumed considerable proportions in recent years, and the profits made on these commodities have been the only redeeming feature of the company's operations in the past few years. Mr. Peter Wallace was the manager of this plant until his recent appointment as acting general manager of the company.

In addition to the canneries mentioned above, which were acquired by purchase, the company also built two new ones, one at Quatsino Sound at the head of Vancouver Island, and the other at Masset Inlet, Queen Charlotte Islands. The Quatsino plant was in a poor location, only having a fair run of fish, and this only in every second year, and has not been operated for a long time. It cannot be considered an asset of any value. The Masset cannery was originally built [in 1911] at Naden Harbour, about 20 miles from Masset Inlet, but the location was found to be unsatisfactory. It was then rebuilt at its present location [Woden/Watun River, Masset Inlet], which is an excellent one, and large packs are secured every second year when the pink salmon run. The cannery building, however, was not erected on as suitable a site as it should have been, and the ravages of teredoes make necessary constant renewal of the foundations. It may be found more economical in the long run to build on the proper, and nearby, site, rather than continue expending so much on keeping up the present structure.

Both factions of the shareholders in the Wallace Fisheries Ltd. are keen for an amalgamation, and its assets can be acquired for much less than their cost to the present owners. The company enjoys an excellent reputation for its products. It is the fifth largest operator in the industry, and third in its production of the valuable sockeye species. In 1925, the company purchased the Mill Bay cannery from the Northern BC Fisheries Ltd. for $45,000 cash.

With the acquisition of Mill Bay the company now owns six operating plants (the Quatsino plant not having been operated for many years), situated as follows: Claxton (Skeena River), Mill Bay (Naas River), Strathcona (Rivers Inlet), Hickey (Smith's Inlet), Masset (Queen Charlotte Islands), and Kildonan (west coast of Vancouver Island). These plants give the company representation in every important sockeye-fishing district, except the Fraser River. The plants are all well located as regards the cheaper grades. The combined annual packing capacity exceeds 250,000 cases, with sufficient supply available to insure capacity packs, except at Masset where pink salmon only run every second year.

In addition to salmon canneries, the Kildonan, Claxton, and Mill Bay operations include cold-storage plants (the latter, however, is dismantled of its machinery), all of which, as well as the canneries at the point mentioned, are operated by water power. Kildonan cannery has a Hiller Reduction Unit for manufacturing oil and fertilizer from pilchards. It has packed large quantities of canned pilchards and herring and many thousand tons of dry-salted herring. Both the reduction and dry-salting operations have shown excellent profits. The company has a can-making plant at Kildonan of sufficient capacity for all of its requirements.

64k. 6/7 Note: "Additional Possibility"

Wm. Hickey & Son. This property [Kingcome Inlet cannery] is not included in the list of those proposed for the amalgamation, as it was sold this spring [to J.J. Stump] and the new owner may not be willing to dispose of his purchase. However, he is a man of no experience in the business, and is reported to have already made mistakes which may dampen his ardour. Therefore, this explanatory note is included in the dossier on the chance that the plant might be acquired.

The cannery was built at Kingcombe Inlet in 1914 [by Guilford Fish Co. Ltd.] but without sufficient investment to complete the undertaking, and the company was, from the first, in financial difficulties. About January 1916, Wm. Hickey, an old and experienced salmon canner, became interested, putting up $10,000 in cash, for which he received a 51% interest. Subsequently, Hickey secured most, if not all, of the company stock. In 1921 he changed the title [of the company] from the Preston Packing Co. to Wm. Hickey & Son. Under Hickey's management the company did well and made good profits up to the time the depression set in in the salmon-canning industry. Between the losses incurred and his banker's unwillingness to finance further operations the company was forced to make an assignment; and the property, which represented an investment of over $50,000, was sold to the present owner for $38,000. If it could be secured for a reasonable increase over its cost to the present owner he might sell, and the property is worth purchasing as it is capable of greater development than it has received in past years.

64m. 6/22 "Companies and Number of Plants Proposed for Amalgamation," c. 1925

Company	Skeena River	Naas River	Rivers Inlet	Fraser River	Van. Isl.	Other Localities	Total	Average No Cases Packed Annually	Estimated or Book Value	Estimated Purchase Price
BC Fish & Pkg. Co.	4	1	3	6		3	17	264,056	$2,431,534	$2,500,000
NBC Fisheries Ltd.	2	2				2	6	124,440	503,262	450,000
ABC Packing Co.	2	1	1			2	6	113,617	600,000	600,000
Gosse-Millerd Co. Ltd.	1		1	1	1	2	6	113,161	600,000	600,000
Wallace Fisheries Ltd.	1		1		1	2	5	100,011	600,000	500,000
J.H. Todd & Sons	1		1		1		3	78,903	400,000	500,000
Provincial Canning Co.			1				1	10,555	75,000	75,000
Kildala Packing Co.	1		1			1	3	45,572	275,000	175,000
M. Desbrisay & Co.		1		1			2	34,287	150,000	100,000
Maritime Fisheries Ltd.	1					1	2	26,626	150,000	150,000
Cassiar Packing Co.	1						1	18,492	94,413	100,000
Summerville [sic] Canning Co.		1					1	13,500	75,000	70,000
Lockeport Canning Co.						1	1	11,000	50,000	40,000
Standard Packing Co.			1				1	4,000	40,000	40,000
Canadian Fishing Co.				1	1	3	5	95,367	500,000	500,000
Canadian F.&C.S. Co.	1						1	22,558	100,000	100,000
	15	6	10	9	4	17	61	1,076,145	$6,944,219	$6,500,000

Above includes all canneries on Skeena River
 "   "   "   " Naas River
 "   "   "   " Rivers Inlet
 "   9 out of 13 "   Fraser River
 "   4 " 10   "   Vancouver Island
 "   15 " 16   in Outlying Districts
 "   61 " 72   of the total of operating canneries in B.C.

61 canneries packed an average of 1,076,145 cases per annum
(an average per cannery, per year, of 17,641 cases).

641. 6/10 Note: "Additional Possibility"

Quathiaski Canning Co. Ltd. This property is not listed amongst those proposed for inclusion in the amalgamation, for, although well worth having, it is not essential to the enterprise, and it is doubtful if Mr. W.E. Anderson, the sole owner, would be willing to sell. The cannery is located in a good fishing area, near Seymour Narrows, 125 miles north of Vancouver[, near Campbell River]. The plant is modern, well equipped, and up to date, and it has been one of the most profitable investments in the canned-salmon industry. Mr. Anderson is an experienced cannery-man, quiet and attentive to business. He devotes all his energies to this one undertaking and has become independently well off from his own-ership of the property. Under the circumstances, he is not likely to consider disposing of it, although its acquisition would be an advantage to the amalgamation. On the other hand, to leave him out would not greatly affect the new company's operations, as the locality is one in which it would have no conflicting interests, nor would he adversely affect its operations elsewhere. As a competitor he would be a friendly one.

65. *2/13 Letter: Doyle to A.M. Lester, California*   RR#1, Ladner, BC
       Packing Corporation, San Francisco   1st October 1925

Dear Sirs:

In submitting to you the proposal that your company should enter the salmon-canning industry in British Columbia I would point out the following advantages:

1. It would help to make up the shortage in the Alaska Packers Association's annual packs occasioned by governmental restrictions in Alaska.
2. It would provide stocks for the Australian business that up to the present you have supplied with American canned salmon. Under the new Australian–Canadian preferential treaty the duty on American canned salmon is prohibitive and the entire trade is now in the hands of Canadian packers. US shipments to Australia and New Zealand for the past 10 years averaged 140,832 cases a year – of which your company held a large percentage.
3. It would keep alive the brands you have established in those markets, which brands have a trade value worth protecting.
4. It would enable you to apply your diminished American packs to the protection of your domestic trade, and give you a supply from British Columbia to take care of your present export business.
5. It would give you a Canadian supply to build up the sale of Del Monte and other brands of salmon in the Canadian home market. With your

canned-fruit products your present Canadian agents are in an exceptionally good position to establish you as influential factors in the canned-salmon trade in this country.

6. It would assist you in extending your operations in the French market, which at present gives Canada more favourable terms on canned salmon than the US obtains.

7. It would maintain and protect the brands you have established in the United Kingdom by making up with BC salmon the shortage occasioned by your lessened supply from Alaska. Should the proposed preference for Canadian canned salmon become a reality, all your present UK trade would be jeopardized, and the impetus given to the BC industry would be so great it would be impossible to buy out existing operators here at anything like the price they would be willing to accept to-day.

8. By delaying any longer to engage in the canned-salmon business in BC you not only are running the chance of not getting in at all, but cannot expect to get as favourable an opportunity as at present. The governmental control of the industry, while thorough and beneficial, is very strict. They have limited the number of canneries to those already in operation, so it is only by buying out existing companies that new interests can enter the field. The virtual monopoly this gives present owners is an asset that will more and more affect their asking prices as the profits from operations retrieve past losses and makes them financially more independent than they are today ...

Accompanying this proposal is a copy of the data I submitted to Mr. Geo. Armsby when I tried to interest him in effecting an amalgamation. While most of this is irrelevant to the present proposition, a study of it will give you a broader knowledge of the situation here, of the existing operators and their past accomplishments. This data was compiled to cover operations up to and including 1923 and I have added the 1924 results to bring it up to date. All is alphabetically arranged. If there is any further information desired I will be glad to furnish it if possible.

Difference in cost of 1 lb. talls and ½ lb. flats was approximately $1.04 per case. In arriving at cost of 1 lb. talls I deducted this sum from ½ lb. flats costs and arrived at above results.

This table shows cost for Skeena River where, owing to the shallow water and numerous snags, the loss of fishing gear is a heavy item. In other districts the cost of this item is materially less than on the Skeena River.

65a. *Attached Tables*

Table A
Cost of packing ½ lb. flats 1924 Season, for 22,000 case pack.

	Sockeyes ($)	Cohos ($)	Pinks ($)	Chums ($)
Fish	4.76	2.02	.60	.32
Nets	.81	.81	.81	.81
Boats	.15	.15	.15	.15
Fish Collecting	.29	.29	.29	.29
Fish Charges	.13	.13	.13	.13
Fish Licenses	.05	.05	.05	.05
Deprec. Boats & Scows	.10	.10	.10	.10
Cans and Boxes	2.18	2.18	2.18	2.18
Chinese Labour [incl. Indian]	.67	.67	.67	.67
White Labour	.23	.23	.23	.23
Sundries	.43	.43	.43	.43
Deprec. Bldgs. & Plant	.17	.17	.17	.17
Freight & Handling	.23	.23	.23	.23
Labelling and Reclamation	.16	.16	.16	.16
Insurance	.09	.09	.09	.09
Commissions	.30	.30	.30	.30
Interest	.08	.08	.08	.08
Taxes and Sundries	.13	.13	.13	.13
Cost per case ½ flats	10.97	8.22	6.80	6.52
Cost " " 1 talls	9.92	7.18	5.76	5.48

Table B
Saving on 65,000 case pack due to larger returns from operating costs, and to purchase of fish from private seiners.

Costs	($)	($)
Fish Boats & Scows	.12	
Steam Fares & Sundries	.04	
White Labour	.37	
Contract Labour	.06	
Repairs & Renewals Bldgs. & Plant	.05	
Heat Light & Power	.04	
Sundries	.11	
		.79
Nets	.81	
Boats	.15	
Fish Collecting	.29	
Fish Licenses	.05	
		1.20 [sic]
Total saving per case		1.99

Skeena packing costs	Sockeyes ($)	Cohos ($)	Pinks ($)	Chums ($)
on 22,000 c/s ½ lb. flats	10.96	8.22	6.80	6.52
Saving on 65,000 case pack	1.99	1.99	1.99	1.99
Estimated cost 65M pack	8.97	6.21	4.81	4.53
on 22,000 c/s 1 lb. talls	9.92	7.18	5.76	5.48
Saving on 65,000 case pack	1.99	1.99	1.99	1.99
Estimated cost 65M pack	7.93	5.19	3.77	3.49

Table C
Selling values 1924 and 1925 BC canned salmon

	Sockeyes ($)	Cohos ($)	Pinks ($)	Chums ($)
½ lb. flats 1924	12.50	9.00	6.75	5.50
½ lb. " 1925	15.50	10.50	8.00	6.00
1 lb. talls 1924	11.50	8.00	5.00	4.25
1 lb. " 1925	14.50	9.25	5.50	4.50

These selling values are net, as costs of labelling, commissions, and handling charges are figured separately in packing costs in Table A.

Table D
Number of fish required per case of 48 lbs. and prices paid fishermen for raw fish.

	Fish to case
Sockeyes	14
Cohos	9
Pinks	17
Chums	8

Prices paid fishermen for raw fish

	Cannery [Owned] Gear ($)	Private [Owned] Gear ($)
Sockeyes each	.25	.37
Cohos "	.15	.22½
Pinks "	.02½	.03½
Chums "	.03	.04

Table E
Proportion of each species packed by the 5 leading companies in 1924

	Sockeyes (%)	Cohos (%)	Pinks (%)	Chums (%)
Canadian Fishing Co.	13	04	37	46
Gosse-Millerd Co. Ltd.	13	05	23	53
BC Fishing & Packing Co.	40	09	30	12
ABC Packing Co.	34	05	47	09
Wallace Fisheries Ltd.	26	01	72	–
Gosse & Wallace combined	17	04	38	39

Since the 1924 season, Gosse-Millerd Co. Ltd. have acquired the Kimsquit Cannery, and Wallace Fisheries Ltd., the Mill Bay cannery. These new holdings will increase their percentages of all species.

The above figures are not a true index of the catch of the different companies, excepting [in the case of] the BC Fishing & Packing Co. and the ABC Packing Co. The Canadian Fishing Co. use most of their catch of cohos and all their bright chum salmon in their fresh- and frozen-fish trade. The Wallace Fisheries Ltd. dry-salt most of their take of chum salmon, and Gosse-Millerd Co. Ltd. also use some of their chums for this trade.

Of the sockeyes packed by the BC Fishing & Packing Co., about 15% is obtained in their Fraser River canneries. This leaves them with approximately 25% for other districts. Of the other companies listed above, only the Canadian Fishing Co. and Gosse-Millerd Co. Ltd. (with one cannery each) operate on the Fraser River.

EMERGENCE OF BRITISH COLUMBIA PACKERS LTD., 1928

66. 2/14 Letter: Doyle to Æmelius Jarvis   *Ladner, BC*
                                                          3rd March 1928

Dear Jarvis:

In the course of our conversation on Tuesday last, you asked me if I know of anyone on the American side I thought would be suitable for the position of General Manager of the BC Fishing & Packing Co.

Subsequently I told some personal friends of our conversation. These friends are not associated in any way with the fishing industry but know all the circumstances surrounding my early connection with the company, the reasons that connection was severed, and the subsequent careers of both the company and myself.

They asked me why I had not advanced my own claims to the general managership. I replied that while I felt every sentiment of right and justice entitled me to expect it, I had thought the offer should be made me instead of my having to seek it. To this they replied that had you not been incapacitated through illness at the time I left the company you would have known all the circumstances, in which event my resignation would never have been accepted, and that I should now fully explain the situation to you and advance my claim to the position, not only on account of the knowledge and experience I possess, but more particularly because the injustice formerly done me should be rectified and compensated for by the company responsible for these injuries. Acting in accordance with their advice, I am herewith stating my position fully. But in doing so I wish to preface my remarks with the statement that I wholeheartedly backed Mr. Whitehead while in the position and would not press my claims had he continued in the management ... When the company directors, in causing me to resign [in 1904], publicly branded me with the reputation of being extravagant and impractical, they inflicted on me a sentence which for more than 25 years has handicapped my efforts and injured my career. No matter how undeserved I may feel this sentence to have been; no matter that Messrs. Evans and Sweeny subsequently altered their opinion; no matter what acknowledgement you and others have made of the knowledge I possess of the fishing industry; so long as the BC Fishing & Packing Co. fail to re-establish me in the position they wrongfully deprived me of, the reputation they then inflicted on me remains a stigma I cannot efface, and which will continue to handicap my future advancement. And with no desire to awaken painful memories I must say that of all men you should be the first to realize the load unjust accusations place upon a person, and how the ill effects continue unless the authors of the wrong publicly acknowledge the error by restoring the victim to the honours and position he formerly enjoyed.

Of the happenings referred to above I have kept a written record, and should you doubt the correctness of my remarks these records are available and can be submitted to you for perusal.

When I severed my connection with the BCPA I determined to so increase my knowledge that the people of BC would be compelled to recognize that in all things relating to the fishing industry I knew more than anyone else. And without being egotistical I think I can safely claim to have accomplished this object. You have told me yourself that I am acknowledged to know the industry better than anyone else. This pre-eminence, I consider, an additional claim to the demands of fair play and justice for the vacant general managership.

Since I left your company it has gone downhill steadily. By your own admissions to me you have realized Mr. Barker's incompetency and its ill effect on the company. To-day your business is disorganized; your staff demoralized; your plants in bad shape; your cannery managers dissatisfied; your operations needlessly extravagant; and your losses excessive. In the light of recent packing costs and plant expenditure it is an insult to class as "extravagant" such expenditure as anything I committed the BCPA to, while if the company's management since my time has been "practical," I thank God for my impracticality.

Looking back over the past 25 years, I can truthfully claim that in every single instance in which I opposed the aims and assumptions of the other canners I was right and they were wrong, and I possess, and can submit to you, the documentary evidence to substantiate this statement. I do not say this boastfully but only to illustrate the advantage my broad knowledge and greater study gave me of the situation, and how the ultimate results obtained backed up and vindicated my judgement.

What your company lacks, and has always lacked, is someone in the actual management and control of operations who is familiar with the technical side of the business, who has the knowledge of the fishing grounds and fishing conditions, the confidence of the cannery managers, and the ability to handle men. In claiming to possess these qualifications I may appear egotistical, but I have kept in touch with the industry all the past years, I know many of your employees and their feelings in the matter, and I think I can truthfully claim to stand higher in their estimation and in the estimation of Government Fishery authorities and the leaders of the Fishermen's Associations than any other canneryman. Under all the circumstances, I feel I can fill the position of general manager of your company better, and with more advantage to the company, than anyone else, and that for this reason, as well as in the demands of fair play and justice, the position should be mine. The formation of the company was my original idea; I had the right to expect compensation through being its general manager; I was deprived of this right through fraud, trickery, and injustice. I am even more entitled to-day to consideration because of what has been kept from me in the intervening years; while in addition the knowledge and experience I possess are assets the company needs and cannot afford to do without. It is on these grounds I base my claim. You profited jointly with me from my conception of what could be done in the salmon industry. Throughout all these years you have enjoyed the fruits of the enterprise, while I, although equally entitled to consideration, have been deprived of the reward. In consideration of what you have been able to gain, I feel you owe it to me to rectify past injustice, restore my good name, and give the company the benefit of the knowledge and experience which you admit I am possessed of.

I will be in Vancouver on Tuesday and can be communicated with at the Club about 1 o'clock; otherwise if you write me [in] Ladner I can get in [to Vancouver] on a day's notice. I would point out that a decision should be made without delay, as the new general manager should be in office before the cannery managers leave for their respective stations, and before plans and preparations for 1926 are too far advanced to be satisfactorily adjusted.

Keeping the Record

For the rest of his life, Henry Doyle tried to keep abreast of developments in the industry by subscribing to fisheries publications and corresponding with officials in the field. His old friend James A. Motherwell, who served as the Canadian government's Chief Inspector of Fisheries for BC from 1921, when F.H. Cunningham resigned, until 1946, secretly supplied him with details of the annual pack. "I know how necessary it is to have this information for your very complete records ... and that you will treat it confidentially," he wrote to Doyle on March 23rd, 1935.[1] Doyle's reputation as the unofficial historian of the industry is also obvious from the requests for historical information he received over the years from such prominent figures as John N. Cobb,[2] Director of the US Fisheries Department and historian of the Pacific fisheries, and H.R. MacMillan[3] (formerly head of the provincial forestry department) when he was president of British Columbia Packers Ltd. in the 1930s.

It is because Doyle maintained his interest and enthusiasm for the industry, and because he did not want to be forgotten, that he donated his papers to public collections. Immediately after World War II, he began rewriting his history of the industry. The original title for the manuscript was changed to "King Salmon," and later to "Rise and Decline of the Pacific Salmon Fisheries." Throughout the 1950s he approached half a dozen publishing houses, both commercial and academic, but all of them rejected the manuscript.[4] Because he had written it largely to vindicate himself in the eyes of his former critics, the fresh criticisms and rebuffs he received from the editors and referees must have stirred up old battles and re-opened old wounds. Yet despite his disappointment, Doyle remained tireless in his campaign to obtain a hearing for his views about the Pacific salmon-canning industry – past and present.

The act of revising the manuscript and submitting it to publishers had obviously become a hobby with him. He loved scrapping with his critics, and he always tried to be one step ahead of everyone else. Perhaps he never intended to publish the manuscript. A few years before his death, in 1961, he wrote to Dr. Peter Larkin, who was then director of the Institute of Fisheries at UBC, asking if the university had a press and, if so, would it consider publishing Doyle's history manuscript.[5] Larkin replied that while a press was being formed, at present it published only in-house material; but could Doyle spare a copy of the manuscript for Larkin to read?[6] Doyle's response was typical of him in his final years:

I would be very pleased if I had an extra copy of my RISE AND DECLINE OF THE PACIFIC SALMON FISHERIES to send you but, as you surmised, I have only the one completed copy and must retain same not only for submission to other publishers (if any), but also to add new material to keep it abreast of the times. For example, last year I added to the Alaska section some data concerning the inroads Japanese "mothership" fishing made in the Behring Sea red salmon runs, and I notice by the September 1957 number of *Pacific Fishermen* the American authorities are now awakening to this very dangerous situation. Also, Vancouver press reports just to hand show the hydro-electric power vs. salmon fisheries dog is not dead yet, and I may have occasion to add to what I already have written on this controversy.[7]

Henry Doyle died at his home in North Hollywood, California, in 1961.

Appendix

Table A1
World Production of Canned Pacific Salmon, 1910-1938
(48-lb. cases)

Year	Alaska	United States	Canada (BC)	Siberia	Japan
1910	2,438,777	3,555,623	762,201	10,000	—
1911	2,820,963	5,173,521	948,965	25,000	—
1912	4,060,129	4,952,279	996,576	77,500	—
1913	3,756,433	6,709,546	1,353,901	133,400	46,000
1914	4,167,832	5,533,743	1,111,039	136,500	65,450
1915	4,489,002	6,506,211	1,133,381	289,009	70,000
1916	4,919,589	6,360,547	995,065	425,800	27,849
1917	5,922,320	8,567,409	1,497,475	511,001	39,644
1918	6,677,369	8,076,143	1,616,157	381,337	35,778
1919	4,591,110	6,630,347	1,393,156	748,511	86,189
1920	4,395,509	5,101,705	1,187,616	595,771	87,516
1921	2,604,973	3,622,612	603,548	705,493	38,122
1922	4,501,355	5,231,675	1,290,326	718,184	25,894
1923	5,063,340	6,411,757	1,341,677	703,669	54,053
1924	5,305,923	6,245,320	1,745,313	799,120	60,190
1925	4,450,898	6,034,321	1,720,622	586,663	133,764
1926	6,652,882	7,491,684	2,065,198	946,188	175,084
1927	3,566,072	5,053,472	1,360,449	817,835	137,462
1928	6,070,110	6,902,447	2,035,637	1,482,469	197,800
1929	5,370,242	6,983,556	1,400,750	1,002,912	632,874
1930	4,988,987	6,044,093	2,221,783	1,752,112	378,404
1931	5,432,535	6,780,492	685,104	1,133,671	458,270
1932	5,260,488	5,914,853	1,081,031	1,720,876	247,251

1933	5,226,698	6,360,742	1,265,072	1,012,905	772,924
1934	7,470,586	8,361,990	1,582,926	1,900,641	892,570
1935	5,155,826	6,037,454	1,529,022	1,207,952	1,467,752
1936	8,454,948	8,983,217	1,881,026	1,689,841	1,198,096
1937	6,654,038	7,526,197	1,509,175	1,073,632	1,335,172
1938	6,791,544	7,274,209	1,697,016	1,198,533	1,113,515

Source: H.E. Gregory and Kathleen Barnes, *North Pacific Fisheries* (San Francisco: American Council Institute of Pacific Relations, 1939), 308, appendix B.

Table A2
North American Production of Canned Salmon by Species, 1899–1938
(48-lb. cases)

Year	King, spring or chinook	Red, sockeye or blueback	Medium red, or silverside	Pink	Chum or keta	Steelhead trout	Total cases
1899	334,974	2,153,388	261,071	401,892	61,932	11,994	3,225,251
1900	338,493	2,046,908	208,026	232,022	155,208	20,597	3,001,254
1901	455,395	3,801,730	126,535	585,017	86,230	20,000	5,074,907
1902	379,641	2,702,045	227,031	549,602	313,603	8,593	4,180,515
1903	403,836	2,231,555	330,319	564,507	61,232	7,251	3,598,700
1904	444,472	1,950,949	168,235	299,333	168,235	9,868	3,041,092
1905	443,794	3,488,322	269,806	253,559	138,642	9,822	4,603,945
1906	424,974	2,122,204	397,346	416,602	450,151	6,500	3,817,777
1907	354,209	1,707,813	397,786	1,114,100	272,135	6,604	3,852,647
1908	379,171	2,186,325	386,745	726,656	303,837	11,863	3,994,597
1909	262,554	3,671,555	373,567	882,410	218,987	17,382	5,426,455
1910	372,901	2,274,780	521,966	589,043	555,908	5,576	4,320,174
1911	627,714	1,869,927	676,141	2,373,595	592,790	8,618	6,104,887
1912	426,338	2,544,435	621,817	1,556,128	808,630	7,198	5,956,953
1913	285,472	4,643,425	300,033	2,392,166	432,812	9,539	8,063,447
1914	509,100	3,121,964	579,980	1,222,013	1,200,433	11,292	6,644,782
1915	641,979	2,492,865	551,821	2,825,570	1,107,707	29,650	7,649,592
1916	646,341	2,432,048	715,815	2,036,077	1,500,332	24,999	7,355,612
1917	673,980	3,248,843	588,749	3,929,332	1,648,313	35,677	10,124,894
1918	697,140	2,987,710	838,088	2,953,245	2,175,031	41,086	9,692,300
1919	704,195	1,707,846	793,175	2,426,414	2,367,481	24,392	8,023,503
1920	705,050	1,892,691	361,566	2,138,959	1,175,001	16,054	6,289,321
1921	419,508	2,034,310	362,943	1,038,090	359,947	11,362	4,226,160

Year							
1922	353,588	2,480,811	510,919	2,241,760	908,283	26,640	6,522,001
1923	389,802	2,309,142	534,225	3,371,917	1,120,591	27,757	7,753,434
1924	406,096	1,902,832	542,682	3,295,739	1,835,251	31,270	8,013,870
1925	550,071	1,581,792	667,817	3,111,320	1,803,371	17,248	7,731,619
1926	485,788	2,550,771	607,778	4,101,422	1,762,134	36,233	9,544,126
1927	538,574	1,738,054	642,522	2,241,304	1,217,338	33,377	6,411,169
1928	354,798	2,214,498	602,203	3,583,433	2,165,652	17,492	8,938,076
1929	375,497	2,100,787	564,826	3,775,764	1,541,213	24,821	8,382,908
1930	427,282	1,710,018	758,451	4,266,301	1,085,351	18,509	8,265,912
1931	418,483	2,084,385	388,140	3,890,755	671,574	13,679	7,467,016
1932	394,698	2,482,800	445,456	2,341,817	1,310,038	14,386	6,989,195
1933	343,442	2,579,891	402,107	3,259,341	1,021,547	19,486	7,625,814
1934	352,352	3,354,863	596,921	4,261,262	1,362,905	16,183	9,944,486
1935	279,693	1,232,852	596,117	4,139,114	1,304,216	15,484	7,567,476
1936	314,195	2,968,184	533,285	5,181,954	1,846,675	20,350	10,864,643
1937	385,040	2,491,655	370,795	4,524,821	1,237,331	18,352	9,027,994
1938	234,041	3,117,421	599,710	3,621,406	1,382,520	16,127	8,971,225

Source: H.E. Gregory and Kathleen Barnes, *North Pacific Fisheries* (San Francisco: American Council Institute of Pacific Relations, 1939), 309, appendix B.
(The entire British Columbia pack included under sockeye before 1903.)

Table A3
BC Production of Canned Salmon by Species, 1903–1936
(48-lb. cases)

Year	Sockeye Fraser River	Sockeye other districts	Total sockeye	Springs	Cohos and bluebacks	Steelheads	Pinks	Chums	Total cases
1903	204,809	163,908	368,717	25,657	51,918	—	27,382	—	473,674
1904	72,688	250,536	323,226	38,675	66,351	—	—	37,642	465,894
1905	837,489	243,184	1,080,673	28,359	44,458	—	13,970	—	1,167,460
1906	183,007	276,672	459,679	32,344	69,132	—	68,305	—	629,460
1907	59,815	254,259	314,074	26,098	87,900	683	118,704	—	547,459
1908	63,126	291,897	355,023	28,164	81,917	1,137	76,448	—	542,689
1909	542,248	298,193	840,441	19,017	61,918	—	46,544	—	967,920
1910	133,045	432,870	565,915	28,789	74,382	140	34,613	58,362	762,201
1911	58,487	325,022	383,509	48,456	119,702	100	305,247	91,951	948,965
1912	108,784	335,778	444,762	80,437	165,102	207	247,743	58,325	996,576
1913	684,596	287,582	972,178	41,049	69,822	—	192,887	77,965	1,353,901
1914	185,483	351,213	536,696	49,328	120,201	—	220,340	184,474	1,111,039
1915	89,040	387,002	476,042	58,104	146,956	2,927	367,352	82,000	1,133,381
1916	27,394	187,395	214,789	66,726	183,623	9,082	280,644	240,201	995,065
1917	123,614	116,234	339,848	76,276	157,589	11,740	496,749	475,273	1,497,475
1918	16,849	259,610	276,459	107,354	191,068	15,916	527,745	497,615	1,616,157
1919	29,628	339,817	369,445	100,551	199,993	4,493	346,639	372,035	1,393,156
1920	44,598	306,807	351,405	118,301	120,033	2,395	520,856	84,626	1,187,616
1921	35,900	128,014	163,914	49,752	124,348	1,220	192,906	71,408	603,548
1922	48,744	250,870	299,614	39,596	109,276	1,657	581,979	258,204	1,290,326
1923	29,423	305,224	334,647	27,142	119,141	1,760	440,932	418,055	1,341,677
1924	36,200	333,403	369,603	27,456	119,989	1,811	657,538	568,916	1,745,313
1925	31,523	361,120	392,643	73,499	199,180	1,996	445,400	607,904	1,720,622

Year									
1926	83,589	253,406	336,995	69,189	181,894	2,165	772,993	701,962	2,065,198
1927	57,085	250,947	308,032	58,977	181,968	1,746	247,617	562,109	1,360,449
1928	26,530	177,011	203,541	18,856	156,757	865	792,362	863,256	2,035,637
1929	60,407	220,899	281,306	19,377	196,444	672	477,969	424,982	1,400,750
1930	107,896	369,782	477,678	38,804	190,954	1,656	1,111,937	401,114	2,221,783
1931	54,688	236,776	291,464	27,147	102,175	1,326	206,995	55,997	685,104
1932	83,447	200,908	284,355	76,060	188,971	1,168	223,716	306,761	1,081,031
1933	53,481	204,626	258,107	20,266	159,052	1,459	532,558	293,630	1,265,072
1934	145,579	232,303	377,882	29,784	225,430	1,282	435,364	513,184	1,582,926
1935	76,415	274,029	350,444	21,920	231,492	596	514,966	409,604	1,529,022
1936	165,651	249,373	415,024	29,854	246,061	1,068	591,532	597,487	1,881,026

Source: Cicely Lyons, *Salmon Our Heritage. The Story of a Province and an Industry* (Vancouver: British Columbia Packers Ltd. 1969), 710. Taken from *Pacific Fisherman Yearbooks* (1928 and 1967). As Lyons points out, the figures do not agree in every instance with some shown elsewhere, but the discrepancies are minor, and the table is shown for purpose of general description.

Table A4
Opening Prices of United States Canned Salmon, 1897–1934
(48-lb. cases)

Year	Sockeyes		Red Alaska		Cohos		Pinks		Chums	
	Talls	½ flats	Talls	½ flats	Talls	½ flats	Talls	½ flats	Talls	½ flats
1897	3.20	—	3.60	—	—	—	2.60	—	—	—
1898	3.20	—	4.00	—	—	—	2.60	—	—	—
1899	4.40	—	4.00	—	—	—	2.70	—	—	—
1900	4.40	—	4.40	—	—	—	3.00	—	—	—
1901	3.80	—	5.00	—	—	—	3.00	—	—	—
1902	4.00	—	3.80	—	—	—	2.60	—	—	—
1903	6.00	7.20	5.20	—	—	—	2.60	—	—	—
1904	6.20	7.60	5.20	—	—	—	2.80	—	—	—
1905	5.40	8.00	4.00	—	—	—	2.80	—	—	—
1906	5.80	8.00	3.80	—	—	—	2.80	—	—	—
1907	6.60	8.80	4.60	—	—	—	3.20	—	—	—
1908	6.40	8.40	4.60	—	4.20	6.00	3.00	—	2.80	—
1909	5.40	8.00	4.60	6.80	4.20	—	2.40	—	2.30	—
1910	6.60	8.80	5.40	8.00	5.00	6.40	3.20	—	3.10	—
1911	7.80	10.40	6.40	9.00	5.80	8.00	4.00	6.40	3.80	6.00
1912	7.80	10.40	5.60	9.20	4.60	6.40	2.60	4.40	2.50	4.00
1913	6.00	8.40	4.60	7.60	3.40	5.60	2.60	4.40	2.20	4.00
1914	7.80	10.80	5.80	8.80	4.60	6.60	3.60	5.60	3.40	5.20
1915	7.80	10.80	6.00	9.20	4.60	6.00	3.00	4.60	2.80	4.20
1916	8.20	11.20	6.00	9.60	5.20	7.20	3.60	6.00	3.40	5.40
1917	11.60	14.00	9.40	13.20	8.00	10.80	6.60	9.20	6.40	—
1918	12.60	16.00	9.40	13.20	9.00	12.80	6.60	9.20	6.40	8.80
1919	—	20.00	13.00	18.00	12.00	16.00	9.00	11.20	8.60	10.00

Year										
1920	—	24.00	13.00	18.00	8.00	12.00	6.00	8.80	4.60	7.20
1921	—	20.00	9.40	16.00	6.00	7.60	4.40	6.40	4.00	5.20
1922	17.00	20.00	9.00	14.00	5.00	8.00	4.60	6.40	4.20	5.60
1923	—	20.00	9.00	13.20	5.60	8.00	5.00	7.20	4.80	6.80
1924	—	18.00	9.00	13.00	6.00	9.60	5.00	7.20	4.80	6.80
1925	—	19.20	14.00	18.00	10.40	14.40	5.40	8.40	4.50	7.00
1926	—	20.00	10.00	16.00	9.00	12.00	5.40	8.40	5.00	6.80
1927	—	22.00	12.40	17.60	9.20	12.60	5.40	8.80	5.20	7.60
1928	—	20.80	9.40	14.80	7.40	10.80	6.60	8.80	6.40	8.00
1929	13.00	20.00	10.60	16.00	7.40	10.80	6.00	8.80	5.40	8.00
1930	12.40	16.00	12.40	16.00	9.00	10.80	4.00	6.00	3.60	5.60
1931	—	16.00	9.40	13.20	7.00	9.60	3.40	5.60	3.20	5.20
1932	9.00	12.00	5.80	8.00	4.40	6.80	3.20	4.80	3.00	—
1933	—	11.00	7.00	9.60	5.20	8.00	4.80	7.00	4.60	5.60
1934	6.80	10.80	6.60	9.60	5.20	8.00	4.00	6.00	3.60	5.60

Source: UBC, Doyle Papers, box 6, file 20 (*Pacific Fisherman Yearbooks*).

Table A5
Opening Prices of BC Canned Salmon, 1905–1934
(48-lb. cases)

Ex. Rate US in Can $	Year	Sockeyes				Cohos				Pinks				Chums			
		Talls		½ Flats		Talls		½ Flats		Talls		½ Flats		Talls		½ Flats	
		(CAN) $	(US) $	(CAN) $	(US) $	(CAN) $	(US) $	(CAN) $	(US) $	(CAN) $	(US) $	(CAN) $	(US) $	(CAN) $	(US) $	(CAN) $	(US) $
—	1905	—	—	6.75	—	—	—	—	—	—	—	—	—	—	—	—	—
—	1906	—	—	7.40	—	—	—	—	—	—	—	—	—	—	—	—	—
—	1907	6.25	—	7.50	—	4.25	—	—	—	—	—	—	—	—	—	—	—
—	1908	6.00	—	7.00	—	4.75	—	—	—	3.40	—	—	—	—	—	—	—
—	1909	5.40	—	6.25	—	4.25	—	—	—	2.50	—	—	—	—	—	—	—
0.9998	1910	6.50	6.50	7.75	7.75	4.75	4.75	6.25	6.25	3.25	3.25	—	—	—	—	—	—
—	1911	7.75	—	8.75	—	6.00	—	7.50	7.50	4.00	—	5.50	5.50	—	—	—	—
1.0000	1912	9.25	9.25	11.00	11.00	7.25	7.25	8.50	8.50	4.00	4.00	5.50	5.50	—	—	—	—
1.0001	1913	6.00	6.00	7.50	7.50	4.00	4.00	—	—	2.50	2.50	—	—	2.20	2.20	—	—
0.9992	1914	8.25	8.26	10.25	10.26	4.75	4.75	6.25	6.26	3.50	3.50	4.50	4.50	3.00	3.00	—	—
1.0039	1915	8.25	8.22	10.25	10.21	4.75	4.73	6.75	6.72	3.25	3.24	4.75	4.73	2.75	2.74	—	—
1.0018	1916	9.00	8.98	11.00	10.98	6.50	6.49	7.75	7.74	3.90	3.89	5.25	5.24	3.25	3.24	4.25	4.24
1.0018	1917	12.00	11.98	14.00	13.97	8.50	8.48	10.25	10.23	7.00	6.99	8.25	8.24	6.25	6.24	7.50	7.49
1.0159	1918	14.50	14.27	16.00	15.75	10.00	9.84	11.50	11.32	8.50	8.37	10.00	9.84	6.75	6.64	7.75	7.63
1.0357	1919	15.00	14.48	16.50	15.93	12.00	11.59	13.50	13.03	8.50	8.21	10.00	9.66	6.75	6.52	7.75	7.48
1.1247	1920	19.00	16.89	20.50	18.23	12.00	10.67	13.50	12.00	6.50	5.78	7.50	6.67	5.25	4.67	6.25	5.56
1.1164	1921	17.00	15.23	18.00	16.12	10.00	8.96	11.50	10.30	4.50	4.03	6.00	5.37	4.00	3.58	5.25	4.70
1.0154	1922	18.00	17.73	19.00	18.71	8.00	7.88	9.00	8.86	5.00	4.92	6.75	6.65	4.50	4.43	6.00	5.91
1.0196	1923	13.00	12.75	14.00	13.73	6.50	6.38	8.00	7.85	5.00	4.90	6.50	6.38	4.50	4.41	6.00	5.88
1.0127	1924	11.50	11.36	12.50	12.34	6.50	6.42	8.00	7.90	5.00	4.94	6.00	5.92	4.50	4.44	5.50	5.43
1.0002	1925	15.00	15.00	16.00	16.00	9.25	9.25	10.50	10.50	5.50	5.50	7.00	7.00	4.50	4.50	6.00	6.00

Year																	
1926	0.9998	16.00	16.00	17.00	17.00	12.00	12.00	13.00	13.00	5.75	5.75	7.75	7.75	4.75	4.75	6.50	6.50
1927	1.0000	16.00	16.00	17.00	17.00	12.00	12.00	13.00	13.00	5.75	5.75	7.50	7.50	5.00	5.00	6.50	6.50
1928	1.0009	16.50	16.49	17.50	17.48	12.00	11.99	13.00	12.99	6.00	5.99	7.50	7.49	5.25	5.25	6.50	6.49
1929	1.0076	17.25	17.12	18.25	18.11	12.00	11.91	13.00	12.90	6.50	6.45	8.00	7.94	5.25	5.21	6.50	6.45
1930	1.0016	16.25	16.22	17.25	17.22	10.25	10.23	11.25	11.23	4.50	4.49	6.50	6.49	4.00	3.99	6.00	5.99
1931	1.0381	12.00	11.56	13.50	13.00	8.00	7.71	9.50	9.15	3.50	3.37	5.00	4.82	3.25	3.13	4.75	4.58
1932	1.1352	12.50	11.01	13.50	11.89	8.00	7.05	9.50	8.37	3.50	3.08	5.00	4.40	3.00	2.64	4.50	3.96
1933	1.0874	13.50	12.41	14.50	13.33	7.00	6.44	8.50	7.82	4.00	3.68	5.50	5.06	3.00	2.76	4.50	4.14
1934	0.9900	13.50	13.64	14.50	14.65	7.50	7.58	9.00	9.09	4.75	4.80	6.25	6.31	4.25	4.29	5.75	5.81

Source: UBC, Doyle Papers, box 6, file 20 (*Pacific Fisherman Yearbooks*); and M.C. Urquhart and K.A. Buckley, eds. *Historical Statistics of Canada* (Toronto: MacMillan of Canada 1965), "Foreign Exchange Rates, 1910 to 1960," 276.

Table A6
Exports of Canned Pacific Salmon to the United Kingdom, 1896–1932
(48-lb. cases)

Year	United States	Canada (BC)	Asiatic	Total
1896	—	—	—	932,226
1897	—	—	—	1,119,093
1898	—	—	—	1,314,985
1899	—	—	—	926,935
1900	—	—	—	1,032,155
1901	—	—	—	1,003,511
1902	—	—	—	1,734,567
1903	—	—	—	907,076
1904	—	—	—	989,063
1905	—	—	—	792,550
1906	—	—	—	1,233,019
1907	—	—	—	501,506
1908	—	—	—	677,442
1909	—	—	—	823,376
1910	—	—	—	1,428,479
1911	—	—	—	842,676
1912	—	—	—	724,680
1913	553,785	573,671	60,260	1,187,716
1914	1,063,204	733,702	331,724	2,128,630
1915	1,157,342	1,431,606	—	2,588,948
1916	1,772,385	998,675	188,064	2,959,124
1917	714,123	460,758	137,038	1,311,919
1918	686,112	377,787	418,590	1,482,489
1919	991,385	1,015,421	199,503	2,206,309
1920	591,219	646,773	445,368	1,683,360
1921	506,490	351,369	464,535	1,322,394
1922	505,913	331,258	434,991	1,272,162
1923	661,849	129,759	407,552	1,199,160
1924	877,863	317,564	544,082	1,739,509
1925	520,383	553,710	412,696	1,486,789
1926	529,536	345,600	433,915	1,309,051
1927	432,018	266,148	742,357	1,440,523
1928	641,990	285,600	921,927	1,849,517
1929	625,919	216,369	798,027	1,640,315
1930	415,128	224,096	1,762,142	2,401,366
1931	440,561	400,479	1,088,312	1,929,352
1932	506,777	334,591	1,167,291	2,008,659

Source: UBC, Doyle Papers, box 6, file 18 (*Pacific Fisherman Yearbooks*).

Appendix

Table A7
BC and United States Canned-Salmon Exports to Australia and
New Zealand Combined, 1915–1933
(48-lb. cases)

Year	United States	Canada (BC)	Total
1915	155,955	82,827	238,783
1916	234,408	127,649	362,057
1917	147,661	98,009	245,670
1918	156,942	81,800	238,742
1919	121,651	111,952	233,603
1920	62,052	74,821	136,873
1921	110,366	65,100	175,466
1922	141,951	95,410	237,361
1923	127,790	96,765	224,555
1924	149,549	152,100	301,649
10-year average	140,832	98,643	239,475
1925	148,451	215,468	363,919
1926	137,485	246,039	383,524
1927	75,439	272,902	348,341
1928	86,264	216,783	303,047
1929	97,371	278,872	376,243
1930	63,338	289,827	353,165
1931	7,408	161,621	169,029
1932	2,317	31,765	34,082
1933	25,000	221,343	246,343

Source: UBC, Doyle Papers, box 6, file 19 (Pacific Fisherman Yearbooks).

Table A8
British Columbia Packers Association and Succeeding Companies:
Results of Operations Since Formation, 1902 to 1935

Year	BC Packers Assn. Cases packed (48-lb. cases)	Profit per case ($)	Assn. pack as per cent of BC pack
1902	283,910	—	43.75
1903	192,119	0.23	40.60
1904	164,696	0.26	35.33
1905	435,501	1.34	37.33
1906	159,547	0.70	25.33
1907	139,805	0.48	25.50
1908	151,673	0.66	28.00
1909	292,578	1.22	30.00
1910	202,413	1.52	26.80
1911	237,413	1.77	25.00
1912	250,624	1.74	25.17
1913	399,486	1.09	29.50
1914	281,367	1.35	25.33
1915	286,104	1.66	25.25
1916	193,946	1.38	19.50
1917	281,893	1.94	18.00
1918	262,396	1.66	16.25
1919	252,237	1.00	16.75
1920	238,769	1.25	20.10
1921	166,294	—	27.50
1922	201,826	0.11	15.67
1923	230,597	0.54*	17.20
1924	272,627	0.47	15.40
1925	286,586	1.11	16.88
1926	531,292	0.99	16.60
1927	407,774	1.58*	30.00
1928	964,619	0.83	47.50
1929	667,838	0.34	47.75
1930	1,059,408	1.19*	41.60
1931	112,652	8.00*	16.50
1932	354,531	0.81*	32.80
1933	440,092	—	34.67
1934	447,324	—	28.25
1935	515,283	—	33.70

Source: UBC, Doyle Papers, box 6, file 1.

* indicates a loss

Table A9
Alaska Packers Association:
Results of Operations Since Formation, 1893 to 1924[1]

Year	Alaska Packers Assn. Cases packed (48-lb. cases)	Profit per case ($)	Assn. pack as per cent of Alaska Pack
1893	462,650	0.99	25.20
1894	556,494	0.83	29.40
1895	526,806	1.09	24.50
1896	699,824	0.89	29.05
1897	818,207	0.65	26.20
1898	775,969	0.77	31.25
1899	877,723	0.78	27.00
1900	1,004,318	0.85	32.25
1901	1,273,566	0.61	25.00
1902	1,306,947	0.55	30.00
1903	1,334,824	0.70	37.00
1904	1,170,474	0.27*	35.70
1905	1,139,721	1.24*	24.75
1906	1,044,676	—	27.38
1907	1,100,035	0.55	31.25
1908	1,160,477	0.57	29.30
1909	1,338,254	0.40	24.80
1910	971,716	0.31	22.50
1911	1,053,015	0.60	17.17
1912	1,202,779	0.31	19.60
1913	1,504,415	0.09	18.25
1914	1,241,980	0.63	18.13
1915	1,024,040	0.54	12.80
1916	1,179,349	1.34	15.05
1917	1,346,292	0.97	12.80
1918	1,251,438	0.64	12.90
1919	583,102	0.88*	7.25
1920	620,978	1.22*	10.00
1921	693,042	1.41*	16.40
1922	940,507	0.32	16.40
1923	748,965	0.46	9.67
1924	627,042	0.22	7.80
Annual Average:[2]			
1920–29	673,500		14.00
1930–37	701,900		11.50

Source:
(1) UBC, Doyle Papers, box 6, file 20.
(2) H.E. Gregory and Kathleen Barnes, North Pacific Fisheries (San Francisco: American Council Institute of Pacific Relations 1939), 96, table 4.

* indicates a loss

Table A10
Ratio of Columbia River Salmon Packed by the Columbia River Packers Association,
Select Years, 1902–1937

Year	Columbia River Packers Assn. cases packed (48-lb. cases)	Assn. pack as per cent of total Columbia River pack
1902	131,500	38.00
1905	128,500	31.30
1914	135,800	29.80
1919	125,500	21.60
1925	116,900	21.60
1929	108,700	25.80
1936	125,100	39.50
1937	191,700	46.00

Source: Pacific Fisherman Yearbooks, compiled by H.E. Gregory and Kathleen Barnes, North Pacific Fisheries (San Francisco: American Council Institute of Pacific Relations 1937), 96, table 4.

Glossary of terms

The main sources for this glossary are Duncan A. Stacey, *Sockeye &*
Tinplate: Technological Change in the Fraser River Canning Industry,
1871–1912 (Victoria, BC: BC Provincial Museum 1982); Patrick W.
O'Bannon, "Technological Change in the Pacific Coast Canned Salmon
Industry, 1864–1924" (Ph.D. dissertation, University of California, San
Diego 1983); and Cicely Lyons, *Salmon Our Heritage: The Story of a*
Province and an Industry (Vancouver: BC Packers Ltd. 1969).

ACID BATH. See LYE VAT.
ALASKA REDS. See SALMON.
ARTIFICIAL PROPAGATION. See HATCHERY.
ATTACHED LICENSE. In BC from 1878 to 1905, only fishing with
  GILLNETS was permitted for salmon in most areas. When
  licenses were introduced, in the 1880s, they were taken out by
  canneries and a few independent fishermen. After an abortive
  attempt on the Fraser River in the 1889–92 seasons at overall
  license limitation, a shift occurred to INDIVIDUAL LICENSES.
  But a majority of licenses continued to be issued to canneries until
  after World War I. With the change from cannery to individual
  licenses came an alteration in methods of payment. Instead of
  fishers and BOAT PULLERS being paid a daily wage, they were
  paid per fish, prices varying by species and fluctuating over the
  SEASON. Unions arose to try to negotiate a fixed minimum price
  per fish for the whole season. (See also SEINE FISHING.)
BATHROOM. Area of a cannery where testing for leaks and cooking
  took place.
BIGHT. Curve or recess of a coast river.
BLUEBACK. See SALMON.

BLUESTONEING. Process of cleansing nets of all slime and dirt and disinfecting to preserve them. Bluestone (copper sulphate and salt) was dissolved in boiling water. Nets periodically received a lengthy soaking in this mixture in special large, wooden, watertight blue-stone vats that lined the net wharves. (See also OILING.)

BOAT PULLER. The person in a two-person GILLNET crew who rowed across the current while the other played out the net. When two-thirds of the net was out, the puller steered the vessel down-stream at right angles to the former course so that the net, when set, approximated the shape of the letter "L," then the boat drifted with the net. In the early decades of the industry in BC, Indian women and boys served as pullers for the Indian fishers.

BOAT RATING. A conservation measure of limiting the salmon catch by canneries. (See also text, chapter 1.)

BODY SEAMER. A CAN-MAKING term referring to the forming of the body of a can body by bending the body piece to shape on a mold or "cylinder," lapping one edge over the other, clamping the seam in place, and hand-soldering it closed.

BOILING KETTLE. In the nineteenth century it was common to cook them cans of salmon twice, in both cases by boiling them in salted water in large iron kettles set over furnaces. After the introduction of cooking in steam RETORTS, toward the end of the century, it was common to do the first cooking in EXHAUST BOXES (though kettles continued to be used in the smaller-scale and mar-ginal operations), the second in the retorts. Double cooking began to lose favour in the first decade of the twentieth century.

BOSS. See CHINESE CONTRACT; JAPANESE FISHERS' BOSS; NET BOSS.

BRAND NAME/TRADE MARKS. Most companies sold canned salm-on under several different brand names and labels to denote the various species, geographical origins of the salmon, and quality of the product. Through advertising and selling of brand-name prod-ucts, both the development of customer loyalties for specific prod-ucts and mass marketing were possible. Canned-salmon brand names and specific label designs were registered under the federal trade marks act. Registration gave the owner of the brand name the exclusive right to the use of the mark in the country in which it was registered.

BROKER/PACKER-BROKER. Brokers were selling agents. The trend in the 1920s was away from the use of an independent broker toward the integration of the canning operations and the selling agents (thus packer-broker).

BUTCHER/BUTCHERER (FISH). Skilled workers who removed the head, tail portion, and fins, slit open the belly, and took out the entrails. Butchering, or slitting, was traditionally assigned to skilled Chinese as part of the CHINESE CONTRACT. A top worker could butcher as many as 200 salmon per hour.

BUTCHERING TABLE. Work station for manual BUTCHERING.

CIF. "Cost, Insurance, and Freight" basis of the ocean shipping of goods.

CAN LOFT. See LOFT.

CAN-MAKING. Hand methods of making can lids and bodies at each individual cannery operation each year (as part of the CHINESE CONTRACT) were replaced by mechanical means, beginning in the 1880s. By the mid-1920s, cans could be bought ready-made from can-manufacturing companies located in New Westminster (later, Vancouver). (See also REFORM LINE.)

CANNERY. Large, plain, technically simple building in which canning took place. Usually set on PILES (occasionally on mud sills), driven into the tide flats, cannery plants were variations based on an L-shaped plan, with a long arm usually paralleling the shore line and the short arm(s) protruding out into deep water, where unloading and storage and docking took place. The interiors were high-ceilinged, open spaces with massive posts and beams. The second floor and attic were used for storage (net and can LOFT). Before World War I, the roofs were wood-shingled and the exterior walls were wood-clad: later on, both the roofs and walls were covered with corrugated galvanized iron. Canneries were routinely enlarged, re-shaped, altered extensively inside, and even moved from one site to another. The term also refers to the larger complex of outbuilding and dwellings.

CANNERY FLOOR. The area in which the main canning operation takes place.

CANNERY GEAR. Refers to fishing using cannery-owned equipment.

CANNERY RATINGS. See BOAT RATINGS.

CANNERY TRUCK. See COOLER/COOLER TRAY.

CANNING, FISH. An advanced processing (thermal) and rigid packaging method for converting the fish harvest into food products which can be stored at room temperature virtually indefinitely. Canning was an intrinsically industrial solution to the problems of food preservation in that it depended on tinplate production and assembly-line factory organization.

CANNING LINE. See LINE.

CAPPER/CAPPING MACHINE. See CRIMPER.

CAR. See COOLER/COOLER TRAY.

CASE. Standard measure of the productivity of a salmon canning operation – PACK. Regardless of the size or shape of tins of fish being packed, each case contains 48 pounds of salmon.

CENTRE HOLE. In the days before the introduction of the SANITARY, or solderless, can, a small hole was left in the lid of the can during the mechanical soldering process to prevent the can from exploding from the build-up of heat and steam inside. (Not to be confused with a VENT hole.)

CHINA CREW/CHINESE. See CHINESE LABOUR.

CHINA HOUSE. A one- or two-storey bunkhouse for the CHINESE LABOUR was standard fare at most salmon canneries on the coast. The cannery owner provided the accommodation as part of his obligation under the CHINESE CONTRACT. The building, which was typically spartan and very overcrowded, with short, narrow bunks stacked four or five high, usually included cooking and eating facilities.

CHINESE CONTRACT. System instituted and run by Chinese merchants, agents, and brokers, who supplied and controlled the CAN-MAKING and packing labour for cannery operators on a per-case basis, with a guarantee of a specified pack per day of the best marketable- or CONTRACT-QUALITY product. The contractor who furnished the gangs of workers, or his subcontractor (the Chinese boss), fed, clothed, transported, supervised, and disciplined them. He had to pay for canned salmon rejected by the manager as improperly packed or unfit for use (though usually there was a small allowance for wastage). Do-overs and fresh-water LEAKS had to be dealt with by the contract crew within a specified time. The contractor received cash advances, for the purpose of engaging experienced Chinese, for example. Usually, the contractor was guaranteed a minimum payment to cover expenses in the event of a poor fishing season, a cannery fire, breakdown of machinery and equipment, and so on. The system continued in Canada until after World War II, but it ended in the US during the 1930s.

CHINESE LABOUR. The work done under the terms of the CHINESE CONTRACT, including manual CAN-MAKING, unloading fish, BUTCHERING, SOLDERING, cooking, testing for LEAKS, possibly WASHING, LAQUERING, LABELLING, crating, equipment repairs, and other work inside and outside the cannery, all of which was done by males who in BC were usually of Chinese ancestry. The work of Klootchmen (Indian cannery workers, usually women), who were FILLERS and SLIMERS, also fell under the general category of Chinese labour.

CHINOOK. For the fish, see SALMON; also, a type of standard jargon developed long ago by the native peoples of Canada for communicating with each other for trade purposes. At the salmon canneries, it was adopted for use among the representatives of various linguistic groups of native peoples, and between natives and non-natives.

CHUM. See SALMON.

CLEANER. A half-dozen cannery workers (usually Indian women and children) were needed on each line to wipe the cans clean after manual or machine soldering. By the turn of the century, operators began substituting mechanical washers (wiping machines), which used steam or hot water to clean the cans.

CLINCHER. A tool with which to grip the overlapping edges of the side seam of the can body while soldering it by hand.

CLOSE PERIOD/TIME (OF FISHING). See SEASON.

COHO/COHOE. See SALMON.

COLD-STORAGE PLANT (FISH). Large, insulated, warehouse-like structure for the freezing, and possibly storage, of fish. By World War I there were cold-storage plants in each fishing district, especially in those near the HALIBUT and HERRING grounds. Freezing involved cleaning or dressing the fish, sharp- or quick-freezing it by refrigeration to below freezing point; then glazing the individual fish with a layer of water to seal it with a protective coating of ice, wrapping it in parchment paper, and boxing it.

COLD TEST. See LEAKS.

COLLAPSED CANS. See REFORM LINE.

COLLECTOR, FISH. See TENDERBOAT; SCOW.

COLUMBIA RIVER BOAT. See ROUND-BOTTOMED BOAT.

CONTRACT QUALITY. See CHINESE CONTRACT.

CONVEYOR (FISH). By 1903, most cannery operations employed elevators and conveyors to remove raw salmon from the SCOWS and transfer them to holding bins in the GUT SHED or CANNERY.

CONVEYOR BELT. A travelling platform (later, an endless looped belt) worked by an endless chain to move the cans through the various stages of production; the employment of such equipment was quite common in the coastal salmon canneries by 1903.

COOKING. See BOILING KETTLE; RETORT.

COOLER/COOLER TRAY. Large, shallow tray, made of flat, iron strips which held several dozen cans. Coolers were stacked on CARS (trucks) which were wheeled in and out of the cooking RETORTS.

CRIMPER/CRIMPING MACHINE. An improved method of soldering the ends of cans, invented in 1882, in which the lids were hand-crimped onto the filled cans securely enough to prevent them fall-

ing off during the soldering stage in the era of mechanical soldering. A mechanical topping-crimping machine was introduced in
the late 1880s to combine the two operations.

CURING, HERRING. A process involving cleaning the fish, mixing it
with salt, and packing it in barrels. The most common processing
method in BC was known as Scotch curing, which differs from
Norwegian curing in that with the former less salt is used.

DIES/DIE PRESS. Prior to the introduction of the SANITARY method
of can-making, the ends of various shapes of cans, with a rim to fit
onto the cylindrical body as a cover, were stamped out on a die
press. Dies were changed according to the required shape and
dimension of the disc.

DIESEL. See GAS BOAT.

DOG SALMON/"DOGS". See SALMON.

DOGFISH/GRAYFISH. A small shark (*Squalus suckeyi*) which preys on
other varieties of ocean fish, especially herring and salmon, and
which was highly destructive of salmon nets. These were caught
and reduced for fish oil on a commercial scale.

DO-OVERS. See LEAKS.

DOUBLE SEAMER. A can closing machine which originated in Europe
and was introduced to fruit and vegetable canning about 1905, but
which was not perfected for salmon canning until its action was
combined with those of others a few years later. After filled cans of
salmon left the EXHAUST BOX, double seamers (which could be
rented or purchased by individual cannery operations) crimped the
ends of sanitary cans in place without the use of solder (instead, a
flange and a sealing compound were used). (See also VACUUM
CLOSING MACHINE.)

DRAG SEINE. See SEINE FISHING.

DRAIN TABLE. Where butchered salmon was piled after being
washed.

DRIFT/REACH. Stretch of water fairly uniform in depth and free of
snags or sharp ledges which could catch and tear the lower portion
of a GILLNET, or cause it to be lost.

DRY-SALTING. Various dry-cure methods exist for preserving herring
and chum salmon by packing the dressed fish in tiers in barrels
with large amounts of dry salt.

ESCAPEMENT. The proportion of the total number of spawning adults
able to complete their journey to the SPAWNING GROUND in a
given year will largely determine the size of the runs to be expected
when their progeny are ready to spawn several years later. Fisheries
officials determined the levels of escapement of returned adults to

the spawning grounds mainly though analyzing the reports of individual Indians who fished the spawning rivers.

EULACHON/OOLICHAN (CANDLEFISH). A small, oily fish (*Thaleichthys pacificus*), it was an important traditional food item for Pacific Coast Indians, who extracted the oil from the spring eulachon catch for subsistence and trade purposes.

EXHAUST BOX. A large, flat, airtight steam chest of wood or metal which removed the air in the headspace of a can filled with fish. The air in the can was replaced by steam, which then condensed during the cooling period, leaving a partial vacuum. As it was introduced into the US and Fraser River salmon-canning industry, in the 1890s, it slowly replaced the first stage of cooking in kettles. (See also VACUUM CLOSING MACHINE.)

FALL FISHERY. Refers to the chum (dog) SALMON FISHERY.

FILLERS. People who placed pieces of salmon into empty cans. In BC, filling was traditionally the work of Indian women and girls, especially in cannery operations in remote locations. Fillers were paid by piece rate (productivity was measured in the number of TRAYS of filled cans).

FILLING MACHINE. A mechanical device for filling empty cans with fish was introduced in the American salmon-canning industry in the 1880s. It was successfully adapted only to packing the one-pound TALL variety (not enough vacuum was created in machine-filled half-pound FLATS). In BC, filling machines were not adopted as quickly or as completely as were many of the other innovations related to salmon canning.

FILLING TABLE. Place where the hand-filling of empty cans with salmon occurred.

FINGER-SOLDER MACHINE. See SOLDER MACHINE.

FISH BOX. Wooden box for holding fresh-caught fish on board fishing vessels and SCOWS, or at the cannery, and for shipping fresh and frozen fish to market.

FISH CUTTER. See GANG KNIFE.

FISH ELEVATOR. See CONVEYOR (FISH).

FISH HOUSE. See GUT SHED.

FISH WHARF. Where fish are unloaded from boats or SCOWS. Usually located at the short end of the traditional cannery's L-shaped design and in the deepest water, to facilitate unloading at all or most stages of the tide.

FISHING CAMP/STATION. An intermediary camp established by a packing company or collection of companies. Fish camps became necessary once the fishing fleets began to move out of the rivers and

inlets, further away from the canning plants. Collectors or TEN-
DER BOATS picked up the daily catch from the fishboats, which
they then delivered to the camp. Packers called at the various
camps several times a day to collect the fish and distribute it to the
appropriate canneries. Some fish camps were floating stations
which could be towed to new locations as required, and they sometimes contained living accommodation for a few employees and
storage facilities for nets.

FISHING METHODS. See GILLNET, SEINE FISHING,
TROLLING.

FISHWAYS. Devices constructed to permit salmon – those on their
spawning run and those on their seaward migration – to bypass
dams and other obstructions in salmon rivers and streams.

FLATS. Flat tins of salmon were put up in half-pound and, in the
early years, one-pound, tins. Typically, the most valuable grade of
salmon, sockeye, was put up in "half flats" for the export trade;
these tended to be packed by hand (hand butchered and hand
filled), rather than by machine, in order to achieve a better appearance in the can. BC canners began packing quarter-pound flats only
in 1933. The term "flats" has a second relevant but quite different
meaning: the mouth or estuary of a river delta, as in Fraser River
flats. (See also FILLING MACHINE.)

FOB. Prices paid for canned salmon on a "free on board" basis at the
cannery or some other specified coastal shipping point meant that
the producer incurred no costs for insurance, transportation, etc.,
from that point on.

FRESH/FROZEN-FISH TRADE. HALIBUT and some species of
SALMON, notably coho and springs, were cleaned, then chilled,
boxed, and sold fresh, or else were frozen in COLD-STORAGE
PLANTS, and sold either locally or shipped in carload lots to
Eastern markets by rail. A minimum rail carload lot of frozen fish
involved about 22,000 pounds (eighty to one hundred FISH
BOXES) in total.

FRESHET. A flood of a creek, stream, or river from heavy rain or
melted snow, which, when it occurred in the spring, would scour
out the salmon SPAWNING BEDS, thus destroying the eggs deposited there.

GANG KNIFE. Machine with a series of revolving knives (gangs),
which cut dressed salmon into properly sized pieces to fill a can.
Foot-powered "gangs" with eight blades could handle two sockeye
salmon at a time in the 1880s. This method began to be replaced by
steam-powered rotary cutters in the 1890s.

GAS BOAT. Fishboats and collectors powered by gasoline motors were introduced on the Columbia River and in Puget Sound in the 1890s, and on the Fraser in the early 1900s, but were prohibited in the northern fishing grounds until 1924. Diesel motors were first introduced in the salmon-canning industry to power TENDER-BOATS in 1914, but the equipment was too large to be practical for powering fishboats for some time to come.

GILLNET. A type of net for fishing sockeye and pink salmon. The gillnet is usually rectangular, with varying MESH SIZES (depending on the species and variety of fish sought and the fishing regulations in place), and ensnares fish by the gills when they strike it. Can be set (anchored) or allowed to drift with the tide or current; in British Columbia only the drift type was permitted. The best marine environment for the gillnet is silt-laden, shallow water of fairly uniform depth and free of snags or sharp ledges, where it can be used effectively night and day.

GLAZING. See COLD-STORAGE PLANT.

GUANO (FISH). Artificial fertilizer made from fish waste.

GUT SHED/FISH HOUSE. A building in which salmon BUTCHER-ING and SLIMING took place; after about 1910 these functions were carried out in the main canning plant.

HALF FLATS. See FLATS.

HALIBUT. Pacific halibut (*Hippoglossus stenolepis*), the largest of the flatfish family (the female halibut has been known to reach 500 pounds in weight), inhabit the waters of the continental shelf and, like Pacific SALMON, are anadromous (see SALMON). Halibut was fished in the early spring months, just after the HERRING season and before the spawning runs of salmon. Fishing with long-lines took place in halibut banks located off the Queen Charlotte Islands and the west coast of Vancouver Island. The depletion of these stocks forced fishers to move further out to sea. Ketchikan, Alaska, Prince Rupert and Vancouver, BC, and Seattle, Washington, were and are the centres of the industry. Canada and the US created an International [Halibut] Fisheries Commission in 1924; its power was strengthened in a new convention signed in 1930. Halibut was (and still is) sold fresh or frozen.

HANGING TWINE. Twine used to hang a net, so called because the MESH is hung by this twine between the corkline (which keeps the top of the net afloat) and the leadline (line on which lead weights are hung to keep the bottom of the net submerged).

HATCHERY. The human-controlled cultivation of the salmon resource by collecting, incubating, and hatching salmon eggs, and rearing the young (fry) in ponds (nurseries, rearing ponds), then releasing the infant salmon that manage to survive into the stream. In Canada, the pioneer hatchery operations were devoted mainly to propagating the sockeye species. Some were owned by government agencies, others by private interests; none of them were especially successful.

HERRING. An important food supply for many varieties of Pacific fish, the herring (*Clupea pallasii*) is a prolific producer, and is much oilier than the Atlantic variety. In the period from 1900 to World War II, herring was caught and used for bait in HALIBUT fishing; processed by CURING, DRY-SALTING (for the Orient, until mid-1930s); and reduced for fish meal and oil in REDUCTION PLANTS. During World War II it was canned (though normally the canned variety would be considered too oily). Herring involved both a summer and a winter fishery.

HUMPBACKS (HUMPIES or HUMPS). See SALMON.

HUNG NET. A fully constructed net consisting of MESH/WEB, leadline, and corkline. (See also HANGING TWINE.)

ICING-DOWN. Process of packing fish with ice, either on board a vessel or in a processing plant, to lower the temperature of its flesh, thus retarding spoilage.

INDEPENDENT GEAR. See ATTACHED LICENSES.

INDEPENDENT/FREE LICENSE. Independent fishers in BC were those holding individual licenses to fish; they sold their catch to canneries on the basis of a fixed price per fish, and divided the proceeds on a contract or share system. (See also ATTACHED LICENSE.)

INDIAN RUNNER/RECRUITER. An Indian who secured Indian fishers and cannery workers in advance each season, on a commission basis.

INSIDE FISHING/LABOUR. Fishing in the river or stream, or working inside the canning plant – as opposed to fishing outside, in the passages, straits, and gulfs, or working around the cannery site.

IRON CHINK. The common name for the (E.A.) Smith Butchering Machine. Its name derives from the fact that the labour it replaced was Chinese. After several years of trials, the first practical version was patented by Smith, of Seattle. It was sold on a small scale in the US in 1905, and was introduced in Canada (Fraser River) in 1906. In the 1907 improved version of this machine, a series of knives rapidly and automatically removed the heads, fins, and tails of salmon under jets of running water, and accomplished the first wash of the fish thus butchered. One machine could serve two canning lines simultaneously. Many improvements, such as making it adjustable to the various sizes and species of salmon, were needed to bring this innovation into common use, after World War I. Of all the innovations adopted by the Pacific salmon-cannery operators, this was the only one developed specifically for salmon canning.

"JAP" LABOUR. By the early 1900s, Chinese contractors in the US and in the Fraser River district of BC began relying on Japanese labourers to fill out their cannery gangs. Japanese also fished for the canneries or worked at building and repairing boats in most districts of BC.

JAPANESE FISHERS' BOSS. The head Japanese who hired and outfitted crews of Japanese fishers to work at specific canneries during the fishing season.

KETTLE. See LEAKS; BOILING KETTLE; LYE VAT/KETTLE.

KINGS. See SALMON.

KLOOTCHMEN/KLOOTCHES/KLOOTCH LABOUR. See CHINESE LABOUR.

L & B. Short form for the firm of Letson & Burpee, a major manufacturer of salmon-canning machinery and equipment, which had started up in New Westminster, then moved to Vancouver in 1895. It also had a shop in Bellingham, Washington.

LABELLING. After it was LACQUERED, a label was applied to each can, either manually, one edge being pasted and the other drawn over, or, by the time of World War I, by machine. Hand labelling was usually performed by Chinese, or sometimes by Indian children. After World War I it was more common not to apply labels at the individual plants, but instead to label at a central distribution point on the coast, or even to ship to export markets unlabelled so that the foreign buyers (importers and wholesalers) could label under their own BRAND NAMES.

LACQUERING. Involved dipping the end of each can into a vat of varnish. This created a protective coating on the tin, thus helping to prevent it from rusting. Machine methods began to replace manual lacquering beginning in about 1900; diffusion was rapid after 1910.

LAY/SHARE. Refers to the traditional payment or share on a fishboat. From the gross returns certain costs are deducted (boat fuel, lubricating oil, etc.). The remainder (net profit) is divided into shares which go to each member of the crew and the owner(s) of the boat and gear.

LEAKS/LEAKERS, MENDING OF. Hand- and mechanically soldered cans had to be tested for leaks after being cooked. Testing was done by plunging the cans into a cold-water bath (test kettles), or by sounding the cans with a mallet or steel rod (a task at which Chinese labourers became highly skilled). Leaky cans were set aside, as DO-OVERS, to be re-soldered.

LIGHT CANS. Underweight tins, when filled, were automatically discarded by the WEIGHING MACHINE, then "patched" to bring the contents up to weight, which was usually done by Indian women or Chinese men at a patching table. The FILLERS could be penalized for producing light and over-filled cans.

LINE. An assembly line or a unit of complementary equipment required for complete processing. The number of lines in a plant was taken as one important measure of its packing capacity. Cannery operators classified lines as fast or slow depending on whether or not an automatic feeder and filling machine were included. Often, cannery operators installed separate lines to pack different sizes or shapes of cans simultaneously, or simply to be on standby should there be periodic gluts of salmon or should the principal line break down. As a term related to fishing, "line" refers to a method of fishing whereby certain varieties of fish, such as HALIBUT and spring SALMON, are caught with lines and hooks.

LINE SHAFT. Traditional, efficient method of powering machines in a factory using a central power source ("prime mover") from which energy is transmitted along a central shaft to power the individual machines and equipment, which are themselves linked to the shaft by a system of belts and pulleys.

LOCK/LOCKED/SIDE SEAM. See BODY SEAMER.

LOFT. Space (usually the attic of the cannery) or separate building (variously referred to as warehouse, net house, or loft) for the storage of nets, floats, ropes, twine, hemp, mooring lines, etc., and/or empty cans.

LYE VAT/KETTLE. After they were filled, tins of salmon received a final bath in a heavy sheet-metal vat or pan containing a strong solution of lye (caustic soda) to clean off the grease and dirt which had accumulated during the canning process.

MEDIUM-RED SALMON. See SALMON.

MESH/WEB. Two loops of twine, joined together with knots to form a diamond shape. Mesh size is determined by the dimension of the mesh from the centre of one knot to the centre of the next, diagonally opposite, knot.

MESS HOUSE. A building at a cannery where some of the fishers, shoreworkers, and officials ate. Because the Chinese, Indians, and Japanese at the canneries usually ate in their own, separate quarters, the mess house was typically for the use of whites only; sometimes there was a separate mess for the officials.

MILD-CURE SALMON. A method of preserving salmon (usually springs) by cleaning, splitting, slightly SALTING, then brining (soaking in a saturated salt solution) in a TIERCE (wooden cask), as the first step in producing smoked salmon. Beginning in the 1890s, mild-cure plants were adjuncts to canneries; by the 1930s, they were independent businesses dominated by Japanese and located mainly around the mouth of the Skeena River and along the west coast of Vancouver Island.

MOTHERSHIP OPERATION. A large ship (later equipped with refrigeration and/or canning lines), to which was attached a fleet of catcher and scout boats. The first of the large-scale operations were initiated by Japanese fish-packing companies in the late 1920s; they were capable of intercepting return migrations of salmon before they entered American and Canadian waters.

NATIVE STREAMS. See SALMON RUNS.

NET. See HUNG NET.

NET BOSS. The superintendent (usually a white employee) of net making, mending, cleaning and preserving, and storing.

NET LOFT/HOUSE. See LOFT.

NET RACKS. Rows of pairs of smooth parallel wooden bars, about twelve feet long and set about five feet apart, for drying and mending nets outdoors after they were cleaned and treated and/or before they were stored.

NETMAN. A person who constructs, repairs, and applies preservatives to nets, fish traps, dip nets, etc. For many years, Indian women made and mended the nets for the cannery operations, especially in the northern districts.

NORWEGIAN-CURED HERRING. See HERRING.

NURSERY. See HATCHERY.

OFFAL. Fish waste (head, tail, and guts) produced in the packing process. In the early decades of the industry, offal was simply dumped into the tidal waters surrounding individual canneries; eventually, cannery operators were forced to reduce the waste, either at the cannery site itself or at a central REDUCTION PLANT, or to have it towed out to safe off-shore areas and dumped.

OILERY. For the reduction of fish oil and fish-liver oil (from varieties such as DOGFISH) for the manufacturing of lubricating oil, beginning in the 1890s. Later, in the 1930s, salmon- and halibut-liver oil was extracted for use in the manufacture of vitamins (a high-value product).

OILING. As a first step in preserving and conditioning fish nets, new nets were treated with linseed oil to keep them "sweet."

OIL APRONS. Protective clothing, made from oilcloth, which was worn by cannery workers.

OUTSIDE FISHING/LABOUR. See INSIDE FISHING/LABOUR.

OVALS. One-pound oval-shaped cans were used on occasion to pack salmon prior to World War I, and, more commonly, HERRING and PILCHARDS (because of the particular shape of these varieties of fish).

PACK. Refers to the output of canned salmon per cannery, canning company, district, or country, as measured in the number of 48-pound CASES of each species and can size, per day or per season.

PACKERS. (for vessels, see TENDERBOATS). Refers to fish-processing companies and their operators.

PATCHING/PATCHING TABLE. See LIGHT CANS.

PICKLING (SALMON). An old method of preserving salmon whereby split, cleaned fish are placed in a cask with great quantities of salt. When the cash is full, weighted boards are placed on the fish to keep them covered by the liquid which forms. Later, the fish are removed, scrubbed, and repacked with fresh salt.

PIG TIN. See TINPLATE.

PILCHARD. A type of HERRING, pilchards were first used commercially in BC in 1917, when a small quantity was canned. From then on, a canned pack was produced annually a until the 1940s, when this variety of fish disappeared from the BC coast. The market for canned pilchards was limited. Beginning in 1925, salmon-cannery operators began processing pilchards (and HERRING) for oil and meal in REDUCTION PLANTS; also, some independent plants were opened on the west coast of Vancouver Island for pilchard reduction.

PILES/PILE-DRIVER (cannery). A steam-driven machine was used for driving heavy posts vertically into the tide FLATS or foreshore; piles provided the foundations for the wharves, the canning plant, and many of the other buildings erected at a coastal cannery site.

PINKS. See SALMON.

POWER KNIFE. See GANG KNIFE.

PURSE SEINE. See SEINE FISHING.

QUADRENNIAL CYCLE. The Fraser River/Puget Sound salmon fishery has historically had a reasonably regular, highly pronounced four-year cycle of abundance: one excellent ("big") year, one not as good, and two poor ("off") years.

QUINNAT. See SALMON.

REACHES. Snags or sharp edges in rivers.

REARING PONDS. See HATCHERY.

RECEIVING FLOOR. An area of the GUT SHED or CANNERY where fish transferred from the boats or SCOWS are piled for gutting.

RED SALMON. See SALMON.

REDUCTION PLANT. For the processing of fish oil, fertilizer, and meal from fish, and from fish waste (head, tail, and guts). Reduction was an important side-line activity for many of the BC salmon-cannery operations in the 1920s and 1930s. (See also OFFAL; OILERY; PILCHARDS.)

REFORM LINE. Process for reforming semi-finished can bodies. Collapsed cans, which were manufactured at a central can-making plant (American Can Co., New Westminster, later Vancouver, was the major producer in BC), were designed for easier and cheaper transport to remote locations. The can-forming line, on which the can bodies were shaped and the bottoms seamed onto them, was synchronized with the canning line. This innovation was introduced in the early 1920s in BC.

RETORT/RETORT CARS/TRUCKS. A large steam pressure cooker, horizontal and cylindrical, of mild-steel construction, with a door that could be bolted into position and made steamtight. Introduced into the salmon-canning industry in late 1870s to replace second-stage cooking using open kettles, it underwent improvements to reduce the cooking and handling time, this increasing productivity and reducing cooking temperatures. Because steam under pressure is a safer, more reliable form of cooking than boiling, cooking in retorts produced a high-quality product and resulted in less waste due to spoilage. The capacity of the retort was expressed in the number of cars/trucks loaded with TRAYS of canned salmon it could hold.

RETORT MAN. One who operates and oversees the cooking process. The position was usually reserved for white workers.

ROUND-BOTTOMED BOAT. An oar – or sail-powered gillnet boat, commonly referred to as a "Columbia River boat," which was used on the Columbia in the 1870s, spread to Alaska in the 1880s, and almost completely replaced the original Fraser River gillnet SKIFF by the 1890s. It also soon became popular in northern BC.

SALMON. Family Salmonide, are of two varieties, Atlantic (genus *Salmo*) and Pacific (genus *Oncorhynchus*). Both are anadromous, that is, they spend most of their adult existence in the ocean but return to their native freshwater streams, etc., to spawn; but only the pacific variety dies after spawning. The Atlantic variety is a form of trout (as is the Pacific steelhead "salmon," *Salmo gairdneri*) and is seldom canned. The native range of the Pacific salmon includes the north Pacific Ocean, the Bering Strait, and the Southwest Beauford Sea, as well as the fresh waters contiguous to those areas. Of the seven distinct species, five are native to the North American coast: these constitute the five "grades" of canned salmon packed in BC and in the US states of California, Oregon, Washington, and Alaska. The most marketable species for canning (in terms of the firmness of flesh, rich, deep-red colour, and fine flavour) is *O. nerka*, known in the trade and labelled as sockeye (in BC and Puget Sound), blueback, or Alaska red. This salmon is relatively small (five to seven pounds), has a four- to five-year life cycle, and runs in July and August. The second most important is labelled pink salmon (*O. gorbuscha*), but was known in the trade as humpback, or humpie. These are even smaller in size than sockeye, but are highly prolific and mature in half the time; the season for pinks follows immediately that of the sockeye. Chum or Keta salmon (also called dog salmon in BC), *O. keta*, which are twice the size of sockeye, mature in four to six years, and constitute the fall fishery. Spring salmon (*O. tschawytscha*) were known as and labelled as spring and tyee on Puget Sound, king in Alaska, chinook on the Columbia and Fraser rivers, and quinnat on the Sacramento River. They are five times the average size of sockeye. Coho or silver salmon (*O. kisutch*) were known in the trade and labelled as medium red, silverside, and coho salmon. (In BC, immature coho were called "bluebacks.") The term "Siberian red" refers to the Japanese fishing industry's equivalent of sockeye salmon.

SALMON RUNS/STREAM. Adult Pacific salmon return from sea to their native rivers, streams, and creeks to spawn and die. They congregate for up to several weeks in the protected inshore waters, river estuaries, and mouths of spawning rivers and inlets before beginning their ascent to the SPAWNING BEDS.

SALT. A flavouring added to salmon in the tins before cooking; also used in large quantities in the cannery building at the end of each canning session, on the floors, BUTCHERING TABLES, SLIMING TANKS, and FILLING TABLES after being washed down, to keep these areas "sweet."

SALTERY. A facility for the dry-salting of fish, especially HERRING and chum SALMON. Some of them were located right at the cannery camps, although, until the mid 1930s, many were run as independent operations by Japanese owners. (See also MILD-CURE; DRY-SALTING.)

SALTING/SALTING MACHINE. A pinch of salt was added to each can before filling. This was a simple hand operation (using a perforated board and a scraper) until the early 1900s, after which time a salting machine was introduced which automatically deposited a measured amount of salt into each can on the line. The machine was powered by, and its action co-ordinated with, the FILLING MACHINE.

SANITARY CAN. Produced on the sanitary line, the technique combined the use of high-speed body-markers, the lap seamer (whereby the side seam was lapped and soldered for a short distance along the seam), and the DOUBLE SEAMER which revolutionized both can making and can sealing. It produced a uniform, more reliable can and eliminated the need for the topper and the SOLDER MACHINE. It was developed for the fruit-canning industry around 1905; and adapted for the salmon-canning industry a few years later.

SCOTCH-CURED HERRING. See CURING, HERRING.

SCOW. Flat-bottomed vessel for transporting fish or ice to the canneries. It was towed by steam-powered TUG or a TENDERBOAT.

SEAMER. See BODY SEAMER; DOUBLE SEAMER.

SEASON. Fishing season refers to the time when fish are available to be caught (in the case of salmon, to when various species are running). The season is also determined by regulation: government officials imposed a weekly close period (usually a 24- or 36-hour period during Saturday to Sunday), and decided on which date the legal fishing season would being and end. The timing of the season (natural or government-regulated) from one district to another depended on local conditions. The canning season was closely related to the fishing season, but the need for start-up and shut-down time at the cannery operations meant that the packing season was longer than the fishing season.

SEINE FISHING. The purse seine uses the principle of encirclement and is used mainly for the "schooling" species of salmon – chums and cohos – and for herring. Purse seines were first introduced to salmon fishing in the Puget Sound and Alaska districts, in the 1890s but were not permitted in BC before 1905. Purses consist of an extensive webbing of tarred cotton; at the top of the net are corks, and at the bottom, lead weights. Brass rings are hung at regular intervals on the leadline; a purseline or draw rope is then passed through these rings. The net is carried out by two vessels, which run in a circle, setting the net. The purseline tightens to trap the fish inside the purse, and is hauled in on a winch. On the Fraser, purse-seine boats (and their winches) were gas-powered by 1907. Beach seines were set from the shore; this method was less efficient for trapping salmon than purse seines. Drag seines operated mostly along the sand bars and beaches near a river's mouth. They were set at low tide, in a semicircle against the current, using a dory and a seine boat. The Dominion government issued exclusive privileges to canners for operating drag seines on certain tidal waters of BC until 1920.

SHARE SYSTEM OF PAYMENT. See LAY/SHARE.

SIBERIAN REDS/SALMON. See SALMON.

SILVERS. See SALMON.

SKIFF. Small, flat-bottomed vessel, usually powered with oars.

SLIMERS/SLIMING TANK. Slimers or washers completed the fish-cleaning process of washing in tanks, removing any blood and loose membranes and entrails, scraping the belly cavity, and scrubbing the skin side with a brush to remove slime (all of which, if not removed prior to canning, could cause the contents to spoil) after the salmon had been BUTCHERED. The washed fish was then thrown onto a DRAIN TABLE. Sliming was generally done by hand by Indian women and old people, but the introduction of the IRON CHINK eventually eliminated the need for hand sliming.

SLITTER. See BUTCHER.

SLOUGH. A slack-water channel in a river.

SOCKEYE. See SALMON.

SOLDER. A fusible alloy used in can making to join the edges of cans, and for sealing the lids closed. Also refers to the process of joining with solder.

SOLDER IRON. A rod used to apply solder when soldering by hand.

SOLDER MACHINE. The chain-solder machine was first introduced to salmon canning in the 1880s to replace the hand-soldering method. Cans were gripped and made to revolve by a heavy chain which, by its friction, hauled them through the long molten solder bath to seal the tops to the bodies. The chain was made to revolve by the action of a man turning the wheel to which the chain was attached. Finger attachments to keep the rolling cans apart began to replace the chain method in the 1890s.

SOLDERLESS CAN. See SANITARY CAN.

SPAWNED FISH. Once Pacific salmon have spawned, they have deteriorated to the point where they are no longer fit for human consumption.

SPAWNING BEDS. Salmon spawn (eggs) are deposited in the gravel beds of shallow, clear, fast-running streams and creeks, where they are fertilized. Every spawning stream supports a genetically distinct salmon population, or race, though, because of the migratory habits of Pacific salmon, the same spawning ground can, and does, support several distinct families of the same species, each one with a different "cycle year." Salmon require a fairly precise set of conditions in order to spawn; changes in the conditions of the spawning ground may cause the extermination of a stream's salmon population.

SQUARE SHEARS. Used to cut the lengths of TINPLATE from which can bodies were made by hand.

STALE FISH. Fish which ran late in the season, or was not canned soon enough after being caught, tended to lose its flavour and richness of colour. If canned, stale fish was marketed as second quality.

STEAM BOX. See EXHAUST BOX.

STEELHEAD. See SALMON.

STOPPING OFF. See VENTING.

SWELLS. Bulges in filled salmon cans that were a result of the contents being contaminated; these products could not be marketed.

SWELL HEADS. Usually referred to the bulge which normally appeared in the lid of a can of fish immediately after the second cooking; cans without swelled heads were suspected of being LEAKS. Sometimes, however, the term was used interchangeably with the term SWELLS.

TAINTED FISH. Fish which became contaminated before or during the canning process. Tainted fish will spoil in the can.

TALLS. The most popular shape for the one-pound can of salmon (pound talls). Talls were used almost exclusively for packing the cheaper grades of salmon; they were the most likely to be machine-filled, and, for that reason, were the size of can packed during periodic gluts in the supply of raw salmon.

TALLYMAN. Cannery employee who entered each delivery of fish by weight, number, and species into the tallybook of the fishing vessel or packer, initialled the entry, and made corresponding entries in his own book.

TENDERBOAT. Vessel powered by steam or diesel engine which was used to transport fish and supplies but did not itself engage in fishing. Small tenderboats which serviced the GILLNET fleet were called collectors, which the larger tenders servicing the SEINE fleet and transporting collector fish to the canneries were called packers. (See also SCOWS.)

TEST KETTLE. See LEAKS.

TICKET PUNCHER. Each FILLER had a ticket; for every TRAY of cans she filled, the Chinese boss or the foreman/floorlady punched a hole in it. The ticket formed the basis of the piece rate to be credited to each filler.

TIERCE. A large barrel for brining or packing MILD-CURE SALMON.

TINPLATE. A thin sheet of iron (or steel) coated with tin which was used for making cans.

TOPPER/TOPPING MACHINE. See CRIMPER.

TEREDO. A saltwater, wood-boring worm.

TRAP FISHING/TRAP NETS/POUND NETS. A carefully constructed assemblage of netting or wire mesh hung from piles driven close to the shore along spawning routes. Salmon were literally corralled once they entered the apparatus. Traps were usually company-owned, the company having to secure the rights to the trap locations. The method was essentially banned in BC from the beginning (the exception being in the Strait of Juan de Fuca areas).

TRAY (CAN). Each tray held a standard number of empty tins (12 tins if FLATS, 24 if TALLS) to be filled. Before World War I, filling the trays with empty cans was usually the work of Indian children.

TRAY (COOLER). See COOLERS.

TROLLING. Fishing with lines and hooks for spring and coho SALMON shifted only slowly from the traditional handlining operation, using small craft, to using powerboats rigged with tall poles carrying as many as six lines and power gurdies to speed up the handling of lines.

TUG. Small, powerful vessel for towing SCOWS and other vessels.

TYEE. See SALMON.

VACUUM CLOSING (SEAMING) MACHINE. The mechanical means to obtain the vacuum in a can necessary to preserve the contents properly. Introduced to the canning of salmon by the early 1920s, it eliminated the need for a separate DOUBLE SEAMER and the steam EXHAUST BOX, and made the modern, high-speed canning line possible.

VENTING. In the days of manual and machine soldering in canning, a vacuum was created to keep the contents of the can fresh. This was done by pricking a vent hole in the lid of each can (halfway between the centre and the edge) after first cooking, thereby allowing the steam to espace. The hole was then stopped off with a drop of solder.

WASHER. See SLIMER.

WASHING MACHINE. See CLEANER.

WASHING TABLE. Where filled cans were wiped after being soldered and before undergoing cooking.

WASHING TANK. See SLIMER.

WEIGHING MACHINE. Introduced into the salmon-canning industry at the turn of the century and widely adopted, especially after 1910, when federal legislation in both the US and Canada was enacted to ensure that the advertised weights of products in those countries were accurate. The machine automatically rejected LIGHT and overfilled cans.

WHITEWASHING. Treating the interior walls of the canneries with a solution of quicklime to reflect the light, and also as a health and fire-safety requirement.

WIPER. See CLEANER.

Notes

PREFACE

1 University of British Columbia Library, Special Collections (hereafter UBC), Henry Doyle Papers, box 5, file 7, "History of the Pacific Coast Salmon Industry"; and University of Washington Libraries, Manuscripts Division (hereafter UWA), Henry Doyle Papers, "Report of the Fourth Convention of the Canadian Fisheries Association," 3–5 June 1920.

2 *Newspaper Reference Book of Canada* (1903), 93.

3 Alfred Chandler, Jr., *The Visible Hand: The Managerial Revolution in American Business* (Cambridge, MA: Belnap Press 1977), 1; Adam Smith, *The Wealth of Nations*, Vol. 1 (New York: Dutton 1910; original 1776), books 1, 2.

4 Howard Lamar, "From Bondage to Contract: Ethnic Labor in the American West, 1600–1890," in Steven Hahn and Jonathan Prude, eds., *The Countryside in the Age of Capitalist Transformation: Essays in the Social History of Rural America* (Chapel Hill: University of North Carolina Press 1985), 294.

5 UBC, Doyle Papers, box 2, file 15, Doyle to E.D. Clarke (Association of Pacific Fisheries, Seattle), 9 July 1936.

6 UWA, Doyle Papers, box 9, scrapbook (1933–35), "Pacific Salmon: A History of the Fish and the Commercial Fishing Industry, by Henry Doyle," 1 April 1905.

7 See UBC, Doyle Papers, box 1, file 6, W.A. Clemens to Doyle, 18 Dec. 1946.

8 Ibid., Howay-Reid Collection of Books.

9 Ibid., Doyle Papers, boxes 1 and 3.

10 Ibid., boxes 2 and 3.

11 Ibid., box 4.

12 Ibid., oversize volumes.

13 Ibid., box 5.
14 Ibid., box 6.
15 Ibid., boxes 10 and 11.
16 Ibid., box 8.
17 Ibid., boxes 7 and 8.
18 Ibid., box 11.
19 Ibid., box 9 and oversize volumes.
20 Ibid., oversize volumes.

INTRODUCTION

1 Canada's historical vulnerability to outside economic forces is the subject of
   Harold Innis's pioneering studies of the cod fishery, the fur trade, and the
   mining industry. See also William L. Marr and Donald G. Paterson, *Canada: An Economic History* (Toronto: Gage 1980), 1–9; and Dianne Newell,
   Technology on the Frontier: Mining in Old Ontario (Vancouver: University of
   British Columbia Press 1986), 1–10.
2 Marr and Paterson, *Canada: An Economic Historic*, 344.
3 J.J. Deutsch, S.M. Jamieson, T.I. Matuszewski, A.D. Scott, and R.M.
   Will, *Economics of Primary Production in British Columbia*, vol. III, "The
   Fishing Industry of British Columbia," (unpublished typescript, University
   of British Columbia Library, 1959), 1–3.
4 M.C.Urquhard, ed., *Historical Statistics of Canada* (Toronto: University of
   Toronto Press 1965), 287–407; Canada, Department of Marine and Fisheries, Fisheries Branch, *Annual Report* [hereafter *Annual Report, Dominion
   Fisheries*] (Ottawa 1887), 9; and Canada, Dominion Bureau of Statistics,
   Fisheries Statistics (Ottawa 1919–30), Capital Invested table.
5 *Annual Report, Dominion Fisheries* (1906), xxii–xxiii.
6 Deutsch, et al., *Economics of Primary Production in British Columbia*, vol. III
   [part II], "The Marketing of the Products of the Fishing Industries," 5.
7 A.W. Bitting, *Appertization or the Art of Canning: Its History and Development* (San Francisco, the Trade Pressroom 1937), 7–8.
8 Keith Ralston, "Patterns of Trade and Investment on the Pacific Coast,
   1867–1892: The Case of the British Columbia Salmon Canning Industry,"
   B.C. Studies, no. 1 (Winter 1968–69): 37–9; and Edward F. Keuchel, Jr.,
   "The Development of the Canning Industry in New York State to 1960,"
   (Ph.D. dissertation, Cornell University 1970), 1–44.
9 Gordon B. Dodds, *The Salmon King of Oregon: R.D. Hume and the Pacific
   Fisheries* (Chapel Hill: University of North Carolina Press 1959). Hume's
   cannery on the Sacramento packed chinook salmon; sockeye did not run on
   this river.

10 Deutsch, et al., *Economics of Primary Production in British Columbia*, vol. VI, "The Importance of Transportation in the Economy of British Columbia," 19.

11 See W.A. Carrothers, *The British Columbia Fisheries* (Toronto: University of Toronto Press 1941); and Joseph E. Forester and Anne D. Forester, *Fishing: British Columbia's Commercial Fishing History* (Saanichton, BC: Hancock House Publishers 1975).

12 See George MacDonald and Richard Ingus, eds., *Skeena River Prehistory*, Mercury Series, Archaeological Survey of Canada, Paper no. 87 (Ottawa: National Museum of Man 1979). This tradition continued into the twentieth century.

13 See Ralston, "Patterns of Trade and Investment," 39.

14 Deutsch, et al., "The Fishing Industry of British Columbia," 4–5ff. For details on all salmon fishing methods, see Duncan A. Stacey, *Sockeye & Tinplate: Technological Change in the Fraser River Canning Industry, 1871–1912* (Victoria: BC Provincial Museum 1982) ch. 2; and Forester and Forester, *Fishing*, 55–86.

15 Arthur F. McElvoy, *The Fisherman's Problem: Ecology and Law in the California Fisheries, 1850–1980* (Cambridge: Cambridge University Press 1986), 10.

16 Ibid., 6.

17 Ibid., 10.

18 See, for example, Francis T. Christy, Jr., and Anthony Scott, *The Commonwealth in Ocean Fisheries: Some Problems of Growth and Economic Allocation* (Baltimore: Johns Hopkins University Press 1965); and James A. Crutchfield and Guilio Pontecorvo, *The Pacific Salmon Fisheries: A Study of Irrational Conservation* (Washington, DC: Johns Hopkins University Press 1969), ch. 1.

19 Sol Sinclair, *License Limitation – British Columbia: A Method of Economic Fisheries Management* (Ottawa: Department of Fisheries 1960). The recent series of crises and bonanzas in the west coast fishery inspired an interesting analysis of the impact of the changing government policy on the social and economic structure of the industry. See Patricia Marchak, Neil Guppy, and John McMullan, eds., *Uncommon Property: The Fishing and Fish Processing Industries in British Columbia* (Toronto: Methuen 1987).

20 Marchak et al., *Uncommon Property*, 1–31, 353–9.

21 Canada, British Columbia Fishery Commission, 1892, *Report* (Ottawa: Queen's Printer 1893), 132–3. Native peoples, none of whom were called as witnesses, had had several thousand years to observe wild salmon.

22 Cicely Lyons, *Salmon: Our Heritage. The Story of a Province and an Industry* (Vancouver: BC Packers' Ltd. 1969), appendix 17, "Salmon Hatcheries Operated in B.C. by the Dominion Government, 1884–1935," 668.

23 See Canada, Commission of Conservation, *Land, Fisheries and Game, Minerals* (Ottawa: King's Printer 1911).

24 Canada, British Columbia Fisheries Commission, *Report and Recommendations, 1922* (Ottawa: King's Printer 1922).

25 For a review of conservation legislation from 1889 to 1924 see Willis A. Rich and Edwin M. Ball, *Statistical Review of the Alaska Salmon Fisheries, Part 1: Bristol Bay and the Alaska Peninsula*, Doc. no. 1041 (Washington, DC: US Dept. of Commerce, Bureau of Fisheries 1928), 47–52. For the post-1930s, see Richard A. Cooley, *Politics and Conservation: The Decline of the Alaska Salmon* (New York: Harper & Row 1963).

26 Despite four decades of commissions, conferences, and treaties, a sockeye-salmon fisheries convention was not formally signed and ratified by Canada and the United States until 1937. See Cicely Lyons, *Salmon: Our Heritage*, appendix 23, 676–8, for a list of conferences leading to the signing of the Sockeye Convention and the establishment of the International Pacific Salmon Fisheries Commission (1937); and Carrothers, *The British Columbia Fisheries*, ch. 7.

27 Homer E. Gregory and Kathleen Barnes, *North Pacific Fisheries, with Special Reference to Alaska Salmon* (San Francisco: American Council Institute of Pacific Relations 1939), 126–52.

28 Frank Millerd, "Expansion and Consolidation in the British Columbia Salmon Canning Industry, 1903–1928" (paper presented at the 13th Conference on Quantitative Methods in Canadian Economic History, Wilfrid Laurier University, Waterloo, Ontario, 16–17 March 1984), 1–3.

29 Canada established preferential trade agreements with France (1923) and Australia (1925, 1931). Carrothers, *The British Columbia Fisheries*, 52–3.

30 See D.G. Paterson, "European Financial Capital and British Columbia: An Essay on the Role of the Regional Entrepreneur," *B.C. Studies* no. 21 (Spring 1974): 33–47.

31 Briton Cooper Busch, *The War Against the Seals: A History of the North American Seal Fishery* (Montreal: McGill-Queen's University Press 1985), 143–5.

32 See Public Archives of British Columbia, Robert Paterson Rithet Papers, Add Mss 504.

33 Ralston, "Patterns of Trade and Investment," 42–4; and Paterson, "European Financial Capital and British Columbia," 33.

34 David Reid has exaggerated both the rate of decline of ABC Packing (a successful British-backed firm which actually remained in family hands for three generations, until the 1960s) and the success of British Columbia Packers Association, which, though registered in the United States until 1910, was always heavily financed by Eastern Canadian investors, in his perception of a trend away from Canadian and British capital to United States capital in the BC salmon-canning industry at the turn of the century.

David J. Reid, "Company Mergers in the Fraser River Salmon Canning Industry, 1885–1902," *Canadian Historical Review* 56, no. 3 (Sept. 1975): 282–302; and ibid., *The Development of the Fraser River Salmon Canning Industry, 1885 to 1913* (Vancouver: Environment Canada, Pacific Region, 1973).

35 Dianne Newell, "Dispersal and Concentration: The Slowly Changing Spatial Pattern of the British Columbia Salmon Canning Industry," *Journal of Historical Geography* 14, no. 1 (1988): 22–36.

36 Ibid., 25.

37 Dianne Newell, "Surveying Historic Industrial Tidewater Sites: The Case of the B.C. Salmon Canning Industry," *IA: The Journal of the Society for Industrial Archeology* 13, no. 1 (1987): 1–16.

38 To my knowledge, no count exists of the American cannery sites, though Guimary surveyed the sites in one section of Alaska. See Donald L. Guimary, "Salmon Canneries in Southeast Alaska: A Documentation of Selected Historic Canneries and Cannery Sites" (typescript, Office of History and Archeology, Alaska Division of Parks, Anchorage, 1983).

39 William M. Ross, "Salmon Cannery Distribution on the Nass and Skeena Rivers of British Columbia, 1877–1926," (graduating essay in Geography, University of British Columbia 1967).

40 Cooley, *Politics and Conservation*, 39–42.

41 Canada, Department of the Naval Service, "Fisheries Inspection Report, B.C., 1915–16," *Sessional Papers* (1917), 244; ibid., 1916–17 (1918), 230–2; ibid., 1918 (1920), 18, 44; ibid., 1919 (1921), 50. The American domestic demand for canned salmon increased during the war; US tariff barriers (of fifteen percent) effectively prevented the importation of canned salmon from Canada, but no such barriers existed for raw salmon.

42 J.C. Weldon, "Consolidations in Canadian Industry, 1900–1948," in L.A. Skeoch, ed., *Restrictive Trade Practices in Canada, Selected Readings* (Toronto: McLelland & Stewart Ltd. 1966), 232–4; and Marr and Paterson, *Canada: An Economic History*, 415.

43 Naomi R. Lamoreaux, *The Great Merger Movement in American Business, 1895–1904* (Cambridge: Cambridge University Press 1985), 1ff.

44 In the American fruit- and vegetable-canning industries, where most of the technological changes occurred first, the rate of adoption was swift and the impact on productivity and labour relations more dramatic. See Martin Brown and Peter Philips, "Craft Labor and Mechanization in Nineteenth-Century American Canning," *Journal of Economic History* 46 (Sept. 1986): 743–56; ibid., "The Decline of the Piece-Rate System in California Canning: Technological Innovation, Labor, Management, and Union Pressure, 1890–1947," *Business History Review* 60 (Winter 1986): 564–601; and Vicki L. Ruiz, *Cannery Women, Cannery Lives: Mexican Women, Unionization, and the California Food Processing Industry, 1930–1950* (Alberquerque: Universi-

ty of New Mexico Press 1987). The development and diffusion of the automatic salmon-butchering machine (known as the "Iron Chink") is discussed
in Patrick O'Bannon, "Technological Change in the Pacific Coast Salmon
Canning Industry, 1900–1925: A Case Study," *Agriculture History* 56, no. 1
(Jan. 1982): 151–66; and ibid., "Waves of Change: Mechanization in the
Pacific Coast Canned Salmon Industry, 1864–1914," *Technology and Culture*, no. 28 (July 1987): 558–77. On the solderless or "sanitary" can and its
development and diffusion in British Columbia, see Stacey, *Sockeye & Tinplate*, ch. 4.

45 Dianne Newell, "The Rationality of Mechanization in the Pacific Salmon-
Canning Industry Before the Second World War," *Business History Review* 62
(forthcoming).

46 The [Victoria] *Colonist*, 6 Sept. 1901; Port Townsend *Call*, 10 Aug. 1905;
and *Pacific Fisherman Yearbook* 3 (1905): 23.

47 The issues of overcapacity and diseconomies of large-scale production in
salmon canning are thoroughly discussed in Gregory and Barnes, *North
Pacific Fisheries*, 110–25. Salmon was hand-packed in many American dis-
tricts well into the 1930s. See "How Salmon is Canned," *Pacific Fisherman
Yearbook*, Supplement (Jan. 1936): 15–20. In British Columbia, the lack of
canning machinery for packing salmon to the specifications of the British
Ministry of Food during World War II was problematic. See Dianne
Newell, "The Politics of Food in World War II: Great Britain's Grip on
Canada's Pacific Fishery," *Historical Papers/Communications historiques 1987*
(1988): 189–90.

48 See Lauren W. Casaday's big study of labour contracting, "Labor Unrest
and the Labor Movement in the Salmon Industry of the Pacific Northwest,"
(Ph.D. dissertation, University of California, Berkeley, 1937); Jack Masson
and Donald Guimary, "Asian Labor Contractors in the Alaskan Canned Salmon Industry: 1880–1937," *Labor History* 22 (Summer 1981): 377–97;
"Pioneer Salmon Cannery Labour Contractors," *Western Fisheries* 12 (June
1936): 8–9; and Alicja Muszynski, "The Creation and Organization of
Cheap Wage Labour in the B.C. Fishing Industry" (Ph.D. dissertation,
University of British Columbia 1986). For the wider application see Patricia
Cloud and David W. Galenson, "Chinese Immigration and Contract Labor
in the Late Nineteenth Century," *Explorations in Economic History* 24 (Jan.
1987): 22–42; and Yuzo Murayama, "Contractors, Collusion, and Competition: Japanese Immigrant Railroad Laborers in the Pacific Northwest,
1898–1911," *Explorations in Economic History* 21 (July 1984): 290–305.

49 Conversation with Gladys Blyth, Port Edward, BC, May 1988.

50 Well documented in Casaday, "Labor Unrest and the Labor Movement
in the Salmon Industry," 82, table 11, "Number of Shoresmen ... [by]
Principal Racial and Nationality Groups, 1907–1934."

51 Gregory and Barnes, *North Pacific Fisheries*, 213.

52 Masson and Guimary, "Asian Labor Contractors," 396–7; and Patrick W. O'Bannon, "Technological Change in the Pacific Coast Canned Salmon Industry: 1864–1924" (Ph.D. dissertation, University of California, San Diego 1983), 344–9.

53 See British Columbia, Department of Labour, *Annual Report*, 1920 to 1943 (Victoria, 1920–43).

54 Deutsch, et al., *Economics of Primary Production in British Columbia*, vol. IV, "Industrial Relations in the Basic Industries of British Columbia," 52. Stuart M. Jamieson and Percy Gladstone, "Unionism in the Fishing Industry of British Columbia," *Canadian Journal of Economics and Political Science* 16 (Feb. 1950): 1–11; ibid., 16 (May 1950): 143–71 (includes lists of organizations of fishers and allied workers' unions and of strikes in the industry to that year); Alicja Muszynski, "The Organization of Women and Ethnic Minorities in a Resource Industry: A Case Study of the Unionization of the Shoreworkers in the B.C. Fishing Industry, 1937–1982," *Journal of Canadian Studies* 19 (Jan. 1984): 89–107; Masson and Guimary, "Asian Labor Contractors," 396–7; George North and Harold Griffin, *A Ripple, A Wave: The Story of Union Organization in the B.C. Fishing Industry* (Vancouver: Fisherman Publishing Society 1974); and H. Keith Ralston, "The 1900 Strike of Fraser River Sockeye Salmon Fishermen" (M.A. thesis, University of British Columbia 1965).

55 See James Conley, "Relations of Production and Collective Action in the Salmon Fishery, 1900–1925," in Rennie Warburton and David Coburn, eds., *Workers, Capital, and the State in British Columbia, Selected Papers* (Vancouver: University of British Columbia Press 1988), 107–8.

56 Canada, Royal Commission on Chinese and Japanese Immigration, *Report. Sessional Papers* (1902), no. 54, 135–64; and W. Peter Ward, *White Canada Forever: Popular Attitudes and Public Policy Toward Orientals in British Columbia* (Montreal: McGill-Queen's University Press 1978), 103.

57 Ward, *White Canada Forever*, 55, and tables 1 and 2, 170–1.

58 The literature is summarized in Gillian Creese, "Class, Ethnicity, and Conflict: The Case of Chinese and Japanese Immigrants, 1880–1923," in Warburton and Coburn, eds., *Workers, Capital, and the State in British Columbia*, 66–8.

CHAPTER ONE

1 Described in Charles E. Goad, *Fraser River Canneries, British Columbia, Including Steveston, 1897*, UBC (a key map is included on sheet 260); W.A. Carrothers, *The British Columbia Fishery*, foreword by H.A. Innis; and

Canada, British Columbia Fishery Commission, *Report and Minutes of Evidence, 1892*, 10c.

2 Keith Ralston, "The 1900 Strike of Fraser River Sockeye Salmon Fishermen," ii.

3 UBC, Doyle Papers, box 1, file 1, "Chronological Record of Henry Doyle's Connections with BC Salmon Fisheries," c. 1957.

4 Ibid., box 5, file 7, "Report on British Columbia Salmon Industry," 5 Dec. 1901.

5 David J. Reid, "Company Mergers in the Fraser River Salmon Canning Industry," 282–302.

6 Cicely Lyons, *Salmon: Our Heritage*, appendix 25, "What Happened to the Plants Acquired by the B.C. Packers Association," 681–3.

7 UBC, Doyle Papers, box 1, file 1, "Chronological Record."

8 Lyons, *Salmon: Our Heritage*, 232. The Bank of Montreal took over Molson's Bank in 1924.

9 The company re-incorporated as a BC company in 1910.

10 The statistics and appraisals are with the Doyle collection but are not reproduced here.

11 Doyle speculated at the time that a line of the Canadian Northern Railway would be built to Port Simpson. The line that was eventually built (1907–14) was that of the Grand Trunk Pacific, connecting Edmonton to Prince Rupert.

12 The story of the timber rush is dramatically told in M. Allerdale Grainger, *Woodsmen of the West*, New Canadian Library No. 42 (Toronto: McClelland and Stewart 1964. First published 1908).

13 See UBC, Brunswick Cannery Records (No. 2, Canoe Pass), 1896–1928. When the partners sold the three plants to British Columbia Packers Association in 1903, operations at No. 1 (at Steveston) were amalgamated with the adjoining Imperial cannery. No. 3 (at Rivers Inlet) remained operational until 1930. No. 2 became a fish camp for the Imperial cannery, also in 1930.

14 See UBC, J.H. Todd and Sons Ltd., Records, 1910–1954. This Victoria-based company acted as a salmon-cannery agent and operated canneries in its own right.

15 Keith Ralston, "John Sullivan Deas: A Black Entrepreneur in British Columbia Salmon Canning," *B.C. Studies* no. 32 (Winter 1976–77): 64–78.

CHAPTER TWO

1 D.B. Deloach, *The Salmon Canning Industry* (Corvallis: Oregon State College 1939).

2 UWA, Doyle Papers, box 1, file 1, "The Deep Sea Life of the Pacific Salmon, 15 January 1905, by Henry Doyle." The injury done to the salmon

fishery by sea lions by World War I was so great that the Dominion government paid a one-dollar bounty for every seal killed.

3 See also British Columbia, "Report of the Fisheries Commissioner of B.C. for 1905," *Sessional Papers* (1906), 6. Babcock wrote that some people believe in the "home stream" theory but that he had his doubts about it.

4 See Duncan Stacey, *Sockeye & Tinplate*, ch. 1; and UBC, G.M. Letson Papers, Letson & Burpee Ltd., machine manufacturers and founders. Founded in New Westminster, the firm moved to Vancouver in 1895; it produced equipment for the salmon-canning industry until World War II. See also UBC, Reliance Motor and Machine Works Ltd. Records. This company produced equipment for salmon-canning and other resource industries in the province beginning in the 1920s.

5 As well as Stacey, *Sockeye & Tinplate*, see Patrick O'Bannon, "Technological Change in the Pacific Coast Canned Salmon Industry: 1864–1924."

6 National Archives of Canada (hereafter NA), Records of the Department of Indian Affairs, RG 10, AW1, R6405, Field Office Correspondence and Miscellaneous, vol. 1454, Indian Agent's Letterbook, New Westminster Agency (1900) 11 July, 741; 13 July, 746; 6 Aug., 38; and Canada, Department of Indian Affairs, *Annual Report, 1900* (Ottawa 1901), Reports of Superintendent and Agents, Kwawkewlth Agency, 9 July. The agent warned "all those [Indians] who were going to the Fraser against joining the Fishermen's union there." The Indians, he reported, "promised to have nothing to do with it."

7 See Cicely Lyons, *Salmon: Our Heritage*, appendix 20, 67. In 1924 the industry arranged with the Canadian Manufacturers Association to have the CMA represent fish processors in BC, through a Canned Salmon Section and a Fish Meal and Oil, and Dry Salt Section. In anticipation of World War II, early in 1939 BC salmon canners cut with the CMA to form a new provincial association: The Salmon Canners Operating Committee, which negotiated the wartime contracts for the BC pack. Once the British Ministry of Food, the main purchaser of the pack, wound up its business in Canada, in 1951, the salmon-cannery operators joined the newly formed Fisheries Association of BC, which constituted the western division of the Fisheries Council of Canada. (In 1984 this was replaced by the Fisheries Council of BC, an independent body.)

8 Rolf Knight, *Indians at Work: An Informal History of Native Indian Labour in British Columbia, 1858–1930* (Vancouver: New Star Books 1978), ch. 6.

9 NA, RG 10, AW1, R6405, vol. 1461, Indian Agent's Letterbook, New Westminster Agency (1904), 1 Aug., 324; 22 Aug., 401; and (the quote) 31 Aug., 468.

10 Lyons, *Salmon: Our Heritage*, 245–46.

11 Ibid., 246.

12 Hugh W. McKervill, *The Salmon People: The Story of Canada's West Coast Salmon Fishing Industry* (Vancouver: Gray's Publishing 1967), 78.
13 UWA, Doyle Papers, box 2, scrapbook (1877–1902), Letter of Agreement dated 22 Feb. 1902.
14 See ibid., box 1, file 1, Robert Ker, secretary-treasurer of BC Packers Association, Vancouver, to Robert Ward & Co. Ltd., Victoria, 13 April 1905; ibid., Ward & Co. to BC Packers Association, 14 April 1905; and UBC, Doyle Papers, box 1, file 14, Ward & Co. Ltd., to Doyle, 15 April 1905. According to Ward, the association's insurance business had been divided among the firms R.P. Rithet & Co., Evans, Coleman & Evans, and Ceperley, MacKenzie & Rounsefell; Ward & Co. were dropped.
15 This is found in a longer account by Doyle, in "Rise and Decline of the Pacific Salmon Fisheries," c. 1950, vol. 2, 226–46 (UBC, Howay-Reid Collection).
16 UBC, Doyle Papers, box 4, notebook 22, "General Notes 1905–06," 19 and 20 Jan., 14, 16, and 19 Feb., 1906.

CHAPTER THREE

1 Kenneth Johnstone, *The Aquatic Explorers: A History of the Fisheries Research Board of Canada* (Toronto: University of Toronto Press, and the Canadian Department of Fisheries and the Environment 1977), 63–8.
2 UBC, Doyle Papers, box 2, file 8, Doyle to Hon. H.C. Brewster, Victoria, 11 Jan. 1916; and Cicely Lyons, *Salmon: Our Heritage*, 360, 382. Reports of the investigation appeared in the annual reports of the provincial department of fisheries.
3 Canada, Dominion Fisheries Commission for British Columbia, 1905–07, *Report and Recommendations* (Ottawa: King's Printer 1908).
4 British Columbia, "Report of the Fisheries Commissioner for 1919," *Sessional Papers* (1920), vol. 2, 69ff.
5 D.G. Paterson, "The North Pacific Seal Hunt, 1886–1910: Rights and Regulations," *Explorations in Economic History* 14 (1977): 97–119.
6 UWA, Doyle Papers, box 1, file 8, "Proposed Government Policy for BC Fisheries, Argument Submitted Hon. S.L. Howe by Henry Doyle, Feb. 1930." The ban on gas motors in the North lasted until 1924.
7 Canada, *Report of the Dominion-British Columbia Boat Rating Commission, 1910* (Ottawa: King's Printer 1911). The commissioners were J.P. Babcock, Deputy Commissioner of Fisheries, Province of BC, and J.T. Williams, Dominion Inspector of Fisheries (Pacific). See Lyons, *Salmon: Our Heritage*, 685–6. A thorough discussion of this salmon-fishing regulation, and the subsequent changes over the next decade, is contained in a paper written by Henry Doyle in 1919 (document 57).

8 *Pacific Fisherman* (Jan. 1913), 37.

9 Lyons, *Salmon: Our Heritage*, 114.

10 Ibid.

CHAPTER FOUR

1 *Canned Salmon: The Ideal Army and Navy Ration, an argument presenting the merits of canned salmon as a nutritious low priced article of food especially suited to military and naval purposes* (Seattle: Association of Alaska Salmon Packers and Puget Sound Canners Association [1915?]).

2 On Canadian canned-salmon purchases during the war, see Great Britain, Board of Agriculture and Fisheries, Parts 1 & 2, Fisheries in the Great War (London: HMSO 1920), xxx–xxxvi, 105–13, table 14 (p. 185); and Sir Thomas George, *The Unbroken Front: Ministry of Food, 1916–1944* (London: Everybody's Books 1944).

3 James Conley, "Relations of Production and Collective Action in the Salmon Fishery, 1900–1925," in Rennie Warburton and David Coburn, eds., *Workers, Capital, and the State in British Columbia, Selected Papers*, 86–116.

4 Cicely Lyons, *Salmon: Our Heritage*, 321.

5 Canada, Royal Commission on the Salmon Fisheries and Canning Industry in British Columbia, *Report of the Special Fishery Commission, 1917* [District no. 2, Northern Coast and Queen Charlotte Islands] (Ottawa: King's Printer 1918). (Also known as the Sanford Evans Commission, after its chairman, who was a Winnipeg economist and statistician.)

6 Canada, Department of Naval Service, *Fishery Inspector's Report, 1916–17* (Ottawa 1918), 231.

7 UBC, Doyle Papers, box 11, file 2, Memo for BC Salmon Canners Association Meeting, 18 Jan. 1921.

8 For this information I rely heavily on UBC, Doyle Papers, box 1, file 1, "Chronological Record"; and Lyons, *Salmon: Our Heritage*, 308, 313, 315, 330, 343.

9 See Lyons, *Salmon: Our Heritage*, 310–11.

10 Good information on the cutbacks exists in British Columbia Fire Underwriters Association, *Plans of Salmon Canneries in British Columbia Together with Inspection Reports on Each, Aug. 1924*; and Canada, Department of Marine and Fisheries, *Annual Report*, 1919 to 1923 (Ottawa 1920–24).

11 UBC, Doyle Papers, box 11, file 2, Memo for BC Salmon Canners Association Meeting, 18 Jan. 1921.

12 A "combination" is distinguished from a consolidation or merger in that with the former, the single control is established by agreement rather than ownership.

14 British Columbia, "Report on Oriental Activities in the Province," *Sessional Papers*" (1927), vol. 12, 17–19; and Joseph E. Forester and Anne D. Forester, *Fishing: British Columbia's Commercial Fishing History*, 159–60. The Japanese successfully fought the policy in court.

15 UBC, Doyle Papers, box 11, file 17, "Evidence, Parliamentary Fisheries Committee," 14 Aug. 1922, testimony of Robert Hanna [Prince Rupert fisherman for the Port Edward cannery], A–17; and NA, RG 10, AW1, R6405, vol. 1349, Incoming Correspondence, Cowichan Agency, 26 July 1909, 86.

16 UBC, Doyle Papers, box 1, file 1, "Chronological Record."

17 See Lyons, *Salmon: Our Heritage*, 356–7. She based her conclusion on the replacement appraisal records held by British Columbia Packers Co.

18 See UBC, Francis Millerd Papers (Gosse-Millerd Ltd., Francis Millerd and Co. Ltd., and Francis Millerd Co.); ibid., Anglo-British Columbia Packing Co. Records; Vancouver City Archives, Bell-Irving Family Papers (Anglo-British Columbia Packing Co.), Add. Mss. 485, vols 1–5; and ibid., Canadian Fishing Co. Ltd. Records.

CHAPTER FIVE

1 UWA, Doyle Papers, box 1, file 5, Doyle to W.P. Powell (Powell & Bros, Vancouver), 30 March 1922; Doyle to Stuart Cameron, Vancouver, 10 May and 31 May 1922; and W.A. MacKenzie & Co., Toronto to Cameron, 23 May 1922.

2 Homer Gregory and Kathleen Barnes, *North Pacific Fisheries*, 134–7; and Alfred Chandler, Jr., *The Visible Hand*, 391–402.

3 See Richard Cooley, *Politics and Conservation*, 107–12.

4 In 1914, British Columbia Packers Asosociation formed a second company, British Columbia Fishing & Packing Company Limited, which it incorporated under a dominion charter; the latter then became the operating company, effective 1 January 1924, when it bought out the original company. See Cicely Lyons, *Salmon: Our Heritage*, 239–40.

5 For the story of the trial in October, 1924, of Jarvis and the Hon. Peter Smith, see Lyons, *Salmon: Our Heritage*, 694–9. See also *Vancouver Province*, 22 May 1926 and 20 Oct. 1928. The signatories to a 1926 petition for a new trial to clear Jarvis's name included such Canadian luminaries as W.G. Gooderman, George H. Gooderham, Sir C.H. Tupper, Sir Clifford Sifton, and Sir Joseph Flavelle. (UWA, Doyle Papers, box 6, scrapbook (1923–26).

6 Lyons, *Salmon: Our Heritage*, 240–1.

7 *Vancouver Province*, 20 Dec. 1926 (UWA, Doyle Papers, box 6, scrapbook (1923–26).

8 See UBC, Doyle Papers, box 1, file 9, various letters from Æmilius Jarvis to Doyle, and box 2, file 14, various letters from Doyle to Jarvis.

9 UBC, Doyle Papers, box 3, file 14, Doyle to C.W. Chesterton (Calgary), 26 May 1928.

EPILOGUE

1 UBC, Doyle Papers, box 1, file 5.

2 Ibid., box 1, file 6, John N. Cobb to Doyle, 30 May 1919.

3 Ibid., box 1, file 4, H.R. McMillan to Doyle, 11 June 1937; Doyle to McMillan, 17 June 1937.

4 Ibid., see various letters box 1, files 13, 14; box 2, files 17, 18; and box 3, file 2.

5 Ibid., box 3, file 2, Doyle to Peter A. Larkin, 21 Aug. 1957.

6 Ibid., box 1, file 3, Larkin to Doyle, 19 Sept., 6 Oct. 1957.

7 Ibid., box 3, file 2, Doyle to Larkin, 2 October 1957. Doyle must have changed his mind; by June, 1959, he had donated the manuscript to UBC. For the letter of acknowledgement see box 1, file 3, Larkin to Doyle, 8 June 1959.

Bibliography

These published sources are included to give readers a start in pursuing for themselves the subject of this book, the rise of the Pacific salmon-canning industry. For a more comprehensive guide to the fuller range of literature, including unpublished studies and manuscripts, see the notes to individual chapters, and Dianne Newell and Logan Hovis, compilers, "British Columbia's Salmon Canning Industry: A Preliminary, Annotated Guide to Bibliographical and Archival Sources" (typescript, UBC Library, Special Collections 1985).

GOVERNMENT REPORTS

Alaska. *Alaska Fishery and Fur Seal Industry*, 1922 to 1937.

British Columbia. Department of Fisheries [title varies]. *Annual Report*, 1902– .

– Department of Fisheries. *The Commercial Salmon Fisheries of British Columbia* Victoria: King's Printer 1938.

Canada. British Columbia Fisheries Commission. *Report and Recommendations, 1922*. Ottawa: King's Printer 1923.

– *The Commercial Fisheries of Canada*. Ottawa: Queen's Printer 1957.

– Department of Marine and Fisheries [title varies]. Fisheries Branch. *Annual Report*. 1868– .

– Dominion Bureau of Statistics. *Fisheries Statistics* [title varies]. 1917– .

– Dominion-British Columbia Fisheries Commission, 1905–07, *Report and Recommendations*, Ottawa: King's Printer 1908.

– *Report of the Dominion-British Columbia Boat Rating Commission, 1910*. Ottawa: King's Printer 1911.

– Royal Commission on Chinese and Japanese Immigration. *Report, Sessional Papers* (1902), no. 54.

– Royal Commission on the Salmon Fisheries and Canning Industry in British Columbia. *Report of the Special Fishery Commission, 1917*. Ottawa: King's Printer 1918.

Carter, N.M. *Index and List of Titles, Fisheries Research Board of Canada and Associated Publications, 1900–1964. Bulletin of the Fisheries Research Board of Canada* no. 164 (1968).

Cobb, John N. *The Pacific Salmon Fisheries*, 4th ed., U.S. Department of Commerce, Bureau of Fisheries Document no. 1092. Washington, DC: USGPO 1930.

Craig, Joseph A., and Hacker, Robert L. "The History and Development of the Fisheries of the Columbia River." US Bureau of Fisheries, *Bulletin* 49 (1940): 133–216.

Drucker, Philip. *The Native Brotherhoods: Modern Intertribal Organizations on the Northwest Coast.* Smitsonian Institution Bureau of American Ethnology, Bulletin no. 168. Washington, DC: USGPO 1958.

Forester, R.E. *The Effect of Power Dams on Pacific Salmon.* Ottawa: Fisheries Research Board of Canada 1952.

– *The Sockeye Salmon [an international compendium of scientific research].* New Westminster: International Pacific Fisheries Commission 1968.

Haig-Brown, Roderick L. *Canada's Pacific Salmon.* Ottawa: Dept. of Oceans and Fisheries 1956, revised 1967.

Jordan, D.S., and Gilbert, C.H. *The Salmon Fishing and Canning Interests of the Pacific Coast.* Report of the Fishing Industry of the United States, vol. 5. Washington, DC: USGPO 1884.

Larkin, Peter A. "Maybe You Can't Get There From Here: A Foreshortened History in Relation to Management of Pacific Salmon." *Journal of the Fisheries Research Board of Canada* 36 (1979): 98–106.

Marlatt, Daphne, ed. *Steveston Recollected: A Japanese-Canadian Experience.* Victoria: Provincial Archives of BC 1975.

Needler, A.W.H. "Fisheries Research Board of Canada Biological Station, Nanaimo, B.C.," *Journal of the Fisheries Research Board of Canada* 15 (1958): 759–77.

Rathbun, Richard. "A Review of the Fisheries in the Contiguous Waters of the State of Washington and British Columbia, 1899." In *Commission of Fish and Fisheries Commissioner's Report.* Washington, DC: USGPO 1899.

Reid, David J. *The Development of the Fraser River Salmon Canning Industry, 1885 to 1913.* Vancouver: Environment Canada, Pacific Region, 1973.

Rounsefell, George, and Keleg, George. *The Salmon Fisheries of Swiftshore Bank, Puget Sound and the Fraser River.* Washington, DC: US Department of Commerce, Bureau of Fisheries, Bulletin no. 27, 1938.

Shaefer, Milner B.; Sette, Oscar E.; and Marr, John C. "Growth of the Pacific Coast Pilchard Fishery to 1942." US Department of the Interior, Fish and Wildlife Service, *Research Report* 29 (1950).

Stacey, Duncan A. *Sockeye & Tinplate: Technological Change in the Fraser River Canning Industry, 1871–1912.* Victoria: BC Provincial Museum 1982.

US Commissioner of Fish and Fisheries, *Bulletin*, 1883–92.

– Congress. Department of Commerce. Bureau of Fisheries. *Report*, 1903–30.

– Department of the Treasury. *Report on the Salmon Fisheries of Alaska* (1892–1905).

– Federal Trade Commission. *Report of the Federal Trade Commission on Canned Foods: Canned Salmon*. Washington, DC: USGPO December 1918.

– Senate Commerce Committee. *Protection of the Fisheries of Alaska: Report to Accompany R.R. 8143*. Senate Report 449, 68th Congress, 1st sess., 21 April 1924.

Washington. State Bureau of Labor. *Special Report on the Salmon Canning Industry in the State of Washington and the Employment of Oriental Labor* (1915).

– State Fish Commissioner. *Report of the State Fish Commissioner*.

TRADE JOURNALS

Pacific Fisherman [Seattle] (1902–29).

Pacific Fisherman Yearbook [Seattle] (1904–29).

BOOKS AND ARTICLES

Beard, Harry R. *Story of Canfisco*. Vancouver: Canadian Fishing Co. Ltd., 1937.

Bitting, A.W. *Appertizing or the Art of Canning: Its History and Development*. San Francisco: The Trade Pressroom 1937.

Brack, David M. "The Ocean Coasts of Canada." *Canadian Geographical Journal* 87 (1973): 4–15.

Brown, Bruce. *Mountain in the Clouds: A Search for the Wild Salmon*. New York: Simon & Schuster 1982.

Browning, Robert J. *Fisheries of the North Pacific: History, Species, Gear & Processes*. Anchorage: Alaska Northwest Publishing Co. 1974.

Busch, Briton Cooper. *The War Against the Seals: A History of the North American Seal Fishery*. Montreal: McGill-Queen's University Press 1985.

Canadian Fishing Co. Ltd. *"CANFISCO" – From Sea to Shelf: The Story of the Canadian Fishing Company Ltd*. Vancouver: CANFISCO 1947.

Canned Salmon: The Ideal Army and Navy Ration, an argument presenting the merits of canned salmon as a nutritious low priced article of food especially suited to military and naval purposes. Seattle: Association of Alaska Salmon Packers and Puget Sound Canners Association 1915 [?].

Carrothers, W.A. *The British Columbia Fishery*. Toronto: University of Toronto Press 1941.

Cepka, Ed. "West Coast Vernacular Canneries." *Architectural Forum* 4 (Sept. 1981): 17–19.

Christy, Francis T. Jr., and Scott, Anthony. *The Common Wealth in Ocean Fisheries: Some Problems of Growth and Economic Allocation.* Baltimore: Johns Hopkins University Press 1965.

Clark, Richard E. *Point Roberts, U.S.A.: The History of a Canadian Enclave.* Bellingham, WA: Textype Publishing 1980.

Cobb, John N. *Canning of Fisheries Products.* Seattle: Miller Freeman 1919.

Conley, James. "Relations of Production and Collective Action in the Salmon Fishery, 1900–1925," in Rennie Warburton and David Coburn, eds., *Workers, Capital, and the State in British Columbia, Selected Papers,* 86–116. Vancouver: University of British Columbia Press 1988.

Cooley, Richard A. *Politics and Conservation: The Decline of the Alaska Salmon.* New York: Harper & Row 1963.

Creese, Gillian. "Class, Ethnicity, and Conflict: The Case of Chinese and Japanese Immigrants, 1880–1923," in Rennie Warburton and David Coburn, eds., *Workers, Capital, and the State in British Columbia, Selected Papers,* 55–85. Vancouver: University of British Columbia Press 1988.

Deloach, D.B. *The Salmon Canning Industry.* Oregon State Monographs, Economic Studies no. 1. Corvallis: Oregon State College 1939.

Dodds, Gordon B. *The Salmon King of Oregon: R.D. Hume and the Pacific Fisheries.* Chapel Hill: University of North Carolina Press 1959.

Forester, Joseph E., and Forester, Anne D. *Fishing: British Columbia's Commercial Fishing History,* Saanichton, BC: Hancock House Publishers 1975.

Freeburn, Laurence, ed. *The Silver Years of the Alaska Canned Salmon Industry: An Album of Historical Photos.* Anchorage: Alaska N.W. Publishing Co. 1976.

Freeman, Otis W. "Salmon Industry of the Pacific Coast." *Economic Geography* 11 (April 1935): 109–39.

Gladstone, Percy H. "Native Indians and the Fishing Industry of British Columbia, Indian Participation and Technological Adoption." *Canadian Journal of Economics and Political Science* 19 (February 1953): 20–34.

Gregory, Homer E., and Barnes, Kathleen. *North Pacific Fisheries with Special Reference to Alaska Salmon.* San Francisco: Institute of Pacific Relations 1939.

Griffin, Harold. "Native Indians Played Important Part in Early Labor Struggles." *The Fishermen* 25, 40 (14 December 1962): 9, 16.

Hume, R.D. "The First Salmon Cannery." *Pacific Fisherman* 2 (January 1904): 19–21.

Hutchison, Bruce. *The Fraser.* Toronto: Rinehart & Co. 1950.

Jamieson, Stuart M., and Gladstone, Percy. "Unionism in the Fishing Industry of British Columbia." *Canadian Journal of Economics and Political Science* 16 (Feb 1950): 1–11, and 16 (May 1950): 143–71.

Johnstone, Kenneth. *The Aquatic Explorers: A History of the Fisheries Research Board of Canada.* Toronto: University of Toronto Press, and Canada, Department of Fisheries and the Environment 1977.

Knight, Rolf. *Indians at Work: An Informal History of Native Labour in British Columbia, 1858–1930*. Vancouver: New Star Books 1978.

– and Koizumi, Maya. *A Man of Our Times: The Life History of a Japanese-Canadian Fisherman*. Vancouver: New Star Books 1976.

Lamar, Howard. "From Bondage to Contract: Ethnic Labor in the American West, 1600–1890." In Steven Hahn and Jonathan Prude, eds., *The Countryside in the Age of Capitalist Transformation: Essays the Social History of Rural America*, 293–324. Chapel Hill: University of North Carolina Press 1985.

Lamoreaux, Naomi R. *The Great Merger Movement in American Business, 1895–1904*. Cambridge: Cambridge University Press 1985.

Lyons, Cicely. *Salmon: Our Heritage. The Story of a Province and an Industry*. Vancouver: BC Packers Ltd. 1969.

Marchak, Patricia, Guppy, Neil, and McMullan, John, eds. *Uncommon Property: The Fishing and Fish Processing Industries in British Columbia*. Toronto: Methuen 1987.

Masson, Jack, and Guimary, Donald. "Asian Labor Contractors in the Alaskan Canned Salmon Industry, 1880–1937." *Labor History* 22 (Summer 1981): 377–97.

May, Earl Chapin. *The Canning Clan: A Pageant of Pioneering Americans*. New York: MacMillan Co. 1937.

McEvoy, Arthur F. "Law, Public Policy, and Industrialization in the California Fisheries, 1900–1925." *Business History Review* 57 (1983): 494–521.

– *The Fisherman's Problem: Ecology and Law in the California Fisheries, 1850–1980*. Cambridge: Cambridge University Press 1986.

McKervill, Hugh. *The Salmon People: The Story of Canada's West Coast Salmon Fishing Industry*. Vancouver: Gray's Publishing 1967.

Nelson Bros. Fisheries Ltd. *The Story of the Canned Salmon Industry of British Columbia*. Vancouver: Nelson Bros. Fisheries Ltd., Occupational Series no. 1-C-1 [n.d.].

Newell, Dianne. "Surveying Historic Industrial Tidewater Sites: The Case of the B.C. Salmon Canning Industry." *IA: Journal of the Society for Industrial Archeology* 13, no. 1 (1987): 1–16.

– "The Politics of Food in World War II: Great Britain's Grip on Canada's Pacific Fishery." *Historical Papers/Communications historiques 1987* (1988): 178–97.

– "Dispersal and Concentration: The Slowly Changing Spatial Pattern of the British Columbia Salmon Canning Industry." *Journal of Historical Geography* 14, no. 1 (1988): 22–36.

– "The Rationality of Mechanization in the Pacific Salmon-Canning Industry before the Second World War." *Business History Review* 62 (forthcoming).

North, George, and Griffin, Harold. *A Ripple, A Wave: The Story of Union Organization in the B.C. Fishing Industry*. Vancouver: Fishman Publishing Society 1974.

O'Bannon, Patrick. "Technological Change in the Pacific Coast Salmon Canning Industry, 1900–1925." *Agriculture History* 56, no. 1 (1982): 151–66.

– "Waves of Change: Mechanization of the Pacific Coast Canned Salmon Industry, 1864–1914." *Technology and Culture* 28, no. 3 (1987): 558–77.

Pacific American Fisheries Ltd. *The Salmon Industry of Puget Sound as Conducted by the Pacific American Fisheries*. Bellingham, WA: Union Printing Co. 1928.

Ralston, Keith. "Patterns of Trade and Investment on the Pacific Coast, 1867–1892: The Case of the British Columbia Canned Salmon Industry." *B.C. Studies* 1 (Winter 1968–69): 37–45.

– "John Sullivan Deas: A Black Entrepreneur in British Columbia Salmon Canning." *B.C. Studies* 32 (Winter 1976–77): 64–78.

Reid, David J. "Company Mergers in the Fraser River Salmon Canning Industry, 1885–1902." *Canadian Historical Review* 56, no. 3 (1975): 282–302.

Skogan, Joan. *Skeena, A River Remembered*. Vancouver: BC Packers Co. Ltd. 1983.

Smith, Courtland L. *Salmon Fishers of the Columbia*. Corvallis: Oregon State College 1979.

Stewart, Hilary. *Indian Fishing: Early Methods on the Northwest Coast*. Vancouver/Toronto and Seattle: Douglas & McIntyre and University of Washington Press 1977.

Thompson, W.F., and Freeman, Norman L. *History of the Pacific Halibut Fishery*. International Fisheries Commission, *Report* no. 5. Vancouver: Wrigley 1930.

Weldon, J.C. "Consolidations in Canadian Industry, 1900–1948." In L.A. Skeoch, ed., *Restrictive Trade Practices in Canada*, 228–79. Toronto: McClelland & Stewart 1966.

Wicks, Walter. *Memories of the Skeena*. Saanichton, BC: Hancock House Publishers 1976.

Young, Isabel N. *The Story of Salmon*. American Can Co. 1934.

RELATED FICTION

Beach, Rex E. *The Silver Horde, A Novel*. New York: Harper & Bros. 1909.

Evans, Hubert. *Mist on the River*. Toronto: McClelland & Stewart 1973 (reprint).

Grey, Zane. *Rogue River Feud*. 1929. Roslyn, NY: Walter J. Black 1930 [?].

Haig-Brown, Roderich L. *Return to the River: A Story of the Chinook Run*. New York: William Morrow & Co. 1941.

London, Jack. *Tales of the Fish Patrol*. New York: McMillan Co. 1905.

McKeown, Marth Ferguson. *The Trail Led North. Mont Hawthorne's Story*. New York: McMillan Co. 1948.

– *Alaska Silver [Mont Hawthorne's Story]*. New York: McMillan Co. 1951.

Sinclair, Bertrand W. *Poor Man's Rock*. Boston: Little, Brown & Co. 1920.

Steinbeck, John. *Cannery Row*. New York: Viking Press 1954.

– *Sweet Thursday*. New York: Viking Press 1954.

Index